Filibuster

Princeton Studies in American Politics: Historical, International, and Comparative Perspectives

Ira Katznelson, Martin Shefter, and Theda Skocpol, series editors

A list of titles in this series appears at the back of the book

Filibuster

Obstruction and Lawmaking in the U.S. Senate

Gregory J. Wawro
and
Eric Schickler

PRINCETON UNIVERSITY PRESS
PRINCETON AND OXFORD

Copyright ©2006 by Princeton University Press

Published by Princeton University Press, 41 William Street, Princeton,
New Jersey 08540

In the United Kingdom: Princeton University Press, 3 Market Place,
Woodstock, Oxfordshire OX20 1SY

All Rights Reserved
Library of Congress Control Number: 2005934980

ISBN-13: 978-0-691-12509-1

ISBN-10: 0-691-12509-0

British Library Cataloging-in-Publication Data is available

The publisher would like to acknowledge the authors of this volume for
providing the camera-ready copy from which this book was printed

Printed on acid-free paper. ∞

pup.princeton.edu

Printed in the United States of America

10 9 8 7 6 5 4 3 2 1

Contents

List of Tables

List of Figures

Preface

"The past is never dead. It's not even past."

(quoting Gavin Stevens in Faulkner 1950, 92)

Five years ago, when we began to explore the dynamics of obstruction in the 19th and early 20th century Senate, our goal was to understand how different institutional rules affect lawmaking. While we hoped that our findings would have some relevance to contemporary debates, proposals to reform the filibuster were virtually absent from the policy agenda in 2001, as we began our research. Since that time, a new phrase—"the nuclear option"—has entered our political lexicon, and the prospect of fundamentally changing the Senate filibuster came to dominate (at least for a period) legislative politics and news coverage. This has been a blessing because it has reassured us that, despite writing about events that occurred long ago, the topic has tremendous staying power and will likely remain highly relevant in the future. We have also had the unusual opportunity of watching our historical argument—namely, that the threat of a "revolutionary" crackdown on obstruction by a determined floor majority limited filibusters in the Senate prior to the adoption of a formal cloture rule in 1917—put to something of a test in today's Senate. Yet the ongoing fight over the future of the filibuster has also been a bit of a curse, in that the day-to-day fluidity of an evolving and increasingly tempestuous political conflict made it extremely difficult to bring closure to our project.

As deadlines for completion came and went, the filibuster battle over several nominees to the federal bench consumed the Senate in the spring of 2005. An armistice was achieved in the form of a compromise by a small group of senators that took the nuclear option off the table, at least for the short term, while allowing some of the nominees in question to be confirmed. Although we are not sure that the compromise was the best thing for the Senate or for the country, it was the best resolution we could have hoped for as authors attempting to finish a book where variants of the nuclear option in the pre-atomic age are a central focus. The compromise was temporary and it is likely that similar conflicts will occur in the future. The deal survived its first test, as minority party Democrats chose not to filibuster John Roberts, the nominee to replace the late Chief Justice William Rehnquist, despite a great deal of uncertainty and concern about Roberts's position on important issues. As we write, however, current events appear to have overtaken us once again as the Senate is beginning to consider Samuel Alito's nomination to replace Sandra Day O'Connor. Given O'Connor's position as the swing voter on several volatile issues, and the potential for Alito to help conservatives shift legal doctrines significantly to the right, talk of a Democratic filibuster and of Republicans' "going nuclear" has returned to the front pages. The Democrats' chances of defeating the nomination may ultimately depend less on the party's ability to muster 41 votes to deprive Republicans of the supermajority necessary for cloture, than it hinges on whether the GOP can secure the necessary floor majority to "go nuclear" and eliminate judicial filibusters altogether. If the GOP has the votes to enforce majority rule, swing Democrats may opt for a "compromise," as in May 2005, in which the filibuster is preserved for the future but is not exercised in this case. In any event, as in past notable instances of Senate obstruction discussed in this book, the key question may be whether a floor majority is willing to go as far as it takes to enforce majority rule.

Thus, we now find ourselves in the unusual position of commenting about events, now in the future, that will be in the past by the time this book reaches the shelves. Yet, this serves to remind us that—as the Faulkner quote so poignantly captures—history should not be thought of as being exclusively in the past. It is also in the present, and paradoxically, in the future. While we cannot be sure about the outcome of the impending (at least at the time of writing) nomination fight, our hope is that at a minimum this book will make clear how historical analysis helps us to understand contemporary and future dynamics of filibusters and, more generally, lawmaking in the United States.

We gratefully acknowledge the following individuals who shared their work, comments, data, and/or code: Scott Adler, Chris Adolph, Richard Bensel, Sarah Binder, Dan Carpenter, Joe Cooper, Avinash Dixit, Erik Engstrom, Gerald Gamm, John Ferejohn, Sophie Gee, Andrew Gelman, William Hamilton, Jennifer Hill, Greg Huber, John Huber, Jeff Jenkins, Bob Jervis, Ira Katznelson, John Lapinski, Orit Kedar, Sam Kernell, Lewis Kornhauser, Robert Lieberman, Forrest Maltzman, Cecilia Martinez-Guillardo, David Mayhew, Walter Mebane, Monika Nalepa, Sharyn O'Halloran, Brad Palmquist, Jeremy Parzen, Eric Petersen, Keith Poole, Andrew Rutten, Elizabeth Rybicki, Wendy Schiller, Steve Smith, Jim Snyder, Charles Stewart, Barry Weingast, Rick Wilson, and participants in seminars at Columbia, Harvard, MIT, NYU, Stanford, UCLA, and UCSD. Charles Cameron, David Epstein, Alan Gerber, Macartan Humphreys, Keith Krehbiel, Nolan McCarty, and Mike Ting were especially helpful with regard to the theoretical components of our analysis. We are also grateful to Ganesh Harish Betanabhatla, Michael Cooper, Joshua Ehrenberg, Michael Kim, Mike Murakami, Kathryn Pearson, Vanessa Perez, John Sides, Melanie Springer, Brian Wagner, and Adam Zelizer for valuable research assistance. Chuck Myers at Princeton University Press, who published both of our first books, has once again demonstrated his consummate professionalism as an editor, and we continue to be deeply grateful for his encouragement and support. Wawro acknowledges the generous support of the John M. Olin Foundation and the Institute for Social and Economic Research and Policy at Columbia University. The authors bear sole responsibility for the contents of this book. Portions of our analysis have appeared previously in "Where's the Pivot?: Obstruction and Lawmaking in the Pre-cloture Senate," *The American Journal of Political Science* 48:758–74 (October 2004) and "Peculiar Institutions: Slavery, Sectionalism, and Minority Obstruction in the Antebellum Senate," *Legislative Studies Quarterly*, XXX: 163–91, (May 2005).

Chapter One

Introduction

In August of 1848, a bill establishing a territorial government for Oregon was considered in the U.S. Senate. The version of H.R. 201 passed by the House of Representatives included a provision—consistent with the Northwest Ordinance—that prohibited slavery in the territory. This provision touched what was arguably the deepest political fault line of the period. Southern senators, extremely wary of any attempt by the federal government to limit the institution of slavery, marshaled their forces to stop the bill with this provision from passing. They did so in part by exploiting procedural rules in the Senate that permitted parliamentary obstruction—a strategy that would come to define the institution although it was not, at least by today's standards, widely pursued at the time. The group of recalcitrant southerners intimated that dropping the offending provision would allow them to support the bill. Supporters of H.R. 201 insisted that the provision remain part of the bill, leading opponents to resort to obstruction in the hope they could prevent its passage before August 14, the date that had been established for the adjournment of the first session. The effort to kill the bill reached a fever pitch on August 12, as the cadre of southerners delivered long speeches interspersed with dilatory motions. Previous votes suggested that the Oregon Bill with the free-soil provision was supported by a fairly narrow majority. Those supporters demonstrated their commitment to waiting out the obstructionists, keeping the Senate in session into the next morning by voting against repeated motions to adjourn. The obstructionist senators finally relented at 9 a.m. on August 13, and votes were taken to recede from Senate amendments so that the bill was identical to that which had passed the House. But this did not bring the battle to a conclusion.

The Senate adjourned on the 13th without holding a final vote on passage. When senators reconvened on the 14th, proponents of the bill were confronted with a parliamentary obstacle because Rule XVII of the joint rules of Congress prohibited bills from being presented to the president on the last day of the session. In order for the bill to become law, the rules would have to be suspended, which at the time could be accomplished by a majority vote. The resolution to suspend the rules would have allowed several other bills to pass, including an army appropriations bill that several senators remarked was desperately needed. But opponents of the Oregon Bill resumed their temporizing tactics. Rather than dispense with the reading of the Senate Journal as was customary, Senator Hopkins Turney (D–TN) insisted that it be read after the morning prayer. Turney then embarked on a speech criticizing the tactics that the majority had used to move the bill toward final passage, claiming they had violated long-standing traditions by imposing a gag on opponents and circumventing the conference committee procedure. Senator Daniel Webster (Whig–MA) raised a point of order, claiming that Turney's words were irrelevant to the subject before the Senate. Webster's move provoked the ire of Senators Henry Foote (D–MS) and John C. Calhoun (D–SC), who came to Turney's defense. After the presiding officer affirmed that Turney was in order—a clear victory for the obstructionists—the southerners began to send signals that they would let the House version pass. Despite Calhoun's assertion that "by the rules of the Senate, the bill was lost, and the majority well knew that" (p. 1084), Foote announced that he "felt authorized to declare that they [the minority] were now willing to yield and let the majority take the responsibility," even though they previously had been fully prepared to consume the remaining time to kill the bill (p. 1085).[1] The resolution was then—rather anti-climactically—adopted without a recorded vote.

Observers of the contemporary Senate should find this case puzzling. The conventional wisdom is that at least a three-fifths majority is necessary, in practice, to pass major legislation today, because the chamber's rules specify that 60 votes are required to force a vote on proposals. Although a bare majority can pass a bill once it reaches a final vote, supermajority support is necessary to reach that stage. At the time the Oregon Bill was considered, the Senate had no rule for cutting off debate and forcing a vote on legislation. How then was a narrow majority able to pass the bill even though its supporters lacked a formal mechanism for stopping minority obstruction? Why did the opponents of the bill relent when the rules of the Senate and time constraints would have enabled them to prevent the bill from passing before the time for adjournment was reached?[2]

The Oregon Bill represents a case where the minority relented despite having a sizable coalition and the parliamentary deck stacked in its favor. But filibustering minorities also had important successes in the 19th century. A particularly consequential—and infamous—filibuster occurred some forty years after the Oregon Bill's passage, culminating in the defeat of the Federal Elections Bill. The bill sought to address the systematic disenfranchisement of African Americans in the South after the end of Reconstruction, by making federal circuit courts, rather than state governors and state certifying boards, the arbiter of congressional election procedures and returns. Even though the bill did not involve the use of federal troops, its opponents—mostly southerners—labeled it "the Force Bill," and fought it vigorously in the Senate. The bill was brought to the floor on December 2, 1890, and

---

[1] The official record of debate is the *Congressional Globe*, 30th Cong., 1st Sess., August 12, 1077–78, August 14, 1083–85. Other accounts include Beeman (1968) and Lyman (1903, 93–100).

[2] The bill would have been carried over to the lame duck session, which began after the fall elections. Given the volatile political conditions of the time, such a delay would have at least generated considerable uncertainty about the bill's ultimate fate.

Democratic senators began speaking at length against it.[3] The bill's Republican proponents responded by committing to "sit out" the filibuster—that is, forcing extended sessions in order to exhaust the obstructionists—as well as threatening a change in the rules that would allow a majority to close debate and bring the measure to a final passage vote.

After four weeks of debate, Senator Nelson Aldrich (R–RI)—considered to be the de facto majority leader of the Senate—proposed a rules change, which would remain in effect for the remainder of the 51st Congress. The rule provided that a floor majority could end debate and force a final vote on a measure, following a "reasonable" amount of debate. Since the opponents of the Elections Bill could obstruct the proposed rules change as well, some method for closing off debate on that proposal would be required. The Senate's sparse rules regarding debate presented both an obstacle and an opportunity. The lack of a motion for the previous question meant that debate could not be easily cut off under existing practices. Yet ambiguities in the rules allowed for the establishment of new precedents that would clear the way for the Aldrich proposal to go forward. These precedents would enable the majority to crush the filibuster of the rules change, which in turn would allow the Elections Bill to pass. The key to the strategy was the cooperation of the Republican Vice President Levi Morton, who under the Constitution was the Senate's presiding officer. The Republicans hoped to use Morton's rulings on points of order to defeat the obstruction (see Crofts 1968, 329–30; "Trampling on the Rules," *New York Times*, January 23, 1891, p. 1). Democrats could have appealed Morton's rulings, and such appeals were subject to debate (and thus delay). But Republicans could then have moved to table the appeal, and a motion to table would not have been debatable. If the motion to table passed, the ruling would then have established a valid, binding precedent. Republicans used this stratagem to overcome Democrats' efforts to prevent the rules change from even reaching the floor (see Chapter 3 for details). The GOP plan was then to use the same approach to force a final vote on the Aldrich resolution, paving the way for a simple majority to pass the Elections Bill.

Newspaper coverage at the time makes clear that the key question was whether a floor majority would stick together to force a vote on the rule change.[4] Both Democratic newspapers (which opposed the Elections Bill and cloture rule) and Republican newspapers (which favored the measures) tracked Aldrich's efforts to build a majority coalition and Democratic efforts to deprive the GOP of a floor majority. For example, the anti-Elections Bill *New York Times* gloated on January 23, 1891, that "in order to pass

---

[3]The bill was initially considered on the floor in the summer of 1890. It was postponed to the post-election lame duck session when it confronted a filibuster that threatened passage of a major tariff bill.

[4]Observers at the time noted that Republicans were emulating the basic approach of Thomas Reed (R–ME), who had used rulings from the chair to crack-down on obstruction by Democrats in the House just a year earlier (see, e.g., "Reed's Humble Followers," *New York Times*, January 29, 1891, p. 1).

the gag law or pass the Force bill there must be forty-five Republicans in the chamber and all but Mr. Allison [who was paired for the bill] must vote in the affirmative. There are not that many gag rule senators now in Washington" ("Trampling on the Rules," p. 1) The staunchly Republican *New York Tribune* countered that the GOP would win, predicting that the GOP could rally the necessary floor majority ("Republicans in Control," January 23, 1891, p. 1). Given his reputation as an extremely practical politician, Aldrich's involvement was taken as a signal that the change had a genuine chance of success (see Crofts 1968, 328; "Closure Comes up To-Day," *New York Tribune*, January 20, 1891, p. 3). But Aldrich's efforts were hampered by a group of silver Republicans who were cool toward the Elections Bill and had earlier joined with Democrats to pass silver legislation.

In the end, the Democrats triumphed by a single vote: on January 26, the Senate narrowly approved a motion to displace the cloture rule with a proposed apportionment bill. While some have claimed this is an example where a filibuster blocked a rules change that may have had majority support (Binder and Smith 1997, 75), the record suggests that Republicans lacked a floor majority for both cloture and the Elections Bill itself (see Chapter 3). It was widely expected that Republicans could use the strategy of a ruling from the chair to force a vote on a cloture rule, so long as they had a majority of the Senate behind their effort. The proponents of the Elections Bill and cloture appeared to have been unable to muster even majority support, however (Upchurch 2004).

Although these cases occurred long ago, they are highly relevant for understanding the operation of the contemporary Senate. Obstruction remains a prominent feature of the institution, with the most recent high-profile filibusters involving a set of nominees to the federal bench. These filibusters share features of the historical filibusters just discussed, including a drawn-out war of attrition and threats to change the rules to stop the obstruction. The conflict gained national attention on November 12, 2003, when for the first time in over ten years, the Senate held an all-night session. The filibuster of the judicial nominees began in February of 2003, as debate on Miguel Estrada, the first nominee voted out of the Judiciary Committee that year, stretched for weeks. The beleaguered nomination drew a substantial amount of attention, as Republicans claimed it was the first time an appeals court nominee was blocked by filibuster. They expressed concern that it was unconstitutional and would set a dangerous precedent requiring three-fifths majorities for the confirmation of judges.[5] Democrats argued

---

[5] As late as March 1, *CQ Weekly* implied the filibuster had only been "threatened" while at the same time conceding the Senate was "stuck" on the nomination ("What's Ahead: Week of March 3," *CQ Weekly*, March 1, 2003, p. 481). The Senate disposed of several judicial nominees during the time that Estrada was under consideration. A handful of previous cases exist where appeals court nominees appeared to have been filibustered, although they were eventually confirmed after cloture was invoked on them by wide margins (see U.S. Congress. Senate. Committee on Rules and Administration 1985, 63; Karen Foerstel, "Dozens of Clinton Nominees Win Confirmation After Lott Strikes Deal With Democrats," *CQ Weekly*, November 13, 1999).

that Estrada's ideological bent put him out of the mainstream and that their opposition was an attempt to prevent the president from stacking the bench with conservative extremists. By the end of March, three cloture votes had been unsuccessful at ending debate over the nomination (Jennifer A. Dlouhy, "Third Vote Can't Charm Lawmakers," *CQ Weekly*, March 22, 2003, p. 697). Debate continued on Estrada, who asked the president to withdraw his name from consideration on September 4. But the controversy continued to simmer as more nominees were added to the list of those being obstructed.

In response to their inability to bring the nominations to a vote, the Republican majority decided to hold the all-night session, which lasted thirty-nine and a half hours. By publicizing the obstruction, they hoped to galvanize public opinion against the Democrats and thereby shake the nominations loose. The Democratic minority happily participated in the event, consuming half of the time allotted for debate, in an attempt to highlight what they viewed as the policy failures of Republicans during a period of unified control of the presidency and Congress. The purpose of the all-night session was not to exhaust the minority (especially considering Republicans held the floor for half of the time), but to wage a public relations campaign. While the event garnered the media attention its planners sought, it did little to mobilize public opinion behind the cause of the obstructed nominees.

Republicans responded with another tactic, one that had potentially far-reaching consequences for the conduct of business in the Senate. Similar to Aldrich's stratagem during the Elections Bill filibuster, Majority Leader Bill Frist (R–TN) pushed the option of establishing a precedent that would enable a simple majority rather than a supermajority to bring nominations to a floor vote (Helen Dewar and Mike Allen, "GOP May Target Use of Filibuster," *Washington Post*, December 13, 2004, p. A01). The so-called "nuclear option" would most likely take the form of a point of order claiming it is unconstitutional to filibuster presidential nominees, followed by a supportive ruling from the presiding officer. Democrats would appeal the ruling, but a motion to table the appeal is non-debatable and thus would require just a bare majority. The Democrats threatened to respond to such a move with every tool of parliamentary obstruction to bring the chamber to a standstill and cause severe disruption of the legislative agenda—hence the term "nuclear option."[6] The establishment of this kind of precedent would affect only the consideration of judicial nominees and would not apply to legislative items. But it no doubt would open the door for applying this approach more generally and thus have dramatic consequences for the protection of minority interests in the Senate.

Republicans' justification for "going nuclear" is that the Senate is no longer functioning effectively. Democrats counter that they are merely ex-

---

[6]Our choice of terms to describe this maneuver is not intended to imply support or opposition to its use. Although Trent Lott (R–MS) is credited with coining the term "nuclear option," Republicans subsequently have favored calling it the "constitutional option" or "Byrd option"—labels they believe are more politically appealing.

ercising the long-standing right of the minority to block extreme proposals, and that eliminating the right to obstruct judicial nominees would eviscerate the Senate's quality as a deliberative assembly. A full understanding of the feasibility, desirability, and potential implications of the proposed changes requires an in-depth examination of the history of obstruction and institutional change in the Senate. For much of its existence, the Senate lacked even the most basic constraints on debate. Yet the Senate appears to have functioned well enough to be a major player in one of the most successful and prosperous democratic nations the world has known. How did the Senate conduct its business and manage to function during earlier periods of its history? Was the restraint exercised by the minority in the Oregon Bill case typical of the 19th-century Senate, and if so, why were minority rights not exploited more fully? What role did threats of rules changes, such as the Aldrich cloture resolution, have in restraining obstruction? Finally, why did the Senate eventually move, in 1917, to adopt formal rules to limit debate, and what was the impact of this reform? These are the critical questions this book seeks to answer.

1.1 THE CENTRALITY OF OBSTRUCTION TO SENATE LAW-MAKING

No activity in the United States Congress captures the attention of political practitioners, pundits, and the public like filibustering in the Senate. The issue of filibusters has tremendous power to get ink for editorial columns flowing and to rouse even the most somnolent students in lectures on Congress. Perhaps this has something to do with fundamental conflicting concerns about the principles of majority rule and minority rights. Perhaps it is simply that filibusters make good political theater, inducing nostalgia for the days when politics was more of a contact sport. Indeed, it is a supreme irony that some of the loftiest democratic ideals like freedom of speech and minority rights are protected through astonishingly ignoble and bare-knuckle behavior. Whatever the reason, the filibuster is deeply ingrained in the political culture of the United States. Case in point: the word "filibuster" appears on a recently produced list of 100 words that is intended to provide a benchmark by which high school students (and their parents) can measure their command of the English language.[7] As Sinclair (2002) points out, if a given person knows anything about the U.S. Congress, they will most likely know that senators can filibuster. Chances are they will know little beyond that, but even well-read students of American politics typically know only the most superficial details about the filibuster and its history.

Even though the filibuster is undoubtedly the most popularly known parliamentary maneuver in the Congress, it has received scant scholarly atten-

---

[7]The list was compiled by the editors of the *American Heritage Dictionaries*. Other politically relevant terms on the list include "enfranchise," "impeach," "gerrymander," "oligarchy," "suffragist," and "totalitarian."

tion. The first book-length treatment of the filibuster was Burdette's classic *Filibustering in the Senate*, published in 1940. Although Burdette bemoaned the dearth of scholarly work on the filibuster at the time, his concerns did not inspire an active research agenda in political science. Since the publication of Burdette's book, Binder and Smith's important work *Politics or Principle?* published in 1997, has been the only book-length treatment of filibuster politics.[8] Although journalistic accounts of filibusters abound, only a handful of scholarly articles on the topic were published during this sixty-year interval (see, e.g., Beeman 1968; Wolfinger 1971; and Oppenheimer 1985). While today it is difficult to find a newspaper article about lawmaking in the Senate that does not include some allusion to the filibuster, there have been few scholarly works that conduct systematic examination of filibusters using modern tools of theoretical and empirical analysis. Discussions that appear in works on Congress are typically descriptive, highlighting some of the details of the usage of the filibuster or notable historical instances of obstruction. The filibuster has simply not been given an amount of rigorous, scholarly attention that matches its place in the popular conscience.

Yet this lack of attention does not appear to be due to the belief that the filibuster is unimportant or irrelevant to understanding lawmaking. As Oleszek (2001, 228) has put it, "The filibuster permeates virtually all senatorial decision making." The principle of unlimited debate and the obstruction that it allows has been a defining feature of the Senate throughout most of its history.[9] Senator Robert Byrd (1988, Vol. II, 162–163) is worth quoting at length on this point:

> We must not forget that the right of extended, even unlimited, debate is the main cornerstone of the Senate's uniqueness. It is also a primary reason that the United States Senate is the most powerful upper chamber in the world today. . . . Without the right of unlimited debate, of course, there would be no filibusters, but there would also be no Senate, as we know it. . . . Filibusters are a necessary evil, which must be tolerated lest the Senate lose its special strength and become a mere appendage of the House of Representatives. If this should happen, which God avert, the American Senate would cease to be "that remarkable body" about which William Ewart Gladstone spoke—"the most remarkable of all the inventions of modern politics."[10]

---

[8] Binder (1997) and Dion (1997) are recent books that address the issue of obstruction. However, since their focus is mostly on the House of Representatives, and in particular on the question of explaining why Congress expands or contracts the parliamentary rights of minorities, they do not address the questions we seek to answer.

[9] It should be emphasized that the term "unlimited debate" means not only the lack of constraints on floor speech, but also a lack of constraints on motions and amendments that can be made on the floor. Debate in the Senate has never been completely without limits. For example, the Senate's rules have always included a provision limiting senators to speaking twice on the same subject in a legislative day without leave of the Senate. See Section 1.2.

[10] See also Rogers (1926, 5–8).

The rules of the Senate have been viewed as important not only because of their effect on the internal dynamics of the institution, but also because of their larger ramifications for the operation of the separation of powers system. Rogers (1926, 256), in arguing that the Senate does "its most notable work" as "a critic of the executive," claimed that "complete freedom of debate and the absence of closure except as a real emergency" are "indispensable" to the Senate's role as a counterpoise to the president. Indeed, in a public relations campaign against senatorial obstruction, Vice President Charles Dawes compared the filibuster with the president's main weapon in inter-branch bargaining, averring that the filibuster "places in the hands of one or of a minority of Senators a greater power than the veto power exercised under the Constitution by the President of the United States, which is limited in its effectiveness by the necessity of an affirmative two-thirds votes" (*Congressional Record*, March 4, 1925, p. 3). Krehbiel's (1998) more recent investigation of lawmaking in the United States demonstrates theoretically and empirically that one cannot hope to understand fully how legislation is passed without taking into consideration the pivotal role that is bestowed on particular senators by their chamber's rules regarding debate.

Unlimited debate in the Senate has often been portrayed as a sine qua non of democratic freedoms. In his maiden speech in the Senate, Lyndon Johnson argued that the rules permitting filibusters were a progenitor of freedom. In the midst of the Cold War, when fears of totalitarianism and threats to democratic forms of government were particularly tangible, Johnson stated that if he "should have the opportunity to send into the countries behind the iron curtain one freedom and only one," he would send "the right of unlimited debate in their legislative chambers," because though "it would go as merely a seed . . . the harvest would be bountiful; for by planting in their system this bit of freedom we would see all freedoms grow, as they have never grown before on the soils of Eastern Europe." To Johnson, unlimited debate was "fundamental and indispensable," standing "as the fountainhead of all of our freedoms" (*Congressional Record*, March 9, 1948, pp. 2048–49).[11]

Although unlimited debate in the Senate has been roundly praised as an essential component of American democracy, usually by those who have benefited from it the most, the filibuster has also been blamed by many for stalling essential legislation and violating the basic democratic value of majority rule. While in one person's view the filibuster is a protection against

---

[11] A more recent statement about the value of unlimited debate to the promotion of freedom in countries lacking democratic traditions was made in regard to Iraq by Senator Johnny Isakson (R–GA). Isakson recounted a conversation with a Kurdish leader regarding concerns about the Shiite majority dominating the Kurdish minority. The leader claimed that the Kurds had a "secret weapon" to prevent this from happening in the form of the filibuster. Isakson claimed that his optimism about the prospects for democracy in Iraq had been bolstered by the Kurdish leader's reliance upon "one of the pillars and principles of our government as the way [the Kurds] would ensure that the majority never overran the minority" (Al Kamen, "Kurds Invoke Senate Rule," *Washington Post*, February 16, 2005, p. A17).

majority tyranny, others view it as a device of tyrannical minorities.[12] White (1968, 228) claims that the filibuster and the Senate's investigative process are the two activities that have most often brought the Senate into disrepute. McCall (1911, 197–98) views unlimited debate as "a vital defect" in the Senate's procedure that did "violence" to "the foundation principle of our government" and rendered the Senate "scarcely as representative an institution as the British House of Lords." Von Holst (1893, 264) argued that the Senate "outrageously tramples under foot the underlying principle of the whole Constitution, if it perverts the right given by Article I, Section 5, Clause 2, to each House of Congress to 'determine the rules of its proceedings,' into a privilege enabling every one of its members to prevent for an indefinite time its acting." While noting that "the total absence of all rules in anyway of limiting discussion" was "the principal characteristic . . . of the procedure of the Senate," Reinsch (1907, 113) emphasized it was "a negative one." More substantively, southern Democrats made extensive use of the filibuster as part of their strategy for blocking civil rights legislation in the 1940s through the early 1960s. This led civil rights groups to make reforming the filibuster a top priority (see Zelizer 2004). Still, those observers who have an unfavorable view of unlimited debate clearly agree with its proponents that its exploitation has enormous consequences for the process of lawmaking in the United States.

If anything, the lack of limits on debate has become more relevant to the uniqueness of the Senate today than it was in the early years of the institution. The Senate, as designed by the Framers, was sui generis among legislative bodies in many ways. Equal representation of the states in the Senate as opposed to proportional representation was viewed at the time as an integral part of the innovative federal system the Framers created, enabling smaller, less populous states to maintain their integrity as sovereign units (Lowi, Ginsberg, and Shepsle 2002, Ch. 3; Riker 1964). Indirect election of senators by state legislatures was viewed as a check on the potential excesses of popular democracy. Both of these features were essential to the Framers' intention to insulate the Senate from the influence of passionate and capricious majorities. However, both of these features are much less important for understanding how the Senate works today. The 17th Amendment removed the insulation provided by indirect elections.[13] The tremendous expansion of the federal government in size and scope has radically altered the Framers' original federal design. Senators themselves have been active participants in using the commerce clause of the Constitution to extend the

---

[12]Indeed, constancy within individuals concerning their views about the normative character of the filibuster is not always forthcoming. As Ornstein (2003) points out "No issue has had more hypocrisy attached to it in Congress than the filibuster. Go back through the decades and read Democrats and Republicans, liberals and conservatives blithely reverse positions as they move from majority to minority or vice versa, or from holding the White House to not" (see also Binder and Smith 1997).

[13]Some have argued that state-level electoral reforms had undercut indirect election long before the passage of the constitutional amendment, however (Haynes 1938, Merriam and Overacker 1928, Riker 1955). We investigate this claim as it relates to obstruction in Chapter 8.

power of the federal government into policy realms that were once the exclusive domain of state governments, dramatically diluting their sovereignty.
Although equal representation still influences Senate outcomes, it does so
in ways that are much different from those anticipated by the Framers (Lee
and Oppenheimer 1999).

The Senate's rules that protect unlimited debate and effectively require
supermajorities for the passage of legislation were not part of the Framers'
blueprint for the Senate. Nevertheless, these rules are consistent, at least
in principle, with their conception of the Senate as a bulwark protecting
minorities and as a brake on precipitate action.[14] Perhaps ironically, the
rules remain as protections while other institutional safeguards the Framers
put into place have become enervated or have disappeared with the passage
of time. If anything, Senate rules and practices concerning unlimited debate
have become *more* important as the Senate has evolved.

Our study explores the dynamics of Senate obstruction during earlier historical eras in order to cast light on the modern Senate and on legislative
politics more generally. The literature on the U.S. Congress has been dominated in the past three decades by research focusing on how institutions
guide behavior and how specific institutional structures are chosen to produce particular outcomes.[15] If congressional scholars share any common
belief, that belief would be that institutions *matter*. But rare is the congressional study where institutions actually *vary*. It is difficult to determine
to what degree institutions matter if we have no variation in their features.
Historical examination creates opportunities for capitalizing on institutional
variance to advance our understanding of how structure, rules, and procedures affect outcomes. It offers practical insight for constitutional architects
in fledgling democracies. Advocates of institutional reform can learn valuable lessons from history, not only in terms of what the actual impact of
their proposals will be, but also in terms of what it takes to bring about the
changes they seek. In this regard, the neglect of the subject of obstruction
by researchers has left huge gaps in our understanding of the Senate, which
is surprising given the centrality of the filibuster to the operation of the institution. This is especially important due to the recent talk of eliminating
or significantly curtailing supermajoritarian features of the contemporary
Senate through the establishment of new precedents. Our investigation explores the viability of this tactic throughout the Senate's history and how it
profoundly affected lawmaking in the body despite the general lack of formal
constraints on debate. Our argument on this point marks a major departure
from previous work on obstruction, which claims that path dependence rendered Senate rules immune from fundamental changes since inherited rules

---

[14]This is not to say that the Framers intended for a minority to be empowered to block
legislation in the Senate. To the contrary, there is good reason to believe that the Framers
anticipated the Senate, like the House, would operate under majority rule (Binder and
Smith 1997).

[15]For an excellent review of this "neo-institutional" work see, Shepsle and Weingast
(1994).

enabled minorities to obstruct attempts to change the rules (Binder 1997; Binder and Smith 1997). We argue that the mutability of the Senate's rules was an important constraint on obstructive behavior in the 19th century. Our historical investigation then provides important insight on the question of what impact this approach to changing the rules will have on the contemporary Senate.

Our study is of relevance for students of legislatures generally and for students of political development in the United States and abroad. Every legislature must decide how it will structure its internal workings, and in particular how to balance the need for action with the need for deliberation and debate—no mean feat given the multitude of interests legislatures are called upon to represent. This balance is typically struck with explicit rules that put limits on how long legislators can speak and on what topics. But striking this balance is an evolutionary process, with legislators adjusting procedures as it becomes clear what works and what does not. Legislatures will evolve in different directions depending on their members' needs and exogenous demands. While a good deal of work has focused on the developmental process in terms of how legislators adopt complex formal institutional structures, much less effort has been devoted to understanding how legislatures might function in the absence of such structure.

We argue that a small collective choice body does not necessarily need extensive, explicit procedural infrastructure in order to meet the demands it confronts. A set of shared, stable procedural expectations can evolve and be sustained over the long term that can serve the collective interests of the body as well as the individual interests of its members, just as well as or perhaps even better than explicit infrastructure. Legislatures that lack extensive formal procedural constraints should not be considered as underdeveloped or immature. They can operate effectively—or at least be effective to the extent required by their members' electoral and policy goals. As the size of the legislature grows and as it experiences (more or less) exogenous policy shocks—possibly severe enough to induce crises—it may become necessary to specify and formalize procedural constraints. But this kind of "institutionalization" may just involve the codification of what had worked well informally.[16] Indeed, our argument focuses on how the threat of codification can help keep the informal system working effectively.

We focus on the Senate in the 19th and early-20th centuries, a period that is important along several dimensions. First, throughout most of this period, the Senate managed to operate—although at times with great difficulty— without even the simplest of provisions like the previous question, which allows a majority to force an immediate vote on a bill or resolution. Explaining how the Senate did so greatly enhances our understanding of how rules, procedure, and informal expectations shape legislative behavior.

---

[16]See Polsby (1968) on the institutionalization of the House and Swift (1996) on the institutionalization of the early Senate.

Second, it was during this period that senators developed a repertoire of obstructive tactics that worked within the Senate's unique institutional context. The first responses to constrain the usage of these tactics were also conceived and deployed. Examining the evolving strategies of senators who support and oppose obstruction informs what we know about how senators pursue their goals, how preferences get converted into policy, and ultimately how representative institutions function, especially in terms of fundamental trade-offs between deliberation and action.

Third, it was during this period that the House of Representatives all but eliminated parliamentary tools that minorities in that chamber used to obstruct. The Senate also adopted a few limits on debate that affected minority rights during this period, some of which were broadly similar to the restrictions adopted in the House. Our analysis illuminates the degree to which the Senate has served as an obstacle to legislation favored by the more explicitly majoritarian House, which in turn tells us about the power of legislative minorities in the American political system.[17] We provide new insight into the the Senate's role as an institutional safeguard in the separation of powers system for securing minority interests, since it is minorities who exploit the Senate's rules regarding debate to obstruct legislation in their attempts to prevent majorities from working their will.

Fourth, we leverage our focus on obstruction to gain additional perspective on two of the central policy battles in American political history: the antebellum struggle over slavery and the recurrent disputes over the use of tariffs to promote American industry. We argue that the threat of minority obstruction often played a significant role when the Senate considered slavery-related legislation, as southerners in particular proved willing at times to push their prerogatives to great extremes in order to prevent changes in the status quo. By contrast, minority obstruction played a much more limited role in tariff politics, which with few exceptions proved majoritarian. We argue that major tariff bills were generally equally salient to both their supporters and opponents, thus making it less likely that a minority could succeed in blocking action. By contrast, southern senators repeatedly have shown a greater commitment on civil rights related issues than non-southerners, a critical advantage in filibuster battles.

Finally, the Senate experienced two of its most fundamental institutional changes in its history during this period: the move to direct election and the adoption of cloture reform. These changes had potential ramifications for obstruction and lawmaking in the Senate, but they are poorly understood on their own and as they relate to each other. Indeed, the basic rules that make obstruction possible and effective as a legislative strategy are not widely appreciated. The next section outlines the institutional context of the Senate to clarify how and why the filibuster came to be so closely associated with the chamber.

---

[17]The Senate's equal representation of states means that legislative minorities cannot necessarily be equated with popular majorities. Such an equation is more plausible in the House, though significant inequities in district size persisted until the early 1960s.

1.2 OBSTRUCTION FUNDAMENTALS

Obstruction is neither unique nor original to the Senate. Parliamentary obstruction is as old as legislative assemblies themselves, with some notable instances of delay occurring as far back as the Roman republic.[18] However, among modern legislatures, the Senate remains one of the last bastions of obstructionists, where parliamentary delay continues to be a part of the institution's quotidian routine.

The uniqueness of the Senate stems from its rules of operation—or lack thereof. The rules that were adopted in 1789 consisted of only twenty-nine items and consumed only one page of the *Senate Journal* (April 16, 1789, p. 13). In 1806, when the Senate dropped the provision for the previous question from its standing rules, they had expanded to forty provisions, but still consumed less than four columns of space in the *Annals of Congress* (see March 26, 1806, pp. 201–4). The rules have granted substantial parliamentary rights to individuals and have placed few restrictions on the exercise of those rights. This was especially the case in the first century of the Senate's existence, and the Senate's standing rules have changed little with respect to the basic rights of senators to engage in debate.

There are essentially three unique features of the rules that form the basis of the institution's tradition of obstruction: the right of recognition, the absence of a previous question rule, and the lack of a germaneness rule.[19] The right of recognition is arguably the most important. Each senator has the right to be recognized by the presiding officer when she seeks the floor. Although several senators can seek recognition at the same time and the chair has some discretion in deciding who sought it first, every senator who seeks to speak must at some point be recognized.[20] By precedent, the presiding officer cannot refuse to recognize a senator who seeks the floor. Thus, "the Senate cannot vote on whatever debatable question is pending so long as any senator wants to be recognized to debate it" (Bach 2001, 2). It is important to point out that these provisions are not explicitly stated in the standing rules of the Senate, and therefore are subject to interpretation and modification through the establishment of new precedents.[21]

---

[18]See Byrd (1988), Dion (1997), and Luce (1922) for histories of the use of obstruction.

[19]The next several paragraphs draw from Bach (2001).

[20]The right of recognition is subject to a "two-speech" limit, discussed below.

[21]The rule from which the right of recognition stems is paragraph 1(a) of Rule XIX, which reads: "When a Senator desires to speak, he shall rise and address the Presiding Officer, and shall not proceed until he is recognized, and the Presiding Officer shall recognize the Senator who shall first address him. No Senator shall interrupt another Senator in debate without his consent, and to obtain such consent he shall first address the Presiding Officer, and no Senator shall speak more than twice upon any one question in debate on the same legislative day without leave of the Senate, which shall be determined without debate." Although this is a broad grant of power to individual members, it leaves open the question of whether a senator seeking to speak solely for dilatory purposes must be recognized. Subsequent precedents—rather than specific, written rules—have allowed senators to speak on whatever topic they choose and have provided that senators are not to be called to order for dilatory speech.

Once a senator has obtained the floor, she cannot be interrupted by another senator without her consent, and can hold the floor for as long as she is physically capable of doing so, since the rules require the senator to stand and address the chair. She can yield for questions without losing the floor, but cannot yield the floor to another senator. As long as she obeys the Senate's rules regarding decorum (e.g., does not impugn the character of another senator or a state of the Union) she continues to hold the floor until she sits down. A debatable question can be moved only when no senator seeks recognition to debate it.[22]

Other legislative bodies typically allow a question to be moved by a majority vote, regardless of whether one or more of its members wishes to continue debate. The Senate deleted the provision for the previous question from its rules in 1806. The provision that was originally adopted in 1789 stated that,

> The previous question being moved and seconded, the question
> from the chair shall be: "Shall the main question be now put?"
> And if the nays prevail, the main question shall not then be put.
> (*Senate Journal*, April 16, 1789, p. 13)

Although the previous question eventually came to be viewed as a means for cutting off debate so that a vote might be taken, this was not the case in the early Senate.[23] Instead, the rule was seen as a tool to delay or kill legislation (Binder 1997; Cooper 1962). If a vote on the previous question was determined in the negative, this typically meant that consideration of the legislation would be postponed until the next day and perhaps indefinitely. The rule provided majorities with a means to remove from consideration items that they did not want to address, rather than a means to force action on items they desired.

Its infrequent use in the Senate, along with the availability of other motions that could accomplish the same ends (e.g., a motion to postpone consideration), led to the deletion of the previous question from the Senate rules. The Senate deemed it viable to rely on the informal constraints of "dignity and courtesy" to prevent its members from abusing the absence of limits on debate and amendments (Luce 1922, 289). As we show in subsequent chapters, however, these informal constraints frayed by the late-19th century, leading to concerted efforts to substitute formal rules, which culminated with the cloture rule of 1917.

One potentially important restriction on debate that has existed from the very first incarnation of the Senate's rules is that a senator is prevented from speaking more than twice on any single question on the same legislative day without leave from the Senate. Regardless of the topic or the length of the speech, it still counts against the quota of speeches on the pending

---

[22]Some motions, such as a motion to adjourn and a motion to table, are not debatable. As we discuss below in more detail, non-debatable motions play a central role in attempts to curtail obstruction by establishing new precedents.

[23]See Luce (1922, 270–73) for the development and changing interpretations of previous question rules.

question.[24] While this rule is typically applied loosely, it can be enforced more strictly when multiple speeches are used for dilatory purposes. It can be especially restrictive when the Senate maintains the same legislative day over several calendar days by recessing rather than adjourning (Bach 2001, 3).

The lack of a germaneness rule in the Senate means that once a senator is recognized, she can speak on any topic of her choosing, although it still counts against her speech allotment on the pending question. The right of recognition and the lack of constraints on topics that senators may address provide in tandem the basis for the tactics most commonly associated with Senate obstruction. Under standard floor procedure, a senator cannot be denied recognition, nor can she be denied from speaking in a desultory way or discussing a topic entirely distinct from the question at hand. Thus, when Huey Long gave his recipe for "potlikker" during his famous 1935 filibuster of a proposed extension of the National Industrial Recovery Act, he was drawing upon a long-standing Senate tradition.

Although obstruction in the modern Senate is equated with extended speeches, this is not the only method senators have employed to hinder majorities. The right of recognition also applies to senators who seek to make motions on the floor. These include motions regarding amendments as well as various procedural motions, such as motions to adjourn, to recess, to postpone, or to table legislative items. Senators can also suggest the absence of a quorum, forcing a call of the roll. These motions do not count against the two-speech limit, although at times certain limits have been placed on their usage. Throughout much of the 19th century, dilatory motions were the primary tactic used by Senate obstructionists. However, by the turn of the century, obstructionists began to use these kinds of motions less and less, relying instead on temporizing speeches. The move away from dilatory motions appears to have begun in response to a series of precedents established in the second half of the century that made it easier to count quorums, along with a 1908 ruling making it harder to use consecutive dilatory motions.[25]

We use the terms "filibuster" and "obstruction" interchangeably in this book to connote the full range of tactics used by opponents to stall legislation. This comports with the traditional understanding that long speeches are but one of a family of tactics used by obstructionists. It is only in the contemporary period that filibusters came to be equated with long speeches, and this shift was largely due to the restrictions on dilatory motions adopted in the late-19th and early-20th centuries.

The basic ground rules that enable obstruction are altered by unanimous consent agreements (UCAs) and, after 1917, when cloture has been invoked.

---

[24]Bach (2001, 3) points out that "senators often can circumvent the two-speech rule by making a motion or offering an amendment that constitutes a new and different debatable question."

[25]See Chapters 2 and 3 for details regarding the establishment of these precedents. Dilatory motions did not disappear completely with these precedents, even though they receded in prominence. Indeed, the cloture rule adopted in 1917 took specific aim at these kinds of motions, providing that "no dilatory motion shall be in order" once cloture has been invoked (*Congressional Record*, March 8, 1917, p. 40).

UCAs work similarly to special rules in the House, placing limits on debate and amendments. The big difference, of course, is that they require unanimity to be put into effect, while only a majority is required to approve a special rule in the House. Although achieving this degree of consensus might seem impossible, the acceptance of UCAs has become the norm for floor procedure in the modern Senate.[26] However, because of the compromises that are necessary to obtain unanimity, Smith (1989, 119) argues that UCAs place "very little genuine restraint on amending activity and debate." Although UCAs were available to senators during the period we investigate, they were not used very often and did not play as prominent a role as they do in the contemporary Senate.[27]

The cloture rule adopted in 1917, which allowed for a two-thirds majority to end debate, also imposed limits on the nature and amount of debate that could take place after cloture is invoked. The original cloture rule allotted one hour of debate to each senator and prevented the offering of amendments that had not been proposed prior to the invocation of cloture. Stricter germaneness rules apply, and the presiding officer is empowered to rule motions and amendments out of order if he deems them dilatory. While questions have been raised about the effectiveness of the cloture rule, which we will address in Chapter 9, its adoption in 1917 provided structure to floor procedure that had been alien to the Senate.

Prior to the regularization of UCAs and the adoption of cloture, the Senate floor was essentially a free-for-all, standing in sharp contrast to the House, which by the end of the 19th century had a highly structured floor procedure with agenda control centralized in the Speaker.[28] Although steering committees and party leaders would emerge and attempt to impose some order on the floor agenda in the upper chamber, they would never achieve the kind of institutional authority that leaders in the House possessed.[29] The formal position of the Senate majority leader was not established until the early-20th century, and even then the position was not endowed with the right of first recognition—arguably the most important power the majority leader possesses—until 1937.[30]

---

[26]See Krehbiel (1986) for a model of how acceptance of a UCA is consistent with individual expected utility maximization. The intuition is that a senator is better off by going along with a UCA that leads to a passage of a bill she does not favor if it allows consideration and passage of a bill she favors by a substantial amount.

[27]The first unanimous consent agreement was used in 1846 during debate over the Oregon territory, although the agreement "was not terribly well-enforced" (Binder and Smith 1997, 76). Furthermore, presiding officers were not obligated to enforce UCAs until a rule change in 1914 (Gamm and Smith 2000). We conduct a systematic investigation of the impact of UCAs in Chapter 9.

[28]Some contend the Senate floor remains something of a free-for-all (Smith 1989).

[29]The development of partisan institutions in the 19th and early-20th centuries is another topic that has been vastly understudied, although recent work has greatly increased our knowledge of this subject (Gamm and Smith 2001b, 2002a,b, 2003).

[30]The right of first recognition means that the presiding officer recognizes the majority leader before anyone else (Smith 1995, 152). This precedent enables the majority leader to structure the agenda before any other senator can offer motions or amendments. While

The congressional literature leaves us with a poor understanding of how the Senate managed to function with so little institutional structure and such extensive individual prerogatives. This book will explore both how individual senators responded to their sparse institutional environment, and how this individual behavior translated into macro outcomes in terms of legislative performance and lawmaking generally. Recent work in economics, anthropology, and sociology has considered how societies function in the absence of a government capable of enforcing clear rules of the game (for a review, see Dixit 2004). Our analysis of Senate politics in the 19th and early-20th centuries contributes to this new literature by exploring how the absence of clear rules limiting debate affected legislative decision-making.

1.3 LAYOUT OF THE BOOK

In the next chapter, we develop our theoretical framework. Much of the prior work on filibusters lacks explicit theoretical development, and the relevant theories that have been developed are largely partisan based (Binder 1997; Dion 1997; Koger 2002). Yet there are several reasons to believe that a party-centered approach will result in an incomplete picture of obstruction and lawmaking given the lack of formal partisan leadership positions and institutions throughout most of the period under examination. Party caucuses and steering committees did not become active until the late-19th century (Gamm and Smith 2001b, 2003), and even then it is open to question how much influence they had over the policy-making process in the Senate. Institutionalized leadership positions have been a focus of partisan-oriented studies of Congress, but these works have dealt almost exclusively with the House (Rohde 1991; Aldrich 1995; Cox and McCubbins 1993). Thus, we seek an alternative to partisan-based theories for answering the questions that we pose.

Although we are sensitive to the potential impact of partisan forces, we begin with a simple focus on the policy and electoral goals of individual senators. We assume that senators are rational, goal-oriented actors who make decisions regarding obstruction that are shaped by institutional context. Extant work on the filibuster has failed to grapple with the simple questions of why senators choose to obstruct rather than simply vote "no" on legislation they oppose or, alternatively, why they would choose not to obstruct legislation that they vote against. Yet the answer to this question has implications for issues that are fundamental to legislative politics, particularly how those

---

this grants the majority leader an important power, it pales in comparison with the formal agenda setting powers of House leaders. See U.S. Congress. Senate (1992, 1093–94, 1098) for details on this precedent. It is worth noting that the precedent establishing the majority leader's right of recognition is in tension with the rule providing that the presiding officer "shall" recognize the first senator who stands and asks to speak. This underscores the extent to which the Senate has used the establishment of precedents to change the actual rules of the game in important ways.

elected to representative institutions use their range of powers and resources to translate constituent preferences into policy outcomes. We address this theoretical point by considering the costs that obstruction entails. These costs involve the physical effort associated with actually holding the floor for an extended period of time, as well as the opportunity costs that result from reduced time to pursue other legislation or to cultivate constituents at home. A similar cost calculus also applies to bill supporters. The key question in pre-cloture filibuster battles was which side had the greater resolve to bear such costs in order to secure its favored outcome. We argue that this institutional context fostered confrontations that were akin to game-theoretic models of "wars of attrition" and that electorally relevant information conveyed through filibuster battles helps to explain why a legislature would choose to allow minorities to obstruct business in the first place. We develop a theory that generates predictions about the conditions under which obstruction will succeed. We argue that even narrow majorities should generally be successful in these wars of attrition, in part due to the implicit threat that the majority will, if necessary, change the rules by resolution or by "revolution" (i.e., by establishing precedents) in ways that eviscerate minority rights. The main exceptions to this generalization occur when the minority has a greater stake in the issue than the majority, and thus has a greater resolve to bear the costs of obstruction. In addition, when final adjournment loomed, the deadline gave an advantage to the minority seeking to run out the clock.

We emphasize that this system involving obstruction was sustainable so long as the Senate was characterized by a set of norms that coordinated expectations about the role of obstruction. Drawing on the literature on "lawlessness and economics," we develop the theory and analyze the dynamics of "relation-based legislating" in Senate deliberations, and we discuss why senators found it more attractive to rely on informal conventions instead of formal rules for a substantial part of their chamber's history. In particular, this system provided a mechanism for senators to credibly convey their preference intensity and for the Senate as a whole to take some rough account of differential intensity. We also assess the conditions that led to institutional change in reaction to the breakdown of relational legislating. This chapter makes clear how a legislature can function even when the actual threshold for passage of legislation is unclear because there is no rule providing for the application of the de jure threshold of majority rule.

Our theoretical approach relies in part on the credibility of threats to establish new rules and precedents restricting obstruction. As noted above, this contrasts with the idea that inherited institutions empowered minorities to ward off changes in the rules of the game (see Binder and Smith 1997). We thus turn in Chapter 3 to an investigation of efforts to change Senate rules and precedents in order to lay a firm foundation for the remaining components of our analysis. We argue that threats to enact precedents restricting obstruction were credible for much of Senate history and, as a result, were a significant restraint on obstruction. We consider two high-

profile cases in which a floor majority allegedly was thwarted in its effort
to change the rules, and we show that the key problem instead was the
absence of a majority in support of the underlying legislation at stake in the
fight. We also document several instances in which a majority on the floor
enacted precedents that helped defeat particular filibusters and that limited
the range of tactics available to obstructionists.

Having established the theoretical foundation for examining obstruction,
Chapters 4 through 6 provide a macro analysis of lawmaking in the Senate
both before and after cloture reform. These chapters constitute a three-
pronged analytical approach to testing predictions from alternative theories, which is motivated in part by the need to consider possible selection
problems that plague the analysis of filibusters. A lack of past systematic
empirical work has given rise to conflicting sets of assumptions concerning
how the Senate operated during earlier periods of its history. Our analysis
helps to resolve these conflicts. With some qualifications, our theoretical
development leads us to expect that lawmaking in the pre-cloture Senate
was generally majoritarian when it came to significant legislation, following
a "median-plus-veto-pivot" model.[31] This stands in contrast with claims
that the lack of a cloture rule induced universal coalitions, because a single senator could credibly threaten to obstruct and kill legislation (Burdette
1940; Heitshusen and Young 2001; McCall 1911; Reinsch 1907; Von Holst
1893). We connect these claims to the theory of universalism—one of the
most prominent theories in the congressional literature regarding coalition
sizes (Weingast 1979; Collie 1988), discussing how this theory relates to obstruction in the Senate. These chapters report empirical work that tests our
theoretical claims against the claims of the theory of universalism.

Chapter 4 undertakes an examination of coalition sizes on significant legislation during the pre- and post-cloture periods to assess which theory more
accurately explains historical patterns. This analysis extends recent work
on the production of significant legislation to a period not yet examined
(Mayhew 1991; Krehbiel 1998; Cameron 2000; Binder 2003). In addition
to presenting a range of statistics regarding coalition sizes, we also examine
variation in coalition sizes, taking into account other pivotal players in the
separation of powers system. We do this by replicating Krehbiel's (1998,
82–90) analysis of the impact of "presidential regime switches," making adjustments for the institutional context of the pre–World War II era. The
analysis in this chapter indicates that although many major bills enjoyed
supermajority support in 1881–1917, coalitions were typically smaller than
in 1917–1946 (and smaller than in the contemporary Senate), with a much
larger proportion of bills passing with only a slim majority in favor. In terms
of coalition sizes on significant legislation, the median-plus-veto-pivot model
does a better job of explaining lawmaking in the pre-cloture Senate than
do the approaches that predict universalism. We also find evidence that

---

[31] We argue that significant legislation is likely to be salient to both supporters and
opponents due its landmark character.

coalition sizes tended to be larger in the final weeks at the end of the lame duck sessions, which is consistent with the "filibusters as wars of attrition" approach developed in Chapter 2.

Chapter 5 continues this line of inquiry by examining the use of obstruction directly. We assess how the size of coalitions opposing obstruction affects whether or not dilatory efforts are successful, incorporating arguments regarding time constraints into the analysis. Specifically, we examine roll call votes on dilatory motions—a central feature of pre-cloture obstructive efforts—to determine how the size of coalitions supporting these motions predicts the failure of the targeted legislation. For example, if unanimity or near unanimity was required to pass legislation, then we should observe that obstruction generally succeeds even when large majorities of senators oppose the dilatory motions directed at a given bill. The results from this analysis are consistent with the results on significant legislation, indicating that unanimity or near unanimity was not necessary to overcome obstruction prior to 1917. Fairly narrow majorities were remarkably successful in passing legislation despite obstruction. While their success rate decreased when the obstruction occurred late in a congress, universal coalitions were still not necessary even during the last few days before the March 4 adjournment deadline. However, as adjournment drew near, there was increasing uncertainty about how large a coalition had to be in order to overcome obstruction. We return to the issue of uncertainty and how it relates to cloture reform in Chapter 9.

Chapter 6 pursues these issues from a different tack, undertaking a case study analysis of obstruction and tariff politics. In addition to being one of the most important policy areas during the period we cover, the tariff is particularly well suited for evaluating our competing hypotheses. Competing conventional wisdoms about the nature of the tariff—as a broadly inclusive distributive policy versus a highly partisan issue area provoking sectional conflict—map tightly onto the models of lawmaking that we consider. Drawing from a wide range of primary and secondary sources, we not only help to settle competing claims about the operation of the Senate, but also divergent views about the politics of one of the dominant policy issues in the history of the United States. The general conclusion that we draw from these different analyses is that despite institutional structures that granted extensive latitude to minorities to prevent the passage of legislation through obstruction, the Senate functioned largely as a majoritarian body, except when end-of-congress time constraints allowed the minority to run out the clock before legislative work was completed. But even then, there was a surprising amount of restraint in the use of obstruction.

Following our three-pronged test of competing theories of lawmaking in the pre-cloture Senate, we turn in Chapter 7 to an individual-level analysis of decisions to engage in obstruction. We take advantage of the unique political context and strategies of obstruction employed during the antebellum period to answer the simple yet crucial question of what drives individuals to move beyond simply voting against legislation and engage in obstruction.

The focus here is on slavery-related legislation, and how southerners' concerns about having minority status drove them to obstruct. We posit that the overwhelming salience of the slavery issue to southern members would make them more likely to obstruct as they became more of a minority in the chamber. While it may seem obvious that southerners would obstruct items related to slavery, our prediction is more nuanced: we predict variation in their use of obstruction in connection with the threat presented by their minority status. We find that both sectional and partisan factors explain antebellum obstruction, with the former being especially relevant for understanding obstruction aimed at legislation related to slavery. This reemphasizes the importance of considering how different policy areas can define minorities in ways that do not always fall neatly along partisan lines. While sectional factors are widely accepted as playing an important role in filibusters of the 20th century, this analysis demonstrates that the sectional divide has been a persistent source of obstructive behavior, dating back to early in the Republic.

While our analysis of coalition sizes in the pre- and post-cloture periods and of antebellum obstruction provide important answers to questions about lawmaking in the Senate, the results also raise several puzzles, especially about the motivation for and impact of cloture reform. Given the success that slim majorities had in passing legislation prior to 1917, why did senators bother to adopt a cloture rule that could be invoked only by a coalition *larger* than had generally been necessary at the time to pass legislation? The congressional literature does not provide a clear assessment of the practical importance of this landmark reform, again producing several competing conventional wisdoms regarding the adoption of cloture.

We approach the critical questions regarding cloture reform from two angles. The first is an attempt to explain why cloture reform happened when it did. Chapter 8 examines changes in the broader political and institutional environment around the turn of the century that undermined the legislative ordering that had existed previously, prompting a move from the reliance on informal conventions to the adoption of more formal rules concerning debate. We investigate how the contextual changes adversely affected the ability of the Senate to operate on the basis of relational legislating as it had during the 19th century. Attention is focused on the development of direct election of senators, which might have affected both the incentives senators had to obey norms against exploiting individual prerogatives as well as the responsiveness of senators to demands for institutional reform. We consider the relationship between incidents of obstruction, turnover, stability, workload, and chamber size, weighing how these different factors might promote or hinder relational legislating. We argue that achieving the cooperative outcome characterized by restraint in the use of obstruction became more difficult due to changes in institutional context.

While several factors may have contributed to the breakdown of informal conventions, our analysis reveals that the increasing size of the Senate and increasing workload were the primary factors. A marked increase in the membership of the Senate due to the addition of new states crippled the effectiveness of relation-based legislating. Other changes in the institutional, political, and economic context intensified the effect of the Senate's expansion, attenuated interpersonal networks, and impaired communication among senators. The systematic evidence that we present exonerates direct election—a prime suspect among the causes of institutional change within the Senate. That reform did not increase turnover or alter individual senators' voting behavior in a manner consistent with the hypothesis that popular control mechanisms motivated senators to adopt more formal rules concerning debate. While direct election may have led the Senate to become more like the House descriptively in terms of members' backgrounds, reforms that reduced and eventually eliminated the role that state legislatures played in selecting senators did not have discernible behavioral consequences for obstruction.

Chapter 9 investigates the impact of cloture reform itself, assessing the degree to which the rule affected lawmaking in the Senate. At the time of its adoption in 1917, the new cloture rule was viewed as a powerful remedy for the ills inflicted on the chamber by its lack of rules regarding debate. However, the prevailing conventional wisdom in the congressional literature is that the cloture reform of 1917 was merely symbolic and had almost no influence on lawmaking in subsequent decades, in part because the cloture procedure was used so infrequently. We develop a simple model that elucidates the benefits of supermajority procedures for shutting off debate, which legislators can realize without actually resorting to these procedures. The model demonstrates how senators can reduce uncertainty associated with passing legislation by enlarging the supporting coalition. The cloture rule offered legislative entrepreneurs a reduction in the uncertainty of passage when they assembled coalitions including two-thirds of the membership. This incentive shift leads one to expect an increase in average coalition sizes and a reduction in their variance after 1917. We adjudicate among the different perspectives on cloture reform, extending our analysis of coalition sizes. Consistent with the predictions of the model, we find a reduction in the variance of coalition sizes on significant legislation, indicating that the adoption of the cloture rule had a substantive impact on the operation of the Senate, contrary to what the conventional wisdom would have us believe. In addition, we evaluate competing hypotheses regarding changes in coalition sizes during this period. Empirical evidence does not support arguments regarding the effects of parties, changes in preference distributions in Congress, the advent of enforcement of UCAs, or changes in the legislative agenda.

Chapter 10 pursues the impact of cloture by examining the effects of cloture on the appropriations process in the Senate. Obstruction was a major source of vexation for senators when it came to exercising their power over the purse strings of the federal government because it often inhibited them from passing spending measures before the fiscal year expired, which threatened severe disruption in government operations. Our analysis considers whether the cloture rule's designation of a sufficient condition for ending debate promoted efficiency in the appropriations process. We argue that cloture worked in tandem with a set of reforms enacted during this period—including the Budget and Accounting Act of 1921 and the recentralization of appropriations jurisdiction in the Appropriations Committee—as the Senate confronted the problems that obstruction posed for enacting fiscal policy. Our quantitative analysis illuminates the impact of these reforms on the ability of the Senate to process appropriations bills by relevant deadlines—namely, the start of the fiscal year—and leads to the conclusion that cloture operated in conjunction with the other institutional changes to improve the Senate's punctuality in passing spending measures. The appropriations analysis thus reinforces the argument that the cloture rule counteracted the uncertainty fostered by minority obstruction.

Chapter 11 concludes with a discussion of legislative behavior, institutional choice, and political outcomes. We discuss the differences between the pre-cloture Senate and the contemporary Senate, and what our historical analysis tells us about the institution and lawmaking today. The costs that undergirded filibusters as wars of attrition are no longer applicable; tight scheduling constraints have led the costs facing obstructionists to become negligible. Yet the right of unlimited debate—though qualified by the cloture rule—persists, even as the informational value of obstruction has faded. We explore the implications of "costless" filibusters for lawmaking in the contemporary Senate. In particular, we focus on the recent debate over the Democratic filibuster of President George W. Bush's nominees to the federal bench. As noted above, the Republican leadership has threatened to execute a "rules revolution" through new precedents, which, if successful, could eviscerate the institution's supermajority requirements and eradicate long-standing protections for minorities. We discuss what our historical perspective reveals about the feasibility and wisdom of the proposed changes, as well as the future of supermajority requirements and limits on debate in the Senate.

Chapter Two

Obstruction in Theoretical Context

2.1 INTRODUCTION

Legislative obstruction is a tool of minorities. If a senator has the votes to pass legislation in the form she wants or defeat legislation she opposes, she does not need to employ dilatory tactics. As the previous chapter emphasizes, the rules of the Senate have historically granted substantial rights to minorities when they have found it in their interest to obstruct. From 1806 to 1917, senators could have asked for the "ayes and nays" in order to bring legislative items to a vote, but minorities could have always responded with dilatory tactics to prevent the votes from actually being cast. Although proposals to reintroduce the previous question were considered intermittently during this period, senators never adopted them to modify the standing rules. This left the Senate with no formal mechanism on the books beyond unanimous consent for ending debate and forcing a vote on proposals until 1917. While senators adopted important precedents to crack down on the exploitation of the lack of rules limiting debate, minorities in the chamber had unparalleled options for hindering majorities from working their will. To be clear, by "minority" we mean a coalition that—at any particular moment—opposes passage of a bill, resolution, or amendment, but would be defeated if that measure were subject to an up-or-down vote.[1]

One of the central puzzles addressed in this book is how the Senate managed to perform its lawmaking functions in the relative absence of rules limiting debate. Why did obstruction not consume the institution despite the wide latitude given individual senators? The most prominent theoretical framework in the literature that has examined the impact of the filibuster on lawmaking is Krehbiel's pivotal politics model. Krehbiel (1998) has shown that this relatively simple model has substantial explanatory power for understanding the complex process of lawmaking in the contemporary United States. The pivotal politics approach assumes that senators can be arrayed along a left-right, unidimensional ideological continuum according to their

---

[1] An important departure of this analysis from the existing literature on this topic is that we do not conceive of the majority and minority in strictly partisan terms. Even a cursory reading of the history of the Senate indicates that divisions over policies that prompt obstruction often ignore party lines. While it might be easier expositionally to say that "the minority" is simply the minority party and then count seat shares to measure the size of the minority, this misses fundamental empirical realities about the causes and consequences of obstruction.

ideal points.[2] For a bill to pass, the coalition supporting the legislation must be large enough to overcome minority obstruction in the legislature and, if the president opposes the bill, it must have enough support to override a veto. Since 1975, Senate Rule XXII has required a three-fifths majority to end a filibuster. As a result, the members at the 40th and 60th percentiles of the distribution of ideal points are filibuster pivots in the contemporary Senate. No legislation can be adopted that is opposed by either of these pivotal members (since a 60% coalition is required to end debate and bring a bill to a vote).[3] A key assumption of the pivotal politics approach is that a pivot is a formally defined, exogenously determined institutional feature. That is, a player is pivotal if under the explicit rules of the lawmaking game, his or her support is required for legislation to pass (Krehbiel 1998, 22). Krehbiel's analysis covers the period after the Senate adopted a cloture rule, thereby establishing the existence and location of the filibuster pivot.

Although pivotal politics provides a useful framework for understanding the impact of filibusters and lawmaking in the contemporary Senate, the pre-cloture context requires several innovations that move us well beyond Krehbiel's basic model. First, Krehbiel implicitly assumes that filibustering is a costless activity. This assumption is consistent with the conventional wisdom that filibustering is for all intents and purposes costless in the modern Senate (Ornstein 2003). Almost no effort needs to be expended to conduct a filibuster in today's Senate, and merely stating a threat to filibuster can keep legislation off the floor. Costless filibustering implies that it is always necessary to have the votes to resort to the cloture procedure to pass legislation. Indeed, coalitions are generally built large enough so that cloture can be invoked even if this procedure is not actually used (Sinclair 2002). Filibusters can be ended straightforwardly by a vote of three-fifths of the chamber, and the procedure for ending debate is often begun before a filibuster even occurs (Bach 2001). As a result, Krehbiel's assumption is a reasonable one for an era in which a hyper-crowded agenda, accommodating scheduling practices, and senators' packed personal schedules allow senators to stop action with the mere threat of obstruction. But for most of the Senate's history, minority obstruction was far from a costless activity.[4]

---

[2] Although this is a fairly standard modeling assumption, we acknowledge that Poole and Rosenthal's (1997) work on ideological scaling indicates that a two-dimensional space is necessary to adequately capture roll call voting behavior for several of the congresses covered in our analysis.

[3] When a veto threat looms, the 67th percentile member (on the same side of the floor median as the president) is also pivotal. Indeed, strictly speaking, Krehbiel rules out by assumption filibusters from senators on the same ideological side as the president due to veto threats. From 1917 to 1975, when a two-thirds majority was required to impose cloture, the filibuster pivots were the 33rd and 67th percentile senators, but again with the same caveat about veto threats making president-side filibusters unnecessary.

[4] Although filibustering is certainly not entirely cost free today, the costs are much lower than in an era when members actually had to hold the floor to maintain their obstruction. There may be occasions when public support for a bill makes obstruction costly, but the actual costs in terms of effort required to delay action do not appear to be prohibitively high.

We argue below that the costs of obstruction were sufficient to deter many filibusters from occurring. Additionally, considering costs allows us to make predictions concerning the circumstances under which obstruction will occur and when it will be effective. Yet, as we argue below, physical costs cannot by themselves explain the relative absence of filibustering in earlier periods.

A second key assumption of the pivotal politics approach is that the institutional rules and procedures that identify the pivotal players are unambiguous, fixed, and exogenous to the game. The need to gain the support of the filibuster pivot is common knowledge in the contemporary Senate: all of the players understand that in the absence of a sixty-vote coalition, legislation will fail to pass. Of ninety major laws enacted between the 1975 cloture reform and 1994, only ten passed with fewer than three-fifths voting in favor. Of these ten, five were budget bills in which statutory provisions mandated that a majority was sufficient for passage. Three of the other five had 59% in favor; a fourth enjoyed a 58% majority. This suggests that the three-fifths threshold is a genuine pivot point for major legislation in the contemporary era, with the exception of bills subject to specific statutory debate limitations (cf. Sinclair 2002).

Furthermore, the basic pivotal politics model assumes that if the players do not like the outcomes that are produced under the existing rules, it is not possible for them to alter the rules in ways that might advantage them.[5] But in the pre-cloture era, the formal rules of the Senate did not specify unambiguously a sufficient condition for passing legislation. Under general parliamentary law, a majority is the threshold for passage. But forcing a vote required that no senator demand recognition, suggesting a potential de facto unanimity requirement. At the same time, nothing in the rules *specified* that the threshold for ending debate is that all senators agree to bring a bill to a vote. The result, in short, is that the rules were ambiguous concerning the threshold required to overcome obstruction.

This ambiguity in the rules also opened up the possibility for a determined majority to use rulings from the presiding officer to crack down on minority obstruction. Indeed, the most crucial way we depart from Binder (1997) and Binder and Smith (1997) is by arguing that the persistence of unlimited debate in the Senate cannot be attributed primarily to the path-dependent development of the chamber's rules. Binder and Smith argue that the absence of a previous question rule after 1806 meant that the Senate lacked a mechanism to facilitate rules changes by a majority. But the absence of clear rules concerning the threshold for obstruction did not preclude a crackdown on filibusters. As we discuss below, floor majorities have at times used creative reinterpretation of the rules to curb obstruction. More generally, we argue that the threat of a "rules revolution"—that is, of the majority using rulings from the chair to eliminate filibustering—had a deterrent influence on obstruction. Senators understood that a determined majority, particu-

---

[5]Under the current cloture rule, the threshold for ending debate on proposed rules changes is two-thirds, thus presumably making it harder to change the rules than to break a filibuster on a specific bill.

larly when supported by a sympathetic presiding officer, could implement new precedents that neutralized minority obstruction.[6] The striking feature of Senate history is that although floor majorities have cracked down on particular kinds of obstructionist tactics through rulings from the chair, actual enforcement of majority rule has not extended beyond threats. We argue that this reluctance to impose majority rule indicates that floor majorities have derived non-trivial benefits from maintaining few limits on debate.

To anticipate our general argument, we claim that costs and threats of rules changes imposed substantial limitations on obstruction. When an issue was salient to both the majority and the minority, the pre-cloture Senate was essentially majoritarian, with the sole caveat being that filibusters in the final few days of a congress posed a genuine threat to legislation (Oppenheimer 1985). But even when the physical costs of filibustering were at their minimum near the end of a congress, senators generally exercised considerable restraint by not blocking legislation. We posit that norms of restraint played a key role in maintaining the viability of a system that depended to a great extent on unwritten conventions rather than formal rules. Rather than creating a de facto supermajority or unanimity requirement, obstruction primarily allowed an intense minority to block action or force concessions from a less intense majority. Thus, the pre-cloture Senate accommodated preference intensity through the device of unlimited debate, while still allowing the majority, as a general matter, to rule. Indeed, we argue that the filibustering system in the 19th century had the advantage of providing a costly signaling device for members to credibly convey the intensity of their opposition or support for proposed legislation.

For such a system to be viable, there had to be a good deal of cooperation among senators in a sparse institutional environment and general agreement about how the system worked. The lurking threat of adopting more formal limits on debate helped to sustain this cooperation, although there was always the potential that individual senators would behave opportunistically, especially at the end of a congress. We argue that the unique formal institutional structure of the Senate fostered the creation of a relatively stable, close-knit membership, which enabled senators to rely on an informal set of constraints to govern the day-to-day functioning of the chamber. The Senate found it beneficial to operate in this mode of "relational legislating" until changes in the larger political and institutional environment—mainly significant increases in the size of the Senate and the mushrooming of the chamber's workload—undercut the effectiveness of the system. In the early-20th century, several senators capitalized on these new conditions to cause

---

[6]We discuss these techniques in detail in Chapter 3. One of the ways to establish a new precedent is for the presiding officer to issue a ruling (e.g., one that takes away a tool used by the minority to obstruct). While the appeal of such a ruling is debatable, from at least the mid-1800s the majority could use a nondebatable tabling motion to kill the appeal. Tabling the appeal is equivalent to sustaining the ruling as a precedent (cf. Beth 2005; Koger 2002). Binder (1997, 199–201) acknowledges the possibility of using rulings from the chair as a caveat, but does not elaborate as to why this option does not undercut the path-dependence argument.

major disruptions, defeating important bills with time winding down before adjournment (Burdette 1940, Ch. 4). These abuses demonstrated to senators that the old system of relying heavily upon informal constraints was no longer working, and thus prompted the adoption of more formal rules for regulating debate. As a result, there was wide support in 1917 for setting up a specific threshold for overcoming obstruction—the two-thirds cloture rule—in order to provide a sufficient condition for ending debate. This change reduced uncertainty for coalition builders: if they built a coalition above the threshold, they could invoke an explicit rule to defeat any obstruction that developed. But filibustering remained costly even in the decades immediately following the cloture rule's adoption. As a result, the post-1917 system preserved some of the information revelation potential of the pre-cloture era. It was not until much later in the 20th century, when the Senate's agenda became so crowded that bill supporters could no longer afford to wait out obstructionists, that time constraints gave rise to costless filibustering (Oppenheimer 1985).[7]

The layout of this chapter is as follows. Section 2.2 discusses the role of cost considerations in affecting the incentives for obstructionists and bill supporters. Section 2.3 analyzes the impact of ambiguous, endogenous rules. Section 2.4 brings the elements together in arguing that the combination of costly filibusters and ambiguous rules generated filibuster battles that in important ways were analogous to game-theoretic models of wars of attrition with incomplete information. These battles offered senators a way to credibly reveal their preference intensity and therefore provided a mechanism for the Senate to account, albeit roughly, for differences in intensity. Minority obstruction was a source of costly delay, but these costs were potentially offset by the beneficial information divulged through filibuster battles. Section 2.5 refines the argument about wars of attrition, emphasizing how these battles were undergirded by norms concerning the appropriate role of obstruction. These norms were especially important late in a congress, when delay was particularly costly and the physical burden on obstructionists was quite small. Section 2.6 summarizes our expectations concerning the dynamics of lawmaking in the Senate.

---

[7] Costs, timing, and possible rules changes are absent from recent theoretical models of lawmaking that place filibusters at the center of their inquiry (Krehbiel 1996; Krehbiel 1998; Brady and Volden 1998). A notable exception is Koger (2002), whose conditional party government approach considers how threats of rule changes affected obstruction. Bawn and Koger (2003) also relax the assumptions of costless obstruction and constancy in the rules. Leaving aside these exceptions, the absence of such considerations as costs and potential rules changes limits the usefulness of extant models for studying earlier periods of the Senate's history. But they are entirely appropriate for studying the modern Senate, where the profound time constraints senators face have altered fundamentally how filibusters are conducted. In the concluding chapter, we will consider how the modern Senate has adapted to address problems associated with time that plagued the institution in earlier periods.

2.2 COSTS AND OBSTRUCTION

A fuller understanding of obstruction and its impact on lawmaking requires us to be more explicit about what motivates an *individual* to obstruct and how individual decisions then aggregate up to produce legislative outcomes. It is essential to consider the cost-benefit calculus that a given senator performs when making decisions to obstruct, paying particular attention to the institutional context of the 19th and early-20th centuries. Senators who oppose legislation do not always obstruct it—they can simply vote "no" to express their opposition. What, then, differentiates senators who oppose legislation by merely voting against it from those who oppose legislation by engaging in obstruction? Given that senators have wide latitude to obstruct—especially in the absence of a previous question rule—why would senators opposed to a piece of legislation ever willingly let it come up for a vote?[8]

Some basic ideas from the spatial theory of voting are useful here to lay out the logic. According to spatial theory, a legislator votes against a proposal if it is further from her ideal point than is the status quo. If enough legislators have similar preferences, then the proposal will not pass. But rules regarding debate often give legislators options beyond voting in order to prevent a change in the status quo. What would prompt the legislator to do more than just vote against the proposal in order to keep it from passing?

Voting against a proposal on the floor is no more costly in terms of effort than voting for a proposal, since the costs of showing up on the floor to vote are the same regardless of the direction of the vote. However, engaging in obstruction has historically carried additional costs. Obstruction traditionally required a senator to spend resources to obtain and hold the floor in an attempt to prevent action on legislation.[9] While the goals of obstruction today can be accomplished by mere threats to filibuster (Sinclair 2002), for much of the Senate's history, conducting filibusters required substantial physical exertion. Obstruction also involves opportunity costs both in terms of other activities the legislator must forgo while obstructing and missed opportunities to pass other legislation. Waging a filibuster means having to stay in Washington, which prevents senators from returning to their states to campaign and interact with constituents. It also prevents them from doing legislative work necessary to enact policies they may care about. The more floor time that is consumed by obstruction of a particular bill, the less time there is to consider other legislation that might pass. If legislation does not pass by the time a given congress adjourns sine die, then the legislation fails absolutely in the sense that it must start from the beginning of the legislative process when the next congress convenes. Obstructionists must decide

---

[8]Extant game-theoretic models of filibuster politics do not answer this question because they do not predict filibusters in equilibrium (see Krehbiel 1998 and Alter and McGranahan 2000), although to be fair, that is not what these studies set out to do.

[9]Several scholars have made this point, but it has been most clearly articulated by Binder and Smith 1997, 13.

whether it is better to live with an array of status quo policies that cannot be changed if a given proposal is pushed and then obstructed. The political calculus thus involves not only whether the obstructed bill will be killed, but also what other bills will be collateral damage to the filibuster. Obviously, bill opponents will be more willing to pay these costs the more intensely they dislike the proposed bill (relative to the status quo) and the more likely they believe that obstruction will succeed.[10] Beyond the legislative benefit of (possibly) blocking a bill that one dislikes, senators will consider whether voters and interest groups will reward them for undertaking the effort necessary to obstruct. The ability to stand in the way of abhorrent legislation offers senators the opportunity to display their dedication to constituents and to raise their profile in the political system as a whole. At the same time, one potential cost of filibustering is that the senator may appear unreasonable to constituents. Several of our case studies suggest that such position-taking calculations have shaped particular filibuster battles (see, e.g., Chapter 6), though they do not lend themselves to quantitative analysis.

A similar calculus applies to bill supporters. Fighting a filibuster imposed substantial costs on those who wanted to see the legislation passed. The main tactic used by bill supporters was to force obstructionist senators to hold the floor for extended periods in the hope that physical exhaustion or changing political winds would bring about an end to the effort. This strategy—known as "sitting out" the filibuster—required bill supporters to be available to oppose dilatory motions on the floor and maintain a quorum, since under the Constitution, the Senate cannot conduct business in the absence of a quorum. If a quorum is not found to be present, the Senate is obligated to either adjourn or dispatch the sergeant at arms to compel the attendance of absent senators. The images of sleep-deprived senators rising from cots to appear on the floor in their pajamas in the middle of the night are humanizing reminders of the costs for those who try to wait out filibusters. Being roused from one's own bed in the wee hours by the sergeant at arms and being forced to return to the Capitol can hardly be less imposing. Indeed, Binder and Smith (1997, 216) argue that "the burden of round-the-clock filibustering actually falls more heavily on proponents than opponents of legislation" because of the need to maintain a quorum. Additionally, those who oppose obstruction must consider the legislative collateral damage they will cause by keeping the obstructed bill on the floor and preventing the consideration of other items they may care about. It is difficult, if not impossible, to assess accurately who bears the greater cost, but suffice it to say that costs are equally a concern of those who oppose obstruction. As with the obstructionists, bill supporters would be more willing to incur these costs the more they value the passage of the legislation and the higher the probability that persevering will ultimately lead to success.[11]

---

[10] The latter follows because the benefits of obstruction are discounted by the probability that the filibuster ultimately defeats (or forces amendments to) the legislation.

[11] One question that immediately follows from our focus is how strategic calculations might differ once individuals are placed in a collective context. We are skeptical that

2.3 ENDOGENOUS RULES

The second limiting assumption of the pivotal politics model is that the institutional rules and procedures that identify the pivotal players are clear, fixed, and exogenous to the game. Yet throughout the Senate's history, the possibility of changes in the rules was an issue that individuals contemplating obstruction had to take into consideration. The rules that allowed for dilatory tactics in the first place could have been altered to remove this alternative to opposing legislation. This was a particular risk in the pre-cloture era because the rules that enabled obstruction did not specify that a minority had the right to use extended debate to stall legislation. Instead, the rules were ambiguous concerning the threshold required to overcome obstruction. To be sure, there were obstacles to changing the rules of the Senate that did not exist in the House or other legislative bodies. Because only one-third of its membership is elected every two years, it has traditionally been accepted that the Senate is a continuing body. This means that the chamber does not adopt a new set of rules each time a new congress convenes, making it more difficult to alter or eliminate rules that enable obstruction, especially since opponents of rules changes can exploit inherited rules to obstruct proposed changes (Binder 1997; Binder and Smith 1997).

Yet it is possible to introduce significant changes without adopting an entirely new set of rules. This could be accomplished by establishing new precedents through rulings from the chair. At any point during proceedings, save when a vote is being taken or the presence of a quorum is being ascertained, any legislator can raise a point of order regarding some aspect of the rules that is unclear, and the chair can issue a ruling based on his or her interpretation. The ruling of the chair is made without debate, but the ruling can always be appealed, and the appeal is debatable.[12] However,

---

collective action problems played a critical role in limiting obstruction. Free rider problems are most acute when each individual's contribution to the collective good does not make a perceptible difference. But in the case of obstruction, each additional participant should have a noticeable impact on the probability of success. An individual obstructionist could give lengthy speeches and offer troublesome dilatory motions that take up considerable time and thus increase the probability that the majority will surrender. Additionally, the coalition supporting the legislation confronts a collective action problem that appears to be at least as severe as that confronting bill opponents. Sitting out a filibuster requires bill proponents to muster a majority of the chamber to the floor on a moment's notice any time the presence of a quorum is questioned. Those conducting the filibuster merely need to have one person holding the floor at any given time. Moreover, the contribution of each individual bill supporter to defeating the obstruction is likely less perceptible than that of each obstructionist. Adding a single obstructionist can mean adding many hours of delay. A single bill supporter's main contribution, by contrast, is staying on or near the floor ready to make a quorum and to defeat any obstructive motions. The probability that any single supporter's presence will be pivotal to defeating an obstructive motion, however, is low.

[12]If senators raise subsequent questions of order while the appeal is being taken, the chair decides them without debate, and any appeals on these decisions are decided at once without debate (*Senate Journal*, March 25, 1868, p. 340). According to precedents, presiding officers can entertain debate on a point of order "for his own enlightenment or

it is relatively easy to prevent obstructionists from taking advantage of this opportunity to debate. A motion to table the appeal is not debatable, and tabling an appeal requires only a simple majority vote.[13] Once an appeal has been tabled, the ruling is considered to be sustained and to constitute a precedent, which is just as binding as a standing rule.[14] Avoiding additional obstruction on the appeal of a chair's ruling would simply require that the chair first recognize an individual friendly to the ruling who will make the motion to table.[15]

Thus, the rules and precedents that allow filibusters and effectively establish the requirement that larger than minimal majority coalitions are sometimes necessary to pass legislation are conditioned by a kind of "remote majoritarianism" (Krehbiel 1991, 19). That is, although in practice certain decisions may require supermajorities, the decision to require supermajorities is ultimately majoritarian itself. Supermajority procedures are the objects of majoritarian choice, and therefore can (in principle) be changed by a majority as long as a supportive vice president or senator is in the chair.[16] It is important to note that the vice president need not be of the same party or policy views as the Senate majority party for this strategy to work. The vice president does not always preside over the Senate when

---

edification" and can close such debate when he sees fit (U.S. Congress. Senate 1992, 765–66). Yet, if a senator insists upon the enforcement of the rule prohibiting debate (which has been part of the Senate's standing rules since 1828), the presiding officer must do so (see *Congressional Record*, June 10, 1914, p. 10131; March 28, 1935, p. 4586).

[13]The precedent that a motion to table is not debatable was in place by 1844 (see Chapter 3).

[14]Indeed, even though the standing rules since 1959 have included the provision that "[t]he rules of the Senate shall continue from one congress to the next congress unless they are changed as provided in these rules," many senators believe that the traditional acceptance of the Senate as a continuing body is an inconvenience that can be changed by a floor majority, given the constitutional provision empowering each chamber to make its own rules (U.S. Congress. Senate. Committee on Rules and Administration 1985; Ornstein 2003).

[15]If the point of order is made in regard to a constitutional principle, then the presiding officer is bound by precedent to refer the matter to the full Senate for decision, which could possibly result in prolonged and obstructive debate. Nevertheless, debate could be avoided simply by not raising the point of order as a constitutional question. We cite several cases below and in Chapter 3 where obstructive efforts were limited in significant ways by using points of order that were not raised as constitutional questions. If a point of order is raised as a constitutional issue and the presiding officer refers the question to the Senate for debate, a senator could make a point of order that the referral is not appropriate. If such a point of order is upheld, it would establish a new precedent not requiring the presiding officer to refer constitutional matters to the floor. Lastly, a presiding officer could simply ignore the precedent and issue a ruling on an arguably constitutional matter (Beth 2005). Vice President Hubert Humphrey did this in 1969, although his ruling was overturned on appeal (*Congressional Record*, January 14, 1969, pp. 593, 994–95). A precedent also exists that the chair is supposed to submit matters of "first impression"— that is, matters not clearly covered by the rules or existing precedents—to the Senate for decision. Yet it is the chair who decides what constitutes a matter of first impression, and chairs often choose to issue rulings rather than referring points of order that arguably fall into this category.

[16]In this sense, the Senate could function as a majoritarian body in the 19th century because the pivotal player on rules changes was the median voter.

it is in session, and a clever majority could simply wait until a sympathetic senator occupied the chair to push new precedents.[17]

One might ask how much flexibility the presiding officer would have in issuing new precedents. Was the existing body of precedents so well known and clear that little creativity was possible? The Senate actually did not compile its precedents in a published volume until 1909.[18] Lacking a ready reference manual for existing precedents, presiding officers and senators on the floor often were not entirely sure of procedural nuances. This presumably left more discretion for creative reinterpretation, as is evidenced by the shifting precedents regarding such matters as whether senators could be removed from the floor for irrelevancy during debate (see Table 3.1) and whether mere debate constitutes business (see U.S. Congress. Senate 1913, 408–9). One might object that such a reinterpretation might then be "lost," since it is not codified. But new rulings that significantly rein in obstruction would be sufficiently salient and noteworthy that they would be especially likely to be remembered. For example, had Aldrich succeeded in establishing a precedent reining in the Democratic filibuster of the 1891 Elections Bill, it is doubtful anyone would have forgotten about the battle. Our theoretical framework then must delineate how supermajority provisions are self-enforceable when majorities have the option of changing them.

2.4 FILIBUSTERS AS WARS OF ATTRITION

The pre-cloture context of costly filibustering and ambiguous, endogenous rules meant that stopping a filibuster against a bill typically required engaging in a protracted battle on the floor, which could lead to the failure to pass other items on the agenda. The class of game-theoretic models known as

---

[17]Indeed, in the presidential administrations during the 1st–64th Congresses (1789–1917), the position of vice president was vacant approximately one-quarter of the time (Ragsdale 1996, Table 1–1), which meant that a member of the Senate had to serve as presiding officer. Nor do a vice president's sympathies necessarily depend on his partisan identification. Vice President Richard Nixon famously conspired with majority party Democrats during the 1950s in an (unsuccessful) attempt to curtail obstruction of civil rights bills by southern Democrats. In 1975, Republican Vice President Nelson Rockefeller worked with liberal Democrats in issuing rulings that helped prompt a reduction in the cloture threshold from two-thirds to three-fifths ("Reformers Consider Filibuster Compromise," *Congressional Quarterly Weekly Report*, March 1, 1975, p. 448).

[18]See Lawrence (2005) on the effects of the publication of precedents on appeals of chairs' rulings and on differences between the House and Senate. The post of Senate parliamentarian was not established until 1937, which meant that presiding officers prior to this time lacked the expertise that the parliamentarian provides for making rulings that are consistent with prior precedents. According to former Parliamentarian Robert Dove, this created opportunities for presiding officers to issue rulings that were contrary to existing precedents. Dove added that prior to the publication of a comprehensive volume of precedents in 1937, the opportunities for presiding officers to depart from past practice were especially abundant.

wars of attrition offers potential insights into the dynamics of obstruction.[19] In a showdown over proposed legislation, opponents of the bill decide in each period whether to obstruct or to allow the bill to come to a vote. Bill supporters decide whether to oppose the obstruction (i.e., by keeping the bill on the floor) or to withdraw the bill.[20] In the absence of a fixed threshold for ending debate, the outcome of such a showdown will depend on which side is willing to bear the opportunity costs of delay for a longer period. The relative "resolve" levels of the two sides and their ability to bear the costs of obstruction will thus be decisive. "Resolve" can be conceptualized in terms of how much each side values its preferred outcome as opposed to the alternative. Thus, the resolve level of bill supporters (opponents) depends primarily on how much more (less) they prefer the proposed bill to the status quo.

If there is complete information concerning the costs and resolve levels, then filibusters should not occur. Since delay is costly to both sides, each can anticipate what would happen if it obstructs or fights the obstruction. If the obstructionists know they are doomed to fail (due to the bill supporters' high resolve level), they will vote against the bill but not filibuster. By contrast, if the bill supporters are convinced that the obstructionists have the greater resolve, they will either not bring the bill to the floor, pull the bill, or displace it at the first sign of trouble rather than waste scarce floor time.[21]

However, if there is incomplete information about actors' preferences, delay becomes possible, and the effort required to obstruct or to battle obstruction becomes a potential information revelation mechanism (see Fearon 1994). The cost of delay in this case is the physical effort required to obstruct, as well as the opportunity costs in terms of reduced time available for other legislative and constituent service activities.[22] In the incomplete

---

[19] For summaries of work on this class of games see Fudenberg and Tirole (1991) and Tirole (1988).

[20] Either side might also offer a compromise on the legislation. This complication does not fundamentally alter the logic of the showdown.

[21] Senators' incentive to posture for constituents and to engage in blame-game politics à la Groseclose and McCarty (2001) could lead to observed obstruction even under these circumstances. But this would require relaxing the assumption of complete information, since blame-game models assume that voters are uncertain about the ideal points of elected officials.

[22] This diverges from Fearon's (1994) model of inter-state crisis bargaining. In Fearon's model, the primary cost of delay has to do with audience costs—the difficulty of backing down once a crisis becomes public. Audience costs tend to rise as a crisis becomes more public. By contrast, the physical costs of mobilizing troops in a crisis are, according to Fearon, less important. In the Senate context, we believe that the costs of delay are best viewed in terms of the physical burden of obstruction and time lost for other activities. Audience costs appear less relevant since it is not evident that obstructing a bill (or fighting obstruction) typically makes it more costly to back down later than it otherwise would have been. In other words, engaging in obstruction seems just as likely to inoculate a senator against complaints about a bill passing as it is to accentuate the penalty. An exception appears to have occurred in the recent fight over judicial nominations, when conservative and religious groups sent signals that Majority Leader Frist's presidential

information situation, each side has an incentive to try to persuade the other that it is committed to its position and will not surrender. When bill opponents engage in obstruction, this provides information about the costs they are willing to bear in order to defeat legislation. Bill supporters' estimates of the opponents' resolve will increase the longer the opponents persist in obstruction. Similarly, by holding continuous sessions and forgoing other opportunities, bill supporters credibly convey their resolve in favor of the legislation.

Information revelation is important in two respects. For the institution as a whole, it helps overcome one of the limitations inherent in majority rule voting systems. As Buchanan and Tullock (1962) argue, majority rule allows the passage of inefficient policies in the sense that a more intense minority can lose to a less intense majority. Vote trading across issues can greatly reduce these inefficiencies, though logrolling has its own transaction costs and enforcement problems (Weingast and Marshall 1988). Costly obstruction can enhance legislative effectiveness by encouraging senators to truthfully reveal how much they value a given legislative alternative. Beyond potentially enhancing the Senate's effectiveness, costly obstruction can provide electorally relevant information for all senators. When bill supporters find that opponents are sufficiently determined to engage in obstruction, this provides information about potential opposition that they may face in their home state concerning their position. Similarly, when bill supporters show that they are determined to overcome a filibuster, this signals to bill opponents that there may be firmer public backing for the legislation. Therefore, filibusters (and efforts to fight obstruction) can signal the intensity of constituent support or opposition to a position, which should prove to be electorally useful information for all senators.[23] This kind of information revelation would be particularly beneficial to senators—as opposed to House members—because of their generally larger and more heterogeneous constituencies. In considering the aggregate benefits of this system of legislating, the value of information revealed through obstruction needs to be weighed against the delay costs confronting both sides. If obstruction becomes too easy for minorities—i.e., the physical costs of obstruction substantially diminish—then it is likely that the information revelation value of obstruction will fall while the costs for majorities in terms of forgone legislative opportunities will increase. This, in turn, can provide a motivation for adopting rules to curtail filibusters.

Indeed, an additional feature of filibusters as wars of attrition is that bill supporters had access to an alternative strategic option other than simply

---

ambitions would suffer if he backed down and did not succeed in getting the nominees confirmed (Charles Babington, "Frist Likely to Push for Ban on Filibusters; Failure Risks Conservatives' Ire; Success May Prompt Legislative Stalemate," *Washington Post*, April 15, 2005, p. A04). It is plausible, though by no means certain, that Frist would have not faced such costs had he avoided escalating the showdown in the first place.

[23] For the importance of reputation and information revelation in war of attrition games, see Kreps and Wilson (1982). For the potential social welfare benefits offered by these kinds of games, see Bliss and Nalebuff (1984).

keeping the obstructed bill on the floor. They could attempt to implement a rules "revolution." As noted above, a committed majority could threaten to create new precedents that undermined—or even eliminated—the tools available to obstructionists. One can think of this as an "outside option" available to bill supporters that is analogous to going to outright "war" in the war of attrition crisis bargaining game. One difference from the typical crisis bargaining game is that only bill supporters would have access to this outside option.[24] The existence of this outside option would be a deterrent to an obstructionist minority when it confronts an especially intense majority, since only such a majority would consider changing the rules to enable the passage of a specific piece of legislation. This feature helps us understand the instances in which the Senate adopted major new precedents amid filibuster fights (see Chapter 3). Attempting to change the rules entails considerable uncertainty and high potential costs for a given majority—particularly in terms of forgone future opportunities to obstruct. As such, when the majority mobilizes vigorously to promote rules changes, this signals that it is particularly intense.

If threats to change the rules are the ultimate weapon of bill supporters, the Senate's fixed adjournment deadline constituted a critical potential advantage for obstructionists (cf. Oppenheimer 1985). In standard war-of-attrition games, the costs of delay continually mount for both sides, and the showdown continues until one side or the other backs down (or, in some variants of the game, engages in all-out war as opposed to continued crisis escalation). But in the Senate context (prior to 1934), all bills not passed by March 4 of odd-numbered years automatically fail. If neither side relents before the last period elapses, the minority automatically wins, since the legislation in question dies and the status quo is maintained. This grants a major advantage to the minority and emphasizes how the strategic situation at the end of a congress differs substantially from that at earlier points. As adjournment looms, the resolve level required to kill legislation falls considerably. Rather than needing to hold the floor for weeks on end, obstructionists would have to obstruct for only a short period. For bill supporters, as adjournment nears, it becomes more costly to keep a stalled bill on the floor since doing so prevents action on other priority bills. Therefore, the costs for obstructionists are likely to be significantly lower near the end of a congress.[25] This suggests that the information revelation value of obstruction

---

[24] As the more numerous group, only bill supporters could threaten to change the rules. Bill opponents could threaten to respond to such rules changes with renewed—and perhaps intensified—efforts to prevent the Senate from functioning. Nonetheless, a committed majority of bill supporters could use the creation of new precedents to curb these minority tactics, resulting in a fundamental asymmetry in the strategic context.

[25] The sheer physical burden for obstructionists should fall as adjournment looms, regardless of whether the obstructionists also fear the loss of other legislative opportunities. In other words, as long as obstructionists do not value the other legislation that remains to be passed *more* than the bill supporters do, it is safe to assume that obstruction becomes relatively less costly to bill opponents the less time is left in a congress. This dynamic suggests that bill supporters may have an incentive to hold back several other bills that

will be reduced near the end of a congress: even a minority that does not have a relatively high resolve level has the capacity to pay the costs to kill legislation. As noted above, this may motivate moves to reform the rules concerning obstruction. Before addressing the specific implications that can be derived from viewing pre-cloture filibusters as wars of attrition, however, it is necessary to consider the role of informal understandings in sustaining the Senate's distinctive approach to deliberation.

2.5 RELATIONAL LEGISLATING AND SENATE OBSTRUC- TION

For battles over obstruction to be effective as an information revelation mechanism, at least two conditions need to hold. First, senators need to have some shared understanding of the "game's" structure. In other words, since the rules themselves featured ambiguity concerning the appropriate role of obstruction and the threshold required for defeating a filibuster, it is necessary for senators to have some shared perception of what the dynamics of battles over obstruction entail. Otherwise, senators will not attain the level of cooperation that is necessary for lawmaking in a legislature with few rules to constrain debate. In addition, there need to be some limitations on senators' capitalizing on the end-of-congress deadline to defeat legislation that a committed majority supports. Otherwise, even minorities with a relatively low resolve level will be able to bear the costs of filibustering to defeat bills in the closing days of a congress.

The emerging literature that Dixit (2004) has labeled "lawlessness and economics" provides theoretical leverage for understanding the development— and eventual decline—of shared understandings regulating Senate obstruction. One of the main arguments in this literature is that actors do not need to rely upon explicit, written rules to structure economic activity. The burden of setting up, maintaining, and employing a policing and judicial apparatus to enforce explicit laws and adjudicate disputes concerning them can outweigh the benefits. It may be less costly to rely on "relation-based governance" of interactions than it is to rely on an authoritative, disinterested third party (i.e., "rules-based governance"). Or it may simply be impossible to rely on third parties. In these cases, "private ordering" can emerge that undergirds economic interaction among self-interested, rational individuals. Such a system is viable in part because the costs and uncertainty of changing to a more formal structuring of interactions dissuade actors from behaving opportunistically.

Long-term relationships are one of the most common forms of private ordering. Such relationships "can be self-enforcing for reasons familiar from

---

the would-be obstructionists want to see passed in order to make end-of-congress delay more costly to the minority. We did not find evidence for this conjecture in the historical record.

the theory of repeated games: the immediate benefit of acting opportunistically can be offset by future losses, because the opportunism leads to a collapse of the relationship and therefore to lower future payoffs" (Dixit 2004, 11). Rather than rely on formal contracts, actors engage in "relational contracts—informal agreements sustained by the value of future relationships" (Baker, Gibbons, and Murphy 2002, 39). Should a given relationship break down, however, those involved in it can shift to a more structured one, involving formal contracts and third party enforcement. The costs that such a shift might entail are a deterrent to opportunistic behavior, and therefore provide incentives to abide by the informal rules that govern behavior.[26] But informal conventions—namely norms—must exist that provide enough predictability to behavior so that individuals will choose to maintain such a system rather than resorting to alternatives. As Ellickson (1991, 167) has put it, "members of a close-knit group develop and maintain norms whose content serves to maximize the aggregate welfare that members obtain in their workaday affairs with one another" (emphasis in original removed).

The canonical model that Dixit develops involves a community of individuals who can potentially benefit from economic interaction. However, they lack the ability to engage in written contracts enforceable by a third party. Instead they must rely on informal mechanisms to prevent opportunistic behavior and realize gains from interaction. If an individual "cheats" in a transaction, information about this behavior is communicated to others in the group and everyone—not simply the person who was cheated—should refuse to transact with this person in the future. Communication is key in these models, both ex ante and ex post to transactions, so that individuals can build shared expectations about acceptable and unacceptable behavior. Game-theoretic models have demonstrated how such a system is sustainable in equilibrium when groups are relatively small, stable, and cohesive, with a particular emphasis being placed on the size of the group. As the size of the group increases, the communication necessary to produce desirable behavioral patterns degrades, and the system begins to break down.

These ideas and concepts can be applied to illuminate the dynamics of the wars of attrition fought during filibusters in the Senate, as well as to explain variation in obstruction, especially as it relates to institutional changes. Legislators can choose the degree to which they structure their interactions through written rules. Historically, senators have chosen a relatively sparse set of rules to govern their chamber, relying less on rule-based governance and more on relation-based governance, particularly when it comes to debate. A senator's behavior is constrained not solely by concerns about violating explicit rules—which, after all, impose only slight restrictions—but also and perhaps more importantly by concerns about his relations with other legislators and how his actions today will affect interactions with them in the future. These relationships encompass shared understandings about

---

[26]It may also be the case that having the fall-back of effective, functioning formal institutions reduces the cooperation that might occur in the absence of this alternative (Dixit 2004, Ch. 2).

appropriate behavior toward one another and what would constitute unacceptable behavior, without being formally specified in the Senate's standing rules. Such understandings or norms would have to be communicated verbally and by a wide range of senators for them to have any constraining effects. Relations among senators would also have to be well established for verbal communication about norms and intentions to comply with them to be credible. But another factor that would promote adherence to unwritten rules is that senators have the option of codifying the constraints, and of doing so in a way that would make some senators worse off than they were before. The threat of moving toward a more rule-based system enhanced the viability of the Senate's relation-based system.

The two approaches to governance have distinctive trade-offs. Written rules tend to have the advantage of specificity and transparency and thus provide clearer guidance as to what is acceptable and what is not. As a result, they are easier to enforce by the presiding officer since it is easier to detect deviation. But this specificity can come at the cost of reduced flexibility. For example, when debate on amendments is limited to five minutes per member as in the U.S. House, then there is little capacity to allow individual representatives to reveal their commitment to a policy through costly action, such as extended speeches. By contrast, unwritten conventions provide greater flexibility, but can be vague and thus open to greater dispute as to what constitutes a violation.[27] Yet, just as it is impossible to write complete contingent contracts, it is impossible to write parliamentary rules that account for every contingency. Widely accepted conventions can serve as constraints on behavior for those situations not covered by written rules. When disputes arise, these conventions can be transformed into explicit constraints in the form of precedents or rules adopted by the chamber. Thus, governance in a legislature (and more generally) is best conceived of as being located on a rule-based to relation-based continuum.

Our theoretical framework spells out how the Senate managed to perform its functions through "relational legislating" and why its members chose to adopt more formal rules at particular points in the chamber's history. The informally governed system of extended battles over filibusters was a component of relational legislating in the Senate: the rules did not completely specify the contours of such wars of attrition, yet we argue senators developed a widely shared understanding of their underlying dynamics.

Relative to other legislative bodies—and in particular, the House—the Senate has long chosen to rely more on implicit—rather than formal—rules to govern itself.[28] In the 1950s and 1960s, when political scientists traced the importance of norms and "folkways" in Congress, the Senate was typi-

---

[27] We concede, however, that sustaining norms may require inflexible application of trigger strategies in repeat play (Gibbons 1992). Additionally, written rules could specifically grant flexibility to agents in certain contexts. But in practice it appears that explicit rules more often reduce discretion in application.

[28] This is not to say that norms were unimportant in the House, but their importance pales in comparison to formal rules when it comes to debate in that chamber.

cally the focus of attention (Matthews 1960). But even a cursory glance at the contemporary Senate makes clear that norms against unrestrained obstruction have withered. Traditional norm-based arguments, such as those made by Matthews, do not provide much leverage for assessing why norms might change or weaken over time. But the "lawlessness and economics" approach, along with the war-of-attrition model, offer hypotheses that can explain changes in reliance on informal norms. In particular, lawlessness and economics suggests that the ability to rely upon norms degrades as group size increases. The war-of-attrition model adds that as time pressures increase (due to a heightened workload), obstruction will be more likely to be undertaken and to succeed. We argue that norms limiting obstruction were reasonably effective in the 19th century, but these norms began to come under strain in the late-19th century as the Senate expanded in size and confronted heightened time pressures. As individual senators became more assertive in flaunting norms of restraint and capitalizing on the end-of-congress deadline to block legislation, the system of relation-based governance began to fray. The adoption of cloture reform in 1917 represented an important response to these changing conditions, shifting the Senate along the relation-based to rule-based continuum.[29]

Demonstrating that norms have a significant impact on behavior poses substantial challenges. Indeed, many congressional scholars, while not denying that norms exist in legislative bodies, adopt the modeling strategy of assuming norms are not operative in order to focus attention on elements of the strategic context that are easier to measure and assess directly (see, e.g., Krehbiel 1998; Weingast and Marshall 1988).[30] However, we believe that careful consideration of norms can be useful in this context because of distinctive features of the Senate. The absence of explicit rules providing a threshold for overcoming obstruction—and more generally, the ambiguities inherent in the Senate's sparse rules and precedents—created a good deal of space for senators' shared expectations about what the rules really "meant" to have an impact. Furthermore, as noted below, the Senate's small size and relatively stable membership created a context conducive to relying to a large extent on informal conventions.

Our analytic strategy in elucidating the importance of norms involves three steps. First, we provide evidence for the plausibility of the assumption that 19th-century senators themselves believed that there were such norms limiting obstruction. In doing so, we pay special attention to those statements where the senator does not have a self-serving motivation to invoke norms. That is, it is more informative when a senator supporting a filibuster

---

[29]Norms of restraint had weakened by 1917, but had not completely disappeared. As late as the 1950s to 1960s, it appears that senators showed at least some restraint in their use of their individual prerogatives. Such restraint is much less common in today's Senate (Sinclair 1989).

[30]Formal models often make use of norms when it comes to off-the-equilibrium path behavior in sequential games (e.g., in decisions about which sorts of off-the-path behavior are plausible and which can be ruled out), but this is typically viewed as a necessary concession rather than as a virtue of such models.

invokes norms as a reason for exercising restraint than it is when a bill supporter attacks the obstructionists for violating norms of restraint.[31] Second, we briefly assess the role of punishment and communication in potentially undergirding Senate norms. Third, and most importantly, our framework generates expectations about the conditions that will lead to the breakdown of the effectiveness of norms. We show that variations in the conditions promoting norms—in particular, chamber size—help explain the increase in obstruction at the turn of the century, which in turn motivated the Senate's shift toward formal rules. Following a discussion of the nature of Senate norms, we take up the first two steps below, and consider the third in much greater detail in Chapter 8).

2.5.1 The Nature of Senate Norms concerning Obstruction

It is true that the war-of-attrition framework offers explanations for filibustering behavior without necessarily attributing a role to norms, except insofar as some shared expectations are necessary for obstruction to serve as a reasonably effective information revelation mechanism. But norms come more decisively into play when one considers end-of-congress obstruction. The low physical costs and the potentially severe collateral damage created by such filibusters meant that battles following the logic of a war-of-attrition would be an extremely problematic information revelation mechanism absent supplementary norms of restraint. In particular, even a small group of obstructionists could capitalize on the end-of-congress deadline to block bills favored by an intense majority. Furthermore, individual obstructionists could easily try to deceive others into believing that they have high resolve in such a context, with a much lower probability of the majority being willing to call their bluff (due to the potential collateral damage caused by late-session filibusters). Such posturing is a central part of war of attrition games with incomplete information. These dynamics produce a collective dilemma for senators: all senators benefit from an informal system that provides considerable latitude for obstructionists, but individual senators will be tempted, particularly late in a congress, to exploit these prerogatives opportunistically. If individual senators do exploit their prerogatives in this manner, then it will undercut the benefits offered by filibusters as mechanisms to account for preference intensity and would prompt changes to the rules to limit prerogatives for everyone. In this context, norms of restraint—buttressed by the threat of rules changes—can limit obstruction. We argue that senators in the 19th century shared an understanding that end-of-congress obstruction was appropriate for killing legislation only when there was a conjunction of an intense minority and less committed majority. The breakdown of this

---

[31]It is true that a senator might cite norms of restraint as a way to save face when surrendering to the majority due to other considerations, such as preferring not to bear the costs of obstruction. Nonetheless, such cases as the filibuster of the Oregon Bill in 1848, in which the costs of delay were minimal for the minority, help to rule out such alternative explanations. Indeed, as noted below, norms likely have the most critical importance when it comes to end-of-congress obstruction.

norm—due to the exogenous changes discussed below—was a major impetus for the eventual shift to a formal cloture rule as a supplement to filibusters regulated by war-of-attrition dynamics.[32]

This restraint and general understanding are consistent with long-standing norms that scholars of the Senate have argued are essential for understanding the institution. Norms or "folkways" have traditionally played an important role in the Senate. Matthews (1960, Ch. 5) cites several of these "unwritten rules of the game," but the most important ones for our analysis are *reciprocity* and *institutional patriotism*. Reciprocity, among other things, entails that senators practice restraint in their exercise of their extensive individual prerogatives, including those that empower them to obstruct. "If a senator *does* push his formal powers to the limit, he has broken the implicit bargain and can expect, not cooperation from his colleagues, but only retaliation in kind" (Matthews 1960, 101, emphasis in the original). One of the most severe forms of retaliation would be the removal of the prerogatives that enabled such behavior in the first place.[33] Thus, the norm of reciprocity is one possible informal constraint on the use of obstruction. Reciprocity took the form of restraint, with senators reciprocally agreeing to limit their use of their individual prerogatives.

The second important norm—institutional patriotism—refers to the expectation that senators make an "emotional investment" in the institution. "One who brings the Senate as an institution or senators as a class into disrepute invites his own destruction as an effective legislator. . . . Senators are, as a group, fiercely protective of, and highly patriotic in regard to, the Senate" (Matthews 1960, 102). As discussed in Chapter 1, excessive filibustering has been one of the primary sources of black marks on the Senate's general reputation.[34] The promotion of institutional loyalty and threats to change the rules should individuals behave in a "disloyal" manner would temper obstruction, as senators sought to protect the legitimacy of their institution. A loss in legitimacy would have hurt individual senators, since it would have decreased the value of a Senate seat—especially if the public supported a transmission of power away from the Senate to other branches in the separation of powers system.

---

[32]One might ask whether the Senate could enact a rule eliminating end-of-congress filibusters but allowing minority obstruction at other times. Proposals featuring this design were floated at different points in the Senate's history, but they ran into the difficulty that such procedures would give incentives to the majority to delay controversial items requiring extended debate until the end of a congress, when they would be shielded from filibusters. As such, it would ultimately render obstruction entirely toothless, even for an intense minority.

[33]Of course, for the majority to exercise this option, it would need to build a coalition of individuals who would be willing to accept new restrictions on their own use of the prerogatives in question.

[34]This point has often been made by those pushing for rules changes in the Senate. For example, see Senator Orville Platt's statement in support of his resolution for majority cloture in 1893 (*Congressional Record*, September 21, p. 1636) and Senator George Vest's (D–MO) statement in the *Congressional Record*, December 5, 1894, p. 46.

These norms have deep roots in the Senate, extending back into the 19th century (Matthews 1960, 116–17). Indeed, the original institutional design delineated in the Constitution established a fertile environment for these norms to flourish. The basic structure of the Senate laid out by the Founders provided the context within which relational legislating—of which norms were a central part—could emerge and be sustained. Comparisons with the House are particularly informative here. The Senate has always been a smaller body than the House, since only two senators are selected from each state regardless of size and population. Malapportionment in the Senate meant that the upper chamber grew at a much slower rate than its counterpart. The smaller size of the Senate provided more opportunities for repeated interaction and enhanced communication among senators within any given congress. The six-year terms of senators, as opposed to the two-year terms of House members, made long-term relationships over successive congresses more likely and extended the "shadow of the future."[35] The staggering of terms—that is, providing that only one-third of the Senate would be up for reelection every two years—induced longitudinal stability in its membership.[36] Indirect election by state legislatures was intended by the Framers to promote additional stability by insulating senators from volatility in the electorate. The conventional view of the Senate is that it approximates a "club," precisely the kind of close-knit group necessary for relational legislating to emerge and remain viable.[37]

It makes sense then that the Senate, especially when compared with the House, could depend more on unwritten conventions to govern their "workaday affairs" and still legislate effectively while allowing for filibusters fought as wars of attrition. As Cooper and Rybicki (2002, 191) observe, the Senate has traditionally "resisted rules changes that would alter its fundamental character as a body that worked on the basis of mutual consent and forbearance."[38] The cultivation of these norms among close-knit senators would promote cooperation among them. To keep senators from excessive posturing and engaging in rampant obstruction, it may have simply been more beneficial to rely on norms that provide disincentives for engaging in this kind of behavior in the first place, rather than depending on rules for dealing with obstructive efforts once they were underway. In particular, norms providing convergent expectations concerning the dynamics of filibusters al-

---

[35] Axelrod (1986) has shown how in relatively small populations with a long time horizon cooperation can evolve through the use of reciprocal strategies such as "tit for tat."

[36] See Shepsle, Dickson, and Van Houweling (2003) for a model of how the overlapping generations feature may affect distributive politics in the Senate.

[37] Ellickson (1991, 177) defines a group as "*close-knit* when informal power is broadly distributed among group members and the information pertinent to informal control circulates easily among them." We are not arguing that the Senate had an "inner club" or "Establishment," which ruled the institution (White 1968, 83–84). Instead, we claim that the Senate as a whole—in the 19th century—shared important features with a close-knit club. See Polsby (1986, 89–97) for a critique of the "inner club" concept.

[38] Cooper and Rybicki (2002, 203) add that "the effects of size were powerfully reinforced by the high regard senators had for their status as senators and the habits of mutual deference that flowed from such regard."

low for the information revelation benefits of the war of attrition, while checking opportunistic behavior—particularly late in a congress.

It is crucial to note that norms refer to widely shared expectations, but they need not be shared by all senators to be effective, and they need not always dominate all other considerations (see Rohde 1988; Sinclair 1989). Instead, for norms to have an impact, it is necessary that violating these expectations be regarded by a substantial group of senators as not worth the costs. These costs may include direct sanctions being imposed on defectors. In addition, we argue that most senators understood in the pre-cloture Senate that excessive obstruction risked provoking rules changes that would limit all senators' prerogatives, and that this risk added to the costs that constrained filibusters.[39]

2.5.2 Senators' Statements about Norms

Evidence that strong norms concerning obstruction existed in the 19th century abounds in the comments of senators in floor debates related to obstruction. These same debates also repeatedly suggest that members understood that rampant obstruction risked generating a crackdown through new rules or precedents. Indeed, obstructionist senators often cite norms as they explain why they relented, indicating that norms were an intimate part of filibuster battles. We discuss several key cases where the evidence indicates that senators held common beliefs about the need for restraint in exercising individual prerogatives and the potential for rules changes. We offer these cases only to support the plausibility of our underlying assumptions regarding norms; they are not meant as tests of our theoretical arguments.

An early statement about the importance of informal conventions to the operation of the Senate and their relation to formal rules was made by Louis McClane (Jacksonian–DE) during the debate in 1828 over the powers of the vice president in preserving order:

> The dignified forbearance and liberal comity which had uniformly marked the deliberation of the Senate, themselves, created a law, and imposed restraints, more efficient than any written rule. They arose from a consciousness of the possession of the ultimate power to enforce respect of the rules of decorum, by other means, when these failed. In such a body, he said, that was the only efficient law. It was the great moral influence of the power of the body for its own preservation, which, like that of punishing contempt, or breech of privilege, required no written code; which

---

[39]It is not clear that such a rules change should be viewed as punishment for those filibustering. Instead, if obstruction repeatedly precludes the Senate from acting on important business, the costs of relational legislating will come to exceed the benefits for most senators. Those favoring the current bill being obstructed will presumably have the most urgent incentive to impose limits on debate, but the institutional change would endure to the extent that senators were responding to the more general proliferation of obstruction.

was within us and around us, accompanied us in all our walks, was our shield and buckler, and, though strong as iron, was yet light as air. He believed the moral force was weakened by too much specialty in regulations of order, as the multiplying of rules of order not unfrequently led to disorder. (*Register of Debates*, February 11, p. 293)

Another early example came in 1841, as the new Whig majority struggled against Democrats seeking to slow the progress of Henry Clay's ambitious agenda. As discussed in more detail in Chapter 3, Clay claimed that procedural changes were necessary to expedite action. Democrats countered by arguing, in the words of William R. King (D–AL), that "a majority of the Senate could always dispose of what was before it very much as they pleased" (*Congressional Globe*, June 12, 1841, p. 46). James Buchanan (D–PA) added that Clay's proposal was unnecessary because "there was a courtesy among the members of that body which rendered it always easy for gentlemen to accomplish their wishes as to the order of business" (*Congressional Globe*, June 12, 1841, p. 45). The Whigs' subsequent success in passing their program—despite Democrats' continued opposition, as reflected in their near-unanimous nay votes—suggests that such statements were not mere empty gestures (see Chapter 3).

The puzzling case of the aborted obstruction of the Oregon Territory Bill (1848), discussed at the beginning of Chapter 1, featured similar statements about how the Senate operates. Several senators explained that the reason they capitulated on the Oregon Bill—even though they were undoubtedly advantaged by the impending adjournment and the standing rules—was that a determined majority had been revealed through the dispute and the minority should not prevent it from ultimately acting. Senator Thomas Rusk (D–TX) argued, "The bill was passed, and according to the course which had heretofore been pursued in the Senate, when a majority, a clearly ascertained majority, had agreed upon a measure, it was proper that he should yield, that they might have the opportunity of passing it, and assuming to God and their country the responsibility of the act" (*Congressional Globe*, August 14, 1848, p. 1084). King of Alabama echoed these thoughts, and though he reemphasized his opposition to the bill, implored his colleagues to let the Senate act, expressing concern about the institution's reputation: "It would comport better with the dignity of the Senate, with their standing in the country, and with public sentiment, than by persisting in opposing this resolution" (*Congressional Globe*, August 14, 1848, p. 1084). Sam Houston (D–TX) added that the demonstration of majority support, however narrow the majority might be, required him to submit and refrain from further delay, since it was a narrow majority that admitted his state to the Union. This kind of reciprocity was essential to relation-based governance.

In March 1873, George Wright (R–IA) introduced a resolution instructing the Rules Committee to investigate the propriety of revising the rules to establish a germaneness provision and a provision for the previous question, possibly by a majority vote. Proponents of the measure claimed that the size of the Senate now required these provisions, and that the abuse of privileges had created serious difficulties that needed to be addressed.[40] In the debate on the motion to take up the resolution, Allen Thurman (D–OH) argued that the claims that senators were going too far in their use of individual prerogatives were exaggerated, and that it was preferable to rely on informal rules for checking this behavior: "There has been no such abuse as is here complained of. Sir, the fewer rules you have and the more you trust the honor of Senators, to their character, to their reputation, their responsibility as gentlemen and as Senators, the more pleasantly and the more readily will you get through the public business" (*Congressional Record*, March 19, 1873, p. 116). Thomas Bayard (D–DE), claiming that he knew of no abuses of unlimited debate that had taken place, argued that "the majority have it in their power to enact measures into laws." He added, "[T]here is a personal responsibility of men to their country and to their constituency on this subject which ought to be sufficient, which, in the past, has proved to be sufficient to protect the country" from the problems presented by unlimited debate. However, he did note the importance of the threat of rules change in keeping obstruction in check, stating that when abuse has occurred, such "rigorous measures" would be warranted (*Congressional Record*, March 19, 1873, p. 114). Matthew Carpenter (R–WI) and Eugene Casserly (D–CA) noted the potential costs of adopting a formal germaneness rule, arguing that it would cause more problems because enforcing it would require additional discussion should a senator be ruled out of order and then the chair's ruling appealed (*Congressional Record*, March 19, 1873, p. 115). These arguments appear to have prevailed, since the Senate rejected the motion to take up the resolution 25-30.[41]

By the end of the 19th century, prominent senators continued to highlight the importance of norms for maintaining the Senate's ability to govern itself in the absence of formal debate limits, even as these same senators noted that these norms were coming under challenge. In a speech articulating the Republicans' strategy in allowing an eventual final vote on the Wilson-Gorman Tariff in 1894, which the party fiercely opposed, John Sherman (R–OH) argued that Democrats had in the Elections Bill case pushed obstruction "far beyond any opposition which has been shown to this bill." Sherman argued that "I am one of those old-fashioned Senators who believe that we have the right to free and fair debate; that we ought to be restrained only by such limits as our own reason should dictate, and not such as should be settled by the other side" (*Congressional Record*, June 9, 1894, pp. 6031–

---

[40] The Senate had seventy-four members at the time.

[41] The twenty-five votes in favor of taking up the proposal suggest that senators may have differed in their judgments about whether obstruction had become excessive at this point. But it is important to note that these were not necessarily votes in favor of change, since there may have been senators opposed to the proposal who nevertheless thought it deserved consideration.

32). This, however, was not permission to obstruct endlessly. Instead, he claimed

> Others around me have expressed the opinion I entertain, that we shall give to this measure only that opposition which is demanded by the interests of our people—not to defeat the will of majority, but so that the will of the majority as exercised here shall not be wrongful, unjust, and destructive to all American industries. That is the way we feel about it. I, for one, do not intend to utter a single word or spend a single minute to prevent the action of the majority on this bill; because I believe it is the constitutional right of a majority to pass such legislation as they think proper; but we must determine for ourselves the extent of our opposition, and how far it shall be carried. . . . Our power to extend debate is almost unlimited. It is our courtesy which has enabled the other side to have the debate carried on under the five-minute rule, and I hope the usual courtesy will be extended to our side. (p. 6032)

One of the clearest statements of the existence and importance of norms regarding obstruction, as well as the credibility of the threat that a majority could change the rules that allow it, was made by Henry Cabot Lodge (R–MA) during the debate over (and filibuster of) the repeal of the Sherman Silver Purchase Law in 1893, which led to the introduction of a resolution for majority cloture by Orville Platt (R–CT). Lodge contended that since the Senate has no rules for compelling a vote,

> they are therefore rules which are based upon courtesy. By the courtesy of the Senate every Senator can speak at any length and at any time. There is, in a word, no method for preventing unlimited debate. But a system of courtesy in the conduct of business of a great legislative body, if it is to be anything or to have any effect, it must be reciprocal. The unwritten law of mutual concession must be observed or a system of courtesy is impossible. . . . When it appears that unlimited debate, the right of which is accorded by courtesy, is used for the purposes of obstruction, then the system of courtesy has become impossible. When a minority not only does not allow a debate to come to a close, but will not even name any date, no matter how distant, at which it will assent to the close of that debate, it is obvious that courtesy has become entirely one-sided: that unlimited debate is to be permitted, but that the right to vote is to be taken away. When the system of courtesy has reached this point it has not only ceased to be practicable, but it has become an abuse and a danger. (*Congressional Record*, September 21, 1893, pp. 1637–38)

He then went on to claim that obstruction exists because the majority allows it, and it is in the hands of the majority to prevent it from occurring. In an article in the *North American Review*, Lodge (1893, 528) contended that "there was never a time when they [the Democrats] could not have brought about a vote with the assistance of the chair, whose occupant was also of their party, if as a party, they had only chosen to do so." Lodge backed the Platt proposal because he believed the minority had reached beyond the limits of courtesy, thereby violating the norm of reciprocity, in their forty-six-day filibuster of the Silver Bill.[42] David Turpie (D–IN) responded by questioning the need for adopting more formal rules, arguing that the measure under consideration warranted neither the extreme of a filibuster nor the imposition of a cloture rule, and instead that what was needed was to "continue to appeal to the wisdom and moderation and the well-known devotion to duty of our fellow Senators" (*Congressional Record*, Sept. 23, 1893, p. 1704).

In the end, the minority did surrender and the bill passed. When the filibuster began, it appeared that enough senators were willing to accept a compromise short of full repeal so that the obstruction might succeed. Majority party Democrats were accused of waffling on a campaign promise to enact the repeal. But President Grover Cleveland made it clear that he would accept only complete repeal, which led many of the Democrats inclined toward compromise to oppose weakening amendments. Once the pro-repeal majority solidified, it used around-the-clock sessions in an attempt to break the filibuster. Threats to change the rules continued and became more intense, with Senator David Hill (D–NY) taking the lead in both proposing rules changes as well as pointing out how precedents could be established to clamp down on obstruction. The *New York Times* credited Hill with bringing about the end of the filibuster, claiming that he was the leader of a "movement that will make repeal possible, and that will render impossible in the future any such disgraceful and senseless filibustering as that conducted by a few Republicans and Democrats for the last eight weeks" ("The Ball Is in Motion Now," *New York Times*, October 18, 1893,

---

[42] Henry Teller (R–CO) disputed Lodge's claim about the importance of courtesy, claiming that senators had a "constitutional right" to obstruct, but acknowledged that it could be taken away and lamented the consequences should that happen. (*Congressional Record*, September 22, 1893, p. 1675). Interestingly, Teller predicted that Lodge would change his position to be less supportive of restrictions on debate in the future when he found himself in the minority on some great question. This prediction came true when Lodge spoke against a cloture motion considered in 1915 (*Congressional Record*, February 15, p. 3786). However, Lodge's conversion is not evidence that senators in this era routinely switched sides on procedural issues as their short-term political interests changed (e.g., as they moved from the minority to the majority). Lodge was in the minority party both in 1893 and in 1915. During his service in the House, he was an ally of the Speaker during the 1890 fight over the Reed Rules. Having advocated forcefully for Reed's rules just three years earlier while a member of the House, the freshman senator Lodge continued to share Reed's disdain for minority obstruction in 1893. The *New York Times* characterized the 1915 proposal that Lodge spoke against as "drastic" and claimed that it lacked support because it would have allowed the majority "to pass any bill, no matter how important or complicated, in two days" ("Owens Outlines Fight for Cloture," December 1, 1915, p. 7). Though still in the minority in 1917, Lodge joined the vast majority of senators in supporting the more moderate two-thirds cloture rule.

p. 5). Such stratagems demonstrated the majority's intense commitment to passage of the bill, whatever the obstacles. Rather than risk a rules change or a permanent break in party ranks, southern Democrats dropped their support for the western silverites' obstruction, even as they continued to oppose the bill. Once the southerners abandoned the westerners, the filibuster collapsed. This example fits the war of attrition framework outlined above nicely, with the lurking possibility of rules changes playing a critical role. Still, the push for rules changes acquired its urgency from the sense among the majority that the obstructionists were violating the shared understanding that filibusters give way in the face of a committed majority.

It is worth emphasizing that such breakdowns (and near breakdowns) in norms were becoming more common at the turn of the century. As discussed below, the expanded size of the Senate undermined norms of restraint, which in turn generated pressure for formal rules to constrain behavior. In March of 1903, William Allison (R–IA) introduced a resolution instructing the Rules Committee to consider changes in debate rules. The *New York Times* claimed that the members of Rules did not support cloture, but that "they are all convinced that there has been grievous abuse of the traditional unwritten law of the Senate and that the country demands a change" ("Proposition to Limit Debate in the Senate," March 12, 1903, p. 5). The sentiment that individual prerogatives were being pushed too far was echoed in other newspapers at the time. The *Washington Post* noted how the Senate was "sensitive to public criticism of its long debates, which criticism is fostered to a large extent by members of the House" (March 12, 1903, p. 4). The *New York Evening Post* stated that "[i]t is not alone Congressman [Joseph] Cannon, not merely the House of Representatives, but the country at large that is growing weary and ashamed of a Senate of grown men which can find no way of escape from its filibusterers and marauders on its own floor." But this outside pressure was not great enough to force serious action by senators. Along with Allison's proposal, Orville Platt introduced a proposal for a three-fifths cloture rule, but his proposal was laid on the table. By 1917, however, as instances of unrestrained obstruction killing widely supported legislation mounted—particularly at the end of a congress—the Senate finally embraced a formal rule for ending debate.

2.5.3 Cooperation, Communication, and Punishment

As the 1873, 1893, and 1903 cases suggest, threats of rules changes were repeatedly used when obstruction was deemed to be becoming excessive. However, the threat of or actual rules changes were a blunt instrument for promoting cooperation and preventing obstruction. Norms helped to maintain the viability of a system with lax or nonexistent formal rules regarding debate where filibusters as wars of attrition could play out. The literature on relational contracting emphasizes the importance of communication and collective punishment in dissuading individuals from violating informal conventions. In our view, communication about Senate norms was essential to promoting adherence to them. While collective punishment may have played an important role, disagreement exists in the congressional literature about its prevalence and effectiveness in sustaining norms (Huitt 1961; Huitt 1962; Matthews 1961). Unambiguous systematic evidence is difficult to find concerning those who appeared to have violated norms against obstruction. A particular difficulty is that when norms are strong—as we argue was the case for most of the 19th century—one should witness few, if any, significant violations and thus little or no actual punishment. When norms fray, violations will become more frequent, but the effectiveness of punishment will weaken in this context. An examination of two of the most notorious obstructionists in the pre-cloture Senate, Matthew Quay (R–PA) and Robert La Follette (R–WI), reveals evidence that there was at least a measure of collective punishment against the them. Both served during the period when norms were coming under severe challenge. Indeed, the vigor of Quay and La Follette's challenges to norms of restraint, combined with the apparent emulation of their tactics by other senators in the 1900 to 1917 period, suggest that those seeking to deter violations by punishing violators were now fighting a losing battle.

La Follette, who served in the Senate from 1905 to 1925, stands out as someone who pushed his individual prerogatives in debate to the maximum. The Wisconsin senator used the filibuster as a high-profile weapon to promote Progressive goals and to fight the conservative leadership of his party. Without question, La Follette's activities drew the opprobrium of his fellow senators: "It is doubtful that any man aroused more bitter antagonisms in the Senate or was ever more reviled by his colleagues than he" (Huitt 1961, 573). And he appears to have been collectively rebuked on at least two occasions for his filibustering behavior. During his 1908 filibuster against the Aldrich-Vreeland Currency Bill, the Senate acted to enforce rules and establish new precedents in a way that could be interpreted as punishment. La Follette staged a highly visible filibuster, delivering marathon speeches that were widely reported in the press and enraged Nelson Aldrich.[43] Senators, in conjunction with the vice president, responded in several ways. First, La Follette's secretary, who had been helping him discern when a quorum was absent, was prohibited from engaging in this activity, even though such assistance had been allowed previously. Second, it was made emphatic that the two-speech rule would be strictly applied to La Follette. Third, new precedents were established regarding successive quorum calls and counting quorums, which essentially doomed La Follette's efforts (Burdette 1940, 83–91). The Wisconsin senator claimed that the rules were being arbitrarily applied to him.[44]

In response to La Follette's role in the filibuster of the Armed-Ship Bill, which was the catalyst for the adoption of cloture in 1917, senators worked collectively to prevent him from delivering a speech on the floor in the waning

---

[43]President Roosevelt was also disturbed by La Follette's actions, calling the filibuster "stupid" and La Follette "an entirely worthless senator" (quoted in Unger 2000, 183).

[44]We examine this case in more detail in Chapters 3 and 8.

hours of the 64th Congress. Majorities voted to uphold a ruling of the chair against La Follette and to allow another senator to exceed his two-speech quota in order to keep La Follette from gaining the floor before time in the congress expired (Burdette 1940, 120–21). La Follette "writhed in the humiliation of being unable to get the floor," and tempers nearly boiled over into physical violence (Unger 2000, 245–46). During the debate over cloture reform in the next congress, La Follette claimed that the vice president had conspired with other senators to again deny him the floor; among other things, the vice president apparently told La Follette that he was not keeping a list of senators seeking recognition, even though he was.[45]

A closer look at another infamous filibusterer provides additional supportive evidence of collective punishment. Matthew Quay, who served from 1887 to 1899 and 1901 to 1904, used his individual prerogatives to a much greater extent than his contemporaries, and often on issues that narrowly affected his state, holding up other Senate business (Burdette 1940; Kehl 1981). An article published on the event of his death noted that he successfully held the Senate up on a "score of instances" where "he seized upon the moment when the situation gave him a power impossible under other conditions at other times." Furthermore, "Quay's achievements were all in defiance of Senate law and parliamentary regulations." He was looked upon "as one ready to sacrifice the interests of party and the public to promote his own purposes." His rapport with his colleagues seemed to suffer as a result. The article claimed that because of his methods he "had few friends and no intimates" and "Republican leaders neither liked him nor trusted him" ("Quay's Senate Power Due to His Methods," *The North American*, May 29, 1904).

The primary evidence of retribution against Quay stems from the Senate's refusal to seat him in 1900, when he was reappointed to his seat by the governor of Pennsylvania after the state legislature failed to reach agreement. Quay had been embroiled in a graft scandal that created controversy in the state legislature, although he was cleared of wrong doing by the time the Senate took up the case. Quay lost by one vote on the Senate floor, and the vote could have easily gone the other way had some notable Republican colleagues supported him. Senator Marcus Hanna (R–OH), then chair of the Republican party, paired against Quay and remarked that "the Republican party would be better off with him" not in the Senate ("Quay's Long Control," *Washington Post*, May 5, 1904, p. 5). Senators seemed to be concerned about the image that Quay's tactics projected, from his perceived bossism in Pennsylvania to his extreme use of individual prerogatives, the ends of which were to maintain his control over the Republican machine in his state.[46]

---

[45] Letter from Robert M. La Follette to his family, March 6, 1917, La Follette Family Papers, Library of Congress. Although his tactics disturbed his contemporaries, Huitt (1961) points out that La Follette has been viewed in hindsight as an "outstanding" senator, receiving special commemoration on the Senate side of the Capitol.

[46] We considered the possibility that the committee assignment process might have been used to punish these senators, given that others have argued that this is an important

Punishment may also have taken less tangible, and therefore difficult to measure, forms. Our difficulty as researchers in observing informal sanctions does not mean such mechanisms were ineffective. Huitt (1961, 573) argues that although punishment even of an informal nature is typically slow in coming, it comes in the form of "a spiritual banishment more conclusive than formal censure and more galling, in its daily erosion of ego, than physical expulsion." Unfortunately "spiritual banishment" does not lend itself to measurement and therefore eludes systematic analysis. Nevertheless, senators had means at their disposal to punish each other. For example, in a body that conducts a good deal of its business by unanimous consent, senators could make life difficult for norm violators by denying their requests for such consent.

While some forms of ex post punishment would have been necessary to sustain relational legislating, ex ante communication about cooperation would have played just as important a role in making possible the gains offered by wars of attrition through filibusters. At the heart of the theory of relation-based governance are game-theoretic models of indefinitely repeated play. While the simple one-shot prisoner's dilemma—the workhorse model for examining collective interaction—predicts individuals will not cooperate in equilibrium, cooperative equilibria exist when this game is played repeatedly. But the Folk Theorem states that any equilibrium is possible, including noncooperative ones, in repeated play settings as long as it is possible for players to receive worse payoffs (Fudenberg and Tirole 1991, 150–55). Crisper predictions emerge if additional factors are brought to bear on the question of how cooperation can be achieved in repeat play settings. An extensive literature bridging several disciplines chronicles a wide array of experiments in which communication produces cooperation in situations where individuals confront collective dilemmas.[47] Communication among players, even if it is costless, greatly increases the likelihood that individuals will choose to cooperate. This improvement has been found to occur even in the absence of formal sanctions for those who defect (Ostrom, Walker, and Gardner 1992). Furthermore, the mode of communication affects the degree of cooperation, with individuals who communicate on a face-to-face basis realizing more

---

tool for rewarding or punishing various behaviors (Cox and McCubbins 1993). While some evidence exists that La Follette was passed over for certain committee assignments, it is difficult to tell whether this was due to his excessive filibustering or to his general ideological differences with his party and its leadership (Stephenson 1930; Brady and Epstein 1997. It is also worth noting that La Follette's committee portfolio throughout the entirety of his career did not indicate that the assignment process was used to punish him. He sat on the Finance Committee for seven out of the ten congresses he served in, which, according to Canon and Stewart's method of ranking the importance of committees (2002, Table 9–2), was near the top of the Senate committee hierarchy during La Follette's tenure. Quay's committee portfolio did not reflect punishment for his behavior, since he occupied seats on both the Appropriations and Commerce Committees, which were ranked second and eighth respectively during his tenure.

[47] For a thorough review of this literature, see Ostrom (1998). Experimental studies have shown that communication can produce cooperation even in one-shot prisoner's dilemmas.

cooperation than individuals who communicate by other means (e.g., sending computerized messages) (Sell and Wilson 1991; Palfrey and Rosenthal 1988; Ostrom and Walker 1991). These experimental results indicate the importance of investigating variation in conditions that promote cooperation through communication.

The small size of the Senate created a wealth of opportunities for interpersonal interaction among senators. Such interactions would be essential for communicating senators' personal commitment to cooperative norms. Face-to-face conversations, as well as formal statements during debates, would have promoted the belief that senators were generally on board when it came to limited use of their prerogatives. The examples discussed above suggest that senators repeatedly articulated the importance of adhering to cooperative norms. This kind of discussion would have been key in preventing defection from norms of restraint and enabling the Senate to function despite its sparse rules regarding debate and deliberation.

2.6 PREDICTIONS ABOUT LAWMAKING

Our approach—with its focus on costs, endogenous rules, and norms—leads us to predictions about the conduct of obstruction itself and to more general predictions about lawmaking and institutional change. The war-of-attrition framework generates several predictions concerning the dynamics of obstruction in the pre-cloture period. First, as the costs confronting obstructionists fall and as the costs facing bill supporters increase, filibusters will be more likely to succeed. This suggests that end-of-congress filibusters are more likely to succeed, and the threat of such obstruction is more likely to affect the calculations of bill supporters (e.g., by inducing them to build larger coalitions to withstand the obstruction). Therefore, our empirical analysis should pay particular attention to the peculiar institutional feature of lame duck sessions, which occurred after the bi-annual congressional elections and had an automatic adjournment date of March 4th in odd-numbered years. A considerable amount of legislating was conducted during lame duck sessions, even though obstructionist senators were substantially advantaged by the existence of the relatively exogenous deadline imposed by the automatic adjournment date, which brought about the death of any legislation not yet passed.[48] The costs to bill supporters of sitting out a filibuster were very high in the lame duck sessions, because it tangibly reduced the chances that other legislation salient to senators would be addressed.

---

[48] We say "relatively exogenous" because the deadline could have been and was changed. However, it took a constitutional amendment to do so, since the automatic adjournment date was based on constitutional provisions setting the length of members' terms. The 20th Amendment eliminated the standard lame duck sessions, and moved the automatic adjournment date to January 3, the day when senators' terms now expire, although Congress typically adjourns well before this date. Thus, it is reasonable to treat the March 4 adjournment date as exogenous to ordinary, day-to-day congressional politics.

Second, as the size of the coalition opposing the bill increases, it should be better able to bear the physical costs of obstruction. Similarly, as the number of bill supporters decreases, it becomes more burdensome to keep enough members on or near the floor to defeat the obstructionist tactics. As a result, the likelihood of success of obstruction should be an increasing function of the coalition size supporting obstruction, although a key question is what size threshold the coalition must cross in order to be successful.

Third, the relative salience of the issue to the minority and majority will be crucial. The probability that obstruction is observed and succeeds will be greater as the resolve level of the minority increases relative to the majority. Differential salience, coupled with timing considerations, are important factors that motivated senators to obstruct, but also figured into the decisions of others regarding whether to fight or capitulate.

Beyond offering predictions concerning when obstruction will occur and succeed, the war-of-attrition framework provides a rationale for why we would observe obstruction in equilibrium, notwithstanding its costs to both sides. Incomplete information about resolve makes delay a possible outcome. Furthermore, it suggests that filibuster politics will often take on the pattern of the minority obstructing, testing the majority's commitment, and then surrendering when the majority shows it is committed to passage. It also helps understand the common view in the 19th century that obstruction was an acceptable strategy to delay legislation, but that if and when the majority showed its commitment to passage—through such devices as keeping the bill on the floor for an extended period—the bill was generally allowed to pass.

This leads to predictions about general patterns in lawmaking. For the 19th and early-20th centuries, majorities will be sufficient to legislate when the end-of-congress deadline is not looming and when the issue under question is equally salient to both sides. Supermajorities—but not unanimous coalitions—will generally be necessary to pass legislation at the very end of a congress or when foes of a bill care more intensely about it than do its supporters. Furthermore, we should see threats of rules changes when the minority insists on obstructing legislation favored by a committed majority. This threat of a majority "revolution" was a key basis for remote majoritarianism, which in turn helped to induce the constrained role played by obstruction in the 19th-century Senate.[49]

Our focus on relational legislating as it pertains to obstruction provides additional predictions concerning institutional change. As noted above, one limitation of arguments about norms is that it is difficult to know how seriously to treat member statements concerning their self-restraint. However, models of relational legislating provide expectations for when norms will fail and formal rules will consequently be adopted. Specifically, the key variables that the economics literature emphasizes when considering the maintenance

---

[49]We realize that our argument about the mutability of Senate rules is controversial. Our predictions regarding a largely majoritarian Senate follow directly from these claims, however. If our theoretical assertions are incorrect, then our predictions should not be borne out in the empirical evidence presented in subsequent chapters.

of relation-based governance are the size and stability of the group. A central argument of Dixit (2004) and others is that relational contracting is more easily sustainable when groups are stable and of a reasonable size. However, as new members are added and group turnover increases, it becomes more difficult to maintain the communication and informal constraints that prevent opportunistic behavior (Dixit 2004, 12–13, 65–66).[50] The temptation to exploit individual prerogatives becomes too great and the communication of norms becomes less effective. As cooperation unravels, the group has an incentive to resort to more formal and explicit constraints on behavior. This does not necessarily mean that the system will experience complete failure, as formal rules can be adopted to address particular shortcomings. Or as Dixit (2004, 85) puts it, "the diminishing returns of a relation-based system can be countered without going to a fully centralized rules-based alternative."

Variation in such factors as the size of the Senate gives us traction on the question of whether or not cooperation is in fact the result of communication and long-term relationships. We use historical evidence to assess whether changes in behavior are consistent with comparative statics predictions derived from the theory of relational legislating. As we show in later chapters, obstruction in the Senate has varied substantially over its history. We investigate whether attempts to impose more explicit rules can be explained by changes in the political and institutional context—such as increases in chamber size—which led to the degradation of relational legislating. The response that we would expect to problems of sustaining cooperation under informal rules is to adopt formal rules for constraining debate.[51] We develop this argument in more detail in later chapters and find that changes in chamber size (consistent with the norms approach) played a role in encouraging greater obstruction, which in turn made rules reform a more attractive option.

The Senate's changing workload, which is related to the number of members of the chamber, should have a systematic impact on obstruction. For much of the 19th century, the Senate's limited workload meant that the cost of waiting out a filibuster was relatively small and that bill supporters

---

[50]One could argue that as the size of a group increases, it becomes easier to enforce relational arrangements since the costs of enforcement are spread over a larger group. Yet the marginal cost of enforcement does not decline with group size since every individual must refuse to deal with a defector. Costs come not in the form of proactive punishment, but in the form of inaction—that is, forgoing potentially beneficial transactions with a known transgressor.

[51]The theory of relational legislating provides leverage on the important question of institutional change and thus is more expansive than Matthews's treatment of norms. Specifically, Matthews says nothing about why legislators would choose to rely more on informal constraints than formal ones, or what would cause them to move along the informal-formal continuum in their institutional choices. Sinclair (1989) examines the breakdown of norms in the post–World War II Senate, but does not cover transitions from informal conventions to formal rules in earlier periods. By tackling these questions, our analysis offers a richer understanding of institutional development than has past research invoking the concept of norms.

could easily afford to keep an obstructed bill on the floor for an extended period. This meant that bill opponents would generally anticipate that their obstruction would fail, and as a result, only an extremely intense minority (particularly one that suspects the majority has a low resolve level) would filibuster. Obstruction provided a mechanism for such intense minorities to slow legislation down so as to test the resolve level of the majority. As the Senate's workload increased, the costs of keeping obstructed legislation on the floor increased as well. This made it more difficult for bill supporters to fight filibusters; for a given level of resolve, they became less willing to bear the costs of delay. This, in turn, encouraged increased obstruction. Even minorities with relatively low resolve levels were tempted to filibuster in order to test the majority's commitment, given the potential for a short filibuster to throw the Senate into turmoil.

Increases in the size of the chamber and workload had a reciprocal effect. New issues and legislative demands were placed on the agenda as new states entered the Union and new senators entered the chamber. A growing workload meant that the time pressures normally associated with the end of the congress were felt earlier and earlier. Concurrently, increases in membership would have weakened the effectiveness of norms that encouraged restraint toward the end of a congress precisely as the time pressures necessitating such restraint became more severe at earlier points in a congress. Time pressures induced by a heightened workload also increased the attractiveness of rules reforms that provided either majority rule or a fixed threshold for overcoming obstruction. That is, wars of attrition over obstruction became a less attractive information revelation mechanism for the Senate as a rising workload increased the scarcity of floor time.

Even as the informational benefits of filibustering were eviscerated over the course of the 20th century, this has not spelled the demise of Senate obstruction. From the start, unlimited debate has empowered senators as individuals and allowed them to display their commitment to their constituents and a broader, national audience. Indeed, the power benefits to individual members have become even more precious in the context of the individualistic, candidate-centered electoral arena confronting contemporary senators. These benefits have helped to sustain the right of unlimited debate even as norms restricting its use have dissipated and as its informational value has become negligible. We argue in Chapter 11 that this has precluded (so far) the development of a floor majority in favor of banning the filibuster.

2.7 DISCUSSION

Filibusters as wars of attrition did not emerge by design. We do not argue that senators attempted to create a set of formal rules and informal conventions that together allowed them to capitalize upon the potential informational benefits of obstruction. Instead, filibusters likely were an unanticipated product of the sparse formal rules of the early Senate. These sparse rules proved sustainable, however, because informal conventions developed that allowed senators to achieve the informational gains provided by filibusters without paralyzing the institution.

Our development of the theoretical underpinnings of parliamentary obstruction and lawmaking in the Senate differs from prominent recent analyses in several crucial ways. First, our theoretical framework emphasizes the costs of engaging in and opposing filibusters, incorporating issues of salience and lost opportunities for legislating. Historically, filibusters involved races against the clock, which became more competitive when time was scarce, as it was toward the end of congressional sessions when it became more apparent how many legislative items could feasibly be addressed (Oppenheimer 1985).

Second, contrary to what the most prominent recent works on obstruction have argued (Binder 1997; Binder and Smith 1997), we contend that path dependence did not render Senate rules immune from major changes. We argue instead that a committed majority could credibly threaten to change the underlying rules and precedents regarding debate and that the mutability of the Senate's rules was a significant constraint on obstructive behavior. Senators contemplating obstruction had to take into consideration a potential response that would remove their individual prerogative of unlimited debate. Concerns about being worse off under a different set of institutional arrangements would make the threat of change a powerful disincentive for obstruction. But individuals can be better off under the absence of formal rules only if some degree of cooperation can be maintained informally. In this sense, the development and maintenance of norms as part of relational legislating were crucial—and vulnerable to breakdown as the broader political and institutional context changed. At a minimum, shared beliefs about what is unacceptable behavior must exist if members of the group are to know what should trigger the adoption of formal rules to govern their behavior. Informal rules or norms that structure behavior are particularly relevant for understanding the macro-consequences of the Senate's sparse, formal institutional environment because they help to explain how the Senate managed to operate and pass laws given that any single senator could use his extensive individual prerogatives to block the passage of legislation he opposed.

Our arguments about relational legislating represent the third major way our theoretical arguments diverge from recent work. Rational choice treatments of Congress under the rubric of the "new institutionalism" and the "positive theory of institutions" assume that cooperation among legislators is difficult to maintain and that they are prone to engage in opportunistic behavior. To address these problems, legislators erect and rely heavily on explicit, formal institutions to constrain and channel their behavior (Cox and McCubbins 1993; Krehbiel 1991; Shepsle 1978; Shepsle and Weingast 1987, 1994; Weingast and Marshall 1988).[52] The remarkably sparse institu-

---

[52] Although positive theories of congressional institutions focus almost exclusively on formal and explicit constraints on behavior, the new institutionalism, which is one of the

tional environment of the Senate raises a major challenge to the explanatory power of received theories about congressional behavior because they place such an emphasis on formal rules. These theories seem appropriate for the "textbook" House of Representatives, where strict rules for floor debate, gatekeeping power for committees, and grants of formal agenda-setting authority to leaders have played a much more prominent role. Unanimous consent agreements to restrict floor behavior—amending activity in particular— were rarely used for much of the Senate's history and are harder to adopt and enforce as compared with restrictive rules in the other chamber.[53] The lack of germaneness rules in the Senate reduces gatekeeping power, since legislation bottled up in committee can be attached as an amendment to something that does come to the floor. As we noted in Chapter 1, the Senate majority leader's floor agenda setting power pales in comparison with that of his counterpart in the House, the Speaker. If one tries to understand Senate lawmaking by focusing on formal rules, it is quite puzzling why the Senate did not degenerate into a morass of legislative impotence given the extensive individual prerogatives that senators possessed. Our theoretical framework explains how senators managed to prevent opportunism in the form of rampant obstruction from resulting in an institutional breakdown. It also enables us to understand institutional change, illuminating why senators eventually chose to adopt formal rules to place limits on debate. Thus, we provide a link between the informal literature on norms and the formal literature on legislative organization. By considering these issues in detail, we have illuminated individual motivations for filibustering, as well as how specific factors contribute to the success or failure of obstruction, and how these apply to legislative behavior and outcomes during critical periods of the Senate's history.

---

main sources of inspiration for these theories, emphasizes that norms are a constitutive part of institutions. Douglass North (1990, 4), the intellectual patriarch of new institutionalism, argues that institutional constraints consist of "formal written rules as well as typically unwritten codes of conduct that underlie and supplement formal rules." See also Greif (2000) and Pierson (2000).

[53]In fact, unanimous consent agreements were not formally recognized as orders of the Senate until 1914, which meant that presiding officers were not obligated to enforce the provisions of such agreements prior to 1914 (Gamm and Smith 2000; Roberts and Smith 2004).

Chapter Three

The Mutability of Senate Rules

One of the most controversial claims that we make in this book is that the threat of rules changes was a significant constraint on minority obstruction in early periods of the Senate's history. For our argument about the constraining effect of potential rules changes to hold, it must be the case that senators believed that it was feasible for the majority to adopt formal rules or precedents to help defeat a filibustering minority. Absent the potential for rules changes, the most determined majority could still be stymied by a committed minority, so long as the minority is large enough to bear the costs of obstruction. We have argued that even if the minority sought to filibuster a resolution proposing a rules change, the majority nonetheless had access to various mechanisms to force a vote on new precedents that would have an impact similar to a rules change resolution. Did senators generally possess the parliamentary savvy necessary to understand what could and could not be done? Strategies for filibustering and fighting filibusters have continually evolved throughout the Senate's history, but a good deal of evidence indicates that the crucial elements for the threat of rules changes to serve as a constraint were in place early in the pre-cloture Senate.

It is important to keep in mind that it was much more feasible to change the rules by majority resolution in the 19th century, and that it may not have been necessary to engage in the same kind of parliamentary maneuvers that appear to be necessary to change the rules today. Obstruction was rare (especially by today's standards) and waiting out filibusters typically was an effective strategy. Filibustering in the 19th century simply did not have the legitimacy or acceptance that it acquired in the 20th century, and it did not appear to be as successful in shaping lawmaking as it is in today's "60-vote Senate" (Sinclair 2002). Nor was the Senate generally recognized as a supermajoritarian institution at that time. While the absence of a previous question rule certainly made changing the rules via resolution more difficult than in the House, it was much more of a possibility in the 19th century than it is today.

In this chapter, we first consider the ways in which rulings by the chair were used in the House to establish important precedents concerning minority rights. These examples from the House are important both because they illustrate the flexibility and effectiveness of rulings from the chair and because senators themselves at times referred to such examples from the House. We then detail how senators used rulings from the chair to restrict, and at times to expand, minority rights in the 19th and early-20th centuries.

These examples demonstrate that the threat of establishing new precedents curbing obstruction was a credible one in the 19th century. We conclude with a detailed analysis of two cases that have been cited as evidence that inherited institutions doomed the Senate to acceptance of rules that permitted filibusters: an 1841 bid by Henry Clay to limit debate and the 1891 effort by Nelson Aldrich to enact a cloture rule to pave the way for passage of the Federal Elections Bill (see Binder and Smith 1997; Binder 1997). A closer look at these cases, however, reveals that the key to these episodes was the existence (or non-existence) of a floor majority in support of the legislation at stake, and that they suggest that a determined majority had the capacity to overcome the obstruction allowed by preexisting institutions.

3.1 RULINGS FROM THE CHAIR AND PROCEDURAL IN-NOVATION IN THE HOUSE

From early in its history, floor majorities in the House have relied heavily upon the establishment of new precedents to determine the contours of minority rights in the chamber. For example, the previous question rule—often regarded as the foundation of majoritarianism in the lower chamber (see Binder 1997)—was actually initially adopted as a precedent, only later to be incorporated into the formal rules of the chamber. Indeed, maneuvering concerning interpretation of the previous question began in 1807, when House Speaker Joseph Varnum attempted to reverse the prevailing practice by ruling that approval of the motion cut off all debate and forced an immediate vote on the pending matter. However, the House voted 103-14 to overturn the ruling (Binder 1997, 50). Four years later, in February 1811, Speaker Varnum was again asked to interpret the previous question. Based on the earlier decision on the floor, Varnum ruled that adoption of the motion did not cut off debate. But the chamber reversed the ruling on a 66-13 vote, transforming the meaning of the previous question motion: now its adoption would cut off debate and force an immediate vote. The change was added to the formal chamber rules when the new congress convened in December 1811. Still, the February 1811 ruling meant that any effort to obstruct adoption of the new rules could be cut off by the previous question motion.

An obvious and important difference between the House and Senate is that the presiding officer in the House is elected by the chamber majority, while the vice president is thrust upon the Senate by the Constitution. While this makes it more likely that the Speaker will be aligned with a floor majority, it is noteworthy that the previous question precedent was adopted by overruling the presiding officer. This example suggests that a supportive presiding officer was not a necessary condition for establishing important new precedents. The overthrow of Speaker Joseph Cannon discussed below is another example.

One of the most significant changes regarding legislative obstruction in the House was accomplished by interpretations of the chair, which were ratified by majorities on the floor. The Reed rules were launched by a set of rulings by Speaker Thomas Reed issued in January of 1890 that eliminated the main tactics that had been used to conduct filibusters in the House. Reed's innovations included counting a quorum and ruling certain motions as dilatory and therefore out of order. The precedents were adopted two weeks later as part of the standing rules of the House. But the rules themselves could not have been adopted in the face of Democratic obstruction if not for the prior precedents established by Reed. This "revolution"—which reversed decades of prior practice—had profound consequences for obstruction in the House, virtually ending its viability as an effective strategy for opposing legislation in that chamber (see Schickler 2001).[1] The severe limitations on individual prerogatives that were imposed in the House demonstrated the possibility that a similar approach to curtailing obstruction could have been pursued in the Senate (cf. Koger 2002). In fact, while the counting of quorums (i.e., counting legislators who are present even though they do not respond to a call of the roll) is more closely associated with Reed's attempts to crack down on obstruction in the House, several rulings in the upper chamber established precedents regarding the counting of quorums long before Reed's revolution.[2] It was clear to senators that they had the option of pursuing a Reed-like solution to problems caused by obstruction in their own chamber.[3]

Twenty years after Reed's revolution, a determined floor majority again boldly challenged existing understandings of the rules. In this case, however, it was the Speaker himself who allegedly stood in the way of majority rule, and thus a floor majority launched a revolutionary reinterpretation of the rules to defeat Speaker Joseph Cannon (R–IL). George Norris (R–NE) presented a resolution to change the rules by removing Cannon from his perch on the Rules Committee, expanding the size of the committee, and elimi-

---

[1]Prior to becoming Speaker, Reed had successfully sought out rulings from the chair that laid the groundwork for the subsequent use of special rules from the Rules Committee to control the flow of business on the floor. In May 1882 and again in February 1883, the Speaker ruled in favor of Reed's maneuvers, which transformed the role of the Rules Committee. Democrats heatedly objected in both cases, but their appeals of the Speaker's rulings were tabled (see Alexander 1916, 197–205).

[2]These occurred in 1858, 1871, 1879, and 1881. The ruling of 1879 was of particular note, even though it applied only to counting senators during a quorum call and not to counting senators who were present but did not participate in a roll call vote. This meant that a majority of the chamber still had to actually participate in a roll call vote for it to be valid (Burdette 1940, 38). When this precedent was raised during the Senate filibuster of the Silver Purchase Repeal Bill in 1893 (see Section 2.5 for details), Reed "wondered why he had not discovered that instance of Democratic support for his contention" regarding the validity of counting a quorum ("The Ball Is In Motion Now," *New York Times*, October 18, 1893, p. 5).

[3]Interestingly, in November of 1890 Reed was reported to be "hatching a new scheme" to get the House and Senate to adopt joint rules, leading to the adoption of the previous question in the upper body ("A Gag Rule for the Senate," *New York Times*, November 29, 1890, p. 5).

nating the Speaker's power to appoint its members. Norris claimed that his resolution was privileged due to the constitutional provision empowering the House to make its own rules.[4] Cannon's allies immediately made the point of order that Norris's resolution was not in order, citing an earlier precedent set by Democratic Speaker Samuel Randall (D–PA). Cannon was correct that House rules and precedents provided that proposals to change the rules should be referred to the Rules Committee and not be allowed directly onto the floor. However, it was also clear that referring the resolution to the Rules Committee would lead to its burial. So the insurgent Republican-Democratic floor majority instead voted 183-160 to overturn Cannon's ruling and thus pave the way for consideration and passage of the Norris resolution. Thus, to overcome a recalcitrant Speaker, the House had adopted the revolutionary precedent that motions to change the rules were now constitutionally privileged. Having accomplished their purpose of curbing the Speaker, a floor majority voted in January 1911 to reverse the precedent that proposals to change the rules were constitutionally privileged. In doing so, leading participants, most notably Democrat Oscar Underwood of Alabama, readily acknowledged that their earlier actions had been "revolutionary" in nature (as quoted in Atkinson 1911, 120). The willingness of floor majorities in the House to adopt such revolutionary new precedents in both 1890 and 1910— which clearly violated prior precedents—is potent evidence of the malleability of existing ways of doing business when confronted with a committed and frustrated floor majority.

One might object that House leaders have relied upon preexisting House rules, such as the previous question, to facilitate procedural innovations. By contrast, a Senate majority, lacking the previous question, would have had a more difficult task in eliminating obstruction (see Binder 1997). The absence of a previous question rule did complicate efforts to end Senate obstruction. But the previous question motion was not the only way to cut off debate. As the 1811 example in the House suggests—along with the examples presented below from the Senate—the set of rules and precedents were sufficiently permissive so that a committed majority had the capacity to use rulings from the chair to force reform. These rulings might have involved violating past precedents, but such violations are by no means unheard of in the Senate, and Reed and Norris had done much the same in the House.[5] The historical record provides numerous examples where floor majorities did at times overcome intense opposition to enact precedents that limited

---

[4]Cannon had inadvertently invited this maneuver the day before when his allies sought to displace Calendar Wednesday—an earlier insurgent innovation to bring matters opposed by the Speaker to the floor—by claiming that a bill concerning the census was privileged under the Constitution and thus could displace Calendar Wednesday. The House initially overturned Cannon's ruling that the census bill was privileged and thus could displace Calendar Wednesday, though it agreed to consider the census bill the next day.

[5]The Senate has traditionally not been resolute in making sure rulings from the chair are firmly consistent with past precedent and rules (see Tiefer 1989, 514), although chairs may refer the decision to the full Senate rather than issue a ruling that contradicts existing rules and precedents (see also Oleszek 2001, 54–55).

the tactics available to obstructionists. It likely would have entailed more uncertainty to use rulings from the chair in the Senate to revolutionize the ways of doing business, simply because a single ruling likely would have left some tactics still available to the minority. But in the end, general parliamentary practice enabled a floor majority to implement rules changes.

3.2 RULINGS FROM THE CHAIR AND PROCEDURAL INNOVATION IN THE SENATE

An examination of the historical development of parliamentary tactics associated with Senate obstruction finds that the necessary components for rulings from the chair to work were in place by the middle of the 19th century at the latest, and that senators expressed an awareness of how to use this approach to overcome obstructionists. One component that appears to have been in place from the dawn of the Republic was the role that the presiding officer would play in determining questions of order (Cushing 1866, 112). Rule XVI of the original standing rules of the Senate stated that

> When a member shall be called to order, he shall sit down until the President shall have determined whether he is in order or not; and every question of order shall be decided by the President, without debate; but, if there be a doubt in his mind, he may call for the sense of the Senate.[6]

The Senate reaffirmed and clarified the role of the presiding officer during the tenure of Vice President John C. Calhoun. As presiding officer, he refused in 1826 to impose order beyond what was explicitly required of him in the Senate rules. Senators' response to Calhoun's interpretation of his role was one of "great surprise" and "gave rise, at the time, to some severe remarks," indicating this interpretation was inconsistent with commonly held beliefs about the role of the presiding officer (Cushing 1866, 112). The Senate explicitly rejected Calhoun's position by amending Rule XVI (making it Rule VI) in 1828, which provided that

> When a member shall be called to order by the President, or a Senator, he shall sit down; and every question of order shall be decided by the President, without debate, subject to an appeal to the Senate; and the President may call for the sense of the Senate on any question of order.[7]

Thus, the Senate reaffirmed that the chair had the authority to rule on points of order and thereby establish precedents, allowing the chair to be a central player in this approach to changing the rules. Indeed, the rule strengthened

---

[6]See *Senate Journal*, April 16, 1789, p. 13.

[7]See *Senate Journal*, February 14, 1828, pp. 158–60. This is part of Rule XX of the current standing rules of the Senate.

the vice president's position in this regard by explicitly granting him the power to call a senator to order. It also explicitly allowed for appeal of the chair's decision, which created the possibility of dilatory action on appeals, although the Senate would later add rules and precedents that circumscribed this possibility.[8]

As of 1841, it does not appear that tabling an appeal of a chair's ruling was a viable strategy for limiting dilatory debate during attempts to establish precedents curtailing obstruction. Yet this did not mean that obstruction prevented the establishment of precedents. On August 5, 1841, Senator Thomas Hart Benton (D–MO) made a motion to print a memorial and resolutions from a meeting of citizens of the county of Fauquier, Virginia opposing a national bank, the distribution of the proceeds of the sales of the public lands, the increase of the tariff, and the creation of a national debt. Clay was clearly upset by this motion and moved to table the motion to print, which passed 21-20. Benton then moved to take up the memorial, and when he began to speak on the subject, was called to order by Clay, who argued that a motion to take up a subject ordered to lie on the table was not debatable. In response to Benton's query about the status of the memorial, the President pro tempore ruled that the decision to table the motion to print carried with it the memorial. Benton appealed the decision and Clay moved to table the appeal "for the purpose of getting rid of the memorial and all its consequences" (Globe, p. 296). Calhoun attempted to explain that Clay's tabling motion was out of order, but Clay called him to order on the grounds that a tabling motion was not debatable. Calhoun claimed that an appeal was a privileged question could not be tabled, and then he and Clay engaged in parliamentary bickering and retaliatory points of order. The chair decided that Calhoun was in order, but the expiration of the morning hour prevented a decision on the main procedural issues in question.

The following day, the chair ruled that the motion to table was in order, stating that "The motion to lay an appeal on the table is one of the modes of sustaining the decision of the chair ... Nothing is more common than this method of sustaining the opinion of the chair. It is practiced everyday in the other House; within the last 24 hours it had been acted upon in that body" (p. 301). Calhoun appealed this decision, arguing that if it were upheld it would be a gag similar to what had been attempted during the Bank Bill debate (see below) and would concentrate too much power in the hands of the vice president, who after all was not selected by the Senate as its presiding officer. On August 7, after more debate over procedure, the Senate voted 9-30 to reverse the decision of the chair that the motion to table was in order. The Senate, however, did sustain Clay's initial point of order that the motion "to take up the subject ordered to lie on the table, should be

---

[8] One of the most important of these changes occurred in 1868, when the Senate limited the use of dilatory debate on appeals by adding to its rules the provision that points of order that arise pending a decision from the chair are decided at once and without debate (U.S. Congress. Senate. Committee on Rules 1883, 16).

decided without debate" on a vote of 25-18 (*Senate Journal*, p. 145). Thus, the Senate curtailed debate by establishing a precedent without resorting to the motion to table an appeal. While there was debate on the points of order, consuming three day's worth of morning business, this does not appear to have been deliberate obstruction and the Senate still managed to vote on Clay's point of order. The main issue of concern appears to have been the right of the Senate to decide directly on appeals—being questions of highest privilege—and not about the ability of individual senators to obstruct an ultimate decision on an appeal. Although Calhoun's argument appeared to have won the day, we do not see this as a victory for obstructionists, since the point about high privilege undercuts the justification for using obstruction for the purpose of preventing the Senate from reaching a decision on the appeal.

It is not clear exactly when it became the accepted practice that tabling motions were nondebatable, particularly those targeting appeals of rulings from the chair. When the Senate revised its rules in 1828, Rule XI stated

> When a question is under debate, no motion shall be received but to adjourn, to lie on the table, to postpone indefinitely, to postpone to a day certain, to commit, or to amend; which several motions shall have precedence in the order they stand arranged, and the motion for adjournment shall always be in order, and be decided without debate.

This appears to expressly prohibit debate only on a motion to adjourn. While some senators in 1841 clearly thought a motion to table was not debatable, a direct decision on that question establishing a clear precedent was not made then. That did not occur until 1844, when John Berrien (Whig–GA) made a motion to table the nomination of Reuben N. Walworth for the position of appraiser of customs for the port of New York. When William Haywood (D–NC) attempted to discuss the question, the President pro tempore Willie Mangum (Whig–NC) "declared that, according to the rules of the Senate, the question to lie on the table was not debatable." Claiming that "the rules of the Senate adopted in legislative session do not bind the Senate in its executive capacity," Haywood appealed the decision, but the decision was upheld by a vote of 32-3 (*Senate Executive Journal*, June 15, 1844, p. 344). Although a Rules Committee report published in 1883, which maps out changes to the standing rules since 1789, indicates the Senate did not change Rule XI between 1828 and 1844, the thirty-two senators who supported the ruling seemed to believe that a tabling motion was nondebatable, whether it be made in an executive or legislative session.[9] At a minimum, this decision established a precedent that senators could stop dilatory debate on an appeal by moving to table that appeal. The standing

---

[9]Indeed, Haywood himself implied that the standing rules prohibited debate on tabling motions, save in executive sessions. Unfortunately, the decision occurred during executive session and the account in the *Executive Journal* does not give any more details on senators' views on this issue.

rules as revised in 1868 explicitly stated that tabling motions were to be decided without debate (*Senate Journal*, March 25, 1868, p. 341). Several other cases (see below) support this contention.

The first time that the Senate voted to table an appeal from a decision of the chair occurred in 1854. On July 31, Senator Charles Sumner (Free Soil–MA) sought leave to introduce a bill to repeal the Fugitive Slave Law and began commenting on the bill. William Gwin (D–CA) made a point of order, stating that Sumner could not debate the question or say anything about the bill unless leave was granted. The Presiding Officer, confessing he was not sure of the rule, decided that debate was not in order. Sumner appealed the decision and Judah Benjamin (Whig–LA) stated, "In order to put a stop to the whole debate, I move to lay the appeal on the table. That is a motion which is not debatable." Sumner questioned whether that motion was in order and the Presiding Officer responded that it certainly was. When John B. Weller (D–CA) attempted to make a remark regarding the rule, the chair held that debate was not in order and that the question must be taken immediately.[10] To remove any doubt about the effect of his motion, Benjamin stated that a yea vote for his motion to table is a vote in favor of the position that "there is no debate upon the permission to offer the bill"—i.e., to uphold the chair's ruling without a direct vote on it. The Senate voted 36-9 to table the appeal and then voted not to grant leave to Sumner to introduce his bill (*Congressional Globe*, pp. 2022–2023). This appears to have firmly established the tactic of using tabling motions on appeals of rulings to create precedents. Throughout the remainder of the antebellum period, there were several occasions where this tactic was used, including seven such instances in the 35th Congress.

Throughout the 19th century, the Senate relied on rulings from the chair to establish precedents that limited the tactics available to obstructionists. To sustain such a ruling, it was not necessary to resort to a replica of the nuclear option, where an appeal is tabled in order to foreclose further obstruction. Instead, there are examples in which the chair made a controversial ruling, and it was then appealed and sustained by a majority vote without a filibuster of the appeal. At other times, the chair referred a matter to the floor for decision—and again the floor voted on the point of order without obstruction, thereby establishing a precedent. In other words, it was not understood that any effort to change the rules or precedents governing obstruction—whether by resolution or rulings from the chair—would necessarily face an all-out filibuster. We have found no examples of appeals of rulings by a chair being successfully filibustered in the 19th century; in addition, when the chair referred a point of order to the floor for a decision, we have found no examples in which the minority blocked a vote on deciding the point of order. In other words, chairs issued controversial new rulings in the 19th century, *and* it does not appear that the minority used obstruc-

---

[10]However, when Salmon Chase (Free Soil–OH) asked the chair if he could make "a single statement," he was permitted to do so.

tion to block such rulings from taking effect. This is consistent with our findings in regard to major legislation (reported in Chapter 4): if floor majorities were generally able to overcome obstruction of significant legislation (with the sporadic exception of end-of-congress filibusters), it makes sense that majorities were also able to win battles over procedure. As Democrat Lewis Linn of Missouri observed, with perhaps some hyperbole, in 1841, "the rules [of the Senate] adopted were always for themselves, and against the minority" (*Congressional Globe*, July 15, 1841, p. 205).

In Chapter 1, we discussed an unsuccessful attempt to use rulings from the chair to impose majority cloture during consideration of the Federal Elections Bill in 1891. But numerous important precedents regarding debate had been established prior to 1891 through rulings of the chair, which could be considered precursors to that attempt to impose majority rule (see Table 3.1). Some, but not all, of these involved tabling appeals to the decision of the chair. Although none of them go as far as establishing de jure majority rule, they support the position that senators believed this was a viable way to change the rules of the game, whether senators wanted to crack down on obstruction or make debate more free. These precedents involved whether senators could be removed from the floor for irrelevancy in debate (1848, 1872), prohibiting discussion of the merits of a bill on a motion to postpone (1859), whether a point of order submitted to the Senate was debatable (1879), and whether and how the chair could count a quorum (1858, 1871, 1874, 1879, 1881).[11]

A telling case occurred during the debate over the admission of Kansas in 1858. Senators favoring the pro-slavery Lecompton Constitution were trying to push for a vote on March 15, which led to an all-night session replete with all of the characteristics of classic filibusters (repeated dilatory motions, disappearing quorums, etc.). At one point during the debate, the presiding officer, Senator John Slidell (D–LA), ruled that a motion by William Fessenden (R–ME) to adjourn was out of order because senators were being summoned to make a quorum. Fessenden appealed the decision of the chair, and Robert Toombs (Whig–GA) moved to lay the appeal on the table, explicitly claiming the appeal was a dilatory effort. This suggests that Toombs knew that a way to deal with dilatory challenges to rulings by the chair was to table appeals.[12] A little later in the debate, Toombs said that it had been well understood that a majority ruled in the Senate and that no previous question provision existed there because it was inconceivable that senators would abuse its absence. He then went on to say that the Kansas bill should be laid on the table and that nothing else should be done "until the business of the House [meaning the Senate] is put in the power of the majority by the previous question. That is the first, the last, and the business this House should do until they get control of the business of the country" (*Con-*

---

[11]Rulings from the chair were used in some instances to unfetter debate, but this only serves to reemphasize the point that rules changes largely depended on the preferences of a majority at a given moment.

[12]The vote on Toombs's motion to table was 20-9, which did not constitute a quorum.

Table 3.1 Important 19th-Century Precedents Restraining Debate or Curtailing Obstruction

Year (Congress)	Description
1848 (30th)	Two rulings on whether senator could be called to order for irrelevancy in debate; no appeal taken on first ruling; on second, chair's ruling that senator was in order overturned; precedent reversed in 1872 (U.S. Congress. Senate 1909, 335).
1858 (35th)	Vice president attempted to count a quorum on a motion to adjourn; names of "absent" senators were then called, and enough answered and cast a vote on the motion to adjourn to produce a quorum (*Cong Globe*, p. 97; U.S. Congress. Senate 1909, 402).
1859 (35th)	Precedent established that it is not in order to discuss the merits of a bill on a motion to postpone; chair ruled it was in order; chair overruled on appeal, 22-29 (U.S. Congress. Senate 1909, 342).
1870 (41st)	Senator can be taken from the floor on a question of order; appeal taken and decision of chair sustained 47-12 (U.S. Congress. Senate 1909, 361).
1871 (41st)	Presiding officer declared the chair could determine the presence of a quorum by counting senators, but it would be up to Senate to decide what to do about those not voting (U.S. Congress. Senate 1909, 403).
1872 (42nd)	Vice president ruled (consistent with amendment to standing rules adopted in 1868) that secondary appeals are decided without debate, again confirming that motion to lay on the table is not debatable (*Cong. Globe*, p. 1292).
1872 (42nd)	Presiding officer ruled that a motion to rescind an order for recess was not debatable since a motion to recess is not debatable; upheld on appeal (U.S. Congress. Senate 1909, 336).
1879 (46th)	Vice President Thurman counted the Senate and announced the presence of a quorum (U.S. Congress. Senate 1909, 402).
1881 (46th)	Presiding officer counted the Senate and announced the presence of a quorum after no quorum voted on a roll call (U.S. Congress. Senate 1909, 403).
1897 (54th)	Presiding officer sustained a point of order that when a roll call has revealed the presence of a quorum and no business has intervened, a Senator cannot immediately suggest the absence of a quorum (U.S. Congress. Senate 1909, 404).

gressional Globe, p. 121). Toombs did not need to carry out the threat to enact the rules change because the opposition essentially surrendered.[13] The 1858 case supports the claim that rulings from the chair were available to limit obstructionists' tactics, even in the antebellum senate. Furthermore, the failure of the filibuster when confronted by Toombs's aggressive tactics reinforces our claim that threats of rules changes were credible in the 19th-century Senate.

Another case that occurred a year later cements our argument about the role of tabling motions in the early-to-mid-19th century. On February 25, 1859, during the debate on an appropriations bill to facilitate the acquisition of Cuba by negotiation, Henry Wilson (R–MA) moved to postpone consideration of the bill. The bill had encountered obstruction prior to this, surviving multiple unsuccessful motions to adjourn. Albert Brown (D–MS) moved to table Wilson's motion, and when William Henry Seward (R–NY) sought to speak to the question of whether Brown's motion was in order, he was called to order himself by the presiding officer, Benjamin Fitzpatrick (D–AL), on the grounds that a motion to table was nondebatable. Seward appealed, but there was some question as to whether John Slidell had moved to table the appeal. The presiding officer said that he had not heard Slidell and had put the question on sustaining the decision of the chair. Brown replied "Very well; we get to the same conclusion," and the Senate sustained the chair's decision 33-9. This case again implies that senators knew that tabling motions could be used to cut off debate on appeals of the chair's rulings.[14] It also indicates that an obstructive minority would not always try to capitalize on appeals for further delay, since the presiding officer was able to get the yeas and nays on his decision (*Congressional Globe*, pp. 1362–63).[15]

The strategy of using rulings from the chair to curb obstruction was not confined to the 19th century. Indeed, a particularly important example occurred in 1908, during Robert La Follette's filibuster of the Aldrich-Vreeland Currency Bill (previously mentioned in Chapter 2). The bill was a salient and significant piece of legislation (identified as such by Petersen 2001), pushed vigorously by the Republican leadership. During an all night session when La Follette made thirty-six quorum calls, Aldrich sought to remove this standard obstructionist tactic by making a point of order that business had not taken place in between successive quorum calls—as required under established rules and precedents—because debate itself did not constitute business. Prior to 1908, debate had been understood to constitute "business." Vice President Charles W. Fairbanks, who was in the chair, did not

---

[13] As Nichols (1948, 164) points out, the Kansas bill passed the Senate in pretty much its original form. The only compromise involved the issue of a land grant that was unrelated to the key concerns of the obstructionists (i.e., whether or not Kansas would be admitted under Lecompton).

[14] It is also consistent with our discussion above of the 1844 decision that motions to table are not debatable.

[15] A few days later, the presiding officer again explicitly stated that a motion to lay on the table—in this case to table the appeal of a decision by the chair—was not debatable. There was no protest of this statement (*Congressional Globe*, March 3, 1859, p. 1633).

rule on the point of order, but instead directly submitted it to the Senate where a 35-8 majority endorsed Aldrich's contention that debate did not constitute business. The Senate then voted 35-13 to table the appeal of the decision. This new precedent helped defeat La Follette's filibuster, as the conference report on the bill was adopted later the same day on a 43-22 vote. Furthermore, it dealt a blow to future filibusters. Burdette (1940, 87) called the importance of the ruling "tremendous" due to the consequences it had for a senator's ability to hold the floor for extended periods: "a senator could call for a quorum if business had been transacted since the last call; but with the transaction of business the speaking senator would lose the floor, and he could regain it only once more on the same subject." Thus, once again, a committed Senate majority showed that it could use procedural innovation—the creation of new precedents—to defeat obstruction of a high-priority bill.[16]

We conclude this chapter by considering two prominent cases that have been presented as evidence that inherited rules enabled the minority to block changes intended to provide for majority rule. These were situations where it is claimed that a majority favored a major bill, faced intense obstruction, proposed rules to curtail obstruction, but ultimately was forced to back down by the obstructive efforts. Such cases would constitute evidence against our argument that threats of rules changes constrained minority obstruction. A closer look at these cases, however, reveals support for our position.

3.3 THE BANK BILL OF 1841

Earlier studies of the Senate filibuster have identified Democrats' filibuster of the Bank Bill of 1841 as one of the first major episodes of obstruction in Senate history and as the first prompting an effort to impose majority cloture (see, e.g., Burdette 1940; Binder and Smith 1997, 91). Whig leader Henry Clay was pushing an ambitious agenda in the special session of the new, Whig-controlled congress. Binder (1997, 179–81) observes that the Whigs faced extensive obstruction of that agenda, particularly the bill to reestablish a national bank. Faced with these Democratic dilatory tactics, Clay threatened a rules change in a floor speech on July 12, 1841 that "should give to the majority the control of the business of the United States Senate" (*Congressional Globe*, p. 184). Leading Democrats, such as John Calhoun, condemned the idea of debate limitations, and William R. King (D–AL) dramatically declared his commitment to a protracted battle by saying, "I will tell the Senator [Clay], then that he may make his arrangements at

---

[16] During the 1908 fight, Fairbanks also expanded upon the 1879 precedent concerning counting a quorum. The 1879 ruling had allowed the presiding officer to establish the presence of a quorum by counting present but silent senators. This precedent was invoked to varying degrees over the ensuing decades, but Fairbanks expanded it by ruling that a motion can be adopted, in spite of a quorum not voting, if the presiding officer finds that a quorum was present.

his boarding house for the winter" (*Congressional Globe*, July 15, 1841, p. 203). Clay renewed the threat on July 15, claiming that he "would resort to the Constitution and act on the rights insured in it to the majority, by passing a measure that would insure the control of the business of the Senate to the majority" (p. 203). Clay never put his proposal into the form of a resolution to change the rules, nor did he seek a ruling from the chair to curtail dilatory tactics. While Binder (1997, 180) acknowledges that it is difficult to determine whether a majority truly favored Clay's reform, she points out that "we do know, however, that Whig senators reached nearly perfect cohesion in voting on the Bank Bill, but without a procedural means of forcing a vote on rules changes, unity over policy goals was not likely to secure procedural gains for the Whig majority." Binder and Smith conclude that "a majority in favor of reform was apparently forced to retreat in face of a determined filibustering minority" (1997, 75).[17]

Beyond King's statement, the main evidence for the assertion that the Democratic filibuster blocked procedural reform comes from Democratic Senator Thomas Hart Benton's description of the events. Like Calhoun and King, Benton decried Clay's proposal, claiming in a floor speech that "when the previous question shall be brought into this chamber, I am ready to see my legislative life terminated" (*Congressional Globe*, July 15, 1841, p. 204). In his book on antebellum politics, Benton claims that Whig senators were willing to support a previous question motion "but when they found out this measure was to be resisted . . . they withdrew their assent" (as quoted in Binder and Smith 1997, 75). Binder and Smith conclude that "under the circumstances, their effort to adopt a previous question rule was bound to be thwarted. Thus, facing a filibuster and not willing to risk their party's agenda, the Whigs folded and abandoned procedural reform" (75). Binder cites the Whigs' troubles with Democratic filibusters in 1841 as evidence that "at least periodically when the Senate debated questions of statehood, slavery, and national expansion, majorities often found themselves unable to bring to a vote favored measures and preferred rules" (178), concluding that the absence of a previous question motion made "it impossible for [the Whigs] to obtain a vote on procedural proposals to secure favored Whig policies" (181).

One difficulty with this interpretation of the Whigs' troubles in 1841 is that Clay actually succeeded in passing his substantive agenda through the Senate. For all of the talk of delay by filibusters, in the end the Democrats did not block the Whig program. Indeed, it is ironic that when Clay urged the Senate to adopt limits on debate, he lacked a floor majority in favor of the Bank Bill (Poage 1936). As the *New York Herald* reported on July 12, "it is ascertained to a certainty, that Mr. Clay's Bank Bill cannot pass the Senate. A Senatorial caucus was held this afternoon, and the discovery was made that only twenty-five votes out of fifty-one can be relied upon for it."

---

[17]In contrast to King's threat of a long filibuster, Democrat Linn suggested that a week's debate would have been required on Clay's proposal. See *Congressional Globe*, July 15, 1841, p. 205.

It is true that several weeks had been consumed in amending the bill, but much of this time involved proposed amendments by friends of the bill. In any case, while Democrats no doubt did try to drag out the proceedings, as of mid-July Clay's own Whig party had four senators opposed to the bill, thus depriving Clay of the needed chamber majority. Indeed, soon after Clay threatened the rule change, King helpfully offered to allow an immediate final vote on the Bank Bill (*Congressional Globe*, July 15, 1941, p. 204). Clay declined, claiming that several Whig senators were absent (204). But even with full attendance, it was clear that Clay lacked the votes for his Bank Bill when he urged the rules change.

On July 27, Clay presented an amendment on the floor that was designed to win over two of the four dissident Whigs; Clay admitted that "the bill, in its present shape, could not pass the Senate, and were the vote taken, it would probably stand 25 for the bill and 26 against it" (*Congressional Globe*, July 27, 1841, p. 254). The amendment passed 25-24, and the bill then was engrossed by the same margin and passed 26-23. Thus, far from minority obstruction blocking a bill with majority support, Clay's rules change threat *preceded* his construction of a majority in support of the bill, and as soon as Clay found a formula for gaining that majority, the bill was approved.[18]

This narrative raises the question of why Clay threatened the rules change in the first place. The record on this point is thin. Poage (1936, 61) argues that Clay had allowed Calhoun to "provoke him" into the threat. It is worth noting, however, that Clay had been pushing from early in the session for procedures to expedite consideration of the Whig program, so as to allow adjournment before the end of the summer. For example, Clay proposed on June 9 that when a bill was unfinished when the Senate adjourned for the day, the chamber would resume consideration of the bill the next day immediately after reading of the journal and following petitions and reports. In defending the proposal, Clay argued that senators should "let their contests be contests of intellect only; and not of brutal physical force; in seeing who could sit out the other, or consume the most time in useless debate" (*Congressional Globe*,

---

[18] Clay's papers, which include letters exchanged with various participants, make clear that the amendment was designed to win over the dissident Whigs and (it was hoped) to forestall a potential veto by President John Tyler. There is no discussion in the papers suggesting that the amendment was intended to mollify the Democratic opposition or to prevent further obstruction. The original bill allowed the national bank to establish branches in the states. The amendment allowed state legislatures to prevent this, if the legislature acted in its first session following passage of the bill. But the bill also provided that a future act of Congress could order branches even in such states. Democrats condemned the amendment as a sham, but it was sufficient to win over two of the Whig dissidents. One might suppose that Democrats allowed the bill to pass because they expected Tyler to veto it anyway. While Tyler ultimately did veto the bill, there was considerable uncertainty about his intentions when the bill passed. Clay's private letters, as well as those of cabinet member Daniel Webster, suggest that participants were not at all confident of Tyler's intentions (see Seager and Hay 1888, v. 9, 581, August 9, 1941 letter to Peter Porter). Secondary sources indicate that the Washington community as a whole was uncertain and consumed with speculation concerning Tyler's likely course (see Poage 1936, 68–69; Van Deusen 1937, 349).

June 12, 1841, p. 45). Democrats objected to the proposal, claiming that it represented an effort to gain undue control of the agenda. James Buchanan (D–PA) argued that such a change was unnecessary because the Senate was generally far ahead of the House in processing legislation, pointing to the quick repeal of the sub-treasury plan in early June (which passed despite strong Democratic opposition, on a 29-18 vote). Buchanan also cited the "courtesy" among members that limited the dangers posed by obstruction (*Congressional Globe*, June 12, 1841, p. 45), noting that if Whigs "persisted in having all the voting on one side of the Senate, and all the speaking on the other, he thought they might hope to get home again in two or three weeks" (45). King of Alabama also opposed Clay's resolution, arguing that he "never had concurred in any attempt to defeat measures by mere delay; yet he insisted that it was the duty of the majority in every public body to allow the minority a full and fair opportunity of discussing every measure proposed" (*Congressional Globe*, June 12, 1841, p. 46). These comments suggest the prevailing beliefs about the limited role of obstruction at the time. A bid by Calhoun to table Clay's resolution was defeated on a 27-19 vote. Clay then accepted an amendment allowing a single hour for the presentation of memorials, reports, and resolutions when the Senate convened, and the resolution was adopted on a voice vote. Several days later, Clay proposed moving the Senate's meeting time up to 10 A.M. from the usual noon hour (June 21, 1841, p. 81). The motion was approved the next day on a voice vote (p. 86). Clay's mid-July threat thus was the third in a string of efforts to quicken the pace of Senate action. The earlier moves had met with at least some success.

Along these lines, a closer look at the deliberations also suggests that Clay's cloture rule threat may have induced greater cooperation by the minority. After initially raising the prospect of a rules change on July 12, Clay renewed the call three days later when Democrats obstructed his effort to shift the Senate's consideration from the Bank Bill to a loan bill that was another Whig priority. Following the discussion of Clay's threatened rules change, the Democrats dropped their opposition to consideration of the loan bill. It was brought to the floor without a roll call, and then was adopted just three days later, by a 23-20 party-line vote. Clay then turned his attention back to the Bank Bill.

In sum, there is little doubt that Democrats used their prerogatives to delay Clay's program in 1841. In addition to the bank fight, Democrats consumed five days battling the Whig plan to dismiss the Senate's printers in March 1841. They also fought Clay's proposal for repealing the sub-treasury plan, as well as the Loan Bill and Land Distribution Bill. Yet, in the end, each of these measures passed the Senate, and with the exception of the Bank Bill, each was enacted into law. Thus, it is clear that a rules change was not *needed* to pass Clay's key proposals in 1841.[19] Obstruction might

---

[19]Later in the same congress, Whigs enacted a major tariff bill by a two-vote margin, over vigorous—but unsuccessful—Democratic opposition (see Chapter 6).

have delayed progress, but in the face of a determined majority willing to threaten changes in rules, the minority relented. King stated the prevailing view when he noted that "[m]uch as he detested a National Bank, he would not create delay by taking captious exceptions; but he and his friends ought to deliberate first, and act afterwards" (*Congressional Globe*, July 15, 1841, p. 204). In arguing against adopting a "gag rule" in the Senate, Calhoun compared the chamber to the House, noting that it is "a body so much smaller, and so distinguished for the closeness of its debate and the brevity of its discussion" (July 17, 1841, p. 215).[20]

We believe that this episode is characteristic of the antebellum Senate. Even as the minority used its prerogatives to slow the majority's program, the expectation in general was that legislation favored by a determined majority would pass. It is hard to explain why the minority, if it had the ability to block rules changes that it opposed, was unable or unwilling in the end to block the legislation that it opposed (and that it had been using its prerogatives to delay). It is more plausible that the majority tolerated rules allowing considerable leeway for obstruction so long as filibusters were not pushed to the extreme of killing priority bills favored by a clear floor majority.[21]

3.4 THE FEDERAL ELECTIONS BILL OF 1891 REVISITED

The case of the Federal Elections Bill of 1890–1891 is such an important chapter in the history of Senate lawmaking and obstruction that it warrants a closer look. Existing accounts leave the impression that a clear majority of senators supported the bill, but were thwarted by southern Democrats' filibuster. Furthermore, the filibuster was also successful in killing the proposed rules change, demonstrating the futility of changing the rules in the face of obstruction (see, e.g., Binder and Smith 1997, 75). It is certainly the case that the Democratic filibuster contributed to the Elections Bill's demise. Indeed, if not for the obstruction, the bill may well have passed in summer 1890, when a slim majority of members apparently were willing to vote for the bill. Nonetheless, in January 1891, Republicans nearly succeeded in amending the rules in order to end the filibuster, and the failure of this bid ultimately was attributable to the absence of a committed majority (or even a nominal majority) at the time in favor of the legislation. The bill lost majority support primarily due to the machinations of a handful of

---

[20]In a recent paper, Wirls (2005) has challenged the notion that the Senate had higher quality deliberation in the antebellum period than the House. Wirls shows that the two chambers consumed similar amounts of time in considering major bills. This reinforces our argument that the Senate in this period was by no means paralyzed by its lack of debate rules. Minorities prolonged consideration of controversial bills in both chambers, yet in the end, majorities generally were able to enact their favored policies.

[21]Although we show in Chapter 5 that obstruction stood a better chance of succeeding in the waning days of a congress, a determined majority could generally avoid this fate as long as its priority legislation was brought to the floor far enough in advance of the March 4 deadline.

silver Republicans who cared far less about civil rights than about adopting currency legislation, which required close cooperation with Democrats
(see, e.g., "Where the Responsibility Lies," January 2, 1891, p. 4; "Senator
Chandler Talks," January 3, 1891, p. 1; "The Lodge Bill in Place," January
16, 1891, p. 1, *New York Tribune*; "Sudden Death of the Force Bill," *New
York Herald*, January 6, 1891, p. 4; Valelly 2004b).[22]

It is essential to note at the outset that Republicans believed that the key
to passage of the rule and the bill was to ensure the support of a majority
of the full Senate. When the Elections Bill was postponed in the summer of
1890 to pave the way for speedy passage of Republicans' top priority—the
McKinley Tariff—George Frisbie Hoar (R–MA) went to his GOP colleagues
and secured a pledge to force a final vote on the Elections Bill during the
lame duck session following the November election, "either by a general rule
like that proposed by Mr. Hoar, and now pending before the committee on
rules, or by special rule of the same purport, applicable only to the Election
Bill" (Hoar 1903, v. 2, 155–56). Hoar proudly noted that he had secured
the signatures of a full majority of the Senate on this pledge (156). When
Democrats renewed their filibuster of the Elections Bill in the lame duck
session, GOP leader Nelson Aldrich presented his resolution to amend the
rules and took up the challenge of securing its adoption.

As we stated in Chapter 1, a pivotal question in the battle over the proposed rules change was whether or not the presiding officer, Vice President Levi Morton, would issue rulings that were favorable to Aldrich's pro–
Elections Bill forces. At the start of the conflict, there was a great deal of
uncertainty regarding what Morton would do. Aldrich and others encouraged him to go on vacation in Florida, which would have left the chair open
for someone who was more clearly sympathetic to the supporters of the Elections Bill. Although Morton had been a strong partisan and vocal supporter
of free and fair elections in the South when he was a candidate for the House
a few years before, he announced his position as vice president required him
to be impartial.[23] Furthermore, Morton lacked parliamentary expertise, and
thus would require considerable guidance from Aldrich's forces in making his
rulings (see, e.g., "Debating the Closure in the Senate," *New York Herald*,
January 23, 1891, p. 4; "Nearing a Vote on the Force Bill," *New York Herald*, January 17, 1891, p. 4; "Cloture in the Senate," *Washington Post*,
December 28, 1890, p. 4).

---

[22]One reason that the Republicans might have had better success in holding onto the
silver Republicans had they pushed for cloture in summer 1890, instead of waiting for
the lame duck session, is that the fall elections likely changed the silverites' calculations.
The Republicans' devastating losses suggested that the long-term success of the free silver movement would require working with the newly ascendant Democrats, rather than
making deals with the Republicans. We owe this point to Richard Valelly.

[23]See McElroy (1930, 189). For Morton's position on elections in the South, see his
speech at the Republican Convention of the 11th Congressional District, 1880, Levi P.
Morton Papers, Manuscripts and Archives Section, The New York Public Library, New
York, NY.

Initially, it appeared that Morton might let down the pro-reform cause. On December 31, Morton ruled that debate was in order when a senator appealed a ruling from the chair. This ruling was entirely consistent with past precedents, and since it seemed to encourage Democrats' continued obstructionist tactics, it enamored Morton with the anti–Elections Bill press (e.g., see *New York Times* Editorial, January 2, 1891, p. 4; "A Caucus on Monday," *Washington Post*, January 1, p. 2). But Morton's ruling was of extremely limited importance and signaled little about his ultimate intentions.[24] Republicans had not yet started their push for a vote on the proposed rules change; indeed, the rules proposal was not yet the pending business. Furthermore, as John Sherman (R–OH) noted on the floor, he could simply move to table the appeal, thus cutting off further debate on the ruling (*Congressional Record*, December 31, 1890, p. 892). The skirmish occupied several hours of debate, but did not establish any precedents contrary to Aldrich's agenda.

The Elections Bill was temporarily displaced in early January when silver Republicans joined with the Democrats to move the Silver Bill to the top of the agenda. Once the Silver Bill was on the floor, GOP leaders chose not to stall its passage in order to allow plenty of time for the Elections Bill fight ("A Vote on Wednesday," *New York Tribune*, January 9, 1891, p. 3). After the Silver Bill had passed, Morton cast the deciding vote to bring the Elections Bill back before the Senate on January 15. While some at the time thought Aldrich's success depended crucially on Morton reversing his ruling regarding debate of appeals, this was not the case. Instead, the GOP needed Morton to rule in favor of a point of order that further debate on the rules change was dilatory and thus out of order, and Morton would then need to rule that a motion to table the ensuing appeal of his ruling was nondebatable. The first would be a departure from past practice, but in the absence of *any* rule providing for a mechanism to end debate, it could be defended as a maneuver consistent with the understanding that ultimately a legislative majority should be able to work its will. Republicans were prepared to argue that the Constitution's provision that each chamber can make its rules precludes the minority from indefinitely obstructing their proposal and thus makes further debate dilatory (see *Washington Post*, "By Aid of the Chair," January 23, 1891, p. 2; ; see also *Congressional Record*, January 22, 1891, p. 1701).[25] The second element—ruling that a motion to

---

[24] Although Democratic newspapers made much of Morton's ruling at the time, the *New York Daily Tribune* noted that the ruling was not the Democratic success that some had claimed ("Filibustering by Appeal," January 3, 1891, p. 2). Indeed, the ruling on debating an appeal stemmed from an initial ruling—sympathetic to the pro–Elections Bill forces—that prevented automatic consideration of a resolution that would have hampered Republicans' attempts to make progress on the measure.

[25] Interestingly, when Clay threatened his rules change in 1841, he also alluded to the Constitution as a basis for his actions (see quotation above, *Congressional Globe*, July 15, 1841, p. 203). When Aldrich first presented the rule, George Edmunds (R–VT) observed that the Constitution as well as common parliamentary law imply that the majority should

table an appeal was not debatable—was unequivocally supported by Rule
XX at the time.

Starting in mid-January, Morton issued a series of rulings that were favorable to the Aldrich forces and suggested to observers that he would cooperate
in forcing a final vote on reform. On January 16, Morton ruled that a motion to table an original amendment carried with it an amendment to the
amendment. When the decision was appealed by the Democrats, a Republican moved to table the appeal. Morton ruled that the motion to table was
not debatable (consistent with past precedent and existing rules) and the
tabling motion carried.[26] Morton's decision firmly established the feasibility
of using a tabling motion to forestall obstruction of a ruling that debate
could be closed by a majority vote.[27]

The following week, Morton went even further in issuing rulings favorable
to the Aldrich forces. These rulings clearly changed Democrats' perceptions
about Morton's impartiality and the prospects for passage of the cloture
resolution. On January 20, Morton ruled a senator cannot yield possession
of the floor to another senator except by unanimous consent (*Congressional
Record*, pp. 1566–67; *Senate Journal*, p. 7; U.S. Congress. Senate 1909,
360).[28] This ruling "removed from the Democrats one of the strongest supports upon which they were leaning" ("Reedism in the House, Closure in the
Senate," *New York Herald*, January 21, 1891, p. 4) It would require each
speaker to hold the floor for an extended period of time, rather than yielding
to colleagues in order to rest. Combined with the two-speech limitation (see
Chapter 1), it would make the obstructionists' task more difficult. On a
subsequent vote to take up the cloture resolution, Morton was accused of ig-
noring John Morgan's (D–AL) plea for recognition ("Reedism in the House,

---

be able to rule in the end. See "The Senate's New Rule," *Washington Post*, December
28, 1890, p. 1.

[26] Although we are hesitant to make too much of it, Morton's personal copy of the
standing rules indicates that he was fully aware of the status of motions to table with
respect to debate. On the pages where Rule XXII appears, the words "not debatable" are
written in the margin next to the text that indicates the precedence of a motion to table.
The section of the rules that states that a motion "to lay on the table, shall be decided
without debate" is also underlined (Morton MSS).

[27] This may not have been clear to everyone at the time, as evidenced by a *Washington
Post* story on January 23 ("By Aid of the Chair," p. 2) that incorrectly outlines this
approach, but the other press coverage and close examination of the floor debate makes
clear what Aldrich, Morton, et al. were doing. An interesting side note: a volume of
Senate precedents published in 1913 lists a ruling by the chair on February 24 of that
year that points of order were not debatable (U.S. Congress. Senate 1913, 402). A note is
included that says this ruling is contrary to Rule XX. Burdette's detailed account (1940,
52–57) misses the key point that dilatory debate on the proposed rules change could be
cut off by tabling the appeal of the ruling of the chair. Burdette's account says nothing
about a move to table an appeal of chair's ruling in favor of Aldrich, instead claiming that
the chair would have had to rule that the appeal could not be debated. Burdette correctly
notes that such a ruling would have been against prior precedents and would have called
into question the vice president's fairness (56).

[28] The *New York Times* claimed that Morton later overruled himself on this point,
although official volumes of precedents do not indicate as such (see "Delaying the Gag
Rule," January 22, 1891, p. 1).

Closure in the Senate," *New York Herald*, January 21, 1891, p. 4; "Cloture in the Senate," *Washington Post*, January 21, 1891, p. 2). Democrats then capitalized on a mistake by Morton, who had neglected to announce the outcome of the vote to take up the Aldrich resolution.[29] The Democrats sought to delay action by forcing a long debate on correcting the *Journal*. A motion to correct the *Journal* is privileged in Senate rules, yet after allowing Democrats to consume several hours with an inconclusive discussion of the motion to correct, Morton ruled that the Aldrich resolution could be considered, without first acting on the motion to correct the *Journal*. This ruling was upheld on a 35-30 vote, despite heated Democratic objections. Finally, Democrats made a point of order that the Aldrich resolution was not properly before the Senate because it violated Senate Rule XL, which requires that resolutions to change the rules specify all of the Senate rules affected. Morton ruled against the point of order. The Democrats appealed, and the appeal was tabled on a 33-28 vote.

This turn of events clearly worried Democrats, and Morton went from being the darling of the anti–Elections Bill press and a paragon of neutral arbitration to an Aldrich lackey who displayed "open contempt for the rules" and used his position to further the partisan ends of Republicans ("Gag Law Set Aside," *New York Times*, January 27, 1891, p. 5). Morton's rulings were characterized as destroying "some of the time honored traditions of the Senate as to the rights of individual senators as opposed to the rights of the majority" ("Fighting Despotism in Both Houses," *New York Herald*, January 22, 1891, p. 3).[30] The *New York Herald* noted on January 23 that the "rulings today clearly foreshadowed [Morton's] purpose to become the tool of his party," ("Debate the Closure in the Senate," p. 4). A few days later, the *Washington Post* noted that "Mr. Morton still holds the key to the situation, and he is apparently only waiting for a favorable opportunity to use it" ("To Close the Debate," January 26, 1891, p. 1).[31]

Once Morton issued his rulings in favor of the Aldrich forces, both Democratic and Republican newspapers agreed that the cloture rule would in all likelihood be adopted. The staunchly Republican *New York Tribune* declared on January 23 that the Democratic obstructionists had been met with a "bold hand" and the "deadlock which their filibustering policy of yesterday had precipitated was broken with an ease and celerity which promise a

---

[29] Morton had announced that the yeas "appeared to have it," but had failed to then add that "the yeas have it." (See "Delaying the Gag Rule," *New York Times*, January 22, 1891, p. 1).

[30] The *New York Tribune* described these as "sagacious, common-sense" rulings.

[31] In retrospect, Morton has been widely regarded as one of the fairest presiding officers of the Senate. When he left the vice presidency, the Senate held a dinner in his honor to demonstrate the chamber's appreciation for his service, which was characterized by his "constant fairness and signal ability" (see Invitation to the Complimentary Dinner to Vice President Levi P. Morton by U.S. Senators, February 16, 1893, Levi P. Morton Papers, Manuscripts and Archives Section, The New York Public Library, New York, NY). Eighty-eight senators attended this unprecedented event. Yet, this was not the view that many had of Morton during the debate over the Elections Bill.

speedy restoration to the majority of its inherent right to control the business of that body" ("Republicans in Control," p. 1). The *New York Herald*, which opposed the bill and the rule (but talked with members on both sides), noted on the same day that "the democrats in the Senate are making the fight of their lives for justice and the freedom of debate. They are liable to get neither" ("Debate the Closure in the Senate," January 23, 1891, p. 4). The *Herald* claimed that "there is not a shadow of doubt" that the rule change would pass, predicting that Morton would refuse to recognize Democrats at the behest of Republican leaders. Similarly, the *Washington Post*, which also opposed the bill, noted on January 26 that "there is strong ground for the prevalent belief that the Federal Senate will make history this week. . . . It is expected that not later than Tuesday evening the majority forces will be thus recruited, and when this happens, the decisive movement that is expected to dispose of the cloture resolution will follow immediately" ("To Close the Debate," January 26, 1891, p. 1).[32]

Nonetheless, these press reports included the cautionary note that even if the rule passed, the Elections Bill itself might well fail since Republicans now lacked a majority in favor of the legislation itself. With fifty-one Republican senators in the eighty-eight-seat body, the GOP could afford at most seven defections. In the end, eight Republicans who opposed the Elections Bill decided to vote against the rule proposal, dooming both initiatives. In its January 23 story, the *Herald* noted that a number of Republicans who had just voted with Aldrich on the procedural battles concerning Morton's rulings "have no sympathy with the Force Bill. . . . some of them have declared their intention to vote against it" ("Debate the Closure in the Senate," p. 4). The next day, the *Herald* observed that "there is no certainty, even though the cloture be adopted, that the Force Bill will pass. . . . The Democrats already have assurances that six republicans, viz.:–Teller, Wolcott, Stewart, Jones, Ingalls, and Washburn will act with them, and it is believed that Stanford, Cameron, Plumb, and Paddock will also vote in the negative if their aid shall be needed" ("A Vice President Useful in Certain Emergencies," January 24, 1891, p. 1). Along the same lines, the *Post* claimed on January 23 that "it does not follow that the adoption of the cloture rule means the passage of the Force Bill. Many senators will vote for the former who will not vote for the latter" ("By Aid of the Chair," p. 2).

---

[32] The Democratic *New York Times* dissented from the view that the Republicans had the necessary majority to pass the rule (or the bill), but nonetheless expected Morton to issue decisions leading to a final showdown in the same time frame (see "Trampling on the Rules," January 23, 1891, p. 1; "The Obstinate Radicals," January 24, 1891, p. 1). The *Times* included a tantalizing hint concerning the Democrats' efforts to build a majority coalition. In discussing the delay caused by Morton's error in failing to announce the outcome of the vote to take up the Aldrich resolution, it noted that "the Democrats are quite content with the situation. They expect the radicals to resort to revolutionary methods to adopt the gag rule . . . for reasons which they do not make public they are confident that if the discussion is not brought to a violent end tomorrow the gag rule will be beaten, despite the very evident fact that Mr. Morton is prepared to go to any length the radical leaders may demand" ("The Senate's Day of Talk," January 21, 1891, p. 5).

As it turned out, a sufficient number of Republicans who opposed the bill voted with the Democrats to sidetrack the rules change.

On January 26, a coalition of Democrats and dissident Republicans shocked the GOP leadership by voting 35-34 to displace the cloture resolution in favor of an apportionment bill. That morning, Democratic leaders had met secretly with "the Republicans who openly opposed the Force Bill" ("Goodby, Closure, Goodby Force Bill," *New York Herald*, January 27, 1891, p. 3). According to the *Herald*, Aldrich had been planning to push for a final vote on cloture the next day. But Democrats now had found the necessary GOP votes to sidetrack the measure. Six Republicans voted with the Democrats—John Jones and William Stewart of Nevada, Henry Teller and Edward Wolcott of Colorado, William Washburn of Minnesota, and James Cameron of Pennsylvania. A seventh, John Ingalls of Kansas, was paired against cloture. Aldrich sought to have the absent Leland Stanford (R–CA) paired in favor of cloture, but Stewart claimed that Stanford wished to be paired against. The dispute left Stanford unpaired, but any hope of resuscitating cloture vanished a few days later when Stanford sent a telegram declaring his opposition to both cloture and the bill. Stanford addressed the telegram to Stewart; in it, he wrote that "on general principles I am in favor of the Closure rule, but I am not in favor of anything that would shut out your proposed amendment to the Elections Bill, providing it will apply only to elections for Congress. Without such amendment, with my present views, I shall be obliged to vote against the Election Bill."[33]

In interpreting the January 26 events, the crucial point is that the source of the GOP defections was opposition to the Elections Bill rather than fear of the consequences of voting for the cloture rule or the belief that it was futile to fight the Democratic filibuster. A close examination of both Republican and Democratic papers makes clear that support for the Elections Bill had always been tenuous within the GOP caucus. From early January, press reports made clear that several Republicans were hostile to the bill, and that a handful of others were indifferent to it at best.[34]

Six of the eight Republican defectors were western supporters of free silver. For these members, the number one priority was passing silver legislation, which required close cooperation with the Democrats. Once the Silver Bill passed the Senate in mid-January, however, these members did not have to worry about the Elections Bill directly disrupting the silver cause. Nonetheless, GOP leaders charged that the silverites had agreed with the Democrats

---

[33]Stanford was in New York City at the time of the critical vote. His position was viewed as pivotal to the cloture rule's chances. Aldrich and Stewart apparently raced to New York to attempt to obtain Stanford's support. When Stanford made clear that he supported Stewart's position, the battle over cloture and the Elections Bill had ended. See "Force Bill Dead beyond Resurrection," January 28, 1891, *New York Herald*, p. 3; "Goodby, Closure, Goodby, Force Bill," January 27, 1891, *New York Herald*, p. 3; Crofts 1968).

[34]It is also worth noting that numerous Republican newspapers had come to the conclusion that adopting the Elections Bill would hurt the GOP's image and thus supported abandoning it (see, e.g., *Congressional Record*, January 22, 1891, pp. 1698–99.)

to oppose the Elections Bill in return for the Democrats' solid support on the currency bill.[35]

Denying any logroll with Democrats, individual silver Republicans argued that they opposed the Elections Bill on principle. Wolcott noted on the floor that he would oppose the Elections Bill even if it were not potentially standing in the way of the Silver Bill or other legislation ("Mr. Wolcott's Speech," *Washington Post*, December 31, 1890, p. 7). Wolcott claimed that the bill interfered with state control of elections and would lead to the resumption of civil strife in the South, which would damage economic growth in the region. Wolcott also cited the threat of the Chinese gaining electoral clout in the West, noting that "the white vote" should always govern there ("Mr. Wolcott's Speech," December 31, 1890, p. 7). Similarly, Jones of Nevada told the *Tribune* that there might already be too much suffrage in the United States ("Washington Gossip: Senator Jones on the Election Bill," January 19, 1891, p. 7). Jones charged that the 15th Amendment had given African Americans the vote too soon, and expressed fear of the consequences should the Chinese gain suffrage on the West Coast. Thus, deep-seated racism likely played a role in motivating opposition among the western Republicans.[36]

Beyond the silver Republicans, a key defection was William Washburn (R–MN). As early as August 1890, it had been reported that Washburn had doubts about the Elections Bill. He claimed at the time that he had "talked with people at St. Paul, Minn., Chicago, and other points, and he says that he can find no general demand for passage of the Force Bill" ("No Gag for the Senate," *Washington Post*, August 11, 1890, p. 1). But in mid-January, Washburn sided with Aldrich on some of the procedural skirmishes surrounding the cloture rule fight. As a result, the *Washington Post* reported on January 17 that "Republicans were much encouraged last night by the action of Senator Washburn in voting with them against adjournment, and they feel that although he may eventually vote against the bill, he will still vote, and thus help to make up the quorum" ("In Continuous Session," January 17, 1891, p. 1). In the end, however, Washburn decided to oppose the cloture rule because "doing so was most effective way of killing the Force Bill" ("Goodby, Closure, Goodby, Force Bill," *New York Herald*, January 27,

---

[35] It is plausible that Democrats used silver Republicans' need for continued assistance on the silver issue as leverage, even in the House. The *Herald* reported on January 17 that "if the [House] republicans from the mining states really care for a silver bill they may learn that the only way to get it is to vote against the Force Bill. They are numerous enough, if they will act together, to kill the Force Bill by absolutely refusing to concur in the Senate amendments and refusing a conference. . . . The fate of the two measures is likely to be inextricably intermingled from now until the end of the session" ("Nearing a Vote on the Force Bill," p. 4). The Silver Bill ultimately failed in the House when a handful of Democratic defectors sided with GOP leaders.

[36] The northern Republican supporters of the bill did not share the same fear of Chinese immigrants as the western Republicans, and also had a stronger commitment to the party's overriding interest in gaining African American votes in the South than did the silverites, who had come to see Democrats as their allies on key issues. See also "Chinaman and Negro," *Washington Post*, December 18, 1890, p. 2

1891, p. 3). Even the staunchly Republican *New York Tribune* admitted that Washburn had "a real solid opposition" to the bill "based upon conviction" ("Washington Gossip," January 29, 1891, p. 7).[37]

The final blow was the opposition of James Cameron of Pennsylvania. In December 1890, the *Washington Post* carried a story from the *Philadelphia Record*, noting "Cameron's opposition to the Force Bill" and explaining that he "was a businessman before he was a Senator, and he has carried some of his business sense with him into the performance of his public function" ("Senator Cameron's Position," December 13, 1890, p. 4). A few days later the *New York Times* observed that Cameron was being condemned by GOP leaders for "his persistent refusal to disregard the fact that many of the most influential and respectable Republicans in Pennsylvania, who have money invested in the South, and who desire to see peace maintained there, believe that the passage of the Force Bill would provoke disturbances, and so keep out the capital that has been going South" ("With Partisan Aims Only," December 23, 1890, p. 5).[38]

Apart from any concern about his constituents' southern investments, Cameron himself apparently had significant investments in the South, which gave him a stake in warm economic relations between the sections (see "Plumb and Cameron's Good Reasons," *New York Times*, August 16, 1890, p. 1). Cameron also had major silver investments, which were publicly exposed in January 1891 and may have reinforced his incentive to work with the Democrats on both the currency and elections issues (see "Cameron's Actions Criticized," *Washington Post*, January 27, 1891, p. 1).[39] As the key vote came on sidetracking the Elections Bill in late January, an investigative committee in the House was probing allegations of corruption on the part of Cameron. Democrat Alexander Dockery of Missouri subsequently testified that he had delayed disclosing Cameron's silver investments due to the fear that it would hurt Cameron's reelection in Pennsylvania. Dockery noted that since Cameron was rumored to oppose the Elections Bill, he did not want to damage Cameron's reelection prospects.[40] Dockery denied the

---

[37] Washburn rarely spoke on the Senate floor, and his reasons for opposing the bill are difficult to determine, but it is clear that he had opposed it for an extended period. For example, the *St. Paul Pioneer-Press* noted in January that "Washburn has never made any secret of the disfavor with which he regarded the Elections Bill" (as quoted in *Washington Post*, "Good for Washburn," January 19, 1891, p. 4).

[38] Several other news reports noted Cameron's hostility to the Elections Bill, but did not speculate on his motives ("Harrison as a Schemer," *New York Times*, December 30, 1890, p. 5; "The Force Bill Buried," *New York Times*, January 6, 1891, p. 5; "Cameron Carries the Caucus," *New York Times*, January 8, 1891, p. 1; "Where The Responsibility Lies," *New York Tribune*, January 2, 1891, p. 4). Cameron himself avoided publicly declaring his views (see "Senator Cameron's Attitude," *Washington Post*, January 3, 1891, p. 1). A few months after the vote, the *Times* claimed that many Pennsylvania Republicans were pleased with the defeat of the Elections Bill since "a good deal of capital [from Pennsylvania] has been invested in the South" (Editorial, March 25, 1891, p. 4).

[39] Cameron was the only northeastern Republican to support free silver in the Senate.

[40] The Pennsylvania legislature reelected Cameron in January 1891. A handful of Republicans opposed him because of his reported opposition to the Elections Bill ("Cameron Carries the Caucus," *New York Times*, January 8, 1891, p. 1).

GOP allegation that there was a quid pro quo, in which the Democrats had used the threat of the disclosure to gain Cameron's vote on the Elections Bill ("Mr. Dockery's Explanation," *New York Times*, January 31, 1891, p. 3; "What Will the Senate Do?" *New York Tribune*, January 28, 1891. p. 2). While each of these factors may have contributed to Cameron's defection, the bottom line is that he had shown signs of opposition to the Elections Bill for some time.

The opposition of Cameron and Washburn—combined with the six western silver Republicans—meant that the GOP had no hope of assembling a majority in favor of the Elections Bill. This, in turn, doomed the Aldrich rules change as well. As the Republicans appeared to be getting closer to success on the cloture resolution, which enhanced the chances for success on the bill, support eroded for Aldrich's maneuver. Put simply, the Republicans who planned to vote against the Elections Bill ultimately decided that the most effective way to defeat the bill would be to sidetrack the cloture proposal. The evidence does not suggest that senators dropped support for the Elections Bill because they saw that it was not possible to break the filibuster. Instead, there was a move to break the filibuster that ultimately failed because there simply was not majority support for the bill, which deprived the rules change of majority support.[41]

Why then did the Democrats not force a vote on passage of the Elections Bill as a way of putting a definitive nail in the bill's coffin? Several of the Republican senators who opposed the Elections Bill faced intense pressure on both sides of the issue. Their official party organizations at home typically backed the bill, but their apparent deals with Democrats to win unified Democratic support for free silver and, in some cases, their personal views on the issue led them to oppose the Elections Bill. For example, the *Washington Post* noted on January 26 that although Cameron "is personally antagonistic" to the Elections Bill, he would "feel constrained, by party ties, to vote for [it] on its final passage" ("To Close the Debate," p. 1). As such, these Republicans preferred to find an indirect way to kill the Elections Bill rather than voting against their party's explicit platform pledge on the floor.[42]

---

[41] Beyond the outright opposition of the eight Republicans who defected in late January, GOP leaders also had to deal with other party members who were indifferent to the bill. For example, when the silver Republicans united with the Democrats in early January to displace the Elections Bill with the currency bill, the *Herald* cited "one western Senator who personally regards the [Elections] Bill with indifference, but was not willing to abandon it now that it was a party measure" ("Sudden Death of the Force Bill," January 6, 1891, p. 4). While this member stuck with his party on the vote to displace the Elections Bill, such indifference likely made the GOP leaders' job of holding together their coalition much more difficult. We have found no evidence that any Democrats regarded the bill with similar indifference.

[42] The *Post* had earlier reported that there were nine GOP senators who opposed the bill, but that "it is extremely doubtful whether enough of them will disregard party domination, the caucus lash, and the administration influence to such an extent as to actually vote against the bill." As a result, the *Post* suggested that the Republicans would seek ways to lay aside the bill without a direct vote on passage ("Mr. Plumb Speaks Out," December 10, 1890, p. 1).

But the evidence is clear that enough Republicans opposed the Elections Bill to prevent a majority in support since all Democrats opposed it. Once free silver had passed the Senate in early January, it does not appear that these Republicans were motivated to oppose the Elections Bill by the desire to move onto other business. From the Democrats' perspective, there was no incentive to allow a final vote on the Elections Bill. The risk of losing, even if small, was far too great given that the bill would hurt the party so much for years to come. In other words, though it certainly looked like Democrats had the votes to beat the underlying bill, they could not be sure that Aldrich would not find some way to pay off a few Republicans and get them to switch. After all, the vote that displaced the Elections Bill with the apportionment bill—thereby killing its chances for passage—was extremely close, 35-34. Given that killing the bill was the Democrats' number one priority, it would not make sense to allow a vote even if the risk of losing was quite small.

This narrative indicates that Aldrich's bid to change the rules to pave the way for passage of the Elections Bill was, in the end, not doomed by the ability of the minority to obstruct the change. Instead, it faltered because Aldrich and Hoar lacked the support of a Senate majority to pass the bill itself. The Democratic filibuster no doubt allowed the southerners time to build coalitions with the silver Republicans and to rally much of the press—including several Republican papers—against the bill. But the filibuster was not sufficient to kill the Elections Bill. Aldrich came tantalizingly close to succeeding in passing his rule, but ultimately failed because he lacked majority support. Writing in 1909, Frederic Haskin noted that had Aldrich succeeded, "the Senate would now proceed under rules practically the same as those obtaining in the House" ("The Force Bill and Cloture," *Washington Post*, December 1, 1909, p. 4). Though this may exaggerate the long-term impact of Aldrich's reform, it would have at the least set an important precedent for de jure majority rule in the Senate. Indeed, in his authoritative study of congressional procedure, Tiefer (1989, 702) notes that the notorious filibuster of the Federal Elections Bill in 1890–91 "revealed quite clearly what it would take to curb the filibuster: a Senate majority determined to change the rules, aided by a vice president in the chair willing to bring the Senate to an immediate vote on the path to a rules change, overcoming all resistance in the process."

Beyond its impact on the Senate, the Elections Bill was arguably the last gasp of Reconstruction. The death of the Elections Bill meant that "the last window for national voting rights jurisprudence had closed for decades to come" (Valelly 2004b, 248). The nominal Republican majority in the chamber had lacked the commitment and unity necessary to reform the rules and pass the Elections Bill, thus abandoning the party's historic commitment to the civil rights of African Americans.

Returning to the war-of-attrition framework outlined in Chapter 2, Republican leaders sought to demonstrate the commitment of their troops through such stratagems as continuous sessions and threats to change the rules.[43] Yet, in the end, the Democrats were far more intense in their opposition to the change than were the Republicans. Where all Democrats agreed that their party would be seriously damaged by safeguarding African Americans' suffrage rights, the GOP included some members who cared deeply about the issue (such as Hoar), as well as others who were largely indifferent to the cause, and others who were either hostile to the underlying measure or quite willing to vote against the bill in exchange for unified Democratic help with their top priority, free coinage. This gave the Democrats a critical advantage as they sought to chip away at the GOP majority in favor of cloture. As Richard Valelly has pointed out, there was a "mismatch between the preference intensity and homogeneity of Senate Democrats, on the one hand, and the preference heterogeneity among the Republicans, on the other" (2004a, 45).

3.5 DISCUSSION

This chapter has provided examples of both successful and unsuccessful efforts to undermine the prerogatives available to filibustering minorities in the 19th-century Senate. On several occasions, Senate majorities put into place new and controversial precedents that curbed obstruction and paved the way for passage of legislation opposed by a minority of senators. In other cases, the threat of a rules change appeared to curb obstruction, without the threat having to be implemented.[44] The unsuccessful bids to change the rules—in particular the 1891 Elections Bill case—reinforce our argument that the committed support of a floor majority was necessary to credibly threaten a "rules revolution." While unanimity—or even supermajority support—was not necessary in the pre-cloture Senate to defeat obstruction or to enact rules or precedents undermining minority rights, the committed support of a majority of the Senate was necessary.

The implication of our theoretical approach is that narrow floor majorities should generally be successful in enacting favored legislation, except when the minority is more intense in its commitment than the majority or when legislation is considered at the very end of a congress. Even in the absence of formal rules restricting debate, majorities typically were able to overcome obstruction in the pre-cloture Senate. The following chapters assess the empirical validity of these claims using a range of types of evidence.

---

[43] The *Post* reported on January 17 that the Republicans were resorting to continuous sessions to rally support for the rules change: "The real purpose is to convince the few Republican Senators who are of conservative opinions that the old-fashioned method of passing a measure obnoxious to the minority by excess of sheer physical endurance is no longer effective" ("In Continuous Session," p. 1).

[44] This is our interpretation of the 1841 events, though it is possible that Democrats would have surrendered and allowed Clay's program to pass even without the threat of a rules change. It is less plausible, in our view, to argue that Democrats allowed the legislation to pass but would have successfully blocked any rules change.

Chapter Four

Where's the Pivot?

4.1 INTRODUCTION

Even though the Constitution implies that only a majority of the Senate is required to pass legislation, the rules of the modern Senate concerning debate effectively mean that supermajorities are generally necessary for passage. Since 1975, three-fifths of the membership has been required to invoke cloture, which places limits on the amount of subsequent debate that can take place so that a final vote on passage may occur. With some variations, two-thirds majorities were required for cloture from 1917 to 1975. But, as highlighted in Chapters 1 to 3, the Senate had no formal rule for ending debate and moving the previous question prior to 1917.[1] What proportion of senators were needed to pass legislation during this period?

To answer this question, we consider competing hypotheses derived from alternative theories of lawmaking: the theory of universalism (Weingast 1979; Collie 1988) and the theory developed in Chapter 2. The predictions generated by these theoretical perspectives comport with the two divergent conventional wisdoms regarding how the Senate operated prior to cloture. On the one hand, some claim that the lack of a cloture rule induced universal coalitions, because a single senator could threaten to obstruct and kill legislation (Burdette 1940; Heitshusen and Young 2001; McCall 1911; Reinsch 1907; Von Holst 1893). On the other hand, some claim that even without a cloture rule, filibusters were rarely successful in blocking legislation and therefore the Senate was essentially a majoritarian body (Oppenheimer 1985; see also Binder and Smith 1997; Koger 2002; Mayhew 2003).

This chapter represents the first prong of a three-pronged approach that we employ to adjudicate between the competing theories (and their associated conventional wisdoms). We examine in this chapter the passage of significant laws during the pre- and post-cloture periods, focusing on the sizes of the coalitions that passed the legislation. In Chapter 5, we analyze the success of obstruction as a function of the size of the coalitions opposing the obstruction. We do this by examining the votes on dilatory motions targeted at specific pieces of legislation. Lastly, in Chapter 6 we investigate obstruction on tariff bills—one of the most important policy areas during this period—to assess the degree to which the politics involving this legislation were majoritarian.

---

[1]The previous question rule in place from 1789 to 1806 was not used to end debate, but rather to postpone action.

This multi-pronged approach helps to address some of the sample selection issues that bedevil analyses of filibusters. For example, one weakness of analyzing the success of obstruction is that one misses cases where minorities chose not to obstruct because they anticipated failure. The analysis of coalition sizes on final passage votes obviates this difficulty in that all successful bills are included, even those for which no obstruction was observed. Both the dilatory motions and final passage votes data suffer from the additional selection problem that one misses legislation favored by a majority that was never brought to the floor due to the expectation of obstruction. The analysis of tariff politics helps overcome this problem because we attempted—with the help of historians—to identify instances in which tariff changes were on the political agenda yet were not acted upon in the Senate.

The results from the different analytical prongs converge on the conclusion that slim majorities were quite successful at legislating in the pre-cloture Senate, which supports the theory we laid out in Chapter 2. In general, oversized coalitions were not necessary to pass legislation; indeed, it was more common for slim majorities to pass major legislation prior to 1917 than in the ensuing three decades. However, the majoritarianism of the pre-cloture Senate is subject to an important qualification: minorities were more successful in obstructing legislation during lame duck sessions when adjournment loomed, although universal support was still not necessary even at the very end of a congress. Based on this result, we conjecture that the cloture rule adopted in 1917 was aimed at reducing the uncertainty posed by small groups of obstructionists capitalizing on the adjournment deadline. We explore this issue further in Chapters 8 through 10.

4.2 COMPETING THEORIES ABOUT COALITION SIZES

The main alternative theoretical perspective regarding coalition sizes that we consider is what we refer to as "distributive universalism." Many empirical studies have noted the tendency in the U.S. Congress to structure legislation to appeal to universalistic coalitions (see Collie 1988 and Shepsle and Weingast 1981 for a long list of citations).[2] Weingast (1979) develops a formal model to explain this phenomenon, focusing on how uncertainty about who will be included in a coalition (and thus obtain distributive benefits from legislation) leads legislators to build maximal coalitions. Weingast (1979, 252) claims that legislators adopt rules to "institutionalize and maintain a tradition of unanimous coalitions" because it serves their reelection and other interests. The Senate's lack of a cloture rule could be viewed as a way of institutionalizing universalism. Without a cloture rule, if one senator or a small group of senators opposed ending debate on a bill, then

---

[2] We use the "distributive" qualifier because most of the work on universalism treats congressional politics primarily in distributive terms (see especially Weingast 1979 and Collie 1988) and in order to distinguish this perspective from the "pivot-based universalism" hypothesis noted below.

technically they could have prevented it from being terminated and therefore prevented the passage of the legislation. Even though the yeas and nays could be called for, the Senate's rules that give every senator the right to be recognized mean that as long as a senator sought recognition to speak or offer motions, the vote could have been prevented from taking place.

A common justification that senators give for their opposition to stricter rules regarding debate is that they want to reserve the option of filibustering in case they are confronted with a bill in the future that they want to obstruct from passing. Even though they may be in a coalition today that could effect a rules change to pass a desired but besieged bill, the uncertainty about being in future winning coalitions motivates their choice of lax debate rules. Thus, uncertainty leads to institutional choices that produce universal coalitions.[3]

This matches one common understanding of how the Senate operated prior to 1917. Burdette (1940, 52, 69, 78–79) discusses several cases in the pre-cloture period where he claims a single senator defeated legislation.[4] In making his case for the adoption of a cloture rule in 1917, Woodrow Wilson argued that "The Senate has no rules by which debate can be limited or brought to an end, no rules by which dilatory tactics can be prevented. A single member can stand in the way of action, if he have but the physical endurance," adding that "the Senate cannot act unless its leaders can obtain unanimous consent" ("Text of the President's Statement to the Public," *New York Times*, March 5, 1917, p. 1). Historian Herman Von Holst (1893, 264) likened the rules permitting filibusters to the *liberum veto* of the Polish Sejm, which gave any single deputy the power to veto resolutions. Reinsch (1907, 118) also made the comparison to the *liberum veto*, arguing that the right of a single senator to block a piece of legislation was "a distinctly feudal principle, by which the desire of one man, however prominent, may defeat the action of the State—a principle similar to which resulted in the political disasters and ultimate downfall of Poland" (see also Matthews 1960, 100). A testable hypothesis based on this view is that unanimous or near unanimous coalitions would have been the empirical regularity in the pre-cloture period.[5]

---

[3]Other models of distributive politics exist that produce predictions of minimum winning coalitions. Yet these models typically assume the existence of a previous question rule, and therefore are inappropriate for the Senate. Consistent with our interpretation of Weingast's model, Baron (1991, 85) points out that requiring unanimity to bring a proposal to a vote produces universalistic outcomes.

[4]In a later chapter, Burdette notes that "most" alleged one-person filibusters "are in reality cooperative enterprises" (1940, 210–11)).

[5]A prediction of smaller than universal coalitions can be obtained from this theoretical perspective. Shepsle and Weingast (1981, 109) conjecture that universalism may at times be restricted to the majority party "in a tightly organized partisan legislature." This would lead to coalitions that closely track the size of the majority party, which would typically be far smaller than the coalitions we would see under the general universalism model. However, the partisan variant of universalism is a poor fit to the pre-cloture Senate since party leadership was quite weak in the upper chamber for most of this period (Gamm and Smith 2002b). Indeed, the Senate has never been a "tightly organized partisan legislature," especially when compared with the House.

The distributive universalism perspective would predict unanimous or near-unanimous coalitions after 1917 as well.[6]

Some questions are immediately raised about the predictive power of this theoretical perspective. Parliamentary rules would have required a single senator to be on the floor at all times and be prepared to hold it for days on end in order to maintain the obstruction. Unless the obstruction occurred at the very end of a congress, bill supporters could have kept the Senate in continual session, making it physically impossible for a lone senator to hold the floor long enough to prevent a vote on the targeted legislation (Rogers 1926, 172–73). For those cases where an allegedly one-person filibuster was successful, there was probably more widespread support for the goals of the obstruction, although the visible effort was undertaken by one senator. A single senator was most likely successful at obstructing legislation because either there existed a sufficient number of less vocal or less active senators who were nonetheless in favor of the obstruction or the legislation was considered with almost no time left in the congress.[7] Nevertheless, the wide acceptance of the contention that the lack of a cloture rule induced universalism demands that we assess it more systematically.

The predictions of the theory of universalism contrast sharply with the predictions that follow from the theoretical perspective developed in Chapter 2. We review the key elements of this framework in order to make clear the predictions regarding coalition sizes that follow from it, and how they would differ from a strict interpretation of the pivotal politics model. The label we give to our alternative is the median-plus-veto-pivot model. While we draw on the basic logic of the pivotal politics model, we find that the additional components discussed in Chapter 2 are necessary to explain variation in coalition sizes in earlier periods of the Senate's history.

According to a strict, rules-based interpretation of the pivotal politics model, a filibuster pivot did not exist prior to the 1917 cloture reform. This gives rise to the theoretical conjecture that the only potentially pivotal players in the Senate then would be either the median or the veto pivot (i.e., the member of Congress whose vote is required to override a presidential veto). The rules and precedents of the Senate, as well as general parliamentary procedure, establish the median as a pivot, because a floor majority is a necessary condition for any motion to pass, while the Constitution defines the veto pivot. If this theoretical conjecture is correct for the pre-cloture period, then the following hypothesis should hold: coalitions were typically

---

[6] According to this model, the lack of cloture would have been but one underpinning of universalistic coalitions. Along these lines, the universalism perspective has been applied to the House as well as the Senate, even though the lower chamber has had provisions to end debate by majority vote since the early-19th century.

[7] For example, the obstruction of the Panama Canal Treaty at the end of the 57th Congress by Senator John Morgan (D–AL) was widely perceived to be a single-person effort (Burdette 1940, 77). However, when Morgan fell ill and had to leave the chamber temporarily, Senators Fred Dubois (R–ID) and Joseph Rawlins (D–UT) continued the obstruction in his absence ("No Progress on the Treaty," *New York Times*, February 27, 1903, p. 3).

just a bare majority of the chamber when the median senator was pivotal and coalitions were approximately two-thirds of the chamber when the veto pivot was the key player. After 1917, the basic pivotal politics model predicts coalition sizes of two-thirds, since the institution's rules now codified this hurdle for gaining a vote on passage.

This theoretical perspective implies that lawmaking in the pre-cloture Senate was majoritarian despite the lack of formal rules for cutting off debate. Simply put, since the chamber's rules required only a majority to adopt a motion, senators understood that in the end majorities would be sufficient to legislate. This is consistent with an alternative conventional wisdom about the Senate. For example, Binder and Smith (1997) claim that at least until the end of the 19th century, minorities did not take full advantage of opportunities to obstruct, implying that the median member of the Senate would typically be decisive when it came to passing laws (see also Koger 2002; Oppenheimer 1985; and Mayhew 2003).

However, one question about the basic pivotal politics perspective that is posed by the history of Senate reforms is that cloture by majority vote was never accepted when it was proposed (U.S. Congress. Senate. Committee on Rules and Administration 1985). The Senate refused, on several occasions, to make the median member the formal filibuster pivot. The position of the filibuster pivot that was officially established in 1917 was the 67th percentile. If narrow majorities were generally required to legislate before 1917, then the effect of the reform would have been to make it *more* difficult to close off debate and pass legislation. This would be surprising, given that reformers were at least ostensibly attempting to rein in filibusters when they adopted the cloture rule.

The theoretical innovations we introduced in Chapter 2 remedy the shortcomings of the basic pivotal politics model when applied to earlier periods of Senate history.[8] The median voter is pivotal on initial passage in that model because under the voting rule, a floor majority is sufficient for passage when a vote is held on legislation. But even though only a majority coalition would be necessary to pass the bill according to the voting rule, without a cloture provision that majority may be obstructed from reaching the voting stage. Bill supporters needed to wage a war of attrition against opponents in order to force action when confronted with a filibuster in the pre-cloture context. We argue that the costs of obstruction, combined with the threats of rules changes (which would induce restraint on the part of the minority), meant that bill supporters could generally expect to win such confrontations so long as the issue at stake was as salient to the majority as to the minority.[9]

---

[8]It is important to point out, however, that the innovations concerning costs and endogenous rules are consistent with pivotal politics' rules-based focus since they are rooted in the institutional features of the pre-cloture Senate. However, our arguments about norms are a significant departure from that model.

[9]While we argue that such restraint by the minority would not be binding when bill opponents are more intense in their views than are bill supporters, our focus in this chapter is on significant legislation, which should be salient to both majorities and minorities.

Thus, the absence of a cloture rule would not have eliminated the median senator's pivotal status. Senators understood that a determined majority would generally be able to apply the voting rule eventually, even in the face of obstruction. If they could not, they had the recourse of adopting new precedents in order to promote majoritarianism.

However, the automatic adjournment date in the lame duck session complicated the majoritarianism of the Senate and thus takes us even further from the basic pivotal politics approach. When adjournment loomed, it no longer could be assumed that the voting rule would eventually be applied, as the reduced costs of obstruction for bill opponents at that time would have tempted senators to exercise prerogatives even in cases where their resolve levels were low. Whether the majority would win the war of attrition and obtain a vote on passage would have depended on the resources the obstructionists possessed to employ dilatory tactics to block action until adjournment. These resources would need to be sufficient to overcome the costs of engaging in obstruction given the time left in the session.[10]

The costs themselves are institutionally rooted since rules and precedents defined the burden senators had to bear to hold the floor in order to prevent the application of the voting rule. For example, as noted in Chapter 1, the rules required senators to stand when they had the floor (which would be physically taxing), limited them to speaking twice on the same question in a legislative day, and forced them to give up the floor upon making certain motions. The ability to bear these costs would depend on the size of the group of obstructionists. The larger their number, the more likely they could have occupied the floor for the amount of time required either to consume the time remaining in the congress or disrupt the legislative process enough to imperil other legislation that was important to the majority. As time constraints became severe at the very end of a congress, the physical costs of obstructing would be lower and thus the size of the coalition required to obstruct successfully would have decreased (cf. Oppenheimer 1985; Binder, Lawrence, and Smith 2002; Sala 2002). The increase in the probability of success of obstruction toward the end of a congress would have made it more tempting to resist violating informal constraints on engaging in this behavior.

It is worth emphasizing that a theory that focused solely on short-term costs and ignored the threat of rules changes and norms of restraint would predict that coalitions for legislation passing in the last few days of a congress would have to be universal. Our approach generates quite different expectations. In the absence of an explicit cloture rule, it was uncertain how many obstructionists were sufficient to bear the costs of outlasting the majority's ability or tolerance to sit out the delay. Our theoretical framework implies that coalitions seeking passage of legislation had to be larger toward the end of a congress, although it was generally not necessary that

---

[10] Costs calculations may have still been relevant for the few decades after cloture reform since filibusters continued to require that senators hold the floor for days on end, even though the reform gave senators an explicit mechanism for forcing a vote on legislation.

they reach universalistic proportions even as the amount of time left approached zero. It was possible for a single senator to have held the floor in the last day or two prior to adjournment to prevent a vote on passage from occurring because the physical costs of obstruction would have been so low. Yet threats of rules changes and norms should generally have prevented this from happening. Thus, the famous one-person filibusters noted by historians need not imply that universal support was *generally* required to overcome obstruction. In fact, the focus on one-person filibusters should not obscure the more general pattern, which is that very few senators took advantage of the extreme time constraints at the end-of-congress deadline to obstruct legislation they opposed.[11]

Therefore, our theory suggests that bare majority coalitions would have been sufficient to pass legislation except when a veto threat was credible. Our arguments about time constraints and costs add the prediction that the coalition size required to overcome obstruction likely was greater than a simple majority when time was running out before the automatic adjournment date, although this did not induce universalism. Contrary to the basic pivotal politics model, we argue that senators would not have always needed to resort to invoking cloture to pass bills in the few decades after cloture reform because the costs to obstructionists at earlier points in a congress would have been too great.[12] Thus, we expect to find that bare majorities continue to enjoy a measure of success even after 1917, due to the continued relevance of costs and threats of rules changes.[13] Our empirical analysis is designed to allow inferences about both pre- and post-cloture lawmaking. In particular, our analysis of coalition sizes on major legislation and on the tariff each provide some potential insights into the post-1917 period, and thus permits a more general test of our theoretical conjectures.

An alternative view of the basic pivotal politics approach is that it implies that universalism should be the empirical regularity in the pre-cloture period, regardless of the specific time constraints imposed by the end of congress deadline. The basis for this argument is the claim that the absence of a cloture rule is tantamount to a requirement of universal agreement for legislation to be adopted. This "pivot-based universalism" hypothesis rests on a definition of a pivot that conflicts with that developed by Krehbiel (1998). Instead of being rooted in the explicit, formal rules of the Senate,

---

[11] The descriptive accounts of one-person filibusters that we have found indicate that each occurred in the final few days before adjournment (Burdette 1940). Yet these accounts belie the fact that many bills passed at these times even though they could have easily been obstructed. In addition, it is possible that other senators supported the obstruction, even if they did not undertake the visible effort of filibustering (e.g., see n. 7).

[12] This is consistent with case-study evidence offered by Mayhew (2003) that indicates relatively narrow majorities were sufficient to legislate in the decades immediately following the 1917 reform (see also Oppenheimer 1985).

[13] This contrasts with the contemporary Senate, in which filibustering has become essentially costless, making the basic pivotal politics model more appropriate and our refinement about costs inapplicable.

the pivot in this perspective would be rooted in the *absence* of a rule specifying how debate could be ended. While we think absences or loopholes in the rules, which create an opening for precedents cracking down on obstruction, are important for understanding obstructive behavior, this moves us far beyond the basic pivotal politics framework. Nonetheless, it is worth noting that such a pivot-based universalism model would make the same predictions as the distributive universalism model for the pre-cloture period, and therefore our empirical analysis gives us some leverage for assessing its validity, notwithstanding our qualms about its conceptual basis. As it turns out, our empirical evidence clearly contradicts the notion that universalistic coalitions were necessary in the pre-cloture era.

We can sum up the predictions of the various models as follows: distributive universalism leads one to expect unanimous or near-unanimous coalitions before 1917. The median-plus-veto-pivot model leads to the prediction of narrow majorities except when veto threats are credible or final adjournment looms. After 1917, the original pivotal politics model predicts that coalitions of two-thirds would be the regularity, although our theoretical framework predicts that we should still observe coalitions of less than two-thirds. By contrast, distributive universalism anticipates that oversized coalitions will persist after 1917.

4.3 COALITION SIZES ON THE PASSAGE OF SIGNIFICANT LEGISLATION

The first way we test the competing hypotheses derived in the previous section is to examine coalition sizes on final passage votes. Krehbiel (1998, 83–84) notes that the pivotal politics model, when applied to the contemporary Senate in which a three-fifths vote is required to invoke cloture, implies that coalitions enacting legislation will generally include at least 60% of the membership. Thus, the size of coalitions in the pre-cloture era, especially when compared with coalition sizes after cloture reform, is informative as to which of the theories best describes reality. The cloture rule in place from 1917 to 1949 required two-thirds of those present and voting to invoke cloture. Since our coalition size data covers 1881–1946 (see below), we focus on the percentage of those voting for the bill, rather than on the percentage of the full membership.

Since opponents may not find it worthwhile to obstruct minor legislation, we follow Krehbiel and others in examining coalition sizes on major laws. This focus implies that we would see little variation in the majority's resolve level with respect to this legislation. That is, we expect that virtually by definition a major law will be highly salient to bill supporters.

A linchpin of our analysis is the identification of a data set of major laws from the pre-cloture era that will render our analysis comparable with Krehbiel's, which uses Mayhew's (1991) dataset of landmark laws enacted from 1947 to 1994. Unfortunately, compiling a list of major laws is made difficult by changes in newspaper coverage and by the lack of such sources as *Congressional Quarterly*. We use as our primary data source a list of significant acts compiled by Petersen (2001), who has attempted to replicate Mayhew's methodology as closely as possible for the period 1881–1946.[14] We are especially interested in comparing coalition sizes before and after the 65th Congress, which Petersen's list allows, in order to examine whether significant changes coincided with the adoption of the cloture rule.

Table 4.1 reports results on coalition sizes for significant legislation.[15] A first noteworthy observation is that the average coalition size in the 47th–64th Congresses (1881–1917) was smaller than in the 65th–79th (1917–1946): on average, 71% voted yea in the pre-cloture era, while the average coalition size was 81% after adoption of the cloture rule.[16] This comparison indicates that legislation in the pre-cloture era certainly did not require unanimous coalitions and that the sizes of coalitions in many cases were smaller than what would have been required after the codification of the filibuster pivot in 1917.

If we consider the percentage of bills that passed with supermajorities before and after cloture, we find strong evidence that an oversized majority was by no means necessary to adopt significant legislation in the pre-cloture Senate. From the 47th through the 64th Congress (1881–1917), 48% of major laws were approved with fewer than two-thirds voting yes and 20% were approved with fewer than three-fifths voting in favor. By comparison, from the 65th through the 79th Congress (1917–1946), just 18% of bills were adopted with fewer than two-thirds voting yea, and an even more paltry 8% were adopted with fewer than three-fifths in favor.[17] Thus, consistent with the median-plus-veto-pivot hypothesis, many bills passed with narrow majorities in the pre-cloture Senate. While a fair number of bills passed with fewer than two-thirds in 1917–1946 as well, which is consistent with our theoretical arguments concerning costs, it was more common for coalitions to exceed the threshold established by the 1917 cloture rule.[18]

---

[14] Petersen acknowledges that a perfect replication of Mayhew's approach is impossible in this earlier time period. However, we believe that Petersen's list is still useful for investigating coalition sizes, especially if care is taken to consider the effects of alternative codings (see n. 23).

[15] Following Krehbiel, the results in Table 4.1 exclude legislation that passed on voice votes since we cannot tell what the actual size of the coalitions on these votes were. The same pattern of smaller average coalition size prior to 1917 remains if voice votes are included and treated as unanimous or near unanimous.

[16] Parametric and nonparametric difference of means tests indicate that the difference between the two averages is significant at greater than the .001 level.

[17] Tests of equal proportions indicate that these differences are significant at the .05 level or better. If we treat voice votes as having greater than two-thirds support (rather than as missing), then 26% of major bills passed with fewer than two-thirds in favor prior to the cloture rule, as compared to 10% after 1917.

[18] We also explored alternative periodization schemes for the data. Due to concerns about changes in workload and the possible peculiarities of the New Deal period, we compared 1881–1901, 1901–1917, 1917–1933, and 1933–1946. The general result that coalition sizes tended to be smaller before cloture reform held up even after we took possible differences among these periods into account.

Table 4.1 Coalition Sizes on Major Legislation, 1881–1946

	Average percentage voting in favor	Percentage enacted with fewer than 2/3 voting in favor	Percentage enacted with fewer than 2/3 voting in favor
47th–64th Congress (1881–1917)	71	48	20
65th–79th Congress (1917–1946)	81	18	8

Notes: Number of laws is sixty-four for the 47th–64th congresses and ninety-seven for the 65th–79th congresses. Following Mayhew (1991), we use the roll call on passage of legislation in each chamber, unless there was a subsequent roll call to adopt the conference report or to accept the other chamber's version of the legislation.

There was also a tendency in the pre-cloture period for there to be fewer close votes on bills passed late in a congress (which we define as the last thirty days before final adjournment), than those passed earlier in the congress. Only 33.3% of major laws passed late in a congress prior to 1917 were approved with less than two-thirds support, as compared to 50% of bills passed earlier in pre-1917 congresses. This comparison implies that timing constraints late in a congress did force legislative entrepreneurs to build bigger coalitions, although unanimity or near unanimity was still not generally required. By contrast, after 1917, there is essentially no difference in the share of close votes for bills passed early and late in a congress.

These results are even more striking when one considers that just ten of ninety major laws enacted between the 1975 cloture reform and 1994 passed with fewer than three-fifths voting in favor. Of these ten, five were budget bills in which statutory provisions mandated that a majority was sufficient for passage. Three of the other five had 59% in favor; a fourth enjoyed a 58% majority. This suggests that the three-fifths threshold is a genuine pivot point for major legislation in the contemporary era, with the exception of bills subject to specific statutory debate limitations (cf. Sinclair 2002). Furthermore, the relatively small average coalition size prior to 1917 is especially noteworthy given that coalitions in recent years are generally larger than one would expect based simply on the pivotal politics model (or, for that matter, based on a median voter model or the majority party's seat share). For example, Krehbiel (1998) finds an average coalition size of

81.9% when analyzing Mayhew's list of landmark enactments from 1947 to 1994.[19] The tendency toward oversized coalitions implies that finding an average coalition size of 70.8% prior to 1917—coupled with the prevalence of legislation passed by narrow majorities—provides strong evidence against the universalism hypothesis and in favor of the median-plus-veto-pivot hypothesis.

The most compelling conclusion to take from our evidence at this juncture is that the adoption of cloture clearly did not result in a shift in the Senate pivot from universalism (or any other value greater than two-thirds) to a pivot at two-thirds. In that case, one would expect *larger* coalition sizes before 1917 than after. Our finding of smaller coalition sizes before 1917 suggests that coalition builders could generally expect to succeed with major legislation if they built a minimal majority coalition, suggesting that obtaining the median's support was the key Senate hurdle.[20]

4.4 COALITION SIZES AND PRESIDENTIAL REGIME SHIFTS

Another way to assess the competing theories about lawmaking in the Senate is to consider the role of the veto pivot explicitly—that is, the member of Congress whose vote is required to override a presidential veto. Krehbiel (1998, 82–90) argues that an implication of the pivotal politics model is that when partisan control of the presidency changes hands, the veto pivot is less likely to be a constraint because the president and both chambers of Congress are more likely to be on the same side of the status quo. The empirical implication of such a "presidential regime switch" is that since vetoes require two-thirds coalitions to be overridden, there should be no change in Senate coalition sizes during the period where two-thirds coalitions were needed to invoke cloture, but there should be reductions in coalition sizes since 1975 when only three-fifths of the chamber has been required to stop a filibuster. For our analysis, if the median-plus-veto-pivot hypothesis is correct for the pre-cloture Senate, then we should see reductions in coalition sizes with presidential regime switches in that period. The logic behind this

---

[19] One rationale for such oversized coalitions that is consistent with a median-plus-veto-pivot model is provided by Groseclose and Snyder (1996). They demonstrate formally that a vote-buying strategy that involves putting together supermajorities can be less costly than a strategy of building minimal winning coalitions, even though only 50% plus one of the legislature is required under the voting rule. Thus, even though the median is the pivotal player, equilibrium coalitions can be larger than minimal winning, but less than universal.

[20] We are not prepared to conclude on the basis of this evidence alone that cloture reform was the dominant causal force behind the increase in coalition sizes after 1917. Other institutional changes, such as the 17th Amendment providing for the direct election of senators, might explain the increase. For example, indirectly elected senators may have been able to vote against popular legislation without fear of reprisal from voters. Directly elected senators may have faced greater pressure to vote for such bills, which might lead to generally larger coalition sizes. We consider other potential causes of coalition size patterns in Chapter 8.

prediction is that if the critical threshold for passage within the Senate is a simple floor majority, then the elimination of veto threats should reduce coalition sizes from roughly two-thirds to minimal majority-sized. But our theory also suggests that we might continue to see some coalitions smaller than two-thirds following post-1917 regime switches. Alternatively, if the distributive universalism hypothesis holds, implying that coalitions had to be greater than what was constitutionally required to override a veto, then we should see oversized majorities (that is, majorities well above two-thirds) regardless of regime switches and in both periods.

To test these predictions, we estimate regression models similar to those used by Krehbiel (1998) to test coalition size predictions in the post-war period (see his Table 4.2). That is, we regress coalition sizes for final passage votes on two interaction variables, one indicating presidential regime switches prior to 1917 and the other indicating presidential regime switches after 1917. We also include a dummy variable for the pre-cloture era, to capture the possibility that coalition sizes were generally smaller prior to 1917.[21] The median-plus-veto-pivot hypothesis predicts a negative coefficient on the pre-1917 regime-switch variable. A coefficient on this variable that is not statistically different from zero would be evidence in favor of the distributive universalism hypothesis.

The results are reported in Table 4.2. The negative and statistically significant coefficient on the main effect for the pre-1917 era reinforces the bivariate results that coalitions were generally smaller in the pre-cloture era than from 1917 to 1946. Consistent with the median-plus-veto-pivot hypothesis, the interaction term measuring pre-1917 presidential regime switches is also negative and statistically significant. Therefore, when the veto pivot was not a constraint, small majorities realized substantial success in legislating. If near unanimity—or even two-thirds—were required to pass major legislation in the pre-cloture Senate, reduced coalition sizes would not coincide with presidential regime shifts. The negative and significant estimate for post-1917 presidential regime shifts indicates that reduced coalition sizes continued to coincide with presidential regime shifts, though coalitions were generally larger after 1917 than before the cloture rule. This supports our conjecture that even after 1917, informal constraints on filibustering (i.e., constraints not directly specified in the standing rules) and the physical costs of obstruction meant that two-thirds majorities were not always a necessary condition for passage of major legislation. Since many pre-cloture conditions remained in place after 1917, it is plausible that minorities at times chose not to obstruct major bills even when they had the votes to

---

[21] Although Krehbiel did not include main effects in his regressions, we include the pre-1917 indicator variable to demonstrate that the regime-shift results are not simply an artifact of smaller coalition sizes pre-1917. If we exclude the main effect, the result on the regime shift interaction holds up. We also depart from Krehbiel by not including House votes in these regressions because the fundamental changes in legislative procedure in that body during this time period would require a much more complicated model. The results for the Senate are unaffected when variables for the House are added to the model. We consider changes in House coalition sizes in Chapter 9.

Table 4.2 Pre- and Post-1917 Cloture Reform Effects of New Presidential Regime on Sizes of Winning Coalitions on Major Legislation, 1881–1946

	1	2	3
Constant	0.820	0.857	0.820
	(0.016)	(0.095)	(0.016)
Pre-1917 Senate	−0.084	−0.086	−0.082
	(0.027)	(0.028)	(0.028)
New Regime × Pre-1917 Senate	−0.066	−0.069	−0.066
	(0.034)	(0.034)	(0.034)
New Regime × Post-1917 Senate	−0.065	−0.066	−0.065
	(0.032)	(0.032)	(0.032)
Majority Party Seat Share		−0.057	
		(0.148)	
Pre-Cloture End of Congress			−0.016
			(0.057)
Adjusted R^2	.138	.134	.133
F value	9.57 ($p < .001$)	7.17 ($p < .001$)	7.15 ($p < .001$)

Notes: $N = 161$. OLS coefficients with standard errors in parentheses.

block cloture.[22] It may seem surprising that the coefficient on the regime change interaction variable is approximately the same both before and after cloture reform, since theory suggests that the effect should be somewhat diminished after 1917. This decrease in the effect is partially captured by the "Pre-1917 Senate" dummy. The overall predicted coalition size is larger for the post-cloture period because of the combined effect of the dummy variable and its interaction with the regime change indicator.

Our model of coalition size is admittedly relatively sparse. However, the results are robust to a variety of alternative specifications. In the model reported in second column of Table 4.2, we include the majority party's seat share, but it has a statistically insignificant impact and does not affect the other coefficient estimates. The null effects for the partisan variable are consistent with our argument in Chapter 2 that partisan approaches to minority obstruction are inadequate.[23] We also tried including a variable to measure end-of-congress effects—see column 3 of Table 4.2—but the coefficient on this variable was not statistically different from zero.[24]

This null finding is probably due to the fact that lame duck sessions were especially prone to voice votes, which are treated as missing data in the OLS regressions, leaving us with many fewer cases. We estimated logit regressions where the dependent variable was whether or not the vote was lopsided—that is, whether or not a greater than two-thirds majority voted in favor of passage, assuming a voice vote indicates greater than two-thirds support for the legislation. The results obtained are reported in Table 4.3. Including voice votes in this manner increases our sample size considerably— from 161 to 284 votes. The main effect for the pre-cloture Senate is negative and statistically significant, which is consistent with the earlier results showing coalition sizes tended to be smaller prior to 1917. The coefficient on the pre-cloture regime-shift interaction is negative and statistically significant as

---

[22] In more recent decades, the Senate's extraordinarily tight time constraints have likely made the costs of obstruction sufficiently low so that they no longer impose a significant constraint on the minority. Nor do informal rules against obstruction appear to be as effective. In the concluding chapter, we consider the transition to low-cost filibustering in the post–World War II period.

[23] It is difficult to determine what predictions a party government approach yields for coalition size (see Krehbiel 1998, 79–82). Therefore, we do not purport to test a partisan model. We also estimated regressions that considered the effects of changes in partisan control of both Congress and the presidency on coalition sizes. We considered three possible configurations: congresses in which there was a switch to unified party government, congresses in which there was a continuation of unified government, and congresses with divided party control of Congress and the White House. These partisan-control models led to the same basic inferences as the party-less models: coalition sizes are smaller when there is a switch to unified party control in the pre-cloture era.

[24] As an additional robustness check, we narrowed the range of legislation to include only those bills identified as significant both by contemporary accounts and by specialized policy histories (i.e., Petersen's replication of Mayhew's (1991) sweep one and sweep two respectively). The results were unaffected. If we instead examine laws identified as significant both by Petersen and by Dell and Stathis (1982), the results are substantively the same. We focus on the Petersen list in the text because the methodology he used to compile his list is clearer than that used by Dell and Stathis.

Table 4.3 Pre- and Post-1917 Cloture Reform Effects of New Presidential Regime on Lopsided Coalitions on Major Legislation, 1881–1946

	1	2	3
Constant	2.303	6.359	2.303
	(0.316)	(1.914)	(0.316)
Pre-1917 Senate	−0.950	−1.285	−1.153
	(0.429)	(0.477)	(0.439)
New Regime × Pre-1917 Senate	−0.842	−1.170	−0.852
	(0.416)	(0.450)	(0.423)
New Regime × Post-1917 Senate	−0.693	−0.945	−0.693
	(0.521)	(0.554)	(0.521)
Majority Party Seat Share		−6.154	
		(2.764)	
Pre-Cloture End of Congress			1.069
			(0.591)
LR test	18.15 ($p < .001$)	21.98 ($p < .001$)	23.43 ($p < .001$)
% correctly predicted	56	69	59

Notes: $N = 284$. Table entries are probit maximum likelihood coefficients with standard errors in parentheses.

predicted, indicating fewer lopsided votes after a presidential regime switch in the pre-cloture era. For two out of the three equations we estimated, the coefficient on the post-cloture regime-shift indicator is not statistically significant. The significance of the coefficient turns on whether we include a variable measuring majority party seat share. The latter variable appears to have the wrong sign, however, since we would expect the likelihood of lopsided votes to increase the more seats the majority party controlled. The end-of-congress variable does have a positive and statistically significant coefficient in the logit model, indicating lopsided votes were more likely very late in a congress.

4.5 COALITION SIZES ON APPROPRIATIONS BILLS

As a robustness check of our analysis of coalition sizes on significant legislation, we performed a similar analysis for appropriations bills. The power over the purse strings is arguably the most important power that Congress possesses. Therefore, the stakes in passing appropriations bills are comparable to those associated with the passage of significant legislation. One particular advantage of this analysis is that it helps to control for changes in the agenda that may have affected coalition sizes, because the number and type of appropriations bills remained relatively constant from year to year. However, during the efforts to reform the appropriations process in the early 1920s, major changes did take place as numerous line items were reallocated under different bill titles. New titles for several regular annual appropriations were created as others were eliminated.[25] But it is difficult to see how these changes alone could have been responsible for any changes in coalition sizes that might have occurred.

One feature of the data on appropriations votes that immediately stands out is how infrequently the Senate held recorded roll calls on final passage. Although the Senate had to pass regular appropriations bills every year, as well as deficiency appropriations to make up for expenditure shortfalls, the chamber's approval usually came in the form of voice votes. This may represent the existence of broad agreement on spending bills. It may also be due to a general eagerness to pass the bills before the expiration of funds prevented government programs from operating. When roll call votes do occur, we should be concerned about the factors that led to a recorded vote rather than a voice vote. It could be the case that the situations where a roll call vote took place are unrepresentative of the way the appropriations process generally worked, which would potentially bias our inferences. However, if we find the patterns to be the same as those that occur with the passage of significant legislation, this bolsters confidence in the general conclusions we reach about obstruction and lawmaking in the Senate.

---

[25] For a detailed accounting of the changes see, the *Congressional Record*, January 18, 1922, pp. 1320–22.

Table 4.4 Coalition Sizes on Appropriations Bills, 1881–1946

	Average percentage voting in favor	Percentage enacted with fewer than 2/3 voting in favor	Percentage enacted with fewer than 2/3 voting in favor
47th–64th Congress (1881–1917)	71	50	27
65th–79th Congress (1917–1946)	78	16	16

Notes: Table entries are from twenty-two roll call votes for the 47th–64th Congresses and twenty-five roll call votes for the 65th–79th Congresses.

We collected data on all appropriations bills passed between 1881 and 1946. The bills and the votes that were taken on them were determined from several sources, including the *Congressional Record*, the *Senate Journal*, the annual Senate document *Appropriations, New Offices, Etc.*, and the roll call codebooks and data produced by Rosenthal and Poole (2000).

The results, reported in Table 4.4, display the same pattern found in the analysis of major legislation. Coalition sizes on appropriations bills (when recorded votes were held) were on average smaller in the pre-cloture period. In fact, the average coalition size for appropriations bills prior to 1917 is identical to the average size for landmark legislation. Although the difference between average coalition sizes before and after 1917 is smaller than what we found for landmark legislation, this difference is still statistically significant according to both parametric and nonparametric tests.[26] Consistent with our previous results, fewer appropriations bills passed without supermajority support after 1917. Prior to the adoption of cloture, about half of the bills with roll call votes passed with fewer than two-thirds, while just over a quarter passed with fewer than three-fifths. After cloture only 16% of the bills in our sample had coalitions that fell below these thresholds (these differences in proportions are statistically significant). Thus, with appropriate caveats about the limits imposed by having few roll calls, the analysis of appropriations votes is confirmatory of the analysis of landmark bills.

---

[26] Both a standard T test and a Wilcoxon two-sample test lead to a rejection of the null of equal means at the .05 level.

4.6 COALITION SIZES AND SILENT MAJORITIES

One potential criticism of our analysis that is worth addressing in some detail concerns abstentions on roll call votes. While senators rarely miss votes in the contemporary Congress, participation rates were much lower during the period we examine. A poor attendance record today provides a challenger seeking to unseat an incumbent senator with a damaging statistic that is easily imparted in a thirty-second campaign advertisement. But in earlier decades senators seemed much less concerned that low rates of roll call voting would be used as a campaign issue against them. High abstention rates could possibly introduce bias into our inferences based on coalition sizes.

Yet the direction of the bias is not clear a priori. Senators who knew they were on the losing side might have seen little benefit from appearing on the floor to cast a vote on final passage since displaying opposition to a successful bill might yield little credit for opponents. However, bill supporters might also have felt less of an imperative to cast votes on successful legislation that would pass without their vote if we accept the view of tenuous connections with constituents prior to direct election. On distributive legislation, senators might have believed it necessary to participate only in earlier stages of the legislative process in order to see to it that their constituencies received their piece of the pie. Coalition sizes would have been larger if everyone who supported these bills thought it necessary to be present to cast a vote in order to have their constituents' interests adequately protected. This would be consistent with the universalism argument, in that if everyone voted, then we would see coalitions that were much larger than minimum majorities.

Poole and Rosenthal (1997, 223–25) provide a way for investigating these conjectures systematically. They test a "silent majority" hypothesis, examining historically whether individuals who abstained would have been more likely to vote with the majority if they had participated in the vote. They find support for this hypothesis only after the 80th Congress and then only on lopsided votes in the Senate.

We replicated Poole and Rosenthal's "silent majority" analysis for the significant legislation included in our analysis. This involved using DW-NOMINATE coordinates to compute predicted votes for senators who abstained, and then taking the difference between the predicted percentage voting yes and the actual percentage voting yes. If coalition sizes would have increased had abstainers voted, then this difference should be positive. Figure 4.1, which plots this difference, shows that in almost every congress covered by the data on significant legislation, the percentage of abstainers predicted to vote yea is smaller on average than the percentage who actually vote yea.[27] Our results on coalition sizes thus do not appear to be driven by

---

[27]The magnitude of these differences is much bigger than what Poole and Rosenthal reported for their analysis of all votes for this period. This appears to be due largely to lopsided votes on significant legislation where most if not all of the abstainers are predicted to vote nay. We should also point out that our data have only a handful of votes per congress, whereas Poole and Rosenthal computed their statistics based on every vote taken in each congress.

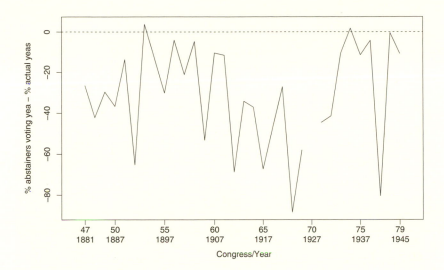

Figure 4.1 "Silent Majority" Analysis for Votes on Significant Legislation

the abstention of bill supporters. Coalition sizes would not have been bigger if abstainers had voted in the pre-cloture era, and there do not appear to be systematic differences in abstention rates on significant legislation across the two periods.

Based on the predicted votes of abstainers, we recomputed coalition sizes for the pre- and post-cloture periods. The results, reported in Table 4.5, make it clear that abstentions did not lead to underestimates of coalition sizes. When abstainers are accounted for, average coalition sizes are smaller for both periods—about 8 percentage points smaller compared with what we reported in Table 4.1. We also see a much larger proportion of bills passing with less than supermajority coalitions in both eras. This analysis adds more explicit confirmation to our contention that abstentions would not alter our inferences regarding the location of the pivot prior to 1917.

4.7 CONCLUSION

The analysis in this chapter indicates that although many major bills enjoyed supermajority support in 1881–1917, coalitions were typically smaller than in 1917–1946, with a much larger proportion of bills passing with only narrow majorities in favor. In terms of coalition sizes on significant legislation, our median-plus-veto-pivot perspective does a better job of explaining lawmaking in the pre-cloture Senate than do the approaches that predict universalism. The results presented here dispel the notion that oversized

Table 4.5 Predicted Coalition Sizes on Major Legislation, 1881–1946

	Average percentage voting in favor	Percentage enacted with fewer than 2/3 voting in favor	Percentage enacted with fewer than 2/3 voting in favor
47th–64th Congress (1881–1917)	63	70	43
65th–79th Congress (1917–1946)	73	34	15

Notes: Number of laws is sixty for the 47th–64th congresses and seventy-three for the 65th–79th congresses. Fewer laws are used in this analysis than that reported in Table 4.1 because of lopsided votes that are not scalable in DW-NOMINATE. Thus, coordinates for predicting yea and nay votes are not available for these roll calls.

majorities were necessary to pass important legislation in the pre-cloture era. The prevalence of small majorities suggests that costs and threats of rules changes were a substantial constraint on obstruction. The fact that coalition sizes did not expand to universal proportions even at end of a congress indicates that norms of restraint also likely played an important role in Senate lawmaking.

Our approach also does well in explaining lawmaking in the three decades after cloture reform. Our analysis incorporating the veto pivot indicated that presidential regime shifts still led to smaller coalitions after the establishment of the filibuster pivot in 1917, even though under the basic, costless pivotal politics model there should have been no change in coalition sizes. This suggests that the cloture rule established the support of the 67th percentile senator as a sufficient, but not necessary, condition for passage. We postpone a deeper investigation of this issue until Chapter 9, although it will come up again in the other prongs of our analysis. Our analysis of dilatory motions, which we turn to next, provides additional support for our conclusion about coalition sizes and pre-cloture lawmaking, as well as providing some clues to the motivations for and impact of the 1917 cloture reform.

Chapter Five

Dilatory Motions and the Success of Obstruction

5.1 INTRODUCTION

Our empirical investigation into the location of the pivotal players in Senate lawmaking has so far kept us above the fray of the parliamentary trench warfare that generates much of the popular interest in filibuster politics. Yet behind the numbers on coalition sizes that we reported in the previous chapter are dramatic legislative battles where sometimes historically consequential speeches are delivered and head-spinning parliamentary skill is on display, and at other times America's ruling elite engage in startlingly brutish behavior. Our analysis of significant legislation did not directly consider whether obstruction occurred and wars of attrition ensued. In this chapter, we pursue a different approach to investigating obstruction and lawmaking that brings us closer to these kinds of engagements. This analysis clarifies why our theoretical refinements to the pivotal politics model are essential for understanding the larger consequences of obstruction in this earlier period of history.

In the pivotal politics model originally derived by Krehbiel (1998), the only resource that legislators have or need to contribute to affect the legislative outcome is their vote. When it comes to stopping filibusters, we need be concerned only with whether senators will vote for cloture or not. The only resource that filibusterers have to obstruct successfully is the votes they can muster against the cloture motion. The obstructionists can give speeches and pursue dilatory maneuvers but these actions are mere window dressing because—given the model's assumptions of costless action and complete information—everyone knows if a cloture vote will succeed in the end.[1]

For the period of the Senate's history where there was no clear rule regarding cloture, more resources came into play. Individuals who opposed obstruction often had to vote against numerous motions to derail a piece of legislation, which required them to be continually available to cast votes if they were to prevent obstruction from succeeding. They could not just show up and vote for cloture when the motion for it was made. They typically had to cast several votes against dilatory motions and other motions to displace the legislation, sometimes across a span of weeks or months. Alternatively, those who opposed the legislation had to do more than simply assemble a

---

[1]Indeed, as stated before, filibusters never actually occur in equilibrium because the players perfectly anticipate each other's moves and thus no proposals will ever be made in the first place that would provoke a filibuster.

coalition of forty-one members to reject the cloture motion. They had to occupy the floor for the amount of time it took either to consume the time remaining in the session or to convince the majority that they were willing to do so, or disrupt the legislative process enough that other important bills would fail to be addressed. The success of the filibuster did not come down to a cloture vote, and instead depended on who was prepared to incur the costs necessary to win the sustained legislative skirmishes that constituted filibusters.

Krehbiel's model seems most appropriate for the "60-vote Senate" where "classic" filibusters in which senators obtain and hold the floor for extended periods are rare (Sinclair 2002). Threats of filibusters rather than actual obstruction are enough to affect legislative outcomes. The issuance of a filibuster threat typically begins a bargaining process where adjustments are made to placate those making the threat in order to avoid obstruction before it starts. The process for dealing with obstruction is highly routinized, with cloture motions often being filed preemptively, prior to the actual consideration of a bill.

The pre-cloture Senate was a very different place, however, since floor procedure was much less structured. For much of the Senate's history, there was not even someone like the majority leader or a centralized party leadership who determined when a piece of legislation would be brought to the floor (Gamm and Smith 2002a). Opposing obstruction during this period required unflagging diligence against dilatory tactics.[2] Opponents of obstruction had to muster enough votes to prevent minority maneuvers such as adjourning the Senate or tabling the legislation under consideration, which typically required keeping majorities on or near the floor for extended periods to maintain quorums and to reject multiple dilatory motions. Thus, while both supporters and opponents contributed their votes, they typically had to do more than just show up on the floor and vote a single time for a motion that, if passed, would have then brought the legislation to a vote on final passage.

The pivotal politics model is primarily concerned with discerning "which of n legislators or the president is pivotal in various lawmaking situations and why" (Krehbiel 1998, 23). For Krehbiel the "lawmaking situation" is completely defined by the locations of potentially pivotal players and policy alternatives on an ideological continuum. This is an extremely useful way for thinking about how preferences map into outcomes. But, as we have emphasized, the situation in the pre-cloture Senate has as much (and possibly more) to do with factors such as the timing of when the legislation is brought to the floor as it does with the configuration of preferences in the separation of powers system.

Our discussion of the resources required for obstruction in Chapter 2 is fundamentally about the size of the minority obstructive coalition and how size interacts with time constraints. The size of the minority required to

---

[2]To be clear, by dilatory tactics we mean activities by senators that are meant to disrupt and delay the legislative process. These tactics can include speeches, quorum calls, and motions meant to stall legislative business.

obstruct successfully depends crucially on the severity of time constraints. Thus, a minority of three may be successful at obstructing in the final days of a congress, whereas a larger coalition would be necessary for success earlier in the session. All but a few members of the minority party may be in favor of legislation being obstructed, but the bipartisan coalition in support could technically be thwarted if little to no time was left for consideration. This is why it is essential to think more broadly about minorities than a partisan perspective permits. An innovation in this chapter's analysis is that it is the first to explicitly measure variation in the size of majority and minority coalitions and investigate the success of obstruction using actual indicators of obstructive behavior. We discuss these measures in the next section.

5.2 UNCOVERING OBSTRUCTION

As part of our second approach to investigating obstruction and lawmaking in the pre-cloture Senate, we examine roll call votes on dilatory motions—a central feature of pre-cloture obstructive efforts—to determine whether the size of coalitions supporting these motions predicts success or failure of the obstruction. For example, if unanimity or near unanimity was required to pass legislation, then we should observe that obstruction generally succeeds even when large majorities of senators oppose the dilatory motions directed at a given bill. However, this analysis runs into the problem that it is difficult to determine when obstruction has actually taken place. The lists of filibusters that exist for the period we are examining are not completely trustworthy for this kind of empirical investigation, especially for the early history of the Republic (Beth 1995). The lists draw almost exclusively on Burdette (1940) for incidents of obstruction for the 19th and early 20th-centuries. Yet his coverage was not meant to be exhaustive, and most likely includes only particularly notable filibusters. Burdette never specifies the criteria he used for the selection of his cases, and it is difficult to tell with any precision from his descriptions how broad the support or opposition was.

One can also question Burdette's interpretation of the outcome of certain cases. For example, Burdette (1940, 28–29) describes a case in 1856 where he claims senators successfully obstructed a bill regarding the admission of Kansas to the Union. Using the tactics of long speeches, frequent quorum calls, and dilatory motions, obstructionists delayed from March 20 to June 25, which according to Burdette forced the bill to be referred back to committee. These parliamentary tactics "served merely to prove that the bill could not be brought to a vote because of unyielding opposition" (28). Although Burdette gives the impression that the bill and the effort to organize Kansas died there, this was not the case.

A bill on the organization of Kansas, S. 172, was indeed recommitted to the Committee on Territories on Wednesday, June 25, in a move intended to free up the Senate to debate other pending issues (*Congressional Globe*, p. 1467). This bill, sponsored by Stephen Douglas (D–IL), was one of the main proposals regarding Kansas that had consumed the Senate in a tempestuous debate for most of the first session of the 34th Congress. The motion to recommit S. 172 took with it several related bills then being considered on the floor. This included another bill to organize Kansas, S. 356, which was a compromise measure drafted by Senator Robert Toombs (Whig–GA).[3] The motion at first was made with instructions to be reported back the following Monday, June 30. These instructions were withdrawn, but the record indicates that senators believed it would be reported then or shortly thereafter. Thus, the approval of the motion to recommit did not lead to the failure of the Senate to pass a bill as Burdette implies. Indeed, S. 172 was reported on June 30, along with its companion bills, S. 342, S. 343, S. 351, and S. 356. S. 356 was taken up on July 2 in the Committee of the Whole by unanimous consent and became the focus of the debate. After a sequence of failed motions to adjourn, the bill was passed 33 to 12 (*Senate Journal*, July 2, 1856, p. 414). The effort to admit Kansas in 1856 was clearly not defeated by obstruction in the Senate as Burdette's account leads us to believe. Instead, the measure died in the House, where "it was hardly even considered" (Nevins 1947, 472).

Still, we should not be too hard on Burdette. His book is an indispensable source on the history of filibusters and a landmark work. Without it, there is no telling how long it would have taken political scientists to move studies of obstruction beyond the jeremiads that characterized what little literature previously existed on the topic. But he did not intend his work to provide an exhaustive list of incidents of obstruction, and it should not be treated as doing so.

Using historical records of debates to create our own list of incidents of obstruction is also problematic. Simply looking at the amount of debate or length of speeches on a particular piece of legislation is inadequate, since it is impossible to tell what the "appropriate" amount of debate on any given bill should be. Some bills can be dispensed with without much comment, while others require extended debate due to their complexities and salience to broad constituencies. Senators' statements during debate are not much help either. Senators protest—often at great length consuming substantial debate time—to the contrary when accused of engaging in dilatory behavior![4]

To circumvent these problems, we constructed a new data set, using dilatory motions to measure obstruction. These motions were an integral part of the temporizing strategies of members of Congress during the 19th century, and are therefore good indicators of incidents of obstruction (Binder and Smith 1997, 47–49; Dion 1997, 12). Binder and Smith define dilatory motions as motions to adjourn or postpone that failed to obtain a majority on a recorded roll call vote. Such motions are likely "intended to consume the time of the Senate in rounding up a quorum and taking a vote" (1997, 225–26, n. 64), thereby drawing out debate and inhibiting progress toward

---

[3]For details of the Toombs's measure, see Nevins (1947, 471–72).

[4]Some senators even questioned whether the famed Armed-Ship Bill filibuster in 1917 was actually a filibuster. See *Congressional Record*, March 8, 1917, pp. 27, 37, 40.

substantive votes. These motions disrupt and delay the legislative process, especially when roll call votes on the motions are forced, and, given their failure, indicate that only a minority supported the obstruction of the legislation's progress. In addition to the general delay caused by these motions, another reason for forcing roll call votes on them is to demonstrate the lack of a quorum, which under the Constitution brings consideration of the legislation in question to a halt.[5] Indeed, in the 19th century, dilatory motions, as much as long speeches, were what members understood to constitute filibusters. Since the individuals making and voting for dilatory motions are identified in roll call records, we can determine who is engaging in and supporting obstruction. Motions to recess, to table legislation, and to go into executive session during the consideration of legislation that is not "executive business" (i.e., treaties and nominations) were also used to obstruct, so we include data on these motions as well.

An examination of a few well-known instances of obstruction is useful to demonstrate that dilatory motions were integral to these efforts. We began Chapter 1 with a discussion of the obstruction of the Oregon Territory Bill in 1848, where dilatory motions were prominently featured. Many similar cases exist.

Dilatory motions were also used by southerners in 1850 to draw out the debate on a bill admitting California. Southerners used a range of parliamentary tactics, exemplified by the debate that took place on August 6. During consideration of the bill, David Yulee (D–FL), introduced a substitute for the bill which "contained forty odd sections" and "occupied some time in its reading" (*Congressional Globe*, August 6, 1850, pp. 1532–33). Yulee then commenced a speech in support of his substitute, where he noted the importance of "a defensive power" to the South through sectional parity and extolled the virtues of obstruction. He cited the dilatory efforts of southerners against a proposal considered in the Congress of the Confederation to relinquish the Mississippi River to Spain, noting that "parliamentary means were successfully and perseveringly employed *by a minority* through a struggle of extraordinary protraction, to defeat an unjust measure" (emphasis in the original). He claimed this was "an example consecrated to the use of southern men of the present day, who should feel no reluctance to adopt a means which honored fathers of the Republic employed to prevent the degradation of their section" (Appendix to the *Congressional Globe*, August 6, 1850, pp. 1163–64).

Other southerners demonstrated their agreement with Yulee's claim by making numerous dilatory motions during his speech. First, Jefferson Davis (D–MS) made a motion to postpone consideration of the bill; the motion

---

[5] A quorum is often not present on the floor during the conduct of debate. Although this is typically overlooked, obstructionists should act to make sure rules regarding quorums are enforced. Even though the time consumed by calling the roll may not be much if all senators are already on the floor, getting senators to the floor can be time consuming and a great inconvenience, especially if the Senate votes to have the sergeant at arms compel the attendance of absent senators.

failed. Then George Badger (Whig–NC), Pierre Soulé (D–LA), and Thomas
Pratt (Whig–MD) made sequential motions to adjourn. Pratt's motion was
challenged on a point of order, because it was made without any business
having been conducted since the previous motion to adjourn was rejected.
The chair sustained the point of order, prompting Soulé to make a motion to
postpone the bill until the following day. "A debate ensued upon the respec-
tive powers of endurance of the friends and opponents of the bill," followed
by an unsuccessful motion to adjourn by Willie Mangum (Whig–NC) (*Congressional Globe*, August 6, p. 1533). After some additional unsuccessful
motions to adjourn and postpone, a debate about the existence of a quorum, and an attempt to have the sergeant at arms compel the attendance of
absent senators, Stephen Douglas noted that several supporters of the bill
had gone home and made a motion to adjourn, which was agreed to. The
remarks of senators during this debate made it clear that opponents of the
bill were obstructing, and the obstructionists acknowledged that their use
of dilatory motions was motivated by their opposition to the bill. Opponents continued to make dilatory motions throughout the debate, but the
bill eventually passed the Senate 34-18 on August 13.

Dilatory motions played a key role in the obstruction of an attempt by
Charles Sumner (R–MA) to add a civil rights provision to the sundry civil appropriations bill in June of 1872. Sumner, despite very poor health, pushed
the civil rights cause relentlessly during the 42nd Congress, only to experience repeated failures (Pierce 1969, 499–504). In his last attempt to enact
meaningful civil rights legislation, he sought to add his anti-discrimination
amendment on June 7 to an amendment that provided funds for the enforcement of voting rights (*Congressional Globe*, p. 4366).[6] The sundry civil
bill had produced a turbulent debate, with some charging that a conspiracy
was afoot to defeat appropriations bills before the Senate's set adjournment
date, which would force the president to call a special session ("Mr. Sumner's Long-Threatened Speech Delivered," *New York Times*, June 1, 1872,
p. 1). Sumner made his move during an evening session held in an attempt to dispose of the bill before the impending adjournment. The debate
was particularly contentious because the Senate had agreed to a temporary
rule limiting debate on pending motions relevant to the bill to five minutes
per senator. Some senators claimed that they would have never agreed to
these limits had they known that amendments like Sumner's—which they
argued was legislative in nature—would be proposed. Senate rules prohibited amendments to spending bills that made legislative provisions if they did
not directly relate to the appropriations contained in the bills. After Sumner
introduced his amendment, a lengthy debate about substantive and parliamentary issues ensued, during which sixteen dilatory motions were made
(all but one by Democrats). The obstruction kept the Senate in session all
night until finally the presiding officer at seven o'clock in the morning ruled

---

[6]For the full text of Sumner's amendment see *Senate Journal*, June 7, 1872, pp. 999–
1000.

Sumner's amendment out of order, a decision that was sustained on a 33-6 vote.[7]

The filibuster that occurred during the attempt to organize the Senate at the beginning of the 47th Congress in 1881 is one of the longest and most acrimonious on record. The election of 1880 had produced a very narrow split between Republicans and Democrats, and each side sought advantage through parliamentary obstruction. Vacancies created by death and the appointment of a handful of senators to President James Garfield's cabinet induced uncertainty as to which party had the votes to organize the institution. At the opening of the special session, the Republicans stalled with dilatory motions until the vacancies were filled and, having won the support of Readjuster William Mahone of Virginia, they were able to pass a resolution for the organization of committees.[8] When the Republicans then tried to replace the Democratic officers of the Senate with Republicans, the Democrats began a fierce filibustering campaign where dilatory motions were again the weapon of choice.[9] The filibuster lasted from March 24 through May 6, until the Republicans finally relented when it became clear that they would be unable to overcome the obstruction. An astounding 114 dilatory motions were made during this period, with business on some days consisting of little else beside these motions.

The purpose of these brief narratives is to establish some historical context and face validity for the argument that dilatory motions played a central role in obstructive efforts. We adopt the approach of using multiple dilatory motions to identify incidents of obstruction targeted at specific bills in order to investigate the success or failure of obstructive efforts.[10] Our analysis employs data from roll call voting records where it could be determined that the motions were targeted at a bill or resolution.[11]

The use of dilatory motions for our analysis is particularly attractive for several reasons. First, the cases of obstruction that were uncovered using this approach matched many on existing lists of pre-cloture filibusters (e.g., see Beth 1994 and Binder and Smith 1997), while also uncovering some that

---

[7]The defeat of Sumner's amendment was the last straw that led him to bolt the Republican party and support Horace Greeley instead of Ulysses Grant in the presidential election of 1872 (Donald 1996).

[8]The vote was a tie, broken in favor of Republicans by Vice President Chester Arthur. James Cameron (R–PA) took the lead in the filibuster, making eight dilatory motions from March 14 to 16.

[9]The *New York Times* explicitly referred to these as "filibustering motions" ("The Bourbon Filibusters," March 26, 1881, p. 1; "Obstinate Minority," March 27, 1881, p. 1).

[10]Burdette (1940, 5) defines filibustering as "the use of dilatory tactics upon the floor of a legislative body." According to this broad definition, then, any use of dilatory motions constitutes filibustering. However, using the more restrictive measure of multiple dilatory motions more accurately reveals the kind of obstruction that is typically thought of as filibustering.

[11]Since only one-fifth of members present are necessary to force a roll call on a motion, we doubt that there are significant sample selection issues induced by omitting dilatory motions where roll calls were not held. Indeed, it is in obstructionists' interests to force roll calls because of the additional time they consume. We exclude from our analysis nominations, treaties, impeachments, and housekeeping measures.

were missing from these lists, but nonetheless appear in histories of particular policy areas. For example, the cases of obstruction of tariff bills in 1883 and 1894 (discussed in Chapter 6), which are not included in existing lists of filibusters, were uncovered by sifting through multiple dilatory motions. Second, it is relatively straightforward to determine which pieces of legislation were targeted by examining descriptions of roll call votes and the debate surrounding the motions. Oftentimes the roll call vote description indicates which piece of legislation was being considered on the floor when the motion was made. If it is not clear from the roll call description, the records of debates in either the *Senate Journal* or *Congressional Record* and its predecessors usually make it clear what is targeted.[12] Finally, the votes on these motions give us a measure of the sizes of the coalitions supporting or opposing the obstruction.

Nonetheless, there are important nuances to measuring coalition sizes on these votes. Our measure rests on two key assumptions that should be made explicit and justified. First, we assume that *opposition* to obstruction rather than support is observable through the votes against dilatory motions. The aforementioned issue of obstructionists using various motions to demonstrate the lack of a quorum indicates that *support* for obstruction is not accurately observable using roll call votes. Obstructionists have an incentive to abstain from voting on these motions if abstaining makes a quorum "disappear," thereby bringing the legislative process to a halt. Thus, the number of those voting *in favor* of dilatory motions would not be a good indicator of the number who engaged in the obstruction. However, opponents of obstruction should more accurately reveal their numbers through their nay votes. They have an incentive to vote in force, both to make sure that dilatory motions are defeated and to try to maintain a quorum in order to keep the consideration of legislation on track. In order to check the validity of the assumption that voting against dilatory motions indicates support for an obstructed measure, we took a sample of twenty of our significantly obstructed measures and checked the correlation between how senators voted on the dilatory motions targeted at them and how they voted on final passage (for those bills that had final passage votes). The median correlation was $-.85$, indicating that those who voted against dilatory motions generally voted in favor of the targeted bill if it could be brought to final passage.

A second assumption is that support for a bill is fairly constant across votes on dilatory motions. One situation in which this assumption might be violated is when compromises lead to defections from the obstructing coalition. However, in our sample of twenty bills, coalitions across votes on dilatory motions appear to be quite durable. For all of the bills in our data, the average standard deviation in the size of coalitions opposing dilatory motions is under four senators. The median correlation across these votes at the individual level for our sample of twenty bills was .8. While it is possible

---

[12]While it is conceivable that a dilatory motion was made during debate on one piece of legislation in order to prevent another from being brought to the floor, our reviews of records of debates did not reveal any cases where this happened.

that some compromises were worked out on certain pieces of legislation that would have decreased support for obstruction, the durability of coalitions across votes leads us to believe that our assumption about the constancy of opposition to obstruction is reasonably accurate.

While the validity of these assumptions gives us confidence in our measures, we also acknowledge their limitations. One such limitation concerns a shift in obstructing tactics that occurred in response to the adoption of precedents that limited the effectiveness of dilatory motions. This shift appears to have occurred in response to a series of landmark precedents that progressively limited the usefulness of dilatory motions and quorum calls (see, Section 1.2, Section 2.3, and Table 3.1). The most important of these precedents appear to have been the 1879 and 1908 rulings allowing the presiding officer to count a quorum, and the 1908 decision limiting the use of successive quorum calls.

In response to these precedents, senators came to rely more and more on protracted speeches to obstruct, which is the tactic most commonly associated with filibusters in the 20th-century Senate. As a result, the number of filibusters uncovered by our method falls prior to the turn of the century. The modification in obstructive tactics is consistent with our general argument about the effectiveness of precedents for changing senators' behavior. But it also suggests our approach to uncovering incidents of obstruction is probably not suitable for constructing a complete time series that covers both the pre- and post-cloture periods. This approach is suitable, however, for determining sizes of obstructing coalitions in the pre-cloture period, especially up through the late-19th/early-20th centuries, when obstructionists began to rely more on long speeches as opposed to dilatory motions. There are no readily available comparable measures for assessing coalition sizes favoring or opposing obstruction for the period covering the switch in strategies because votes on cloture motions do not become available until after 1917.

Figure 5.1 displays the frequency of counts of dilatory motions targeted at pieces of legislation. The first bar gives the number of pieces of legislation targeted with two dilatory motions. For this analysis we focus on incidents of "significant" obstruction, which we define as three or more dilatory motions targeted at a piece of legislation.

While identifying incidents of obstruction is a difficult task, determining the success or failure of dilatory tactics is even more complicated because the goals of obstructionist senators are often not obvious. It is easy to tell whether a filibustered bill passed the Senate, but the goal of the filibuster may have been to force compromise rather than kill the targeted legislation. It could also be the case that one bill is blocked in order to kill, force consideration of, or compromise on a different measure. Given the difficulties of determining senators' goals, we consider only whether or not obstructed bills passed the Senate in the congress in which they were considered. This is an admittedly extreme measure, but it is the outcome that has typically been the focus of analyses of filibusters and the major concern of normative assessments of the Senate's rules regarding limits on debate.

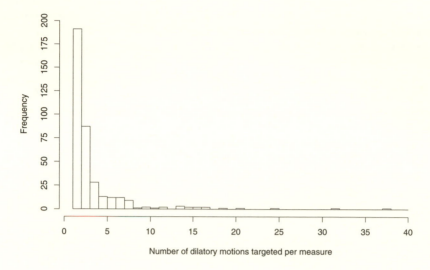

Figure 5.1 Histogram of Dilatory Motions

Different opinions exist about the extent to which filibusters have caused the demise of legislation. Burdette (1940, 39) argues that, until the 1880s, the filibuster "had been a device remarkably unsuccessful; almost every obstructed measure was eventually passed despite the filibustering opposition." Burdette (209) claims for later periods, including the post-cloture period, that the power of filibusters was "almost unrestricted." Wolfinger (1971), however, contends that Senate filibusters actually killed very few bills in the 1930s to 1950s. Using our measures, we find that 19% of significantly obstructed measures failed in the antebellum period, which is comparable to the number that failed in the period from the Civil War to the turn of the century.

5.3 MODELING THE SUCCESS OR FAILURE OF OBSTRUCTION

The dependent variable in our empirical model equals 1 if the bill passed and is 0 otherwise. We model the success or failure of a piece of legislation as a function of the maximum size of the coalition opposing dilatory motions. To compute this measure of coalition size, we use the largest number of votes cast against the dilatory motions targeting a given piece of legislation for the numerator of our measure. The denominator is the number of senators who were members of the Senate at the time of the vote. We do not use the total number of votes cast (i.e., ayes plus nays) as the denominator because of the disappearing quorum problem. The number of senators present in the chamber varies substantially from vote to vote because of turnover and absenteeism. Some error is likely to creep into our measure because senators who oppose the obstruction may not be present in the chamber to vote. Therefore, we may underestimate opposition to obstruction in some cases, but the use of maximum coalition size should mitigate this problem. Some might be concerned that using the maximum coalition size could overstate the size of the coalition that bill supporters could consistently muster to try to stop delay. Fortunately, the results did not change appreciably when we used the average coalition size instead.

We expect that larger coalition sizes will increase the probability of passage. The key question though for testing the hypotheses developed in Chapter 4 is by how much at particular sizes.[13] The distributive universalism hypothesis suggests supporting coalitions will tend toward unanimity to be successful; the median-plus-veto-pivot hypothesis implies narrow majorities will generally overcome obstruction.[14]

We strongly expect the effects of coalition size on the likelihood of passage will depend on when obstruction occurs. As discussed in Chapter 2, as the end of a congress draws near, time constraints and thus the costs of waiting out the obstruction increase (see also Burdette 1940, 215). We tap into these time constraints by including a variable measuring the number of days remaining in a congress when the obstruction occurs, along with a dummy variable indicating whether the obstruction occurs in the final thirty days of a congress. The coefficient on this dummy variable should be negative, implying that a given coalition opposing obstruction will be less successful late in a congress. Our model also includes interactions between the coalition size variable with the number of days until the end of the congress and the end of congress indicator. The end-of-congress effect should be attenuated as the coalition size and the number of days left increase.[15]

---

[13]Another nuance is that the probability of passage of legislation might not increase continuously with coalition size, implying that a step function with different thresholds for coalition sizes is appropriate. However, we chose to estimate a model with coalition size as a continuous variable for several reasons. First, it is difficult to know what thresholds should be specified. While the politics of cloture reform suggest some thresholds are particularly relevant (e.g., 67%), we might miss others that are relevant if we do not slice up the distribution of coalition sizes into very fine intervals. But taking such fine slices consumes many degrees of freedom, which is a problem with our relatively small sample size ($N = 157$). More degrees of freedom are consumed when we include interaction terms. Estimation of a model specification using the step function with only a few steps (namely, 51%, 55%, 60%, and 67%) proved to be problematic, as we experienced problems with convergence, very poor fit to the data, and very imprecise coefficient estimates. Using a continuous measure does not throw away information and also has the advantage of telling us what the probability of passage is with any particular coalition size.

[14]One complication is that it is plausible that filibuster threats kept bill supporters from bringing matters to the floor when they expected obstruction to be successful. The convergence of the results from our multi-pronged approach gives us confidence that this potential selection issue is not leading to incorrect inferences, however.

[15]One question that is raised by our arguments about end-of-congress obstruction is why senators would ever consider important items late in the congress. One answer to this question is that they do not always have complete control over timing. Items may be forced onto the agenda due to exogenous circumstances in the polity. Other items may

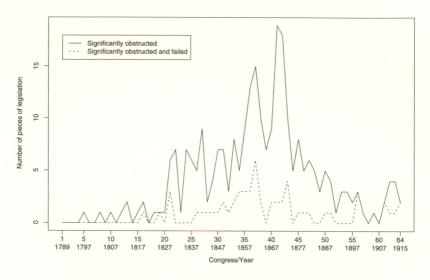

Figure 5.2 Time Series Plot of Incidents of Obstruction

Figure 5.2 displays a time series plot of the number of incidents of significant obstruction in the 1st through 64th Congresses. By this measure, obstruction increased substantially throughout the 19th century, peaking in the 41st Congress (1869–1871) with nineteen incidents, and then declined thereafter. The plot shows that a fair number of obstructed measures— 22%—failed to pass during this period.[16] This plot also demonstrates the difference between this measure of obstruction and previously compiled measures of filibusters. Although our measure indicates the amount of obstruction was declining toward the end of the 19th century, extant lists of filibusters indicate that obstruction was increasing (Binder and Smith 1997). The plot illustrates the shift in obstructionists' tactics in response to the precedents that limited the usefulness of dilatory motions. The peaks in the figure correspond to historical accounts that suggest obstruction increased in frequency as slavery and secession rose on the agenda in the 1840s and 1850s, and during the battles over Reconstruction. But we emphasize that the figure understates the prevalence of filibusters at the turn of the century, as obstructionists turned to long speeches in place of dilatory motions.[17]

---

take time to work their way through the House or the committee stage in the Senate. In Chapter 6, we discuss how senators do seem to have responded to the problems obstruction posed for tariff legislation by considering tariff bills earlier in congresses.

[16] One might object that the high success rate in passing obstructed bills reflects concessions made by bill supporters to win over a subset of the obstructionists. Our case studies, however, suggest that slim majorities were generally successful even in the absence of significant concessions (see especially Chapter 6).

[17] While our method does a reasonably good job of identifying filibusters that others have documented through the 1870s and 1880s (while also uncovering many additional cases), it does not pick up several prominent cases near the end of the pre-cloture period.

Table 5.1 Descriptive Statistics for Analysis of Passage of Obstructed Measures, 1st–64th Congresses

Variable	Mean	Median	Std. Dev.	Min.	Max.
Coalition size	0.520	0.506	0.104	0.302	0.833
Days left in Congress	167.200	170.000	169.710	0	714.000
Coalition size × Days left in Congress	18.186	9.818	22.881	0	141.509
End of Congress	0.318	0	0.467	0	1.000
Coalition size × Days left in Congress × End of Congress	1.596	0	3.363	0	15.000

Note: $N = 157$.

Table 5.1 reports descriptive statistics for the explanatory variables in the model. The proportion of obstructive incidents that occurred at the end of the congress (i.e., the mean of the end of congress variable reported in the table), indicates the importance of our concerns about the effects of final adjournment. Approximately 32% of the incidents in our sample occurred in the last thirty days of a congress, even though on average this time period constituted less than 10% of the total time that congress spent in session.

The results of the probit analysis of the passage of significantly obstructed legislation in the pre-cloture period are reported in Table 5.2. The coefficients on the variable measuring the size of the coalition opposing obstruction and the end-of-congress obstruction indicator variable are statistically significant and have the expected signs. The larger the size of the coalition opposing obstruction, the more likely a bill is to pass, although this effect is tempered if the obstruction occurs at the end of a congress. The coefficient on the three-way interaction between coalition size, days left in the congress, and the end-of-congress dummy is positive and marginally statistically significant. This result, combined with the statistical insignificance of the coefficients on the main effect for days left in the congress and its interaction with coalition size, indicate that time constraints materially have an impact only at the end of a congress.[18]

---

[18] We also estimated a model in which an end-of-session dummy replaced the end-of-congress dummy. The coefficients on this variable and its interactions were not statistically different from zero. These results indicate that time constraints increased obstructionists' leverage only when final adjournment loomed. This makes sense given that pending legislation can be carried over from one session to the next, except after final adjournment. Given our concerns about the validity of our measure of coalition sizes after the establishment of precedents limiting dilatory motions' usefulness, we repeated our analysis excluding congresses after 1879. The results were very similar to what we report here. The change in obstructionists' tactics after the establishment of these precedents limits

Table 5.2 Probit Analysis of Passage of Obstructed Measures, 1st–64th Congresses

Variable	Coefficient	Std. Err.	p value
Constant	−0.475	0.703	0.499
Coalition size	2.483	1.223	0.042
Days left in Congress	0.0002	0.001	0.851
Coalition size × Days left in Congress	0.006	0.007	0.391
End of Congress	−0.821	0.407	0.043
Coalition size × Days left in Congress × End of Congress	0.093	0.051	0.070
Likelihood ratio test	15.76	($p = 0.008$)	
Expected percent correctly predicted	69		

Note: $N = 157$.

In order to adjudicate among the competing hypotheses, we simulated the probability of passage associated with particular coalition sizes for obstruction occurring early or late in a congress (again, "late" here means the last thirty days prior to adjournment). The other variables in the model were set to their median values. We account for uncertainty in the simulations by employing the method advocated by Herron (2000, 87) to compute 95% confidence intervals around the predicted probabilities.[19] A plot of the results that include the confidence bounds and indicate thresholds of theoretical interest appears in Figure 5.3.[20]

If the coalition opposing the obstruction is 51% and the obstruction takes place early in a congress, a bill has a .80 probability of passage with a 95% confidence interval of [.65, .90]. Late in a congress, an obstructed bill has a probability of passage of .68 for a coalition of this size, with confidence

---

our ability to explore different periodization schemes for the time frame spanned by our analysis.

[19] This method involves drawing a set of coefficient values from a multivariate normal distribution using the estimated coefficient vector as the mean vector and the estimated variance-covariance matrix as the variance matrix for that distribution. We then sort the set of simulated coefficient values and use the values at the .025 and .975 percentiles for the bounds of the confidence intervals.

[20] Note, however, that we do not observe the complete range of coalition sizes—from 0 to 100%—in our sample; the highest value we observe is .83.

Early in a Congress

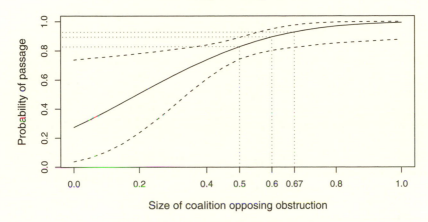

Size of coalition opposing obstruction

Late in a Congress

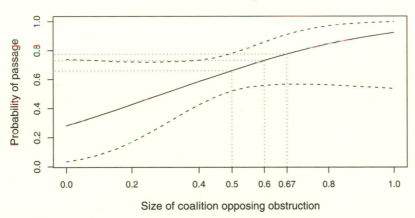

Size of coalition opposing obstruction

Figure 5.3 Simulated Probabilities of Passage, Varying Size of Coalition opposing
Obstruction

bounds of [.56, .79]. On the last day of a congress, the predicted probability of passage is .51 [.34, .68]. A bill with a bare majority thus has a very good chance of passage early in a congress, but its chances are less if it is considered late in a congress. However, contrary to the universalism hypothesis, those chances are never near zero. The largest coalition size in our sample—.83—gives approximately the same predicted probability regardless of when the obstruction occurred: .95 [.81, .99] early in a congress and .94 [.77, .99] late in a congress. Therefore, building oversized majorities was one strategy for counteracting time constraints, yet these constraints did not appear to demand coalitions to be of universal proportions in order to defeat obstruction.

These results are consistent with the analyses of significant legislation, indicating that unanimity or near unanimity was not necessary to overcome obstruction prior to 1917.[21] Fairly narrow majorities were still very successful in passing legislation despite obstruction. As implied by our theory, their success rate decreased when the obstruction occurred late in a congress, but unanimity was still not required. As adjournment drew near, there was increasing uncertainty about how large a coalition had to be in order to overcome obstruction.

More support for this result is provided by linking our analysis of coalition sizes on dilatory motions to our analysis of coalition sizes for the passage of major legislation. To do so, we identified those significant laws (from Petersen's list, as described in Section 4.3) that were targeted with multiple dilatory motions and examined the coalition sizes on these motions. As it turns out, seven significant laws adopted from 1881 to 1946 were obstructed according to our measures. These were the tariff bill of 1883 (adopted with 51% voting in favor), the Pendleton Civil Service Reform Law of 1883 (adopted with 88% voting in favor), the International Copyright Act of 1891 (59% in favor), the Silver Purchase Repeal of 1893 (57% in favor), the Wilson-Gorman Tariff of 1894 (53% in favor), the Canadian Reciprocity Act of 1911 (66% in favor), and the creation of the Federal Trade Commission in 1914 (90% in favor).[22] Interestingly, the mean supporting coalition size across these cases is 66%, which is what the pure pivotal politics model would predict for the post-cloture period. However, two of the seven passed with very slim majorities in favor, and three passed with coalitions smaller than what was required by the 1917 cloture rule. Only two of these bills had coalitions that approach universal proportions. This confirms our rejection of the hypothesis that unanimous or near unanimous coalitions were necessary to pass major legislation in the pre-cloture Senate, even when obstruction was clearly a feature of deliberations.

---

[21] Unfortunately, given the change in tactics of obstruction in the late-19th century discussed above, we are not able to compare our results in the pre-cloture Senate with a parallel analysis of the post-cloture Senate, simply because of the lack of comparable measures of the size of coalitions opposing obstruction.

[22] Of these the Silver Purchase repeal, Canadian Reciprocity Act, and Federal Trade Commission Act appear on extant lists of filibusters (Beth 1994).

5.4 DISCUSSION

These results are consistent with the analyses of significant legislation, indicating that unanimity or near unanimity was not necessary to overcome obstruction prior to 1917. Fairly narrow majorities were still very successful in passing legislation despite obstruction. Their success rate, however, decreased when the obstruction occurred late in a congress. This increased the level of uncertainty for legislative entrepreneurs seeking to build coalitions that could win the war of attrition.

The findings in this chapter reinforce our basic argument that the precloture Senate was characterized by a high degree of majoritarianism, notwithstanding the sparse institutional structure that left minorities with considerable opportunities to obstruct. The costs confronting obstructionists likely help explain the high success rate of slim majorities early in precloture congresses. But, even as greater majorities were required at the very end of a congress, universal support was by no means necessary to overcome obstruction. This finding again suggests the role of norms of restraint, in tandem with threats to change the rules of the game, in limiting obstruction in the pre-cloture era. We argue in Chapter 8 that as these norms began to break down in the late-19th century, even large majorities were by no means assured of success in the waning days of a congress. This breakdown of informal restraints, in turn, motivated senators to move toward a formal cloture rule that reduced the uncertainty posed by late-congress filibusters by small minorities (see Chapter 9).

This chapter has brought us closer to examining the "politics as contact sport" element of obstruction. We have focused on the kinds of legislative battles that needed to be fought in the trenches of the Senate floor. Small majorities fared well in those battles, except when minorities exploited particular institutional advantages, such as the end-of-congress deadline. But the quantitative analysis in this chapter still strips away much of the richness and detail of the political combat that often has shaped major policy choices in American history. The next chapter discusses a case study of tariff politics that maintains this richness while confirming the conclusions that we have reached so far.

Chapter Six

Obstruction and the Tariff

6.1 INTRODUCTION

In earlier chapters, we have relied primarily upon general, quantitative tests to assess the impact of unlimited debate in the pre-cloture Senate. We take a different tack in this chapter, tracing the role of obstruction in a single policy area over a long stretch of history. One advantage of such an approach is that it enables us to draw upon both a rich historical literature and primary sources to gain a nuanced understanding of the dynamics of coalition building. Our case study of tariff politics from the 1820s through 1930 allows us to assess the robustness of our finding that policymaking in the pre-cloture Senate was generally majoritarian, with the exception that obstruction posed a somewhat greater—but not absolute—threat late in a congress. The case study approach also allows us to examine whether compromises were frequently made by bill supporters in order to defuse threats of obstruction. Finally, the tariff analysis circumvents the selection issues involved in analyzing obstruction in a particularly useful way: it enables us to identify instances (if they exist) in which proposals to change tariffs were on the political agenda yet were not acted upon in the Senate because of the fear of filibusters.

We focus on the tariff for several reasons. First, it was one of the dominant political issues in the United States for much of the 19th and early-20th centuries (see, e.g., Bensel 2000). No issue reached the top of the political agenda more often. For much of the hundred years from the rise of Jackson through the presidency of Herbert Hoover, the tariff was one of the key issues distinguishing Democrats from Whigs and Republicans. It is especially important that major tariff bills were in general highly salient to both supporters and opponents: the backers of high tariffs viewed protection as the linchpin of economic progress, while their foes believed that high tariffs resulted in a host of evils, such as high prices, discrimination against agricultural producers, and the fostering of monopolies.[1] A further noteworthy feature of tariff politics is that the Constitution requires that revenue bills

---

[1]This may distinguish the tariff issue from policy questions concerning slavery and civil rights, in which southerners likely often cared more about decisions than did their political adversaries in Congress. See Chapter 7 for a discussion of obstruction on slavery-related issues in the antebellum period.

be initiated in the House before being considered in the Senate.[2] The House bill provides a useful baseline for assessing whether compromises were made in the Senate in order to overcome threats of obstruction. Detailed examination of changes from the House bill enables us to gain additional insight into the question of compromises in the face of obstruction.

The tariff is also particularly well suited for evaluating our competing hypotheses. Some view the tariff as largely a distributive policy (Schattschneider 1935; Lowi 1964), and Weingast's (1979) formal model that produces universalistic equilibria was specifically designed to apply to distributive policies. Others view the tariff as a contentious, partisan issue central to sectional battles over redistribution, which suggests that coalitions would be far from unanimous (Bensel 2000; Epstein and O'Halloran 1996; O'Halloran 1994). Our focus on coalition formation and size should illuminate to what extent tariff policymaking fits these competing models.

One might object that the distributive nature of the tariff suggests that the unidimensionality assumption of the pivotal politics model may be incorrect. We employed a technique, developed by Poole and Rosenthal (1997, 29–30), for determining whether the final votes on tariff legislation included in our analysis were multidimensional, by examining the reduction in classification errors for roll call votes that occurs when another dimension is added to the main issue dimension produced by the NOMINATE scaling procedure. The gain in the aggregate proportional reduction in error obtained from adding the second dimension was only .05, which is far below the threshold of .2 that Poole and Rosenthal use to identify issue areas that are multidimensional. Although deliberations concerning specific tariff rates likely involved distributive concerns, it appears that decisions on final passage simplified to the single-dimensional issue of higher versus lower rates, which corresponded closely to the sectionally defined ideological cleavage for much of this era. In other words, though tariffs may in principle have been multidimensional distributive issues, decisions on the basic question of passing versus rejecting a specific tariff bill typically mapped closely onto a single overriding ideological dimension.[3]

A further issue highlighted by the analysis of tariffs is the role of party politics. Our quantitative analyses to this point have generally not focused on partisan dynamics, though we have attempted to address the possible influence of partisan variables where appropriate and feasible. However, there is good reason to expect party affiliation to play a significant role in shaping members' behavior on tariff politics. For much of the 19th and early 20th centuries, the tariff was a critical element of each party's "label" or reputation among voters (cf. Cox and McCubbins 1993). Furthermore, there is empirical evidence suggesting that individual senators' votes on tariff bills were partly shaped by party ties (Brady, Goldstein, and Kessler 2002).

---

[2]Congress occasionally sidestepped this requirement; see Stanwood (1903) for examples.

[3]We thank John Ferejohn for this point, which fits nicely with the account of tariff politics in Bensel (1984).

Nonetheless, we view the potential influence of party in this context as an opportunity to extend and refine our analysis, rather than as undercutting it. Even if parties shape individual members' votes on tariff bills, it does not follow that this party influence affects the *threshold* required to overcome obstruction and pass legislation. If the Senate operated under a de facto majority rule standard in the pre-cloture era, then the majority party presumably sought to pressure a sufficient number of members to gain a floor majority. If, on the other hand, a wider margin was required to legislate, party leaders would aim to put together a commensurately larger coalition.[4] In either case, coalition size would still be informative for understanding the threshold necessary for passage.[5]

The partisan stakes of tariff battles also bring particular benefits to the analysis. First, it allows us to delve more deeply into the impact of preference intensity on obstruction. In particular, we repeatedly found instances in which the minority party opposed a tariff bill, but many of its members believed that fully capitalizing on their right to obstruct would either damage their party's reputation with the public (due to the bill's popularity) or would endanger these members' other priorities. In these cases, the minority relented once the majority showed its commitment to passing the bill. The result is a more nuanced understanding of preference intensity, which is not simply attributable to how much the minority dislikes the proposed policy change but also incorporates information about the perceived public reaction to obstruction. A highly intense minority is one that both opposes the substance of the legislation and believes that its constituents will reward it for pushing that opposition to the limit, even at the cost of other legislative priorities.

Second, Democrats' long-standing opposition to high tariff rates provides leverage for assessing the claim that tariff politics are an example of universalistic, distributive politics. Since Democrats generally favored cutting rates, instances in which Democratic majorities pursued lower tariffs will allow us to explore whether coalition-building dynamics differed when a proposed policy incurred specific, identifiable costs on a significant subset of senators (that is, when rate cuts directly threatened the interests of senators from states benefiting from the existing higher rates). This, in turn, speaks to the universalism versus majoritarianism debate.

In the end, the case for majoritarianism found in earlier chapters is bolstered by the tariff analysis. It is particularly telling that Democrats were able to pass bills that unquestionably reduced broad categories of rates, thus imposing significant costs on a substantial number of senators. The 1846

---

[4]It is worth emphasizing that this chapter does not attempt to test the impact of party versus constituency on member behavior. Rather, we seek to understand how obstruction affected coalition building on an issue that had clear partisan stakes.

[5]One possible distortion would be if the majority party seeks to ensure all of its members vote in favor of final passage in order to form a coherent party image. In this scenario, it is possible that coalition sizes would be larger than the threshold required to overcome obstruction. However, the prevalence of minimal majority coalitions on tariff final passage votes suggests that this is not a serious concern in practice.

case—in which Democrats enacted a broad reduction in rates by a single vote over intense Whig-led opposition—belies the claim that tariff politics was sufficiently distributive that the minority simply relented due to being "paid off" with concessions on rates salient to individual members. As Mark Hansen (1990, 545) argues, "19th-century tariff making was a far cry from the 'reciprocal non-interference' that marked the 20th century."[6] Instead, distinct sectional political economies dictated that the export-dependent South paid the costs of high tariffs with few corresponding benefits, while northern manufacturers generally gained from higher rates, with the West the key swing region (Bensel 2000).[7]

To mitigate problems of selection bias, we attempted to identify all successful and unsuccessful efforts to adopt general tariff bills.[8] We excluded narrow tariff bills that affected only a small subset of duties.[9] We also do not focus on bills that failed due to lack of sufficient support in the House.[10]

We rely upon two well-known histories of tariff politics, by Stanwood (1903) and Taussig (1931), along with analysis of roll call votes, the *Congressional Record* and its precursors, the *Annals of Congress*, the *Register of Debates*, and the *Congressional Globe*. Since Stanwood's book does not include tariffs adopted after 1897, we also searched periodical indices for rel-

---

[6]Similarly, Hiscox (2002) argues that party lines concerning the tariff began to solidify by the 1840s, and sharp sectional/partisan cleavages defined tariff making into the early-20th century.

[7]Louisiana sugar interests were the main exception in the South. A complication confronting the tariff analysis is that the need for additional revenue at times forced Congress to adopt rate hikes. This might undermine the assumption that a single dimension concerning protectionism shaped tariff policymaking. Our finding that final passage votes empirically did generally fall along a single dimension partially mitigates this concern. The cases in which Democrats sought tariff reductions are helpful as well in this regard since tariff *cuts* were (generally) not driven by fiscal deficits. It is also worth emphasizing that tariff rates were at times so high that a rate reduction would have actually generated greater revenue. This suggests that senators had some flexibility in designing rates to respond to changing fiscal realities. We should also note that we exclude the tariff bills adopted during the Civil War because the fiscal emergency of the time, rather than protectionism, appears to have been the dominant issue. Five significant tariff bills were approved from August 1861 through March 1865. These bills generally passed with little controversy.

[8]We also reviewed Stanwood's (1903) comprehensive history of tariff politics in the 19th century, looking for any instances of changes in policy that were not proposed due to fears of minority obstruction. While Stanwood discusses several examples in which a subset of legislators favored a change but it did not reach the floor, each of these appears to have failed due to a lack of majority support in one chamber or the other, or due to presidential opposition, and thus these potential changes are not relevant for exploring the location of the senator who is pivotal when it comes to filibusters.

[9]The sole exception is the Woolens Bill of 1827, which is included because of the importance of wool products to the antebellum economy.

[10]These include proposed changes in 1830, 1844, 1868, 1878, 1884, and 1886. Each was defeated by a majority vote on the House floor. In some cases (e.g., 1844), minority obstruction in the lower chamber may have also played a role in inhibiting change. The Ways and Means Committee also proposed a rate reduction in 1876, but instead a floor majority voted to refer a resolution to the committee stating that no legislation affecting the tariff was advisable at this time. As we point out in footnote 7, we also exclude the tariff bills adopted during the Civil War.

evant articles on tariff legislation considered from the 1890s on, and we drew
upon the regular summaries of congressional politics published in the *American Political Science Review* and *Political Science Quarterly*. We consulted
newspaper coverage, member biographies, and other secondary sources in
those cases where the other sources did not allow us to assess the role of
minority obstruction.

Several conclusions concerning the role of minority obstruction in the pre-
cloture Senate emerge from our analysis of tariff politics. First, slim majorities were generally quite successful in adopting significant changes in the
tariff. Consistent with our analysis of major legislation in Chapter 4, the
median-plus-veto-pivot model does a good job of explaining coalition sizes on
the pre-cloture tariff. Second, minority obstruction posed a greater threat to
passage as adjournment loomed. In the late-19th and early-20th centuries,
this threat appears to have encouraged bill supporters to shift tariff bills to
special sessions convened early in each congress. Finally, we find repeated
cases in which the minority party vigorously opposed a tariff bill yet chose
in the end not to fully capitalize on opportunities to obstruct the legislation.
In some cases, such as the 1846 tariff, it appears that norms concerning
the appropriate role of the minority played an important role in encouraging restraint. In other cases, minority members evidently decided that their
party's electoral standing would be promoted by allowing the majority to legislate. But the bottom line is that threats of minority obstruction had little
substantive impact on the content of tariff bills in the pre-cloture Senate. On
this high-salience issue for both supporters and opponents, majoritarianism
is the dominant theme.

6.2 ANTEBELLUM TARIFF MAKING

Table 6.1 presents a summary of tariff bills considered in the antebellum
period. With the exception of a single bill considered late in a congress,
slim majorities evidently were generally able to pass highly controversial
tariff changes. The sole example of successful obstruction occurred in the
Senate in 1827, during the lame duck session of the 19th Congress. The
House had passed its version of the bill to raise rates on wool products on
February 10, less than four weeks before the statutorily mandated March 4
date for adjournment. A narrow Senate majority appears to have favored
the bill. Senators voted 25 to 21 on February 13 to refer the bill to the
more tariff-friendly Manufacturing Committee rather than to the hostile
Finance Committee (Stanwood 1903, v. 1, 257). When the Manufacturing
Committee reported it to the floor a few days later, opponents offered a
series of motions to recommit and to refer the bill. Each was defeated by
a margin of one to six votes.[11] As it became clear that these motions were
preventing the Senate from considering other business, a large majority of

---

[11] Bill supporters argued that the sole purpose of the motions to recommit and to refer
was to defeat the bill through delay. For example, bill supporter Benjamin Ruggles of

Table 6.1 Summary of Major Tariff Bills Considered in the Antebellum Senate

Year/ Congress/ Session	Bill No. and Direction of Change	Senate votes (date)	Senate Deliberations	No. of Obstruc- tive Motions	Coalition Size on Obstructive Motions	Outcome and Conclusion
1827/ 19th/ Lame Duck	H.R. 362: Wool tariff increase	Tabled 21-20 (February 28)	Supporters narrowly defeated series of motions to refer or recommit the bill. But tabled by single vote, apparently due to sense that too late to pass.	0	N/A	**Failed.** Successful obstruction case (it appears majority favored bill based on motions to refer, recommit)
1828/ 20th/ Regular	H.R. 132: Increased rates ("Tariff of Abomination")	Adopted 26-21 (May 13)	Senate Finance reported bill with amendments on April 30. Debated May 5–12. Key pro-wool amendment adopted 24-22.	0	N/A	**Enacted.** Appears majoritarian (narrow margin and no discussion of obstruction).
1832/ 22nd/ Regular	H.R. 584: Decreased rates (small but general cut)	Passed 32-16 (July 9); receded from several amendments by wide margins	Considered for one week on floor; series of amendments to restore protection were adopted by narrow margins.	3	.63	**Enacted.** Fairly quick consideration. But also had wide margin.
1833/ 22nd/ Lame Duck	S. 115 and H.R. 641: Gradual but substantial cut	Passed 29-16 (March 1)	Clay proposal introduced February 19. Passed after short consideration.	3 on S. 115	.59	**Enacted.** Fairly wide margin.
1837/ 24th/ Lame Duck	S. 176: Reduced duties	Passed 27-18 (February 25)	Passed after brief consideration (four days of amending).	0	N/A	**Failed.** Apparently due to lack of House support.

Table 6.1 Summary of Major Tariff Bills Considered in the Antebellum Senate (continued)

Year/ Congress/ Session	Bill No. and Direction of Change	Senate votes (date)	Senate Deliberations	No. of Obstruc- tive Motions	Coalition Size on Obstructive Motions	Outcome and Conclusion
1842/ 27th/ Regular	H.R. 472 and H.R. 547: Increased duties	Passed H.R. 472 by 25-23 (August 5); after veto of H.R. 472, passed H.R. 547 by 24-23 (August 27)	Initial version passed after less than two weeks of consideration; revised version passed after three days of amending.	0	N/A	**Enacted.** Tyler veto forced Congress to drop one provision, but intra-Congress politics appear majoritarian.
1846/ 29th/ Regular	H.R. 384: Cut tariffs	Passed 28-27 (July 28)	Debated from July 13 to 28. Both sides competed for pivotal voter to gain majority support.	2	.49	**Enacted.** Majoritarian politics.
1857/ 34th/ Lame duck	H.R. 566: Compromise bill (reduced rates but also helped manufacturers via freer raw materials)	Initial passage without a division (February 26); conference report agreed to by 33-8 (March 2)	Not reported until February 24th. Discussed, amended, and passed in single long day.	0	N/A	**Enacted.** Does not appear that there were filibuster threats, but also note the wide margin.
1860–61/ 36th/ Regular and Lame Duck	H.R. 338: Increased rates (Morrill Tariff)	Passed 25-14 (February 20, 1861)	Initially delayed by anti-tariff Finance majority, but after secession a select committee reported it to floor. Passed three weeks after reported.	7	.52	**Enacted.** Obstructionism attempted in both House and Senate; wide majority supported bill.

38-7 voted to postpone the bill until the next day (*Register of Debates*, February 19, 1827, p. 390). The Senate returned to the tariff proposal on February 28 but immediately confronted a motion to table. Vice President John Calhoun broke a 20-20 tie by voting for the tabling motion. According to Stanwood, a narrow majority had favored the bill, but the motion to table succeeded because of "time having been frittered away until it was obviously too late to secure the enactment of the bill" (Stanwood 1903, v. 1, 258). The sponsor of the motion to table, bill opponent Robert Hayne of South Carolina, argued that "it was obvious that this bill could not be acted on" so late in the session (*Register of Debates*, February 28, 1827, p. 496). Press accounts prior to the vote to table show that observers doubted the bill's prospects, in spite of the narrow majority backing it: for example, the *Daily National Intelligencer* noted on February 22, 1827, that "the short time that now remains for debatable subjects renders it, we think, very improbable" that the Senate will pass the woolens bill ("Washington," p. 3).[12] Thus, it appears that a large and determined minority had succeeded in blocking a bill that likely had the support of a bare majority in the waning days of the 19th Congress.[13]

Examining the rest of the tariff bills considered in the antebellum period suggests two patterns: first, the only bills to pass in lame duck sessions had supermajority support. Second, bills considered in the regular long session were able to pass with the support of a bare majority. This juxtaposition suggests that filibusters posed little threat during the regular session when it came to tariff bills, though they may have posed more of a danger during the lame duck sessions when only a slim majority favored legislation. Turning first to the lame duck sessions, the successful bill in 1833 to reduce rates substantially (though gradually) was adopted by a 29-16 margin in the Senate.[14] Similarly, the tariff bills enacted during the lame duck sessions of the

Ohio argued that if the motion to refer the bill to the Finance Committee prevailed, "the bill would be killed; for when reported upon, it would be too late to act upon it during this session" (*Register of Debates*, February 19, 1827, p. 384). After each motion to recommit or refer was defeated, bill opponents immediately responded with an alternative motion to recommit or refer, which was later defeated in a virtually identical vote. Bill sponsor Mahlon Dickerson of New Jersey argued that the motions to recommit with instructions could just as easily be offered as amendments to the bill—thus avoiding the unnecessary delay of returning the bill to committee (February 19, 1927, pp. 387–89).

[12] Though some might suspect that the Senate agenda was sufficiently sparse that obstruction could not succeed in the 1820s, press accounts suggest otherwise. For example, the *Intelligencer* noted that "before [the Senate] is depending at this moment a greater amount of indispensable business than probably ever before has been at so late a period of the Session" ("Washington," February 24, 1827, p. 3).

[13] Note that the motions used to delay the bill in this case are not counted as obstructive using the methodology outlined in Chapter 5 (see column 6 of Table 6.1). Although the criteria we use for identifying dilatory motions are reasonably effective, they do not capture all of the possible tools available to obstructionists. But it is also important to note that this incident does not appear on extant lists of filibusters, which usually mark 1841 as the first time that a filibuster occurred in the Senate's history.

[14] This was a somewhat unusual case in that protectionist Henry Clay (Whig–KY) championed the cuts in duties, believing that gradual reductions would actually save the

34th Congress (the Tariff of 1857) and the 36th Congress (the Morrill Tariff of 1861) each had wide support. The former was adopted with 73% of the members voting in favor, and the latter was adopted with 80% voting yea.[15] A fourth tariff bill also passed the Senate during a lame duck session in 1837 with just 60% voting in favor, though this bill was not acted on in the House and thus it is possible that opponents chose not to obstruct it knowing it would not be enacted.[16] But the general pattern appears that successful bills in the lame duck sessions had fairly wide supermajority support (70% or more), while the one instance of a closely divided Senate resulted in failure to pass a bill.

The regular long sessions are a much different story. The Senate adopted tariff bills by both narrow and wide margins, and minority obstruction was consistently innocuous. One of the best examples of the ability of slim majorities to legislate occurred in 1842, when a bill to raise duties was adopted by a 24-23 vote. The House and Senate had initially passed a slightly different version of the legislation—also by extremely narrow margins—which was then vetoed by President John Tyler, who opposed a provision of the legislation regarding the distribution of funds from land sales. After the veto, both chambers dropped the funds distribution provision but kept the rest of the bill essentially unchanged (Stanwood 1903, v. 2, 26–28). The revised bill was considered on the Senate floor from August 25 to August 27, 1842, when it was approved on a 24-23 vote.[17] It is noteworthy that the president's veto had forced some changes to the bill even as the opposition of over 45% of the Senate did not appear to exact concessions. Of course, proponents of the original bill would have been able to keep the funds distribution provision in if they had two-thirds support, but the binding constraint was the veto pivot rather than the threat of a filibuster. This is consistent with the results in support of the median-plus-veto-pivot model for coalitions on significant legislation discussed in Chapter 4. It is also consistent with the conjecture that "relational legislating" created the expectation that majorities would generally be sufficient to pass controversial bills in the pre-cloture Senate.

One might suspect that the minority allowed the 1842 bill to pass because its opposition was not particularly deep; perhaps, along the lines of the "distributive" tariff of recent decades, benefits and concessions were spread

tariff system from the political onslaught of the Jacksonian Democrats. Roughly equal proportions of pro-Jackson and anti-Jackson senators voted for the bill. Such an instance belies the usual spatial interpretation, in that several protectionists appear to have voted for a bill that they liked less than the status quo, based on the belief that it would forestall a more dramatic shift in policy in a subsequent congress. But this sort of alignment proved extremely unusual in the tariff bills we have analyzed.

[15] The 80% figure refers to the vote on the conference report. The other key vote in 1857 was on adoption of the Finance Committee chairman's substitute version of the bill; 64% voted yea on that roll call. The final (pre-conference) passage vote was a voice vote, but it appears that opponents of the tariff bill had focused attention on the vote on the Finance substitute.

[16] As noted above, the Constitution requires that the House initiate revenue bills. This was one occasion where this requirement was sidestepped (see Stanwood 1903).

[17] The key test was on the vote to engross and send the bill to a third reading.

broadly. But such a claim is difficult to sustain. During the three days of debate on the final bill, low-tariff Democrats attacked the legislation fiercely. As Stanwood (1903, v. 2, 28) observes, "opponents of the bill made repeated and strenuous attempts to modify it radically, but every motion to that end was defeated." James and Lake (1989, 14) conclude that "passage of the 1842 'black tariff' threw the South into a panic. Not only did Southern interests shudder at the economic costs imposed by the new duties and the possibility of foreign (viz., British) retaliation, but, more important, the bill's redistributive component threatened to recast economic and hence political power in favor of northern manufacturers and abolitionists."[18]

The 1842 tariff was not the only instance of a major rate change being adopted by a bare majority in the regular sessions. In 1846, the Senate adopted a substantial reduction in tariff rates by a 28-27 vote. With the low-tariff Democrat James Polk in the White House, supporters of the tariff reduction did not need to fear a veto. Interestingly, the outcome in this case appears to have been up in the air for several weeks as both sides fought over the vote of Tennessee Whig Spencer Jarnigan, who personally supported high tariffs but whose legislature's instructions mandated a vote for tariff cuts. The Democratic triumph in the end speaks powerfully to senators' understanding of the appropriate role of obstruction in the mid-19th-century Senate.

Concerns about time constraints played an important role in the 1846 battle, yet it is striking that the Whig opponents of the bill sought to gain majority support for delaying the bill, but did not opt to use dilatory tactics to kill it once the Democrats displayed that they had clear majority support for passage. After the House approved the bill in early July, Senate Democrats moved to dispense with the customary reference to the Finance Committee, and instead asked that the bill be made a special order for the following Monday and be made the unfinished business until its consideration was completed (*Congressional Globe*, July 6, 1846, pp. 1053–54). The Whigs sharply condemned this maneuver. James Morehead (Whig–KY) claimed that the bill "was a measure which was about to revolutionize the country to its very foundation," and thus required committee consideration before reaching the floor (p. 1054). Democrats countered that Finance was evenly divided due to a member's absence, and that there was little chance any members would change their minds on the bill. Even at this early stage, the Whigs made clear that they opposed the bill vigorously but would not attempt to defeat it through obstruction: when Democrat Ambrose Sevier (D–AR) argued for dispensing with the committee reference due to the short time left in the session (1054), Willie Mangum (Whig–NC) replied that he

---

[18]Since the 1842 bill promised to increase government revenue, it may be the case that fiscal pressures made it more difficult to defeat the bill through obstruction. However, Democrats denied that the fiscal situation required that such a harmful bill be enacted (*Congressional Globe*, August 27, 1842, pp. 958–59). Furthermore, the 1846 tariff cut—discussed below—followed a similar majoritarian dynamic in the Senate, and in that case, the fiscal situation likely cautioned *against* the revenue reductions likely to result from passage.

"could assure the gentlemen that there was no purpose on this side to procrastinate and prolong debate upon this subject, or to defer the final action of the Senate" (1054). Mangum, however, condemned the bill on the merits, claiming that it "will work an entire revolution in the system of collecting revenue" (1054). After a motion to refer the bill to Finance was defeated 24-22, the Democratic motion to make the bill the special order for next Monday was accepted on a voice vote (1057).

The bill then was considered on the floor from July 13 to 28. While the bill was on the floor, Whigs pushed for the Senate to fix an early date for final adjournment of the session. Democrats successfully resisted a bid to set July 20 as the adjournment date, but eventually were narrowly rolled on a vote to set August 10 as the final day of the session.[19] Whigs voted 21-1 in favor of the August 10 date; Democrats voted 15-14 against, with northern Democrats (who were less enthusiastic about the tariff bill) voting in favor of setting the date, and southern Democrats voting 11-3 against.

Even so, Whigs did not push this advantage to the limit. During the two weeks of debate on the bill, there were a series of extremely close votes. Whigs sought to defeat the bill by defining the issue in ways that would allow Jarnigan to vote against the Democratic proposal. Thus, Jarnigan voted on July 27 to refer the bill to the Finance Committee with instructions to report a revised bill that would raise sufficient revenue but avoid discriminating against domestic manufacturers. The motion, which its sponsor John Clayton (Whig–DE) avowed was intended to kill the bill, carried 28-27 (Stanwood 1903, v. 2, 78; *Congressional Globe*, July 27, 1846, pp. 1143–45).[20] But the Finance Committee reported back the next day, asking to be discharged from the bill because the instructions were impossible to comply with in the short time left before the end of the regular session. Jarnigan then shifted ground and voted in favor of discharge, claiming that even though "I do not approve of this bill," his instructions obliged him to vote to discharge the committee since that now amounted to the question of whether the bill would pass or be defeated (*Congressional Globe*, July 28, 1846, p. 1151). The motion to discharge carried 28-27, as did the vote on final passage. Jarnigan cast the decisive vote allowing the bill to pass. This appears to have been a quintessential case of majoritarian politics, with both sides bidding for the support of the senator who turned out to be the median voter.[21]

---

[19] The vote took place on July 16.

[20] Clayton freely admitted on the floor that "one of the primary objects he had in view in offering these resolutions of instructions had been to defeat the bill. That and that alone, was his object. He was anxious to destroy it" (*Congressional Globe*, July 27, 1846, p. 1144). Moments before presenting his successful motion to refer, Clayton had proposed a simpler resolution to recommit the bill with instructions to restore the duties of the 1842 tariff act. That resolution had been defeated by Jarnigan's vote, but the Tennessee senator argued that his instructions left him at liberty to vote for the second resolution "so as to render [the bill] as little injurious as possible to the business and interests of the country" (*Congressional Globe*, July 27, 1846, p. 1144).

[21] Interestingly, it appears that Jarnigan's instructions are what made him the median voter in this case. Jarnigan's NOMINATE scores place him squarely in the mainstream of the Whig party, yet he was the only Whig to vote for the bill.

With so little time left in the session, Whigs surely could have used their prerogatives to delay the bill until the lame duck session convened after the election. Their restraint in not fully exploiting their prerogatives by no means reflected compromises made en route to passage to mitigate the opposition. The Senate adopted only one floor amendment to the bill. The amendment did not affect any of the rates in the legislation; instead, it eliminated a provision allowing the government to seize goods and sell them at auction whenever it suspected that an importer had lied about the goods' value. The amendment passed because Thomas Hart Benton (D–MO) sided with the Whigs, arguing that the original provision was an unconstitutional expansion of federal authority (Stanwood 1903, v. 2, 79). But the Senate left in place all of the rate changes proposed by the Democrats, which together promised a radical reorientation of U.S. tariff policy. As James and Lake (1989, 1) observe in their essay on the 1846 act, it "reversed the protectionist principles embodied in the 'black tariff' of 1842 and inaugurated a decade and a half of freer trade." The act set rates that "were substantially lower" than those set in 1842 (10). Similarly, Faulkner (1929, 13) argues that the 1846 act "brought radical reductions" in tariffs.

The Whigs clearly understood the high stakes of the fight and fiercely denounced the bill. Clayton considered "the bill as so destructive and ruinous in its character on all the great interests of the country, that it must be altered entirely before it could receive the least approbation from him. If he should set out to amend it, there was nothing to amend by" (*Congressional Globe*, July 27, 1846, p. 1143). Daniel Webster (Whig–MA) claimed that the bill "has the face and front of an aristocratic bill, oppressive of the poor and workingman, and in every respect it corresponds to its face and front" (*Congressional Globe*, July 28, 1846, pp. 1152–53). John Crittenden (Whig–KY) charged that "this measure is destructive and ruinous in all its features—raw materials and all—and it should not pass" (1155).

Even as they fiercely condemned the bill, the Whigs made clear that they saw their duty to be probing for any weakness in the majority supporting the bill, but not to defeat it by obstruction. Democrat Hopkins Turney of Tennessee referred on the floor to a "rumor which was whispered in the Senate that it was intended by the opponents of the bill to protract the debate until the vacancy created by the resignation of Mr. Haywood could be filled" (July 27, 1846, p. 1144)[22] The Whigs denied, however, that they were using a strategy of delay. Mangum claimed that "there was no such purpose entertained in any quarter," adding that it would be at least twenty days before a new senator replaced Haywood, "long before which time the fate of the bill would have been decided in the Senate" (1144). Democrats also claimed that Clayton's bid to have the Finance Committee revisit the rates in the bill would cause time to run out before the August 10 adjournment date that Whigs had advocated (July 28, 1846, p. 1150). Clayton responded

---

[22]William Haywood (D–NC) had resigned on July 25, 1846. He was replaced by a Whig.

that if the August 10 date provided insufficient time for Finance to consider changes to the bill, he would vote for a resolution to extend the session (July 28, 1846, p. 1152).

While the sincerity of Clayton's offer may be open to question—given his overriding goal of defeating the bill—bill opponents did not prolong consideration once it became clear that their amendments could not win approval. Clayton noted that "it was not his intention to enter into the details of the bill. He wished to test the views of the Senate on the great principles of the bill itself" (*Congressional Globe*, July 27, 1846, p. 1143). When Democrats proved they had the votes to defeat all of his amendments, Clayton observed that "I regret it. But having done my duty, I do not feel that I am under any obligation to do anything more in this matter. . . . If they all fail, I do not intend to wear out gentlemen on the other side of the House by offering amendments. It is not part of my purpose, sir, to delay action on this matter. . . . I have said enough to warn gentlemen of the mischievous consequences which will follow the passage of this bill, and having thus discharged my duty, I abide the consequences" (*Congressional Globe*, July 28, 1846, p. 1152). After a series of efforts to recommit the bill failed narrowly, Simon Cameron (D–PA) moved another amendment. Crittenden expressed "regret" that Cameron had "thought proper to introduce any further amendments" (*Congressional Globe*, July 28, 1846, p. 1155). Cameron responded that he "felt it his duty to use all honorable efforts to get it into some shape" so that the bill would be less harmful (1155). Cameron's amendment was then rejected on a voice vote. A few moments later, John Niles (D CT) made a last-ditch effort, moving to postpone the bill until December. Niles observed that "he should not consider that he had done his whole duty in opposition to this extraordinary measure, without making this, the last effort, to arrest its progress. . . . His object was to give his northern friends an opportunity to arrest or postpone the measure without a direct vote on its merits" (*Congressional Globe*, July 28, 1846, p. 1156). At the end of his speech, Niles remarked that "I have now discharged my last duty in relation to this measure, which I suppose is to be passed. . . . A delay of a few months is too much, I suppose, to hope for" (1157).[23] The motion to postpone was defeated, 28-27, and the bill was passed by the same margin. Thus, a major change in tariff policy was enacted by a single vote, while confronting the vigorous opposition of protectionists. Bill opponents creatively sought to find a way to persuade the swing voter Jarnigan that he might side with them without disobeying his instructions. But when all of these efforts failed, the opponents believed that they had fulfilled their responsibility as senators, and allowed the majority to work its will.

While there were other instances of tariff bills in the regular sessions that were passed by wider margins, the 1842 and 1846 cases suggest that a slim majority was sufficient in the regular sessions for the adoption of significant changes in this highly controversial policy area.[24] Antebellum tariff politics

---

[23] Cameron and Niles were two of just three Democrats to vote against the bill.

[24] The so-called Tariff of Abominations, passed during the regular session of the 20th

thus emerge as essentially majoritarian, with the caveat that veto threats and consideration of bills near final adjournment posed risks when only a narrow majority favored a bill.

6.3 THE TARIFF FROM 1865 TO 1889

In the decades following the Civil War, the tariff peaked as an issue central to American politics and party competition (Hiscox 2002). The large GOP majorities in the Civil War relied heavily upon high tariffs to finance the war. Once the conflict had ended, Republican leaders sought to maintain as much of the high rates as was politically feasible despite the presence of a fair number of Republican members who favored lower rates and considerable public pressure to lower import taxes. Democrats continued to be the strongest supporters of tariff reductions, but their party also included a small, yet often decisive faction of pro-tariff northerners.

As Table 6.2 suggests, tariff legislation appears even more clearly majoritarian in this new era than in the antebellum period. Simply put, despite occasional threats of minority obstruction, a bare Senate majority proved sufficient to adopt significant changes in tariff policies, regardless of whether the proposal was considered in a lame duck session or in a regular session.[25]

The tariff increase of 1875 is a telling case. Republicans had lost their House majority in the 1874 election, and on their way out of office, House Republicans narrowly succeeded in passing a bill to raise rates. The legislation repealed the 10% reduction in duties on manufactured goods that had been adopted in 1872, while adding 25% to the duty upon molasses and sugar of all kinds, and increasing the internal taxes on tobacco and whiskey (Stanwood 1903, v. 2, 188). The bill went to the Senate with fewer than four weeks remaining before adjournment. The Finance Committee reported it to the floor on February 26. After an extremely short but bitter debate, it was adopted on March 2, by a vote of 30-29. The Senate did not amend the House bill; as a result, the proposal went directly to President Grant and was signed on March 3.

This case initially seems puzzling because it would have hardly stretched the limits of physical endurance for the bill's opponents to filibuster it to

---

Congress (1828) was also approved by a fairly narrow margin of 26 to 21. However, the margin may be deceiving as several of the bill's opponents appear to have privately hoped it would pass in order to discredit the protective system as a whole (see Stanwood 1903, v. 1). As a result, this case is not well suited to evaluating whether a majority was sufficient to pass legislation. The 1828 and 1833 case (discussed above) were the only instances of tariff bills in which the qualitative literature gave reason to suspect insincere voting played a role.

[25] Minority obstruction did occur in the House as well in this period and at times forced the majority to resort to unusual parliamentary stratagems. However, it appears that in the end the majority was generally able to overcome this obstruction (see, for example, the 1875 and 1883 tariff changes, which were adopted after overcoming Democratic obstruction in the House).

Table 6.2 Summary of Major Tariff Bills Considered in the Senate from 1865 to 1889

Year/ Congress/ Session	Bill No. and Direction of Change	Senate votes (date)	Senate Deliberations	No. of Obstruc- tive Motions	Coalition Size on Obstructive Motions	Outcome and Conclusion
1866–67/ 39th/ Regular and Lame Duck	H.R. 718: Proposal to increase rates	Passed 27-10 (February 1, 1867)	Long Senate debate; Senate bill more moderate than House version.	3	.36	**Failed.** Apparently due to obstruction in House.
1870/ 41st/ Regular	H.R. 2045: Reduced duties	Passed 43-5 (July 5); no roll call on conference report	Considered from June 24 to July 5.	3	.41	**Enacted.** Democratic filibuster in House and limited obstruction in Senate. Wide margin.
1872/ 42nd/ Regular	H.R. 2322: Reduced duties	Passed 50-3 (May 30)	Quick consideration (May 27–30).	6	.41	**Enacted.** Large supermajority support.
1875/ 43rd/ Lame Duck	H.R. 4680: Increased duties	Passed 30-29 (March 2)	Reported February 26 and passed very quickly.	2	.40	**Enacted.** Majoritarian politics, though some obstruction in House.
1883/ 47th/ Lame Duck	H.R. 5538: Mild rate reductions	Passed 42-19 (February 20); approved conference report 32-31 (March 3)	Senate took minor House-passed tax bill and substituted tariff bill. Protracted floor debate; evidence of filibustering.	13	.37	**Enacted.** A good deal of filibustering, but passed with narrow majority at end of session.
1888–89/ 50th/ Regular and Lame Duck	H.R. 9051: House proposed reductions	Passed 32-30 (January 22, 1889)	Senate passed bill to raise rates despite knowledge that no chance of agreement with House.	2	.36	**Failed.** Due to House-Senate disagreement (did not even go to conference).

death in the closing days of the session. The absence of any Senate amendments indicates that no compromises were made to buy off potential obstructionists in the upper chamber. Furthermore, since the next congress had a Democratic House and a Republican Senate and president, it appeared likely that any tariff increases enacted would endure for several years. Indeed, the next significant change in rates was not adopted for another eight years.[26]

Newspaper coverage strongly indicates that the bill's opponents deliberately chose not to obstruct the tariff's passage due to concern about being blamed for the special session that would have ensued had business come to a halt prior to passage of the end-of-session appropriation bills. The *New York Times* declared that the "opposition held out as long as possible without forcing business into such a condition that they would become responsible for an extra session, and then allowed action to be taken" ("The Revenue Bill," March 3, 1875, p. 1), and concluded that "the bill finally passed almost by the mercy of its opponents rather than by the strength of its friends" ("The Senate on the Revenue Bill," March 4, 1875, p. 6). Even as they allowed the tariff bill to pass, Senate Democrats blocked a voting rights bill with an overt filibuster threat (see, e.g., "Editorial," *New York Times*, March 1, 1875, p. 4; and *Congressional Record*, March 1, 1875, pp. 1939–40, and March 2, 1875, p. 2035). Democrats were willing to risk blame for a special session in order to defend their top priority—control of the South's voting process—but not to stop a tariff increase.[27] The contrast between the voting rights and tariff cases indicates that obstructive minorities were selective in deciding when to push their prerogatives to the limit, and that political calculations—focused on issue salience and the expected public (dis)approval for the disruption caused by an end-of-congress filibuster—played a critical role.[28]

---

[26]The 1875 changes were by no means trivial. Stanwood claims that Democrats and low-tariff Republicans "opposed the bill uncompromisingly" (1903, v. 2, 188). In addition, obstruction in the House forced supporters to resort to the tactic of striking the enacting clause in order to move the bill from Committee of the Whole to the House (190). Stanwood concludes that the bill restored duties to the "giddy height" they had attained during the war and represented a "bold, even audacious defiance of the opposing party" (191). See Tarbell (1911, 81) for a similar assessment, as well as "The Week," *The Nation*, March 4, 1875, p. 142; "The Results of the Session," *New York Herald*, March 5, 1875, p. 6; and "Tax and Tariff in the Senate," *New York Tribune*, March 3, 1875, p. 1. It is also worth noting that the *New York Herald* listed the tariff as one of six laws of "national importance" approved by the 43rd Congress ("Important Enactments of the Forty-Third Congress," March 5, 1875, p. 7). Though the Senate floor debate was relatively quick, bill opponents condemned it in sharp terms and proposed a series of crippling amendments that would have forced the bill to a conference committee (see *Congressional Record*, March 1, 1875, pp. 1951–53, 1960–65, 1971–76, 1981; March 2, 1875, pp. 2059–64). Each amendment was defeated by a narrow margin.

[27]Although Democrats strongly opposed the tariff change, their intensity on the issue did not match their core commitment of consolidating white control of the South's electoral process.

[28]Republicans argued that revenue pressures required the tariff increase, but bill opponents disputed the need for increased revenues and claimed that more extensive use of internal taxes rather than import tariffs would better remedy any revenue shortfall (see, e.g., *Congressional Record*, March 1, 1875, pp. 1951–53).

The tariff bill of 1883, adopted in the lame duck session of the 47th Congress, also suggests the ability of slim majorities to adopt significant tariff changes. This case is a bit more complicated, however, because the legislation adopted by the Republican congress on the whole resulted in *reduced* rates. A tariff commission created by Congress had recommended substantial reductions in rates. The initial Senate bill followed this formulation and passed with broad bipartisan support. But the ensuing conference committee inserted numerous increases, so that the final bill angered many Democrats who believed Republicans were attempting to defuse the tariff issue without actually changing the system appreciably. The final vote on the conference report in the Senate was 32-31, and it occurred late on the night of March 3, as Congress was about to adjourn.

This again raises the question of why bill opponents allowed a vote on final passage. As late as March 2, there was considerable speculation on the Hill as to whether Democrats would block the conference report ("A Report on the Tariff," *New York Times*, March 3, 1883, p. 1). Indeed, the two Senate Democrats on the conference committee had resigned in protest of the House's insistence on maintaining the higher rates in its bill; they were replaced by a Republican and a Readjuster when no Senate Democrats agreed to take their place ("The 47th Congress," *Washington Post*, March 2, 1883, p. 1). But in the end, bill opponents appear to have decided that the public's demand for immediate action counseled restraint in the use of obstruction. The long legislative battle over the bill had apparently demonstrated to the minority that there was a general public demand for the legislation, even as Democrats believed that the long-term effects of the bill would be negative. The *New York Herald* ("High Protectionists at Work in Conference Committee," March 2, 1883, p. 4) quoted a leading Democrat's observation that "[i]t would probably hurt us with the people if it could be said that the Conference bill was lost through our obstruction. . . . But, aside from that, this conference bill will stand before the country as a perfected Republican measure. . . . My belief is that the bill will precipitate a commercial and industrial derangement. . . . that will make our work of reform in the next congress much easier."[29] This unusually frank assessment provides a glimpse into the complex—but at times important—position-taking calculations that also informed the minority's decisions concerning obstruction.

It is worth emphasizing that much of the significant tariff legislation occurred in the lame duck sessions during this period, which suggests that members were not particularly afraid of obstructionists capitalizing on the lack of available time to kill proposals.[30] There were, of course, a handful of

---

[29]Republicans had indeed sought (with some justification) to blame Democrats for obstructing the bill's progress ("Conference Ordered," *New York Tribune*, February 28, 1883).

[30]Two tariff bills considered in lame duck sessions during this period failed. But both can be explained without reference to minority obstruction in the Senate. The first, an 1867 proposal to increase rates, died in the waning days of the session. Minority obstruction may have played a role here, but it was in the lower chamber: the Senate had amended the House-passed bill to make it more moderate. House leaders initially sought to gain votes on each Senate amendment individually. This ended up dragging

efforts to change rates in the regular sessions. The two successful bids—in 1870 and 1872—were both adopted by immense majorities. Each was an instance in which a Republican congress proposed moderate reductions in rates in response to the apparent unpopularity of the extremely high rates adopted during the Civil War.[31] Several other bids to change rates failed, but this was generally due to a lack of majority support in the House for Democratic proposals to cut rates.[32]

In sum, tariff politics in the 1860s–1880s reinforce the antebellum finding that narrow majorities were generally sufficient to pass major policy changes in the pre-cloture Senate. The maneuvering in the lame duck sessions suggests that obstruction continued to pose a greater threat when final adjournment neared, but that even when time constraints were severe, the minority repeatedly proved reluctant to push its prerogatives to the limit and kill legislation demanded by a determined majority. When it came to issues salient to both sides—such as the tariff—this restraint appears to have outweighed the minority's temptation to capitalize on the end-of-congress deadline.

6.4 THE TARIFF FROM 1890 TO 1930

The majoritarianism of the 1860s–1880s began to fade somewhat in the 1890s. This coincides with our argument that obstruction became a bigger problem at the turn of the century as the size of the Senate increased markedly (see Section 2.5.3 and Chapter 8). When one examines the tariff bills considered from 1890 through 1930, it is noteworthy that only once—in 1921—was a significant tariff change considered in a lame duck session (see Table 6.3 for a summary of the tariff bills in this period). Indeed, several of the key proposals—the 1897 Dingley Tariff, the 1909 Payne-Aldrich Tariff, the 1913 Underwood Tariff, and the 1921 Emergency Tariff bill—were adopted in special sessions convened soon after the preceding congress had adjourned.[33]

The use of special sessions likely was a lesson derived from Republicans' experience with the McKinley Tariff of 1890. The adoption of that bill

---

on for several days. In response, Republican leaders sought a two-thirds vote to suspend the rules in order to discharge the Committee of the Whole from consideration of the bill so that it could be sent to conference. The vote on the motion was 102-69, and the bill was dropped (see Stanwood 1903). After the general tariff bill failed, Congress enacted a narrower change in the tariff on wool and woolen goods. The Senate approved this change by a 31-12 vote. The second failed in 1889 (50th Congress), when the Democratic House passed a bill to reduce rates and the Republican Senate passed a bill to raise rates. The vote on Senate passage was quite narrow—32 to 30—but all involved understood that no bill would be enacted given the wide gap separating the House and Senate proposals. The House never even took up the Senate-passed version and chose not to request a conference committee.

[31] Stanwood claims that House Democrats filibustered the 1870 proposal in protest of its failure to go further in reducing rates. We found multiple dilatory motions were made against the bill, indicating that there was obstruction in the Senate as well.

[32] See footnote 10 above for a list of these cases.

[33] Even the Smoot-Hawley Tariff of 1930 was initially considered in a special session, though it was not finally adopted until the regular session.

Table 6.3 Summary of Major Tariff Bills Considered in the Senate from 1890 to 1930

Year/ Congress/ Session	Bill No. and Direction of Change	Senate votes (date)	Senate Deliberations	No. of Obstructive Motions	Coalition Size on Obstructive Motions	Outcome and Conclusion
1890/ 51st/ Regular	H.R. 9416: Increased rates (McKinley Bill)	Passed 40-29 (Sept. 10); conference report agreed to 33-27 (Sept. 30)	Finance reported bill on June 18. Considered for roughly seven weeks before unanimous consent agreement setting final vote.	0	N/A	**Enacted.** Majority sufficient to pass bill but faced filibuster threat in Senate (see text).
1894/ 53rd/ Regular	H.R. 4864: Reduced rates (Wilson-Gorman Tariff)	Passed 39-34 (July 3)	Finance and special Democratic committee reported hundreds of amendments. Long delays due to GOP speeches and Democrats' initial lack of majority support.	8	.39	**Enacted.** Despite early GOP filibustering, Senate politics generally majoritarian (key was getting enough Democratic votes).
1897/ 55th/ Special session	H.R. 379: Increased rates (Dingley Tariff)	Passed 38-28 (July 7); conference report approved 40-30 (July 24)	Finance reported bill May 4. Considered for about 6 weeks. Increased raw material rates further to gain floor majority by winning over dissident westerners.	0	N/A	**Enacted.** Appears majoritarian. Minority able to slow action but no evidence of concessions to minority.
1909/ 61st/ Special session	H.R. 1438: Included both reductions and increases (Payne-Aldrich)	Passed 45-34 (July 8); conference report approved 47-31 (August 5)	Debated for eleven weeks. Considered huge number of amendments from Finance. Several long speeches attacked rates, but little evidence of intent to obstruct.	0	N/A	**Enacted.** Taft veto threat forced cuts at conference stage. Otherwise, despite a few filibuster threats, appears majoritarian.
1913/ 63rd/ Special session	H.R. 3321: Reduced rates (Underwood Tariff)	Passed 44-37 (Sept. 9); conference report approved 36-17 (Oct. 2)	Two months of debate but does not appear to have been filibustered (large number of amendments to consider).	0	N/A	**Enacted.** Appears majoritarian (no evidence of filibuster threat; narrow vote on initial passage).

Table 6.3 Summary of Major Tariff Bills Considered in the Senate from 1890 to 1930 (continued)

Year/ Congress/ Session	Bill No. and Direction of Change	Senate votes (date)	Senate Deliberations	No. of Obstructive Motions	Coalition Size on Obstructive Motions	Outcome and Conclusion
1920–21/ 66th/ Lame Duck	H.R. 15275: Increased rates on farm products	Passed 44-30 (February 16); conference report approved 49-36 (February 28)	Democrats filibustered bill initially, but agreed to date for vote after cloture fell short of necessary two-thirds margin.	0	N/A	**Failed.** Veto killed bill. Approved with fewer than two-thirds voting yes (despite filibuster), but possibly due to anticipated veto.
1921/ 67th/ Special session	H.R. 2435: Increased rates on farm products (Emergency Tariff Bill)	Passed 65-29 (May 11); conference report approved 53-26 (May 20)	Reported April 30 and passed less than two weeks later.	0	N/A	**Enacted.** No discussion of obstruction but did have wide margin.
1922/ 67th/ Regular session	H.R. 7456: Increased rates (Fordney-McCumber)	Passed 48-25 (August 18); conference report approved 43-28 (Sept. 19)	Finance reported nearly 2,000 amendments. Democrats obstructed bill, but dropped filibuster a few weeks after failed cloture motion.	0	N/A	**Enacted.** Democratic filibuster but approved with just under two-thirds support.
1929–30/ 71st/ Special and regular sessions	H.R. 2667: Increased rates (Smoot-Hawley)	Passed 58-36 (March 24, 1930); conference report approved 44-42 (June 13, 1930)	Senate considered for roughly five months. Added 1,253 amendments to House bill.	0	N/A	**Enacted.** Some delaying tactics used at times, but note very narrow final approval vote.

one month before the midterm election was blamed for immense Republican losses, as Democrats claimed the tariff increases had caused a sudden spike in consumer prices. Republicans concluded from this experience that it was safer to pass a tariff bill well before an election, so that the law's beneficial effects would be obvious (Stanwood 1903, v. 2, 378). On its own, such a calculus might have led members to favor the use of lame duck sessions, since it would maximize the distance to the next election. The avoidance of the lame duck sessions, however, indicates concern that minority obstruction now posed a more severe problem, particularly when time was short.[34]

The basis for such concern emerges fairly clearly when one considers the actual record of tariff bills in this period. It became quite typical for the consideration of each bill to drag on for anywhere from one to six months in the Senate.[35] This was partly due to the immense number of amendments typically proposed by the Finance Committee to the House-passed legislation, which led to numerous additional floor votes. But the minority's increased use of procedural tactics and long speeches fueled the delays. Indeed, where accusations of minority obstruction were relatively uncommon when tariff bills were considered in the 1860s–1880s, they were a recurrent feature of Senate tariff debates after 1890. Yet though the minority often did prolong the consideration of tariff bills, it still appears that supermajority support was not necessary to gain the adoption of significant changes—at least so long as the short lame duck sessions were avoided.

The legislative odyssey of the McKinley tariff of 1890 underscores how Senate obstruction was becoming a more significant problem for bill managers, even as it did not require supporters to assemble supermajority coalitions to gain passage. The tariff bill sped through the House in May 1890, but then ran into much slower going. After being reported from the Finance Committee with hundreds of amendments on June 18, the bill occupied the Senate floor for nearly two months and became entangled in a Democratic filibuster of a civil rights measure, the Federal Elections Bill (see Chapters 1 and 3 on the Elections Bill). The Democrats threatened to bring the tariff bill down with the elections proposal. To forestall such an outcome, high-tariff diehard Republican Matt Quay of Pennsylvania made a deal with Democratic leaders: in exchange for a promise of a vote on the tariff bill by September, the Republicans would delay the Elections Bill until the lame duck session (Hirshson 1962; Kehl 1981). Despite the objections of a handful of Republican senators who cared more about the Elections Bill than the tariff, the agreement stuck and the Senate approved the tariff on September 10 by a vote of 40-29. The final conference report was approved three weeks later, by a 33-27 roll call. The subsequent success of the Democratic filibuster of the Elections Bill reinforced the belief that minority obstruction posed a serious threat to controversial legislation, particularly in the short session.[36]

---

[34] This is also consistent with Binder and Smith's (1997, 63) finding that end-of-session filibusters were particularly effective in this period.

[35] Meanwhile, the use of restrictive special rules often resulted in much briefer consideration of tariff legislation on the House floor.

[36] See Chapter 3 for a discussion of the 1891 bid for cloture reform.

This case represents a logroll on procedure, but not on substance. That is, Republicans agreed to delay the Elections Bill in order to clear the way for the tariff, but they did not make substantive concessions on the tariff bill to Democratic opponents. Indeed, the bill raised rates to unprecedented levels, with Democrats condemning it as "intensely and scandalously sectional" ("The Senate Tariff Plan," *New York Times*, September 11, 1890, p. 1). Zebulon Vance (D–NC) closed the debate for his party, arguing that the "bill had but one redeeming feature, and that was its intense and naked selfishness, which would be the means of arousing the conscience of the American people and of leading to its repeal" (p. 1).

Four years later, the Democrats held both chambers of Congress and the White House. The House approved a substantial cut in tariffs on February 1, 1894. The bill placed several raw materials on the free list, including sugar, lumber, wool, iron ore, and coal, while reducing rates on numerous manufactured items. The bill ran into two major obstacles in the Senate. First, Democrats' narrow margin in the upper chamber meant that the concerns of six high-tariff dissidents—spearheaded by Democratic leader Arthur Pue Gorman of Maryland—were sufficient to deprive the bill of even majority support. Second, staunch high-tariff Republicans such as Quay engaged in dilatory tactics to stall the bill's progress. It appears, however, that the former proved the more significant constraint.

The Finance Committee reported its initial version of the legislation on March 20. As floor debate began on April 2, the Democrats lacked majority support for their version (See "Working for an Agreement," *New York Times*, May 1, 1894, p. 1, and Stanwood 1903, v. 2, 326–28). James Jones (D–AR) approached each of the dissident Democrats to find out their price for supporting the bill. Jones described his approach as follows: "I went from the beginning to the end through the bill, with man after man, on this side of the chamber, spending days and days in the work" (*Congressional Record*, July 23, 1894, p. 7804). Following this extensive consultation, Jones presented a revised proposal on May 7 with an additional 428 amendments designed to win over the necessary Democratic votes. Newspaper coverage and floor debate suggest that the strategy was to win over a floor majority and not to build a supermajority through converting Republicans to support the bill.[37]

Nonetheless, Republicans did use obstruction in fighting the bill, evidently with a modest degree of success. In particular, Quay delivered a multi-part speech that took up over two hundred pages of the *Congressional Record*. According to Quay's biographer, this campaign of obstruction resulted in

---

[37]Both the Democratic *New York Times* and the Republican *New York Tribune* depict the amendments as an effort to win over a floor majority through concessions to dissident Democrats, rather than as an effort to mitigate GOP opposition (see "Working for an Agreement," *Times*, May 1, 1894, 1; "Two More Items Disposed Of," *Times*, May 13, 1894, p. 1 and 2; "Mr. Gorman's Victory," *Tribune*, May 9, 1894, p. 1; "Editorial," *Public Opinion*, May 24, 1894, p. 180). See also the discussion in Chamberlain (1946, 92) and in Stanwood (1903, v. 2, 328–40).

several amendments to the bill to mitigate the damage to Quay's constituents (Kehl 1981; see also Tarbell 1911). However, an examination of the *Record* and of newspaper coverage provides little evidence of major concessions to Quay.[38] Quay's obstructive campaign is indicative of the more general observation that norms against obstruction had begun to fray by the 1890s.

Beyond Quay's individual campaign, Republicans engaged in a more organized obstructive campaign in early to mid-May, but eventually backed down amid internal divisions over strategy as Democrats threatened to hold continuous sessions and to seek a cloture rule. Republican Eugene Hale of Maine had claimed on May 12 that if Democrats attempted to pass legislation similar to the tariff rates approved in the House, "no bill of that sort will be permitted to go through. The minority will find a way to prevent it" ("Two More Items Disposed Of," *New York Times*, May 13, 1894, pp. 1–2). A week later, the *New York Times* claimed that Democrats were just five votes short of a majority for a proposal to impose a rules change for majority cloture ("May Shut off the Closure," May 19, 1894, pp. 1–2). According to the *Times*, Democratic Vice President Adlai Stevenson indicated to bill supporters that he would facilitate the move for majority cloture by ruling that the Constitution allows a majority to change the rules. Such a ruling from the chair could have been appealed, but Democrats could have moved to table the appeal ("Majority Rule in the Senate," *New York Times*, May 20, 1894, p. 17). But Republicans dropped their filibuster around May 19. The press reported that though Republicans still were unified in opposition to the bill, "it [had] become clear that the Republican senators [would] not unite to defeat the bill by filibustering or by prolonging debate indefinitely" ("Political," *Public Opinion*, May 24, 1894, p. 180). Several Republicans still favored such a plan, but there were others in the party who argued that the Democrats should be given the opportunity to pass the bill. For example, Republican Fred Dubois of Idaho argued on the floor that though he opposed the bill, which he claimed would "cause great loss" to his state,

---

[38] Tarbell and Kehl do not provide specific evidence of duties altered by Quay's filibuster. The best example we could find of an amendment in which Quay's filibuster may have played some role concerned the duties on woolen dress goods. Jones had proposed that woolens that were valued at over 60 cents per pound receive a 50% duty, while cheaper goods receive a 40% duty. This sparked opposition from Democratic senators James Smith (D–NJ) and Edward Murphy (D–NY), as well as from Quay, and wool manufacturers (led by a Democratic lobbyist, Walter Stanton). Quay sought to have the dividing line instead placed at 40 cents per pound, so that less expensive goods would also have the higher duty ("Sidetracked by Mr. Quay," *New York Times*, June 15, 1894, p. 5). The *Post* quoted a "prominent Democrat" (presumably Smith or Murphy) on June 16 threatening that he had a majority behind an amendment to reduce the dividing line from Jones's proposed 60 cents down to 50 cents per pound (see "More Trouble Ahead," p. 1). The Democratic leaders surrendered to this demand, and an amendment setting the dividing line at 50 cents was approved with just five nay votes. The *Post* reported that Quay would not stop talking "until the concessions demanded by Messrs. Smith and Murphy, reinforced by the Senator from Pennsylvania, had been conceded" ("Approaching the End," June 18, 1894, p. 2). Quay's filibuster likely enhanced the Democrats' incentive to give in to Smith and Murphy's demands, but it is worth emphasizing that the coverage in the *Post* suggests that a floor majority favored the revised rate.

the Senate nonetheless had the duty to reduce economic uncertainty through "speedy action on the bill before us" (*Congressional Record*, May 16, 1894, pp. 4809–10).[39] Another bill opponent, Henry Teller (R–CO), noted that though he believed in the right of the minority to force debate and discussion, "the people have a right to have some kind of legislation upon this subject. . . . They voted for it and they are entitled to it" (*Congressional Record*, May 17, 1894, p. 4883). Teller went on to note that though all Republicans oppose the bill, it will be approved "if there is a full vote on the other [Democratic] side" (4883). This dissension over GOP strategy was important because it made it much harder for the minority to deprive Democrats of a quorum to do business. The *Post* thus reported on May 24 that at least eight Republicans would cooperate in helping Democrats achieve a quorum if the majority party opted for continuous sessions and that "the impression is at last penetrating the Republican side that the Democrats have enough votes to pass the bill, and this knowledge has its effect in discouraging the opposition" ("Democrats as a Unit," p. 1; see also "Washington Information," *Wall Street Journal*, May 22, 1894, p. 4). By late May, newspaper coverage predicted a final vote would be obtained by early July and that the bill would likely pass by a narrow margin.[40] These forecasts proved accurate: the bill was adopted 39-34 on July 3. On the day the bill passed, ardent protectionist Anthony Higgins (R–DE) "directly charged the silver Republicans with being responsible for the passage of the tariff by refusing to enter into a filibustering combination" with their fellow Republicans ("Hill Against It," *Washington Post*, July 4, 1894, p. 1).[41]

When one considers the main changes made to the bill by the Democrats prior to passage, it is clear that the primary logic was one of building a majority, rather than preempting obstruction. For example, Democrats dropped sugar from the free list due to the demands of Louisiana's Democratic senators, while iron ore and coal were dropped due to demands from Alabama and West Virginia's Democratic senators (Stanwood 1903, v. 2, 326–28, 238–51; Lambert 1953; "Iron Ore Forty Cents a Ton," *New York Times*, May 24, 1894, p. 5). These were among the most controversial changes to the bill, yet they were required to gain enough Democratic votes for passage (see "Gorman Tells All," *Washington Post*, July 24, 1894, pp. 1–2). By contrast, wool was kept on the free list because no Democratic senators were threatened by this change. The *Wall Street Journal* noted that Democratic leaders were

---

[39] Dubois predicted that speedy passage would help the Republicans, since the temporary benefits of the bill for the economy would subside well before the election (*Congressional Record*, May 16, 1894, p. 4810).

[40] See "Editorial Summary," *Public Opinion*, May 31, 1894, pp. 202–3 and "Tariff Filibustering to End," *New York Times*, May 20, 1894, pp. 1–2. A handful of Republicans, most notably Quay, continued to slow progress on the bill into June, but press coverage indicates that senators (correctly) expected the bill to reach the final passage stage.

[41] Higgins' speech suggested he believed Quay's filibuster had paid some dividends. Higgins claimed Quay had used obstruction to gain concessions, and that with the silverites' cooperation, the GOP might have defeated the bill as a whole (*Congressional Record*, July 3, 1894, p. 7093).

insisting on free wool even though the provision was especially damaging to western Republicans, and "under these conditions, Republicans will consent to no agreements of any kind and the debate on free wool may continue until there is an attempt to force a vote by continuous session" ("The Tariff Situation," June 15, 1894, p. 4). Republicans made repeated unsuccessful efforts to restore protection for wool; the last failed on a 37-32 perfect party vote (see "Hill Against It," *Washington Post*, July 4, 1894, p. 1; and "Wool to Go on Free List," *New York Times*, June 16, 1894, p. 1). Lumber was also placed on the free list, despite vigorous GOP opposition, because it was the price for the vote of Nebraska's Populist senator, William Allen (see "Now the Income Tax," *Washington Post*, June 21, 1894, p. 1). Once Jones brought in the amendments to win over the high-tariff Democrats, Gorman claimed that it is no surprise that Republicans attacked the bill, since "it had not been framed to please them" ("Democrats are a Unit," *Washington Post*, May 24, 1894, p. 1). Gorman encouraged his Democratic troops by observing that "there has never yet been a time in the history of this Senate when a clear majority was unable to enact a law" (p. 1).

It is especially striking that Democratic leaders' own accounts attributed the revisions to the House bill to the need to win over dissident Democrats rather than to GOP obstruction, even though the latter explanation may have helped shift blame for the often-unpopular changes. President Grover Cleveland accused the Senate Democrats of "party perfidy and dishonor" (Lambert 1953, 229) and claimed that the "deadly blight of treason has blasted the counsels of the brave in their hour of might" (Stanwood 1903, v. 2, 355). In the midst of such internecine warfare, the need to defuse GOP obstruction might have provided a convenient way for Senate Democrats to excuse their alleged apostasy. Yet Democrats Gorman, Jones, and George Vest (D–MO) did not resort to such excuses when they responded to attacks from Cleveland and House Democrats (see Lambert 1953; Stanwood 1903, v. 2, 332, 346–52). For example, Gorman stated that Senate Democrats had revised the bill only after finding that "it could not receive forty-three votes. . . . Every Democratic senator was seen and was talked to. His views and suggestions were ascertained and a memorandum was made of every amendment proposed" ("Gorman Tells All," *Washington Post*, July 24, 1894, p. 1). Gorman explained that the slim party majority meant that Democrats from manufacturing states such as New York, Maryland, New Jersey, and Ohio had to be satisfied with any proposed tariff changes for a bill to pass (p. 2).[42]

It is essential to note that Republicans continued to regard the bill as harmful, but did not make full use of their prerogatives to block it. John

---

[42]Notwithstanding the fierce criticism of Cleveland, the Senate Democrats held firm to all of their chamber's amendments, again due to the need to maintain a majority for the bill: "it is said that if the slightest change is made in these [disputed] schedules . . . at least one, and perhaps two, Democratic Senators stand ready to move an indefinite postponement of the consideration of the conference report" ("The Future of the Bill," *Washington Post*, July 24, 1894, p. 2).

Sherman (R–OH) summarized the prevalent view: if Republicans "chose to do it, they could defeat the bill by availing themselves of the rules of the Senate. There was not a Senator on his side of the chamber who did not regard the measure as injurious to the people of the United States. . . . And Republican senators would be justified in resisting the measure, and he sometimes thought, would not be excused if they did not resist it to the same extent as Democrats had defeated an important measure a few years ago [viz., the Elections Bill]. But Republican Senators would give to the pending bill only that opposition which was demanded by the interests of their people—not to defeat the majority, but to show that the proposed measure was wrongful, unjust, and destructive to American industries" ("Mr. Vest's Speech," *Washington Post*, June 10, 1894, p. 3). Republicans voted 31-0 against passage. Indeed, as discussed below, the GOP pushed for a substantial revision in the Wilson-Gorman rates as soon as they gained unified control of government in the 1896 elections (see below).

Consistent with our theoretical framework, a committed majority had threatened to use continuous sessions and to change the rules in response to an obstreperous minority. Although the Republicans did not acknowledge that these threats played a role in their surrender, the timing is consistent with this hypothesis.[43] More generally, the case supports our argument that excepting perhaps end-of-congress obstruction, a determined majority could count on being able to legislate when it came to the tariff. The key constraint confronting Democrats was constructing a floor majority in favor of the bill.

The Dingley Tariff of 1897, the Payne-Aldrich Tariff of 1909, and the Underwood Tariff of 1913 were each the subject of lengthy debates and numerous roll call votes, but it does not appear that there were substantial efforts to kill or amend the legislation through obstruction. Each was initially adopted by a majority of less than 60%.[44] While there was some discussion of threats of obstruction in 1909, these threats did not result in significant changes to the legislation.[45] In 1913, newspaper and magazine coverage indicates that Republicans explicitly decided not to obstruct the bill, instead using their speeches to produce a record of the flaws of the legislation, so that they could later blame Democrats for the tariff reductions' harmful effects on the economy.[46] Indeed, press coverage of the various tariff bills in this

---

[43] Regardless of whether the threat of a rules change was credible—given that Democrats were a few votes short in their bid to build a coalition for majority cloture—it is clear that Republicans did not push their prerogatives to the limit once it became evident that a floor majority supported the bill and that Democrats would use such tactics as continuous sessions to push it to passage.

[44] The conference report in 1909 commanded a wider majority of 47 to 31, perhaps because the conference committee had acceded to President William Howard Taft's demands for some decreases in the duties in the initial Senate bill. The conference report in 1913 also was approved by a wider majority than the initial Senate bill (36 to 17, as compared to 44 to 37 on initial passage). It is unclear why opposition declined at the conference stage in 1913, given that the Senate, House, and conference versions were extremely similar to one another (see, e.g., Chamberlain 1946).

[45] See, e.g., Willis (1910) for discussion and assessment.

[46] For example, the "The Progress of the World," *Review of Reviews*, reported in August 1913 that "well-informed Republican Senators expressed themselves in private last month

era suggests that making a record of opposition through a war of attrition was often considered a more salient goal to foes than was actual defeat of the legislation. For Republicans in 1913, with tariffs seeming to be waning in popularity, it may have been an especially inauspicious time to obstruct the new president's program of reduced rates.[47]

A consideration of post-1917 tariff bills suggests that threats of imposing cloture became an element of legislative battles over tariffs, but that supermajority support was by no means a necessary condition for passage. A proposal to adopt an emergency tariff increase for agricultural products was considered in the lame duck session of the 66th Congress. This was the first time a major tariff bill was considered in a lame duck session since the 1880s. Interestingly, the bill confronted a lengthy Senate filibuster in January 1921. Boies Penrose (R–PA) presented a cloture resolution on January 31, arguing that nearly two-thirds of the Senate backed the legislation yet Democrats were blocking its passage. The cloture resolution failed, with 36 senators voting yea and 35 opposed. Some Republicans who backed the tariff bill, such as Hiram Johnson of California and Asle Gronna of North Dakota, opposed cloture, arguing that it was inherently objectionable (see *Congressional Record,* February 2, 1921, pp. 2431–32).[48] Oscar Underwood (D–AL) noted prior to the cloture vote that though he opposed both the bill and cloture, he would not have objected to a unanimous consent request for a vote on the bill, since its passage would have demonstrated to the country what sort of policies Republicans favored (*Congressional Record,* January 31, 1921, p. 2313). This may sound like an empty promise, but right after the cloture resolution failed, the ranking Democrat on the Finance Committee, Furnifold Simmons (D–NC), offered a unanimous consent agreement calling for a final vote on February 18. While another Democrat, John Sharp Williams of Mississippi, objected to the agreement, Simmons promised that a sufficient number of party members would join with the Republicans to force a vote by mid-February (*Congressional Record,* February 2, 1921, p. 2433). As it turned out, the legislation was adopted by a 44-30 vote on February 16; the 49 to 36 vote on the conference report was also successful. Still, President Woodrow Wilson vetoed the bill so it may be that Democrats chose to end their obstruction because they were confident the president would kill the bill.[49]

---

as confident that the bill would have the requisite majority and would become law after a due period of debate. . . . There was not much indication that any members of the opposition would filibuster or use obstructive means" (v. 48, no. 2, pp. 134–35). See also a similar assessment in "The Tariff in the Senate," *The Nation,* v. 96, no. 4299, May 22, 1913, p. 514.

[47] However, Republicans did not have qualms about obstructing other parts of Wilson's program that they deemed to be less popular (see Chapter 8).

[48] Based on their NOMINATE scores, both Johnson and Gronna were predicted to vote in favor of cloture. Nonetheless, both voted against ending debate.

[49] Underwood predicted the veto during his January 31 speech (p. 2316). A similar bill was eventually enacted in the special session of the 67th Congress, which convened in Spring 1921. With a Republican in the White House, a veto was no longer a threat to the bill's prospects. In any case, the Republicans' increased majority in the new congress

But the next instance of a filibuster on a tariff bill followed a remarkably similar course, without a veto at the last stage. The Senate Finance Committee added nearly two thousand amendments to the House-passed tariff bill of 1922. This necessitated a lengthy floor debate, which was exacerbated by Democrats' strategy of engaging in protracted discussion of even the least important amendments. Republicans accused Democrats of engaging in a new type of filibuster. Henry Cabot Lodge (R–MA) argued that "technical filibustering is taking advantage of every parliamentary point, and insisting on roll calls and quorums, and raising points of order, and an infinite number of things" (*Congressional Record*, July 5, 1922, p. 9984). Democrats were instead adopting an alternative approach to filibustering in which "time was wasted [through lengthy debate] on wholly insignificant things." Lodge might have also mentioned that a series of precedents established during earlier filibusters had made such dilatory motions a less viable strategy for obstructionists; thus, the turn to lengthy speeches was a sensible adaptation to changed rules of the game.[50]

In response to the delays, Republicans offered a cloture resolution, which fell short of the necessary two-thirds support on a 45 to 35 vote (54 votes were needed).[51] At the time, Underwood argued that it was too soon for cloture given that Democrats had not yet had the chance to present their amendments (*Congressional Record*, July 5, 1922, p. 9982). There is no evidence that anyone thought that the defeat of the cloture motion meant the defeat of the tariff bill. Instead, observers expected that the failure of cloture would be followed by negotiations between GOP and Democratic leaders on a unanimous consent agreement to limit debate on key schedules so that a vote could be reached by the middle of August ("Want Bonus Passed, Subsidy Shelved," *New York Times*, July 7, 1922, p. 15). A few weeks later, on August 2, Democrat Simmons once again proposed a unanimous consent agreement providing for a final vote. After some haggling over the precise terms, a date for a vote on final passage was set. The bill was adopted with nearly two-thirds support, though the final vote on the conference report was a bit closer, with just 61% voting yea. Although it is not entirely clear why Simmons made the offer, it followed Democratic accusations that Republicans might choose to delay final action on the tariff bill until after the November elections ("Tariff Bill Slated to Pass August 17," *New York Tribune*, August 3, 1922, p. 1; "Vote on the Tariff Now Seems in Sight," *New York Times*, August 3, 1922, p. 17; "Chemical Wood Pulp Is Put on Free List," *New York Times*, August 4, 1922, p. 4). As the tariff proposal was receiving considerable criticism in the press—including from some Republican

---

resulted in greater than two-thirds support for the bill, which was approved 53 to 26 (see Table 6.3).

[50] The GOP countered the obstruction by refusing to adjourn the Senate. This resulted in the longest legislative day in Senate history to that point, which stretched from April 20 to August 2. By recessing instead of adjourning, Republicans took advantage of the various precedents established in recent decades that had limited the procedural tools available to obstructionists.

[51] There were six paired votes.

papers—it is plausible that Democrats calculated they would benefit more from allowing the Republicans a vote on the measure than in continuing to be blamed for obstructing its progress (cf. Groseclose and McCarty 2001).[52]

The last major tariff bill of this era—and the last of the traditional tariff bills in American history—was the Smoot-Hawley Act of 1930. Consideration of this bill dragged on from September through November of a 1929 special session, and continued into the spring of 1930. While foes of the bill engaged in dilatory tactics at various points (see Chamberlain 1946, 130), on the whole the politics appear majoritarian. Initially, a coalition of Democrats and dissident Republicans had the upper hand, and won a series of amendment battles that reduced rates on eastern manufacturers and raised duties on western raw materials. In the second session, however, many of these amendments reducing rates on manufactured goods were defeated on reconsideration, as conservative Republicans used vote trades to win over the dissident Republicans (MacMahon 1930, 922–23). Although the bill was adopted on March 24 by a wide margin (58-36), the conference report was approved by a scant two votes in mid-June, suggesting again that supermajority support was not a necessary condition for major changes in tariff laws, even thirteen years after adoption of the cloture rule. Once again, it is likely that political calculations made obstruction an unattractive option in the spring of 1930: with the economy in a tailspin, filibustering a major piece of economic legislation would have subjected Democrats to charges of worsening the economic crisis that they otherwise were quite able to blame on the Republican president and Congress.

6.5 CONCLUSION

Our evidence suggests that a floor majority was sufficient to pass major tariff legislation in the Senate for much of the period before and immediately following the adoption of the cloture rule. Prior to the cloture rule's adoption, obstruction by a large and determined minority at the end of a congress appears to have posed considerable uncertainty for coalition builders. The death of the wool tariff in 1827, as well as the shift to special sessions and

---

[52] For examples of this criticism from Republican newspapers, see *Congressional Record*, August 1, 1922, pp. 10842–47). One might hypothesize that Simmons introduced the unanimous consent agreement because changes to the bill had moderated its content. In presenting his resolution, Simmons noted that since the important wool schedule had now been dealt with, it made sense to set a date for a final vote. However, the Senate had approved the high wool rates proposed by the Finance Committee ("Wool Fight Ended, High Duties Stand," *New York Times*, August 1, 1922, p. 21; "Vote on Tariff Late in August Now Predicted," *New York Tribune*, August 1, 1922, p. 3), and therefore it is unlikely that concessions motivated Simmons or the other Democrats. More generally, the Senate bill was extremely protectionist (and all but three Democrats voted against its passage). The Republican caucus approved a proposal to amend the rules to allow for majority cloture on appropriations and revenue bills, but the proposal was never brought to the floor. We were unable to ascertain whether a floor majority would have favored the proposal. In the end, majority cloture was not needed to pass the tariff bill.

the avoidance of lame duck sessions after 1890 each suggest the disruptive potential of late-session obstruction. But once again it appears that a floor majority was sufficient to adopt new tariff laws so long as the lame duck sessions were avoided.

As a final element of our analysis of tariff politics, we analyze the coalition sizes on final passage votes and compare these to the coalition sizes on all major legislation (see Chapter 4). A first observation is that tariff bills were typically controversial: none of the tariffs passed on a voice vote in the Senate. By comparison, when the universe is all major legislation, 44% of bills enacted from 1881 to 1945 were approved on a voice vote.[53] A second observation is that final passage votes on tariff bills were often quite close: across the entire time span, 68% of Senate final passage votes had fewer than two-thirds in favor; in nearly half of the final passage votes (47%), fewer than 60% of the senators voted yes. Close votes were especially common after 1881: 78% of the final passage votes after 1881 had fewer than two-thirds voting in favor, as compared to 60% prior to 1881. This is much greater than the proportion of close votes for the universe of all major legislation during this period (see Table 4.1).[54] On the whole, the average coalition size supporting successful tariff bills was just 62.8%, as compared to an average size of approximately 80% on all major bills. The prevalence of close votes supports the claim that the median voter was generally pivotal for tariff bills. An additional nuance is that coalition sizes were 4.5% greater for tariff bills passed under divided government. This conforms to the median-plus-veto-pivot model's prediction: since divided government makes a veto more likely and thus the veto pivot relevant, coalition sizes tend to increase.[55]

While generally consistent with the median-plus-veto-pivot model, our case study of the tariff also suggests two refinements of our understanding of obstruction that are not detectable in the earlier, quantitative analysis of all major legislation. First, as the 1846 case attests, norms of restraint at times played an important role in leading minorities to choose not to

---

[53] If the list of major laws is narrowed to 1881–1930 (to correspond to the end point of our tariff data), then 46% of the bills were adopted on voice votes.

[54] We also tested the "silent majority" hypothesis for the bills in our sample. That is, we investigated whether coalition sizes would have been bigger had those who abstained participated in the roll call votes. We computed the statistic measuring the difference between the percentage of senators who actually voted in favor and the percentage of abstainers who were predicted to have voted in favor (had they cast votes). Of the thirty final votes on tariff legislation for which we could compute this difference (four votes had no abstentions), only seven had positive values, indicating that in most cases, abstainers would not have increased the size of the coalitions voting in favor if they had participated.

[55] One might counter that the prevalence of logrolling on tariffs makes final vote tallies uninformative, as members may have voted against bills even though the legislation included major concessions for their district. This argument is not very plausible. As Bensel (2000) argues, tariffs were highly redistributive in this era; they benefited industrial districts and hurt the South and most other agricultural areas. With a few minor exceptions, each bill in Tables 6.1 to 6.3 moved tariffs either substantially up or down and had clear implications for each member's constituency. A close look at the floor debate, newspaper coverage, and the amendments made to each bill lends little support for the idea that members were frequently voting insincerely.

exploit their prerogatives fully. Second, electoral calculations at times also contributed to the decision of bill opponents to relent. On a handful of occasions, obstructionists appear to have decided to drop their filibuster due to some of their number believing that it was politically advisable to let the majority legislate, even as these members continued to oppose the bill on final passage. Although not completely unheard of in the contemporary Senate,[56] it may well have been more common in the pre-cloture Senate when filibuster battles were fought as wars of attrition. As noted in Chapter 2, such battles provided a mechanism for the credible revelation of preference intensity. In these cases, individuals in the minority showed that they were unwilling to continue to bear the costs of obstruction, apparently signaling that the bill was not sufficiently abhorrent to their constituents to test the majority's will any longer. It is worth emphasizing that such cases of minority surrender occurred only *after* the majority made it clear—at times even through threats of rules changes—that it was committed to bearing the costs of fighting obstruction indefinitely.

The near majoritarianism on one of the leading issues of 19th-century politics is indicative of how much has changed in more recent times. In the contemporary Senate, with the exception of budget legislation and other bills where statutory requirements restrict minority obstruction, it is safe to assume that a 60% majority is generally necessary to adopt major legislation. In the pre-cloture Senate, no such assumption appears appropriate. The results from each of the prongs of our investigation into lawmaking in the Senate lead us to roundly reject the conventional wisdom that the absence of a cloture rule led to universalism. In the context of costly obstruction, when filibusters were fought as wars of attrition with the threat of rules changes lurking in the background, an intense majority could typically count on being able to pass favored legislation

---

[56]A prominent recent example was Gordon Smith (R–OR), who voted for cloture on the Bipartisan Campaign Finance Reform Act of 2002 even as he continued to oppose the bill's passage. Even more recently, as a result of the compromise that was reached over judicial nominees in 2005 (see Chapter 11), several Democrats voted in favor of invoking cloture on the nominees but then voted against confirmation.

Chapter Seven

Slavery and Obstruction in the Antebellum Senate

7.1 INTRODUCTION

The previous three chapters analyzed the macro-effects of obstruction on lawmaking. In this chapter, we push our analysis down to the micro-level by investigating what factors motivate individuals to engage in and support obstructive efforts. We undertake an analysis of obstruction in the antebellum Senate, exploiting the special political context of this period to further test some of the key theoretical conjectures developed in Chapter 2—specifically, those relevant to salience and intensity. In particular, we focus on the importance of minority status as it relates to sectionalism and the salience of issues involving slavery in driving minority obstruction. Our discussion so far has indicated how alternative theoretical perspectives make different—and sometimes competing—predictions about the dilatory strategies of minorities and when obstruction should occur. The empirical analysis we discuss here clarifies the causal relationships among relevant factors at the individual level, providing a deeper understanding of why individuals at times choose to obstruct and at other times refrain from doing so.

As we have noted in earlier chapters, prior empirical research has generally examined obstruction through the prism of partisanship (Binder 1997; Binder and Smith 1997; Binder, Lawrence, and Smith 2002; Dion 1997). While party-based theories of obstruction have had success in explaining obstruction in the modern Senate, other factors—namely, sectionalism—may be equally or more important for explaining this behavior prior to the Civil War. A substantial amount of historical work emphasizes the importance of balance in representation in the Senate between free and slave states in understanding the politics of this period. Sectional cleavages, particularly over slavery and related issues, make it imperative to consider these factors in addition to partisanship in order to understand minority obstruction. Southerners, regardless of party, were especially concerned about having minority status in the chamber because their paramount interests in the institution of slavery were threatened as their relative numerical strength in the Senate declined. Understanding obstruction in the Senate during this period is important because the upper chamber has been viewed by many as crucial in maintaining political stability over the issue of slavery, which would eventually rend apart the Union. While it is well known that southern senators used filibusters to block civil rights legislation during the 20th century, we do not know the extent to which obstruction was part of their strategic arsenal during the antebellum period.

This chapter investigates this question by using data on dilatory tactics aimed at legislation on slavery-related issues, as well as legislation unrelated to slavery. The variation in salience associated with these two different classes of legislation enables us to probe a key component of our theoretical argument. Our analysis is also unique in that it treats the senator as the unit of analysis.[1] Previous studies have examined what factors are related to obstruction only in the aggregate, and thus are vulnerable to ecological fallacies. We conduct an individual-level test to investigate our hypotheses regarding the relationship between issue salience and obstruction. This is not simply an effort to demonstrate that sectionalism mattered; instead we show—as predicted by our theoretical framework—that sectionalism drove senators' willingness to engage in and support obstructive efforts in certain, predictable situations but not in others. When southerners constituted a numerical minority in the chamber, they exploited the peculiar rules of the Senate regarding debate to obstruct legislation related to the "peculiar institution" of slavery. The use of and support for dilatory tactics by southern senators increased as they became a smaller minority. The finding that dilatory tactics were used to protect southern white interests during the antebellum era has deeper historical significance. It indicates that the use of obstruction in battles over civil rights were part of a long-standing reliance on dilatory tactics by southerners to protect against perceived federal infringements on their section's system of racial subordination.

7.2 PREDICTIONS FOR EMPIRICAL TESTING

Our main goal is to test a simple prediction that emerged from our theoretical discussion. In Chapter 2, we argued that the resolve level of bill opponents will be crucial in leading them to resort to obstruction. This resolve should be a function of the issue's salience to the individual member. It also will be a function of the spatial distance between the member's ideal point and the median voter, as compared to the distance between the member's ideal point and the status quo.[2] It is worth emphasizing that we are not assessing the success of obstruction in this chapter; instead, we are examining the conditions under which individual senators will use dilatory tactics.[3]

---

[1] Some studies have conducted individual-level analysis of support for cloture motions, however (see Binder and Smith 1997, 92–125 and Krehbiel 1998, Ch. 5).

[2] More precisely, obstruction becomes more attractive as the distance between the member's ideal point and the median increases relative to the distance between the member's ideal point and the status quo. This prediction emerges from the maintained assumption of floor procedure under an open rule, where outcomes can be expected to converge to the median voter. Such an assumption is consistent with our results indicating that the Senate was majoritarian during the antebellum period.

[3] As we argue in Chapter 2, we expect obstruction to succeed only when the minority cares substantially more about the issue than the majority, or at times when adjournment made time constraints pressing. Even in the latter context, norms and threats of rules changes limited the frequency of minority success.

The issues of threats to the status quo and salience were linked in an especially potent way in the antebellum period. The Constitution "implicitly recognized the legality of slavery as the status quo" in the United States (Riker 1982, 214–15; see also Ransom 1989, 27–33; Miller 1996, 16–21; North and Rutten 1987, 26). Southerners were overwhelmingly concerned about attempts to pass federal legislation that would have substantially curtailed or abolished slavery, since the passage of such legislation would have thrown the South into utter economic and social turmoil.[4]

Slavery was inextricably related to several of the important issues that Congress dealt with during this period. Southerners viewed legislation involving internal improvements and public lands as having profound consequences for their interests in slavery. These issues affected the South's political and economic strength in the Union, and went to the heart of constitutional questions about the reach of the federal government and its ability to regulate slavery (Bensel 1990, 38–39; Kohlmeier 1938; Potter 1976, 390–92; Stanwood 1903, 244, 291–302; Taylor 1951, 21, 95). If the issue of slavery was not explicitly raised during debates surrounding legislation addressing these policy areas, it was never far below the surface.

Of particular concern to the South was western expansion and the admission of new states. Some have argued that the key to preventing sectional cleavages from tearing apart the Union was the maintenance of balance in representation in the Senate between southern slave states and the free states of the North (Carpenter 1990; Meinig 1993; Nichols 1963; Potter 1976; Ransom 1989; Weingast 1998, N.d.).[5] According to this argument, as long as each state had equal representation in the Senate and there were an equal number of slave states and free states in the Union, the South had an effective veto over any federal legislative initiative that infringed on the property rights of slave holders (assuming the vice president broke tie votes in the South's favor). The admission of new states to the Union threatened the institution of slavery because it had the potential to upset this balance. If balance was upset in a way that relegated slave states to the minority in the Senate, anti-slavery forces could have had enough votes to pass legislation that was inimical to southern slaveholder's' interests (assuming it had the support of the president and the House).

Southern senators should have been strongly motivated to exploit their rights as a minority in order to protect their interests in slavery. Binder and Smith (1997, 56–58) argue that John C. Calhoun's doctrine of the "concurrent majority" was intertwined with southerners' justification of the right to unlimited debate as a protection of minority interests. Calhoun, who led the

---

[4]Disagreement existed, however, about whether anything short of a constitutional amendment was valid for changing the status quo with respect to slavery. Although the Supreme Court in the *Dred Scott* decision implied that a constitutional amendment was necessary to limit slavery, southerners were militant against any legislative effort that even remotely called the institution into question (e.g., see Miller 1996 and Richards 2000).

[5]For arguments questioning the importance of balance see Elster (2000) and McCarty, Poole, and Rosenthal (2002).

often-discussed Bank Bill filibuster of 1841, offered "the most fully developed and probably decisive theoretical justification" for the use of unlimited debate for obstruction, which southerners adopted to defend "rules of debate that would best protect their interests: here, their region's interest in protecting a culture and economy based on slave labor" (58). Thus, obstruction had been identified by contemporaries as a means for protecting sectional interests.

Our central hypothesis then is that when southerners became a numerical minority, a given senator from that section should be more likely to obstruct, digging in against the threat of legislation that affected the issues that were overwhelmingly salient to the South. As their numerical disadvantage increased and it became more likely that free state senators could change the status quo on slavery and related issues, southerners should have been more likely to obstruct.[6]

Variation in free and slave state representation during the antebellum period enables us to test this prediction. In twenty-one out of the thirty-six antebellum congresses, there were unequal numbers of free and slave state senators, with slave state senators constituting a sectional minority in eighteen of those congresses (see Table 7.1). In the 1850s, the South's disadvantage grew worse, and by the end of the decade they were down by six senators. While the difference in the number of senators from each section may seem trivial, it is important to keep in mind that the small overall size of the Senate during this period meant that the addition of even just two senators could have a substantial impact. Although slavery was not an issue in many of these congresses and the South could draw support from some northern "doughfaces" (Richards 2000, 85–100), the minority status of the South raised the possibility that entrepreneurial senators would try to make political gains by pushing anti-slavery legislation (cf. Riker 1982). Weingast (1998, 168–69) points out that anti-slavery measures regularly passed the House during this period, and southern senators were concerned about preventing *any* legislation that threatened slavery from passing their chamber, lest the abolition movement gain momentum. But did southern senators exploit the lack of debate limits when they constituted a minority, and did they become more obstructive as their numerical disadvantage worsened?

While previous research has shown that sectional influences became important in roll call voting behavior during this period (Silbey 1967; Poole

---

[6]This would contradict Dion's (1997) prediction that partisan minorities should obstruct more as their size increases, if the logic of his partisan argument was generalized to any kind of minority. Our argument raises the question of why southern senators would have ever let legislation pass that increased the likelihood that they would have been relegated to the minority. New free states could be admitted only by acts of Congress, and some of the greatest battles where the weapons of obstruction were deployed by southerners concerned this kind of legislation (Burdette 1940, 25–30; Lyman 1903, 93–100; Potter 1976, 151–52). However, exogenous factors, such as the viability of slavery in the territories, would have made it difficult for the South to have maintained parity with free states in the long run (McCarty, Poole, and Rosenthal 2002, 425–32). While the South would have no doubt preferred to maximize the size of its coalition in the Senate, the realities of western expansion appeared to have made it inevitable that slave states would constitute a minority of the Union.

Table 7.1 Free versus Slave State Representation in the Antebellum Senate

Congress	Session dates Begin	End	Free states	Slave states	No. of days in session not in balance
1	3/4/1789	3/3/1791	7	6	All
2	10/24/1791	3/2/1793	8	7	All
3	12/2/1793	3/3/1795	8	7	All
4	12/7/1795	3/3/1797	8	8	175
5	5/15/1797	3/3/1799	8	8	0
6	12/2/1799	3/3/1801	8	8	0
7	12/7/1801	3/3/1803	8	8	0
8	10/17/1803	3/3/1805	9	8	134
9	12/2/1805	3/3/1807	9	8	All
10	10/26/1807	3/3/1809	9	8	All
11	5/22/1809	3/3/1811	9	8	All
12	11/4/1811	3/3/1813	9	9	177[a]
13	5/24/1813	3/3/1815	9	9	0
14	12/4/1815	3/3/1817	10	9	82
15	12/1/1817	3/3/1819	11	10	98
16	12/6/1819	3/3/1821	12	11	82
17	12/3/1821	3/3/1823	12	12	0
18	12/1/1823	3/3/1825	12	12	0
19	12/5/1825	3/3/1827	12	12	0
20	12/3/1827	3/3/1829	12	12	0
21	12/7/1829	3/3/1831	12	12	0
22	12/5/1831	3/2/1833	12	12	0
23	12/2/1833	3/3/1835	12	12	0
24	12/7/1835	3/3/1837	13	13	52[b]
25	9/4/1837	3/3/1839	13	13	0
26	12/2/1839	3/3/1841	13	13	0
27	5/31/1841	3/3/1843	13	13	0
28	12/4/1843	3/3/1845	13	13	0
29	12/1/1845	3/3/1847	14	15	All
30	12/6/1847	3/3/1849	15	15	176[c]
31	12/3/1849	3/3/1851	16	15	112
32	12/1/1851	3/3/1853	16	15	All
33	12/5/1853	3/3/1855	16	15	All
34	12/3/1855	3/3/1857	16	15	All
35	12/7/1857	3/3/1859	18	15	All
36	12/5/1859	3/3/1861	18	15	All

[a]Louisiana was admitted on April 30, 1812, restoring balance.
[b]Arkansas was admitted on June 15, 1836 in between the 1st and 2nd sessions. The 2nd session started on December 5, 1836, creating imbalance for 52 days until Michigan was admitted on January 26, 1837.
[c]Wisconsin was admitted May 29, 1848, ending the imbalance that existed for most of the 1st session.

and Rosenthal 1997), we do not know the degree to which they systematically affected obstruction. Parties helped to defuse the sectional cleavage over slavery, so it may be that partisan factors will explain behavior better than sectional factors. Even though the Senate did not have formal party floor leadership positions until the late-19th/early-20th centuries (Gamm and Smith 2002a), party caucuses emerged and became functional in the antebellum period (Gamm and Smith 2001b). Although their activities were limited in scope, especially compared with party caucuses at the beginning of the 20th century, some research shows party agenda control dynamics in the Senate even in the absence of highly developed partisan institutions (Campbell, Cox, and McCubbins 2002). In the next section, we determine the empirical support for the theoretical conjectures regarding the importance of partisan and sectional factors in explaining the use of dilatory tactics.

7.3 EMPIRICAL ANALYSIS OF THE USE OF DILATORY TACTICS

A key problem that our empirical analysis must address is determining which senators are involved in obstructive efforts. Again, extant lists of filibusters are not helpful here since they do not always indicate who conducted the filibusters and likely miss many instances of obstruction in the antebellum era. If we are to test hypotheses regarding individuals' decisions to obstruct, we need to identify who actually engages in obstruction. As in Chapter 5, we employ dilatory motions to indicate incidents of obstruction. Not only do roll call records reveal which senator made a particular motion, but they also reveal which senators supported or opposed these motions.

In order to assess our key hypothesis, we first estimate empirical models where the dependent variable is the number of dilatory motions made by a senator in a given congress.[7] We first consider motions that were aimed at legislation related to the issue of slavery, which we define broadly to include proposals that impacted the sectional balance of power, such as bills concerning western expansion and the admission of new states, tariff changes, internal improvements, and public lands.[8] Targeted legislation and their subjects were determined by analyzing records of debates, roll call descrip-

---

[7]We use congresses as the unit of analysis rather than congressional sessions (see Binder, Lawrence, and Smith 2002), because the latter would give little to no additional variation in the variables examined. For the event count analysis, all congresses in the antebellum era except the 36th are included. It is not clear how to treat the 36th Congress since seven states had seceded by the end of it, dramatically changing the dynamics within the Senate. Fortunately the results in the quantitative analyses reported below are generally robust to including or excluding that congress.

[8]Several of these classes of bills were salient not just to southerners, but also to non-slave senators. For example, as we argue in Chapter 6, major tariff bills were typically salient to both supporters and opponents because they were closely tied to economic development more generally, even as they were connected to sectional interests as well. But for purposes of this chapter, the key claim is that the sectional stakes of such fights for southerners were higher as slave states suffered a numerical disadvantage. Our results are robust to excluding the cases of obstruction against the bills discussed in Chapter 6.

tions, and issue codes used to classify roll calls (Rosenthal and Poole 2000; Poole and Rosenthal 1997, 259–62). In order to weed out trivial instances of obstruction, we include only those motions that were part of an obstructive effort where multiple dilatory motions were targeted at a bill, although we do not require that all of the motions in a given obstructive effort be made by the same senator.

The explanatory variables in the model measure sectional, partisan, and ideological factors. We include a dummy variable that equals 1 if the senator represents a slave state and is 0 otherwise. To capture southerners' concerns about being in a minority, we include a measure of the degree of sectional parity in terms of free state advantage, which was coded as 0 when free and slave states were equally represented, 1 for when free states had a one state advantage, −1 when slave states had a one state advantage and so on. This produces a variable that ranges from −1 to 3. It is important that the variable is allowed to be both positive and negative, instead of using a dummy variable for imbalance, because a more accurate test requires that obstruction by southerners decrease when slave states have a numerical advantage. We interact this variable with the slave state dummy to account for multiplicative effects. Positive coefficients on these variables when predicting obstruction on slavery-related issues would support arguments about how section and salience affected the use of dilatory tactics.[9]

We account for partisan factors with several variables. First, the model includes a dummy measuring membership in the minority party, which should have a positive coefficient. Second, we include the measures of majority and minority party strength used by Binder, Lawrence, and Smith (2002) for purposes of comparability with past work (see also Binder 1997, 220–22). These variables are a function of the parties' seat shares and their cohesiveness. One potential virtue of the measure is that it should speak more directly to arguments about threats to the status quo than do measures that rely only on the size of the majority party. The partisan perspective implies that it is mainly minority party members who will be sensitive to changes in aggregate party strength, so we interact the indicator for minority party membership and the party strength variables. The arguments of Binder, Lawrence, and Smith (2002, 409–10) suggest we should see positive coefficients on the interaction terms, implying that minority party members obstruct more as the strength of either the minority or majority party increases.

To account for partisan factors generally, we include dummy variables indicating the party affiliation of the senator. The party dummy variables indicate Democrats, Whigs, Republicans, and a residual "other" category for minor parties, making Federalists the reference category.[10] The inclusion of

---

[9]We also tried including a measure of the percentage of seats held by southerners, but the main effect and the interaction term were so highly correlated (at greater than .99) that the standard errors for the coefficients on the variables were very large.

[10]Senators' party affiliations are those identified by Martis (1989) and coded by Rosenthal and Poole (2000). A party was put in the "other" category if it appeared in only

these variables in the model enables us to distinguish party from sectional effects further and should assuage concerns that any findings of sectional effects are spuriously caused by partisanship.

The model also includes variables measuring the absolute value of the distance between the senator's NOMINATE score and the score of the median senator for the first and second dimensions. It is necessary to include measures for both dimensions because the second dimension often proved important in the antebellum period (see Poole and Rosenthal 1997, 91–100). Our theoretical approach indicates that the coefficient on these variables should be positive, since the benefits of obstruction will exceed the costs for more extreme senators.

Finally, the model includes a measure of workload in order to account for the probability that obstruction will be successful. As workload increases, placing more demands on scarce time for considering legislation, senators are more likely to capitulate to an obstructive colleague. This, in turn, will increase the incentive to obstruct. One difficulty is finding a good exogenous measure of workload for this period (cf. Dion 1997, 37). Measures of workload that have been used in the literature, such as the number of public laws passed and the number of days in session, could be consequences as well as causes of obstruction. Binder, Lawrence, and Smith (2002) include in their aggregate-level analysis a variable measuring the number of civilian federal employees in a given year as a proxy for external policy demands placed on the Senate. Unfortunately, this variable does not exist for all of the congresses covered by our analysis.[11] Instead, we rely on the workload variable used by Binder (1997, 218–19), which is a factor score produced by a principal component analysis of the number of public laws enacted, the number of days in session, and the number of senators in each congress.

The effects of explanatory variables are estimated by methods for event count data. To account for the prevalence of zero values for the dependent variables, we estimated a zero inflated negative binomial (ZINB) model where a time trend predicts whether an observed count is zero.[12] This also helps to account for the gradual development and acceptance of the use of dilatory tactics during the antebellum period.

---

one or two congresses in the analysis or if it accounted for only a handful of senators. One could argue that the Jacksonians should be folded in with Democrats and the Anti-Jacksons combined with Whigs, since the Jacksonians mostly became Democrats and Anti-Jacksons mostly became Whigs. However, when it came to obstruction, statistical tests revealed differences in the behavior of the individuals whom Martis identifies as members of these different partisan factions. Lumping them all together raises the risk of specification bias, so we treat them as distinct.

[11] Other variables employed by Binder, Lawrence, and Smith (2002), such as the existence of a tracking system for bills and a fixed adjournment date, do not vary in the antebellum period, and therefore are not included in the specification.

[12] The ZINB model allows the process generating zeros to be different from that generating positive counts, thereby avoiding bias, and is recommended whenever a large percentage of zero counts are observed. For an accessible discussion of these kinds of models, see Long (1997, 242–50). A likelihood ratio test indicated that a ZINB model fit the data better than a zero inflated Poisson model, and a Vuong test favored the ZINB over a standard negative binomial model.

The estimation results for legislation related to slavery are reported in Table 7.2. The coefficients on the slave state dummy and the free state advantage variable are positive as expected and are bounded away from zero. The interaction between these two variables is not statistically significant, but a look at the marginal effects indicates that slave state senators were more likely to engage in obstruction when they were in the minority. In order to assess marginal effects, we computed the probability of a non-zero count for the dependent variable using the simulation method advocated by King, Tomz, and Wittenberg (2000).

The results—reported in Table 7.3—show that when slave and free states had equal representation in the Senate, southerners were over twice as likely to obstruct as were free state senators. Their probability of obstruction increased slightly when they were down one state, and they were still about twice as likely to obstruct as were free state senators. Toward the end of the antebellum period, when southerners were at their greatest numerical disadvantage, their likelihood of obstruction increased by about 8 percentage points, and they were about 9 percentage points more likely to obstruct compared with their free state colleagues. It is worth emphasizing that the data indicate that, overall, senators exercised abundant restraint in their use of obstruction. About 70% of the senators in the sample made no dilatory motions during their careers. Thus, any departure from a zero count is significant. Although by contemporary standards the marginal effects may seem small, they are substantively significant for the antebellum period where obstruction of bills was much less common. Free state senators also saw increases in their obstructive behavior with deviations from parity, but slave state senators were still always more likely to obstruct.

Although the variables capturing southerners' concerns about their minority status have significant effects, we also see effects for the partisan variables. The variable measuring majority party strength and its interaction with the minority party indicator have coefficients that are statistically distinguishable from zero. But even though the sign on the interaction is as expected, a look at the marginal effects in Table 7.3 indicates that the predictions from the partisan model are not entirely borne out. Because the negative coefficient on the main effect for majority party strength dominates the positive coefficient on the interaction, a one standard deviation increase in majority party strength led to a slight decrease in the probability that a minority party senator obstructed. Consistent with expectations, a majority party senator was less likely to obstruct (by about 3 percentage points) when his party's strength increased by one standard deviation. None of the other variables in the specification have effects that are statistically significant at conventional levels, so we do not report marginal effects for them.

In order to fully test our hypotheses about salience, we estimated the models for legislation not related to slavery (see Table 7.4). The sectional variables do not have statistically significant effects on the usage of dilatory motions, which provides critical support for the arguments about how the salience of the slavery issue for southerners drove them to obstruct. The

Table 7.2 Factors Affecting Senators' Use of Obstruction on Legislation Related to Slavery

Variable	Coefficient Estimate	Standard Error	p value
Inflation model			
Constant	9.989	2.358	0.000
Trend	−0.458	0.116	0.000
Negative binomial for count			
Constant	1.941	1.461	0.184
Slave state senator	1.175	0.205	0.000
Free state advantage	0.381	0.158	0.016
Slave state senator × free state advantage	−0.128	0.168	0.448
Min. party senator	−1.613	1.526	0.290
Maj. party strength	−9.709	2.368	0.000
Min. party strength	1.238	2.656	0.641
Min. party senator × maj. party strength	7.783	3.835	0.042
Min. party senator × min. party strength	−2.220	4.280	0.604
Deviation from median on dimension 1	0.323	0.421	0.444
Deviation from median on dimension 2	0.322	0.237	0.175
Workload	1.220	0.746	0.102
Democrat	−0.973	0.993	0.327
Whig	−1.142	0.991	0.249
Republican	0.508	0.854	0.552
Jacksonian	0.578	1.117	0.605
Anti-Jackson	0.079	1.039	0.939
Other	−0.918	1.007	0.362

Notes: Table entries are maximum likelihood estimates from a zero-inflated negative binomial model.
Number of observations = 1678.
Number of observations with non-zero counts = 192.
Log-likelihood = −623.29. Likelihood Ratio $\chi^2 = 121.66$ ($p < .001$).
Likelihood ratio test of $\alpha = 0 : \chi^2 = 20.68$ ($p < .001$).
Vuong Test of ZINB versus Negative Binomial: $Z = 3.29$ ($p < .001$).

Table 7.3 Simulated Probabilities of Non-zero Counts, Legislation Related to Slavery

Free/Slave State Split	Free State Senator	Slave State Senator
Parity between free and slave states	0.069 [0.009, 0.282]	0.160 [0.029, 0.414]
One slave state advantage	0.050 [0.005, 0.256]	0.137 [0.022, 0.390]
One free state advantage	0.094 [0.015, 0.317]	0.187 [0.038, 0.438]
Three free state advantage	0.158 [0.033, 0.398]	0.243 [0.061, 0.485]
Value for party strength	Maj. Party Senator	Min. Party Senator
Baseline prob. for party strength variables	0.069 [0.009, 0.282]	0.089 [0.014, 0.304]
One std. dev. increase in maj. party strength	0.037 [0.005, 0.206]	0.080 [0.013, 0.287]

Note: The results are based on 5,000 simulations of the coefficient vector from the zero-inflated negative binomial model. The simulated probability is the median of the distribution of the simulations, and the bounds of the confidence interval (in brackets) are the .025 and .975 percentiles.

variables that do appear to drive obstruction on these kinds of bills are majority party strength (irrespective of whether a senator is in the majority or minority party), ideological deviation on the first and second NOMINATE dimension, and workload, all of which have positive effects on obstruction. Yet the confidence intervals for marginal effects for these variables (reported in Table 7.5) all have zero for their lower bound, suggesting caution in attributing substantive significance to these effects.

These results provide support for the theoretical argument that issue salience drives individuals' use of obstruction. Particularly telling is the finding that southerners were more willing to engage in obstruction on slavery-related issues when their region was at a numerical disadvantage, but that this relationship does not hold for non-slavery legislation. Partisan factors also influenced whether a given senator engaged in obstruction on slavery-related legislation, yet we did not find similar effects for non-slavery legislation, even though we expected to see them.[13] Variables capturing ideological

---

[13] In particular, minority party status was insignificant.

Table 7.4 Factors Affecting Senators' Use of Obstruction on Legislation Not Related to Slavery

Variable	Coefficient Estimate	Standard Error	p value
Inflation model			
Constant	14.732	9.259	0.112
Trend	−1.409	1.127	0.211
Negative binomial for count			
Constant	−0.829	1.281	0.518
Slave state senator	0.065	0.178	0.716
Free state advantage	0.019	0.171	0.913
Slave state senator × free state advantage	−0.186	0.207	0.368
Min. party senator	0.272	1.499	0.855
Maj. party strength	4.279	2.401	0.070
Min. party strength	−2.825	2.317	0.220
Min. party senator × maj. party strength	1.991	3.639	0.580
Min. party senator × min. party strength	−2.257	3.368	0.500
Deviation from median on dimension 1	0.654	0.385	0.090
Deviation from median on dimension 2	0.428	0.243	0.078
Workload	2.309	0.608	0.000
Democrat	−0.076	0.494	0.877
Whig	−0.646	0.462	0.162
Republican	−0.306	0.382	0.423
Jacksonian	−0.257	0.640	0.689
Anti-Jackson	−0.562	0.528	0.287
Other	−0.689	0.484	0.155

Notes: Table entries are maximum likelihood estimates from a zero-inflated negative binomial model.
Number of observations = 1678.
Number of observations with non-zero counts = 154.
Log-likelihood = −553.19. Likelihood Ratio χ^2 = 43.42 ($p < .001$).
Likelihood ratio test of $\alpha = 0 : \chi^2 = 21.26$ ($p < .001$).
Vuong Test of ZINB versus Negative Binomial: $Z = 5.12$ ($p < .001$).

Table 7.5 Simulated Probabilities of Non-zero Counts, Legislation Not Related to Slavery

Baseline probability	0.085 [0.000, 0.213]
One std. dev. increase in maj. party strength	0.110 [0.000, 0.266]
One std. dev. increase in median dev. (1st dim.)	0.098 [0.000, 0.234]
One std. dev. increase in median dev. (2nd dim.)	0.096 [0.000, 0.237]
One std. dev. increase in Senate workload	0.144 [0.000, 0.324]

Note: The results are based on 5,000 simulations of the coefficient vector from the zero-inflated negative binomial model. The simulated probability is the median of the distribution of the simulations, and the bounds of the confidence interval (in brackets) are the .025 and .975 percentiles.

extremism and the probability of successful obstruction (i.e., workload) became apparent when the sample included legislation that did not concern slavery.

7.4 SUPPORT FOR OBSTRUCTIVE EFFORTS

In order to further test our arguments about the obstruction calculus at the individual level, we examined what factors predict whether or not a senator supports dilatory motions. Supporting dilatory motions is a measure of participation in an obstructive effort, since it indicates that senators are bearing the costs to be present on the floor in order to endorse the actions of those making the motions. Thus, the same factors that motivate senators to obstruct should motivate them to support obstruction. We investigate whether or not this is the case by estimating the effects of the explanatory variables used in the count models on a senator's support for dilatory tactics. The dependent variable is the number of roll call votes cast in favor of dilatory motions divided by the number of votes on such motions cast by each senator per congress.[14] The expectations for the effects of the explanatory variables are the same as in the event count analysis. We do separate analyses for motions made by slave state senators on slavery and non-slavery issues.

---

[14]The disappearing quorum problem discussed in Chapter 5 affects this analysis. For each observation, we include only those votes where the senator cast a recorded vote. Hence, we may underestimate the degree of support for obstruction among those members who abstained in an attempt to break a quorum.

Parameter estimates were obtained using an extended beta binomial (EBB) model (King 1998, 119–21; Palmquist 1999). The EBB model is designed for analyzing grouped binary data where heterogeneity and dependence exists within and across observational units. It is especially well suited, therefore, for analyzing series of roll call votes, since binary vote outcomes for a given senator are likely to be correlated across votes within a given congress.[15]

The results for slavery-related measures are reported in Table 7.6.[16] The estimate of the coefficient on the slave state indicator variable is positive and bounded away from zero, indicating that slave state senators were more likely to support dilatory motions made by senators from their section. The positive and significant coefficient on the free state advantage variable indicates they were even more likely to do so when free states had numerical superiority. Table 7.7, which reports simulated probabilities produced by the King, Tomz, and Wittenberg (2000) method, demonstrates the magnitude of the effect of these variables. The probability that a southern senator supported obstruction by a colleague increased by 3 percentage points when free states had a one-state advantage, and fell by a similar amount when slave states had a one-state edge. During the congresses where the South had the smallest minority, a senator from that section was 9% more likely to support obstruction. A slave state senator was always more likely to support this kind of obstruction than was a senator from a free state.

Interestingly, all of the coefficients on the variables that measure party strength are also statistically significant. The simulated probabilities reported in Table 7.7 show that a minority party senator was generally more likely to support obstruction by a slave state senator on slavery-related legislation, and was about 17% more likely to do so with a one standard deviation increase in majority party strength, and about 9% more likely with with the same increase in minority party strength. Thus, partisan and sectional factors did not necessarily work in competing direction, with minority party members supporting the obstructive efforts of slave state senators.

The variables measuring the member's distance from the median on each dimension are statistically significant. As a senator became one standard deviation more extreme on either dimension, he was between approximately 2 and 3% more likely to support obstruction. Senators identified as Anti-Jacksons by Martis (1989) and senators from parties in the "other" category

---

[15] A grouped logit model assumes independence of the binary vote outcomes and thus would not be appropriate. A panel model for the series of votes, while allowing for heterogeneity and dependence across votes, is not appropriate here either because the explanatory variables of interest do not vary across votes within a given congress. Note that the 1st though 9th, 11th, 14th, and 19th Congresses are not included in this analysis because no legislation in these congresses was targeted with multiple dilatory motions. The 36th is also not included because of the onset of the secession crisis.

[16] The γ and ϕ estimates reported in the table give a sense of the correlation across votes. Both of these estimates are bounded away from zero. The value of ϕ, which can be thought of as the within pairwise correlation coefficient, confirms that correlation across votes does exist and must be accounted for.

Table 7.6 Factors Affecting Senators' Support for Obstruction of Legislation
Related to Slavery

Variable	Coefficient Estimate	Standard Error	p value
Constant	2.177	0.628	0.001
Slave state senator	0.746	0.093	0.000
Free state advantage	0.129	0.064	0.045
Slave state senator × free state advantage	−0.008	0.074	0.918
Min. party senator	−7.423	0.824	0.000
Maj. party strength	−5.975	1.199	0.000
Min. party strength	−5.569	1.312	0.000
Min. party senator × maj. party strength	19.082	1.892	0.000
Min. party senator × min. party strength	11.170	2.049	0.000
Deviation from median on dimension 1	0.631	0.214	0.003
Deviation from median on dimension 2	0.301	0.125	0.016
Workload	0.472	0.348	0.175
Democrat	−0.356	0.258	0.167
Whig	−0.011	0.168	0.949
Republican	−0.277	0.269	0.304
Jacksonian	0.141	0.312	0.650
Anti-Jackson	−0.630	0.251	0.012
Other	−0.801	0.266	0.003
γ	0.264	0.021	0.000
ϕ	0.209	0.020	0.000

Notes: Table entries are maximum likelihood estimates from an extended beta binomial model. The dependent variable is support for motions made by slave state senators.
Number of observations = 893.
Log-likelihood = −7403.05. Likelihood Ratio χ^2 = 3111.02 ($p < .001$).
Likelihood ratio test of $\phi = 0 : \chi^2 = 1261.11$ ($p < .001$).

Table 7.7 Simulated Probabilities of Support for a Slave State Senator's Obstruction of Legislation Related to Slavery

Free/Slave State Split	Free State Senator	Slave State Senator
Parity between free and slave states	0.268 [0.179, 0.380]	0.436 [0.322, 0.558]
One slave state advantage	0.244 [0.156, 0.360]	0.407 [0.291, 0.534]
One free state advantage	0.294 [0.201, 0.406]	0.466 [0.347, 0.589]
Three free state advantage	0.349 [0.238, 0.486]	0.526 [0.384, 0.662]
Value for party strength	Maj. Party Senator	Min. Party Senator
Baseline prob. for party strength variables	0.268 [0.179, 0.380]	0.485 [0.383, 0.587]
One std. dev. increase in maj. party strength	0.211 [0.140, 0.304]	0.652 [0.545, 0.746]
One std. dev. increase in min. party strength	0.207 [0.135, 0.301]	0.570 [0.454, 0.672]
Other variables		
One std. dev. increase in median dev. (1st dim.)	0.301 [0.204, 0.415]	
One std. dev. increase in median dev. (2nd dim.)	0.288 [0.195, 0.401]	
Anti-Jackson senator	0.163 [0.106, 0.240]	
"Other" party senator	0.141 [0.086, 0.219]	

Note: The results are based on 5,000 simulations of the coefficient vector from the extended beta binomial model. The simulated probability is the median of the distribution of the simulations, and the bounds of the confidence interval (in brackets) are the .025 and .975 percentiles.

are both around 10% less likely to support obstruction by a southerner, relative to Federalists (the upper left cell of Table 7.7 serves as the baseline).

Tables 7.8 and 7.9 report the results for support of obstruction of non-slavery-related measures. The free state advantage variable and its interaction with the slave state indicator both have statistically significant coefficients, but the coefficient for the latter is negative, indicating that slave state senators were less likely to support non-slavery-related obstruction when they were at a numerical disadvantage. This is consistent with our arguments about salience, in that it suggests southerners were making something of a trade-off across issues in deciding when to obstruct: when at a numerical disadvantage, they obstructed slavery-related legislation at an increasing rate, while refraining from obstructing other legislation. All of the party variables have coefficients bounded away from zero. The marginal effects for these variables indicate that minority party members were always more likely to support obstruction than were their majority party counterparts. Minority party members were even more likely to support obstruction as either majority party or minority party strength increased (about 11 and 6 percentage points, respectively). Both of the median distance variables have statistically significant effects, as do the indicators for Whig, Jacksonian, and "other" senators. An increase of one standard deviation on the first or second NOMINATE dimensions led to approximately 8 and 4 percentage point increases in support for obstruction, respectively. A member of the Whig party was about 16% more likely to support obstruction, while Jacksonian and "other" senators were about 13% more likely.

To summarize the results, sectional factors predict the use of and support for dilatory tactics on slavery-related legislation in a manner consonant with the theoretical approach presented in Chapter 2. As expected, section did not have effects for the use of dilatory motions on legislation not related to slavery, and we found that southerners decreased their support for dilatory motions on this kind of legislation when they were in the minority. The sectional variables had consistent and sensible effects across the different models and samples considered. Partisan factors are also predictors of the usage and support for obstruction on both kinds of legislation examined, but these effects did not trump those found for the sectional variables. General indicators of party affiliation also helped to explain variation in obstruction in a few instances. Ideological distance mattered for use of obstruction against non-slavery-related legislation and for support of obstruction for both kinds of legislation. Workload had effects only on the use of dilatory tactics for non-slavery legislation, although the lack of robust results for this variable may be due to the difficulty of measuring workload accurately.

7.5 CONCLUSION

This chapter has sought to further our understanding of parliamentary obstruction by considering what factors would lead a legislator to obstruct

Table 7.8 Factors Affecting Senators' Support for Obstruction of Legislation
Not Related to Slavery

Variable	Coefficient Estimate	Standard Error	p value
Constant	0.131	0.515	0.799
Slave state senator	0.084	0.076	0.269
Free state advantage	0.158	0.058	0.006
Slave state senator × free state advantage	−0.212	0.075	0.005
Min. party senator	−5.270	0.616	0.000
Maj. party strength	−3.284	1.053	0.002
Min. party strength	−3.759	1.017	0.000
Min. party senator × maj. party strength	12.100	1.759	0.000
Min. party senator × min. party strength	7.843	1.541	0.000
Deviation from median on dimension 1	1.260	0.182	0.000
Deviation from median on dimension 2	0.309	0.108	0.004
Workload	−0.263	0.235	0.264
Democrat	0.073	0.217	0.736
Whig	0.696	0.217	0.001
Republican	0.153	0.139	0.271
Jacksonian	0.487	0.255	0.056
Anti-Jackson	0.306	0.229	0.182
Other	0.456	0.226	0.044
γ	0.180	0.018	0.000
ϕ	0.153	0.018	0.000

Notes: Table entries are maximum likelihood estimates. The dependent
variable is support for motions made by slave state senators.
Number of observations = 1265.
Log-likelihood = −5055.471. Likelihood Ratio χ^2 = 1057.73 ($p < .001$).
Likelihood ratio test of $\phi = 0$: χ^2 = 291.40 ($p < .001$).

Table 7.9 Simulated Probabilities of Support for Obstruction of Legislation Not Related to Slavery

Free/Slave State Split	Free State Senator	Slave State Senator
Parity between free and slave states	0.285 [0.205, 0.382]	0.302 [0.219, 0.403]
One slave state advantage	0.254 [0.172, 0.358]	0.313 [0.223, 0.423]
One free state advantage	0.318 [0.236, 0.409]	0.291 [0.212, 0.387]
Three free state advantage	0.390 [0.294, 0.494]	0.270 [0.183, 0.376]
Value for party strength	Maj. Party Senator	Min. Party Senator
Baseline prob. for party strength variables	0.302 [0.219, 0.403]	0.337 [0.256, 0.433]
One std. dev. increase in maj. party strength	0.267 [0.191, 0.363]	0.447 [0.354, 0.546]
One std. dev. increase in min. party strength	0.254 [0.181, 0.346]	0.399 [0.301, 0.508]
Other variables		
One std. dev. increase in median dev. (1st dim.)	0.370 [0.278, 0.480]	
One std. dev. increase in median dev. (2nd dim.)	0.324 [0.237, 0.430]	
Whig senator	0.465 [0.399, 0.532]	
Jacksonian senator	0.413 [0.360, 0.469]	
"Other" party senator	0.407 [0.328, 0.491]	

Note: See notes to Table 7.7 for details on table entries.

rather than simply vote against legislation he opposes. We posited that in the antebellum Senate, the overwhelming salience of the issue of slavery to southern members would make them more likely to obstruct as they became a smaller minority in the chamber. We also considered how ideological extremism figured into dilatory strategies. These theoretical considerations were placed alongside partisan-based models, which have been applied previously at the aggregate level to examine obstruction. We found that both sectional and partisan factors explain antebellum obstruction, with the former being especially relevant for understanding obstruction aimed at legislation related to slavery. This emphasizes how different policy areas can produce minorities that do not fall along partisan lines. While sectional factors are widely accepted as playing an important role in filibusters of the 20th century, this analysis demonstrates the systematic influence of these factors during a much earlier period.

In 1949, V. O. Key wrote in *Southern Politics in State and Nation* that southerners were "justifiably proud of the technical virtuosity of their politicians" because, though "the South lost the crucial battles . . . its politicians won The [Civil] War—at least for three-quarters of a century." Although Key did not live to see it, the passage of the Civil Rights Act of 1964 and the Voting Rights Act of 1965 meant that southerners had held out against the cause of racial equality for nearly one hundred years after Appomattox. They did so in part by employing a "strategy of obstruction," providing "an instructive illustration" of the significant negative power of "cohesive and determined minorities" (Key 1949, 317). The quantitative evidence presented in this chapter suggests that at least one factor contributing to their success was that their senatorial ancestors had developed and honed the tools of parliamentary obstruction in the antebellum period, lending the weight of history to the effectiveness of the strategy of exploiting the Senate's unique rules of debate for maintaining a southern social and economic order based on racial subjugation.

Nonetheless, it does not appear that obstruction was a viable strategy for protecting southern interests in slavery for the long term. As the case of the Oregon Territory Bill suggests (see Chapter 1), even when legislation directly touched upon the sectional balance of power, minority obstruction was often limited by norms of restraint. In that case, southerners used dilatory motions to delay passage, yet ultimately allowed the bill to pass when it became clear that a committed majority favored the legislation. While such norms would almost surely not have been strong enough to lead southerners to relent when confronted with a bill directly curbing slavery, southerners had good reason to believe that they would not have prevailed in such a fight if confronted by an intense free-state majority. Ultimately, southerners chose to secede rather than pursuing solutions through existing democratic institutions. Their fears about democratic solutions were well founded since existing institutions—which did afford them protections as a minority—could have been changed in ways that would have led to the passage of legislation to curtail and eventually end slavery. When the issue became equally salient for non-southerners, the pressure would have been tremendous to change the rules in ways that would have undercut the effectiveness of dilatory tactics, just as pressure built when non-southerners found that they could no longer ignore the civil and voting rights abuses of Jim Crow.

Chapter Eight

Obstruction and Institutional Change

8.1 INTRODUCTION

While our analysis of coalition sizes in the pre- and post-cloture periods in previous chapters provides important answers to questions about lawmaking in the Senate, it also raises several puzzles, especially about the motivation for and impact of cloture reform. Most notably, if slim majorities could generally pass legislation prior to 1917, why did senators bother to adopt a cloture rule that would require coalitions to be *larger* than was typically necessary at the time? Historians and political scientists have a poor understanding of the practical importance of this landmark reform, and several competing conventional wisdoms exist regarding the reasons for the adoption of cloture.

In this chapter, we investigate the question of why cloture reform happened when it did, while the impact of the reform is addressed in Chapters 9 and 10. While many believe that cloture reform was attributable to the overwhelming public outcry against the filibuster that killed the Armed-Ship Bill in the 64th Congress, this intuitively appealing explanation does not seem to be the whole story. The Armed-Ship Bill filibuster was not the first occasion that the public became incensed about obstruction of popular measures. Why was public opinion at this time so influential on the chamber specifically designed to be the more immune to these kind of inflamed passions?[1] If public opinion was responsible for the change, how were voters fooled into accepting an allegedly toothless reform, especially if, as Burdette (1940) claims, filibusters continued virtually unabated?

Understanding the many complexities of cloture reform requires taking into consideration the general political and institutional environment of the early-20th century, focusing on changes that might have undermined relation-based legislating. Particular changes in the environment occurred that might have led to the failure of existing informal constraints on behavior, prompting moves to adopt formal rules. As senators began to use the filibuster more aggressively to kill legislation—particularly capitalizing on the end-of-congress deadline—demand for an explicit, formal mechanism to limit debate grew. The theory presented in Chapter 2 provides comparative statics predictions that identify how changes in context would have affected

---

[1] A nearly identical reform was considered in 1916, but did not come to a vote. Koger (2002) examines votes related to this case.

the Senate's ability to continue to rely upon informal norms to regulate obstruction. One of our main focuses is on reforms providing for the direct election of senators, which might have affected both the incentives senators had to obey norms against exploiting individual prerogatives as well as the responsiveness of senators to demands for institutional reform.

We consider the relationship between incidents of obstruction, turnover, stability, workload, and chamber size, weighing how these different factors affect relational legislating. We argue that the cooperative system in which senators were restrained in their use of obstruction broke down as the institutional milieu changed around the turn of the century. Rising chamber size, turnover, and workload all had the potential to make the Senate a less close-knit body and increase the temptation for individual senators to fully exercise their prerogatives. We argue that these changes undermined the cooperative, relation-based equilibrium and increased the incentive to shift toward more formal, rule-based operations. Examining such variation provides leverage for assessing our arguments about the importance of informal conventions. While arguments based on norms can often be ambiguous, this kind of comparative statics analysis provides crisper tests of our arguments because of our institutionally grounded claims concerning variation in the impact of norms.

8.2 CHANGES IN THE POLITICAL AND INSTITUTIONAL ENVIRONMENT

In Chapter 2, we discussed the features of the Senate that enabled the chamber to function under relational legislating. A relatively small membership, six-year terms, and overlapping cohorts provided the kind of durability and stability to intra-Senate relationships that would have been necessary for a heavy reliance on informal constraints to be viable. As the evidence from previous chapters makes clear, senators were able to cooperate legislatively to a remarkable degree prior to the 20th century even though the absence of formal constraints granted extensive individual prerogatives. There appears to have been a system of generally accepted informal conventions, which—in conjunction with threats to change the rules themselves—made the Senate more or less a majoritarian body.

However, there is evidence that this system started to break down around the turn of the century. According to Burdette (1940, 79–80),

> Filibustering had now quite clearly assumed astounding proportions in the Senate. In the last two decades of the nineteenth century storms of obstruction had swept the chamber. . . . [I]t was the heyday of brazen and unblushing aggressors. . . . The premium rested not upon ability and statesmanship but upon effrontery and audacity.

This account makes clear that not only was filibustering increasing in amount and scope, but that long-standing conventions of the Senate had begun to erode. Binder and Smith (1997, 69–70) argue that "any norm of restraint that had flourished in the early Senate was severely strained by the end of the century." This erosion had an effect on the legitimacy of the institution:

> During the Gilded Age—the era of its greatest power—the Senate sunk from the heights of public esteem to the depths. Its inertia was a subject of public ridicule—"The Senate does about as much in a week as a set of men in business would do in half an hour," one newspaper correspondent wrote—as was the corruption that infected it. And it was the subject of public anger. (Caro 2002, 33)

Frustration with the Senate was particularly acute during the filibuster of the bill to repeal the Sherman Silver Purchase Law in 1893. The *New York Times* reprinted several editorials from both Democratic and Republican newspapers throughout the country criticizing what they deemed to be a dysfunctional Senate ("Let the Majority Rule," October 21, 1893, p. 4). The *St. Louis Republic* claimed that "[t]he Senate is lower in the opinion of the Nation than is good for either the Senate or the Nation." The *Detroit Free Press* even went so far as to call for the "abolition" of the Senate:

> Its usefulness has long been seriously questioned, but it has not been regarded heretofore as hostile to the spirit of our institutions. The adoption of a compromise as a concession to a beggarly minority will settle its position in that regard and show that it is dangerous instead of useless. And when that is shown the Senate must go.

Standard counts of filibusters indicate that their frequency was increasing around the turn of the century, providing quantitative support for the perception that obstruction was getting worse. Figure 8.1 displays a plot of the number of filibusters in the Senate in the 1st through 79th Congresses.[2] Although the number of filibusters pales in comparison to today's Senate, the dramatic increase in obstruction at the turn of the century alarmed observers. The infrequency of filibusters and their low success rate in the 19th century appears to have led to great hue and cry when they were used successfully. Precisely because senators had not used filibusters to derail legislation that often, when they did pursue this option, it led to outrage at the perceived subversion of majority rule.

In the 63rd Congress (1913–1915), seven filibusters occurred, which by conventional counts set a record for the number of filibusters in a single congress in the pre-cloture period. The discussion in Burdette (1940, 95–103) indicates that the nature of much of this obstruction had implications

---

[2]Again, we remind readers of the limitations of the data on filibusters. In this chapter, we rely upon Beth's (1994) count of filibusters rather than on the incidents of obstruction identified by examining dilatory motions (see Chapter 5). Recall that dilatory motions became a less useful indicator of obstruction by the late-19th century, as precedents limited their usefulness and bill opponents shifted tactics to rely more upon long speeches and less upon obstructive motions.

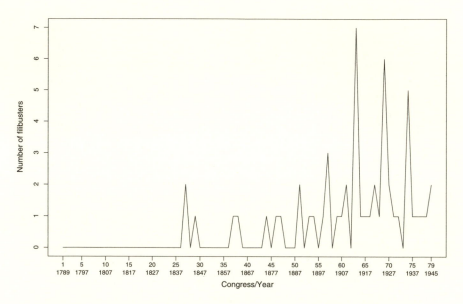

Figure 8.1 Filibusters in the Senate, 1st–79th Congress (1789–1946)

for beliefs about Senate norms. The 1912 elections had given the Democrats unified control of the government, with a 51-44 seat majority in the Senate. This was the first time the Democrats had a majority in the Senate since the 53rd Congress (1893–1895) and only the third time they controlled the chamber since the Civil War. Although Burdette (1940, 95) claims that "[f]ilibustering against major issues was not the program of the Republican minority," his description of the filibusters and newspaper reports indicate that Republicans were behind most of the obstruction that occurred.[3] This raised the possibility that Republicans were violating a norm of reciprocity by inhibiting the Democrats from taking advantage of unified control to enact their agenda. This contrasted with past experience, in which the minority party typically obstructed only a small portion of the majority party's program.[4]

During a prolonged Republican filibuster of a rivers and harbors bill, the consternation of Democrats became apparent in a flip-flop on the establishment of a precedent that would have imposed a severe limit on debate. On

---

[3]For those instances where Burdette is not specific about the source of the obstruction, see "May Not Try to Ban Unfair Practices," *New York Times*, July 29, 1914, p. 9; "Will Delay Trade Bill," *New York Times*, July 9, 1914, p. 1; "Wants Tolls Issue Put Up To People," *New York Times*, May 3, 1914, p. 10; "Blocks Agreement To Vote On Tolls," *New York Times*, May 21, 1914, p. 10. Two of the seven filibusters appear to have been led by Democrats.

[4]For example, Democrats seriously obstructed only the federal elections bill in 1890, allowing the rest of the GOP's ambitious program to pass the Senate.

September 17, a majority voted 28-24 to establish a precedent that would have required unanimous consent for a senator to yield to other senators for any purpose, including yielding for a question. This decision would have eliminated the respites that filibustering senators took when sympathetic colleagues would query them at length about the issue under debate. But it also would have severely hampered substantive informational exchanges between senators on the floor. The following day, the Senate reversed itself on a vote of 15-35, with ten Democrats switching their votes to oppose the precedent (Burdette 1940, 97–99; Koger 2002, 231–32).[5]

An indicator of the growing frustration that the increasing frequency and potency of filibusters caused is the amount of interest in changing the rules that existed at this time. The more obstruction is seen as problematic, the more likely senators will embrace moves toward formal limitations on this behavior. Data on attempts to change the rules reveal that such an increase did occur around the turn of the century. Figure 8.2 reports a time series of attempts to change the rules from 1789 to 1946. Included in these counts are efforts to limit obstructionist tactics—either through the introduction of resolutions or through the establishment of precedents—that were intended to be permanent. Thus, for example, the five minute limit on debate in secret sessions relating to the Civil War that was adopted in 1862 is not included in these counts, since it expired with the end of the rebellion.[6] While the data give us only a rough sense of the desire for change since the counts do not account for the severity of the proposed innovations, the data do indicate that there were two periods when the Senate saw substantial increases in attempts to modify the rules. The first started in the 1870s and continued until the mid-1890s. After a lull in attempts at the very beginning of the 20th century, they picked up again as the Senate moved into the 1910s. These efforts to impose more formal restrictions on debate indicate that at least some senators thought the informal constraints were no longer doing an adequate job. In several cases, the specific filibusters that provoked the threats to change the rules failed in the end, thus obviating the need to actually enact the rules changes. But by the early 1910s—as noted by Burdette and others—filibusters were now killing more legislation, suggesting that *threats* of rules changes would need to be backed up by their actual implementation.

The theory discussed in Section 2.6 predicts this kind of unraveling would occur if the incentives for obeying informal conventions decrease, which

---

[5] Although the Democrats chose to rescind the precedent, their ability to use a narrow majority vote to change the long-standing precedent regarding yielding for questions again points to the ability of a determined majority to use new precedents to crack down on obstruction.

[6] The source for these data is U.S. Congress. Senate. Committee on Rules and Administration (1985), which indexes the data by years rather than congresses. In some cases, the committee print was not specific about the year in which certain proposals were made, but instead gave an aggregate number for a range of years. We distributed these cases evenly over the period given. Other judgment calls were necessary regarding the extent to which a proposal would have lasting impact.

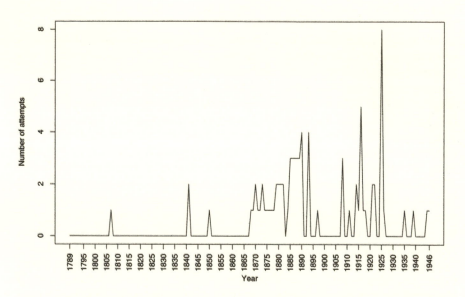

Figure 8.2 Time Series of Attempts to Limit Debate in the Senate (1789–1946)

would in turn prompt attempts to change the institution. If those threats do not sufficiently deter obstructionists, then actual rules changes will eventually result. What factors would have changed the tendency to defect from the cooperative norm, such that it would have led senators to seek more formal rules to constrain their behavior? A decline in the "close-knittedness" of the Senate would have reduced the communication among senators that had promoted cooperation. As argued in Chapter 2, the primary cause of the breakdown of a relation-based system is an increase in the size of the group. As more members join the group, interpersonal relations decline along with the communication among members regarding adherence to informal conventions that undergird the system.

Around the turn of the century, the Senate experienced a surge in its size, which our theory predicts would have reduced the effectiveness of informal constraints. Figure 8.3 displays a time series of the total number of senators in the institution from the 41st to the 79th Congress (1871–1946).[7] The size of the Senate increased considerably at the end of the 19th century, with the admission of North and South Dakota, Montana, and Washington in November 1889 and Idaho and Wyoming in July 1890. All of the senators from these states began serving in the 51st Congress (1889–1891). Four more states—Utah, Oklahoma, New Mexico, and Arizona—were added between 1896 and 1912. This meant that the Senate expanded by 30% in twenty

---

[7]This period begins after the readmission to the Union of all of the southern states that had seceded.

years, which was one of the largest expansions in a period of this length in the Senate's history and marked the last significant increase in the membership of the institution.

The substantial influx of new senators would have produced a decline of interpersonal relations and communication in the chamber, making it harder to convey shared beliefs about how the system worked. Senators expressed concern about how the size of the Senate was creating problems for the reliance on lax rules regarding debate. For example, during the Elections Bill fight, George Edmunds (R–VT) observed that "with a Senate of more than eighty members" it was clear that the chamber now required a rule allowing the majority to end debate ("The Senate's New Rule," *Washington Post*, December 28, 1890, p. 1). Similarly, an editorial reprinted in the *Washington Post* stated that "Republicans know the fact that Democrats as well as Republicans realize the necessity, in view of the present size of the Senate, of having some means of putting a limit upon debate. The old rule which allowed unlimited debate was good enough half a century ago, when the Senate was only about half its present size; but now, when the Senate numbers eighty-eight members, it is deemed utterly impracticable to permit debate to go on without limit or hindrance" ("Cloture in the Senate," December 28, 1890, p. 4).[8]

Just four years later, Democrat George Vest (D–MO) emphasized the Senate's increased size in arguing for a cloture rule. Vest noted that when he came to the Senate in 1879, there were seventy-six senators:

> It now consists of eighty-eight, with the certainty that in a very few weeks it will be increased to ninety-two, and the probability, almost a certainty, that in the near future it will be increased to ninety-eight. . . . This is a most significant fact as demonstrating not only the increase of the number of Senators, but the vast increase of the adverse and conflicting interests of the whole country. When there were in the Senate but forty or fifty or sixty Senators, adjustment of public questions was comparatively easy. The social intercourse and friendly relations which existed among that number of Senators also largely facilitated the absence of friction and the antagonism and attrition that come even from partisan conflict. But the country has vastly increased. We will soon have, as I have said, nearly one hundred members in this body. The statement of that fact it seems to me is convincing that there must be a change in our rules so that the interests of the immense domain which we are here representing can be adjusted to a finality and not put under the control of a minority of this body, even of a factional few much less than a respectable minority. (*Congressional Record*, December 5, 1894, p. 45)

---

[8] During the filibuster of the silver repeal bill in 1893, Senator John Sherman (R–OH) cited exactly the same rationale for his support for cloture reform (*Congressional Record*, October 17, p. 2596).

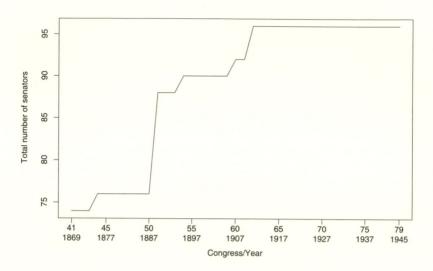

Figure 8.3 Size of the Senate, 41st–80th Congress (1871–1948)

Vest concluded the most serious objection to the rules and resulting filibusters was that "they have brought the Senate of the United States into
disrepute and have destroyed its influence" (p. 46).

Another trend that began around the turn of the century that would have
affected senators' interactions concerns attendance in the chamber. Poole
and Rosenthal (1997, 218–19) note that prolonged absences from the Senate
chamber (as measured by absences on consecutive roll call votes) increased
from the 45th to the 60th Congress (1877–1909), such that "by the 60th
Congress, representatives were missing chunks of votes as large as those
missed a century earlier." They attribute this pattern to changes in transportation technology rather than to changes in institutions, based on the
high correlation between House and Senate abstention rates. For our argument, the key point is that in the latter half of the 19th and early part of
the 20th centuries, senators were frequently absent from the chamber and
presumably from Washington, which would mean less interaction and less
communication with their colleagues.

The Senate also experienced heightened turnover in the early-20th century,
which would have presented challenges to the maintenance of relational legislating. The last two decades of the 19th century saw significant stability in
the chamber's membership, with Senate careerism taking root in the 1880s
(Stewart 1992, 74). Senate membership during this time was much more
stable than that of the House. This changed, however, with the beginning of
the new century. Figure 8.4 shows the percentage of freshman in the Senate
during this period. As Stewart (1992, 74) has pointed out, "Senate elec-

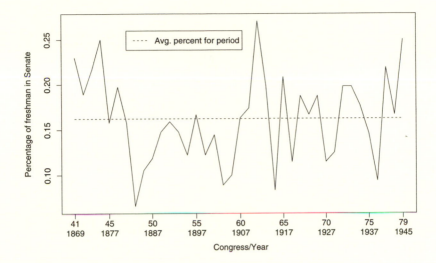

Figure 8.4 Percentage of Freshmen in the Senate, 41st–80th Congress (1871–1948)

tions between 1906 and 1912 produced higher-than-average turnovers in the chamber." The 62nd Congress (1911–1913) set a record for the percentage of freshman in the chamber in the period between the end of the Civil War and World War II, with 27% of senators serving in their first congress. The instability associated with higher turnover, exacerbated by the expansion of the chamber, would have been especially problematic for the informal conventions that helped to keep obstruction in check previously. Heightened turnover would have decreased senators' expectations about the likelihood of remaining in the chamber, increasing senators' discount rate for the future and thus making them more willing to risk an eventual shift to more formal rules in exchange for an immediate gain through unrestrained obstruction. An increase in turnover and an increase in size would have had an interactive effect, as new senators—not just from recently admitted states—would have had less personal interaction with their colleagues than had been typical in previous congresses. This would have made it difficult to effectively communicate the importance of cooperative norms, placing a severe strain on relation-based legislating.

An influx of senators who had served in the House could also have undercut relation-based legislating. House members were socialized in a very different institutional context than senators. Formal rules played a much more significant role than informal conventions in governing floor debate in the House. They may have had difficulty making the adjustment to the relation-based environment of the Senate and the freedom from constraints on debate that members of that chamber enjoyed. This is consistent with Dixit's (2004,

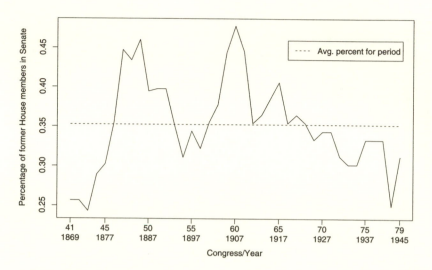

Figure 8.5 Percentage of Former House Members in the Senate, 41st–80th Congress (1871–1948)

84) arguments about clashes that can result when individuals from relation-based and rules-based systems begin to interact.[9] It is a common complaint in the contemporary Senate that senators who were socialized in the House bring with them "a political philosophy that disregards time-honored Senate rules designed to counter the majoritarian House and protect the minority party as well as the individual senator" (Allison Stevens, "Senators Pack a Sharper Edge," *CQ Weekly*, December 13, 2003, p. 3069).[10]

Figure 8.5 shows that in the final fifteen years of the pre-cloture period the percentage of senators who were former House members generally exceeded the average for the 41st–79th Congresses. The 58th through the 65th Congress all had higher than average percentages of members who came from the other chamber. Figure 8.6 indicates that freshman senators during these congresses were more likely to come from the House than was typical prior to World War II.

It is also worth noting that some argue that changes in the leadership of the Senate took place that may have further undercut the viability of

---

[9]This does not necessarily mean that former House members would tend to engage in obstruction more. But if they generally did not support the informal infrastructure or had difficulty establishing relationships necessary for success in legislative endeavors, it would weaken the system's effectiveness for all senators.

[10]Former Senator Alan Simpson (R–WY) recently summed up this argument: "So many House members have come to the Senate and brought the poison with them, and we haven't found the antidote yet. The rancor, the dissension, the disgusting harsh level came from those House members who came to the Senate. They brought it with 'em. That's where it began" (quoted in Stevens, "Senators Pack a Sharper Edge").

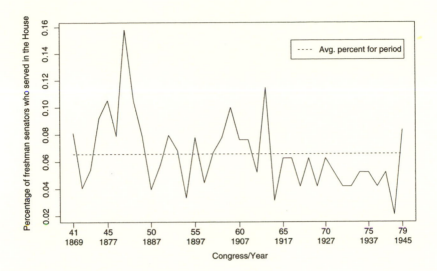

Figure 8.6 Percentage of Freshman Senators who Served in the House, 41st–80th Congress (1871–1948)

relation-based legislating. Beginning in the mid-1890s, a group of Republican leaders emerged who worked to provide a degree of organizational order that had previously been lacking in the chamber. "The Senate Four," as the group was known, consisted of Senators Nelson Aldrich, William Allison, Orville Platt, and John Spooner (R–WI). These individuals used their formal positions in the institution, mostly as committee chairs and working through the Republican steering committee, to direct the agenda-setting process (Gamm and Smith 2002a; Keller 1977, 303–4; Rothman 1966). The mid-1890s to the middle of the first decade of the 20th century is considered a high point of leadership influence in the Senate's history. After the first decade of the 20th century, however, the Senate Four no longer held sway as deaths and retirements ended the group's long reign. The loss of strong leaders and the coordinating services they provided would have made the Senate floor a more chaotic place and the chamber more vulnerable to obstruction. Although formal floor leadership positions emerged in the Senate at this time, the occupants of these positions evidently wielded less effective influence than had the Senate Four.[11]

The changes in the external political environment would have also increased the temptation to defect from anti-obstruction norms. The dramatic changes brought on by the industrial revolution and the concomitant increase in societal complexity taxed the capacity of Congress as new de-

---

[11]It is difficult to tell if the decrease in party unity that occurred in the Senate at this time was due to the absence of strong leaders or whether decreasing party unity prevented leaders from having much of an impact.

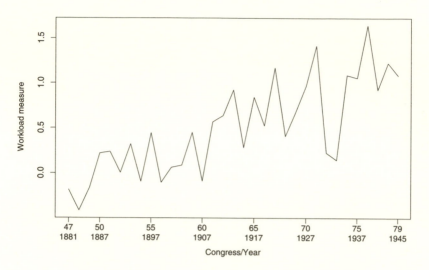

Figure 8.7 Workload in the Senate, 47th–79th Congress

mands were placed on governing institutions (Keller 1977, 300–1; Gilligan and Krehbiel 1987, 326). As the national government grew tremendously in size and responsibilities at the turn of the century, the chamber's legislative agenda expanded. Binder and Smith (1997, 66–67) note the significant increase in the workload of the Senate, as its agenda mushroomed to address these demands (see Figure 8.7 for a plot of Binder's [1997] workload measure). The increase in the Senate's size reinforced this trend of increasing workload in the chamber. As more senators entered the Senate, each with his own legislative goals and priorities, demand for scarce floor time increased. Binder and Smith contend that obstruction "was significantly easier and more effective in a policy-making environment in which Senate leaders had a sizable unfinished agenda at stake." Disobeying existing norms would have become increasingly profitable—and thus more and more tempting—as the majority's ability to tolerate delay declined.

All of these factors would have made a move to formal rules governing debate more appealing to senators. In order to investigate the influence of these factors more systematically, we estimated a count model where the dependent variable is the number of attempts to change the rules in a way that would limit debate that occurred in a given congress. This variable was compiled from the list of such attempts included in the committee print on the Senate cloture rule (U.S. Congress. Senate. Committee on Rules and Administration 1985; see n. 6). The number of attempts to change the rules is a good indicator of the degree to which senators believed informal conventions were no longer working and that a move to more formal rules was warranted. The explanatory variables included in this model are the size of the Senate (measured as the number of seats), the percentage of freshman, the percentage of freshman who served in the House, Senate workload, and Binder's measure of majority and minority party strength. Binder's theory (1997) of the expansion and contraction of minority rights suggests that these latter variables should be included in the specification, although her quantitative analysis of rules changes in the Senate does not find effects for these variables (see 171–76). In order to allay concerns that any effects for size might be due to increased ideological diversity brought on by the admission of new states, we include variables measuring the standard deviation of DW-NOMINATE scores for the first and second dimensions. We also include a trend variable in order to avoid making spurious inferences due to upward trends in attempts to change the rules.

Descriptive statistics for this analysis appear in Table 8.1 and the results from the estimation of a negative binomial model appear in Table 8.2.[12] The key variable that we expect to see effects for—chamber size—has a statistically significant and positive coefficient. The addition of two new senators through the admission of a new state to the Union produces an increase in the expected count of attempts to change the rules by approximately 19% (with 95% confidence bounds [3%, 38%]). In the case where four states were admitted within a year, which is what happened with North and South Dakota, Montana, and Washington, the expected count would increase by approximately 102% [12%, 258%].

The workload measure also has a coefficient that is bounded away from zero with a 90% confidence interval. A one standard deviation increase in this variable gives about a 106% increase in the expected count of attempts to change the rules (with a wide 90% confidence interval of [3%, 311%]). The measure of minority party strength also has a statistically significant effect, the magnitude of which is a 60% increase in the expected count for a one standard deviation change in this variable (the confidence bounds are [10%, 135%]). The measure of ideological deviation and the trend variable both have statistically significant and negative coefficients, which is contrary to what we anticipated for these variables. The other variables in the model do not have coefficients that are bounded away from zero. This analysis confirms that Senate size seems to be the key to the unraveling of relational legislating. As the Senate began a period of marked growth in size starting in 1889 and as it strained under its expanding workload, norms constraining obstruction were undermined. As filibusters became a more severe threat to legislation with wide support, this led to increased threats to change the rules. When these threats proved insufficient to deter obstructionists, the Senate resorted to more formal rules limiting debate.[13]

---

[12]Tests for overdispersion indicated that a Poisson model was inappropriate for these data. Given the number of zero observations for the dependent variable, we also performed a Vuong test of the standard negative binomial model against a zero-inflated version. The test did not indicate that a zero-inflated model was more appropriate.

[13]We estimated a similar model in which the dependent variable was the number of filibusters that occurred in a given congress. The results on the size variable were essentially the same, while the effects of other variables were not as robust.

Table 8.1 Descriptive Statistics for Analysis of Attempts to Limit Debate, 1st–79th Congress (1789–1946)

Variable	Mean	Median	Std. Dev.	Min.	Max.
Count of attempts to limit debate	0.513	0.000	1.116	0.000	8.000
Size of Senate	66.924	66.000	23.828	24.000	96.000
Percentage freshman	0.197	0.184	0.118	0.066	1.077
Percentage freshman from House	0.092	0.079	0.057	0.000	0.324
Workload	−0.342	−0.500	0.849	−1.592	1.645
Maj. party strength	0.344	0.338	0.069	0.204	0.540
Min. party strength	0.231	0.236	0.071	0.104	0.408
NOMINATE std. dev. (1st Dim.)	0.420	0.420	0.061	0.248	0.579
NOMINATE std. dev. (2d Dim.)	0.576	0.572	0.044	0.489	0.687

Note: N = 158.

Table 8.2 Analysis of Attempts to Limit Debate, 1st–79th Congress (1789–1946)

Variable	Coefficient	Std. Err.	p value
Constant	90.004	49.014	0.066
Size of Senate	0.087	0.037	0.019
Percentage freshman	1.995	1.407	0.156
Percentage freshman from House	−2.533	4.300	0.556
Workload	0.842	0.502	0.093
Maj. party strength	−2.838	2.480	0.253
Min. party strength	6.660	2.711	0.014
NOMINATE std. dev. (1st Dim.)	−1.062	5.302	0.841
NOMINATE std. dev. (2d Dim.)	−13.948	4.930	0.005
Trend	−0.048	0.026	0.072
Gamma	−0.202	0.561	0.719
Log-likelihood	−85.49		
Likelihood ratio test	45.58	$(p < .001)$	

Note: $N = 158$.

8.3 DIRECT ELECTION

The Senate experienced another landmark institutional change during this period: the move from indirect to direct election of senators, provided for by ratification of the 17th Amendment in 1913. In assessing the sources of cloture reform, it is important to understand fully what direct election did and did not do. The small body of research that has examined the effects of direct election has produced conflicting results. Some contend it had minimal to no effect (Brady, Brody, and Epstein 1989; Haynes 1938; Merriam and Overacker 1928; Riker 1955). Other work indicates that the Senate became more similar to the House as a result of the 17th Amendment (Crook and Hibbing 1997;Lapinski 2000a; Stewart 1992).

We examine several ways that direct election might have mattered for obstruction, and in doing so, fill in some considerable gaps in the congressional literature. Our examination falls into two categories. First, we investigate whether direct election made it more difficult to sustain relational legislating. At first glance, it appears plausible that direct election, by making senators more attentive to the general public and thus less likely to be focused on intra-institutional norms, undermined relational legislating and therefore is responsible for the shift to formal rules limiting debate. However, we show below that there is little support for the notion that direct election, on its own, was responsible for the breakdown of norms constraining obstruction.

Second, we assess whether direct election affected preferences in such a way as to make senators more interested in changing rules regarding debate. Specifically, direct election might have made senators more responsive to popular demands to change the rules. Some have claimed that the reason the Senate stubbornly stuck to rules that appeared antiquated for a "modern" legislature was that the mode of selection of senators had created too much of a buffer between a public often incensed about obstruction and their senators who, because of the protection afforded by state legislatures, felt no need to change their rules despite alleged problems.

Along these lines, Dion (1997) argues that direct election was the reason senators responded the way they did to the public outcry against filibusters in 1917. However, Dion does not attempt to test this conjecture systematically. Indeed, an examination of the actual debate that led to the rules change, including analysis of roll calls on the change, would not be terribly revealing, since the proposal provoked surprisingly little debate and was approved 76-3. And it would be difficult to parse the change to direct election from other major changes and events that took place at approximately the same time, including the creation of formal floor leadership positions (Gamm and Smith 2002a).

If direct election led to cloture reform, one would expect to see evidence that it either directly undermined relation-based legislating–through increased turnover, for example–or that it changed senators' voting behavior in ways that would indicate senators were forced to be more responsive to their constituents. In the sections below, we examine a range of indicators that aim to tease out the impact of direct election. But the results provide little support for the notion that the two landmark reforms of this era were closely related to one another.

8.3.1 Direct Election and Turnover

Did direct election lead to instability in terms of increased turnover? When one considers that elections of senators by state legislators were often volatile affairs, the answer is not obvious. Far from being a smooth process where political elites conspired and easily reached consensus in choosing whom to send to Washington, Haynes (1906) points out that these contests were often plagued by prolonged balloting that sometimes lasted several weeks, deadlocks where a decision could not be reached, and in some cases even violence.[14] It was common for the selection process to appear chaotic—in the social choice sense—producing winners who were not even candidates on early ballots. Hence, the volatility that often accompanied state legislatures' selection of senators may not have produced more membership stability than direct elections.

Nonetheless, Crook and Hibbing (1997) give the impression that the reform did produce greater turnover, pointing out that in the ninety-six cases

---

[14]See also Schiller and Stewart (2004).

where direct election of senators occurred between 1908 and 1918, 44% of the incumbents in seats subject to direct election did not return to the Senate.[15] From this they conclude that "[c]learly, a large portion of the indirectly elected Senate was not prepared to cope with direct election" (849).

However, a closer comparison of directly and indirectly elected senators indicates that direct election did not cause particular electoral difficulty for senators. Table 8.3, which reports the results of our analysis, shows that our numbers for turnover rates where direct elections took place are very similar to Crook and Hibbing's original analysis, although we found 101 cases as opposed to 96.[16] Fifty-nine percent of these individuals were reelected, while 41% either lost their bid for reelection or did not pursue such a bid. We find a serious discrepancy, however, in the comparison with cases where incumbents were not confronted with direct election: 47% were reelected, while 53% did not return to office. Thus, contrary to Crook and Hibbing's claim, incumbents who faced direct election coped with it just fine, experiencing *lower* turnover than those who were indirectly elected (the Pearson Chi-squared statistic for the difference gives a p value of .09). This result seems to be driven in large part by the significant turnover that occurred in the 61st and 62nd Congresses, both of which took place before direct election for all senators began (see Figure 8.4). One could argue that the large number of senators who did not seek reelection in the 62nd Congress (fifteen total) could be due to anticipation of direct elections.[17] However, if these individuals had survived indirect elections during this congress, they would have not had to face whatever problems the new electoral context presented for another six years. Of the twenty-five senators that sought reelection in 1914—the first year where an entire class of senators were subject to direct election—only two were unsuccessful, with one losing in the primary and one losing in the general.[18]

---

[15] According to Riker (1955), direct election reforms were adopted in Nebraska, Nevada, and Oregon prior to the implementation of the 17th Amendment. Engstrom and Kernell (2003) claim that a direct preference vote was adopted in several other states prior to 1914. However, they did not collect data for southern states, and it is not clear whether or not they would have found additional cases there had they done so. Rather than introduce a possible sectional bias, we rely on Riker, as do Crook and Hibbing, for our analysis. Lapinski (2000b) indicates that Arizona adopted a popular vote reform in 1912, but the results are the same whether or not Arizona is added to Riker's list.

[16] We tracked down several senators whose fates were listed as "unknown" by the ICPSR biographical data file (Inter-university Consortium for Political and Social Research and McKibbin 1997), which was the data used by Crook and Hibbing. Of the five individuals we located, four of them were reelected.

[17] Crook and Hibbing claim this number is thirteen. Three of these cases involved short-term appointments where those appointed to fill vacancies created by death or resignation did not seek reelection. If these cases are dropped, the Chi-squared statistic no longer attains statistical significance, leading to the inference that there is no difference between directly and indirectly elected senators. However, the evidence still does not lead to the inference that direct election increased instability.

[18] We also find that the percentage of senator's who did not return to their seats during this period was 15.8, in contrast to the 21.5% figure that Crook and Hibbing provide.

Table 8.3 Contingency Table for Turnover and Direct Elections, 1908–1918

	Turnover		
Direct Election	No	Yes	Total
No	43	48	91
	(47%)	(53%)	(47%)
Yes	60	41	101
	(59%)	(41%)	(53%)
Total	103	89	192

Note: Pearson $\chi_1^2 = 2.843$ ($p = .09$)

Therefore, senators were somewhat less likely to return to office in the few years prior to the implementation of direct election at the national level than following the reform. We should not yet conclude from this that direct election reforms had no impact on senators' likelihood of staying in office. In fact, according to Lapinski (2000b, 196–97), thirty-three of the forty-eight states in the Union had implemented some form of direct control over the selection of senators prior to the 17th Amendment.[19] These reforms—which included direct primaries, voluntary party regulation, and preference votes—may have contributed to the instability in the Senate in the early-20th century.

However, an examination of state-level reforms indicates that this is not the case. We conducted an analysis of turnover from the 47th through the 63rd Congress, the last congress before direct election was instituted at the national level.[20] As reported in Table 8.4, the rate of turnover of Senate seats for this period was only slightly (and insignificantly) higher in those states that adopted some mechanism for popular control of their senators. When a senator was up for reelection, the likelihood that his seat turned over was about 42% in states that did not have any form of popular control versus 45% in states that did (again, not a statistically significant difference). It is important to note that our measure is whether or not the holder of a given Senate seat changed and is not just focused on electoral defeat, since some senators may have strategically retired rather than face the new campaigning difficulties that might have attended popular control. Examining electoral defeat, we find that the proportion of incumbents who were unsuccessful in their reelection bids was 19% for senators from states that had no such controls and 22% for senators from states that did—also not a statistically significant difference.

---

[19]Engstrom and Kernell (2003) report similar figures for non-southern states: twenty-four out of thirty-seven had adopted direct control reforms before 1914.

[20]According to Lapinski (2000b), the first state-level direct election reform was adopted in 1883 by Nevada, which instituted a direct primary. Of the states that adopted some form of popular control, most of them did so between 1900 and 1910.

Table 8.4 Contingency Table for Turnover and State-Level Direct Election Reforms, 1881–1912

Direct Election	Turnover		
	No	Yes	Total
No	231	167	398
	(58%)	(42%)	(79%)
Yes	59	49	108
	(55%)	(45%)	(21%)
Total	290	216	506

If we examine turnover and electoral defeat by Senate election class, we do not see significant differences longitudinally in states with and without popular controls. Figure 8.8 displays time series of the percentage of seats up for reelection in each congress where there was turnover or an electoral defeat. While there appear to be differences between the two kinds of states early in the series, this is due only to the fact that so few states had implemented popular controls during these congresses and the differences are not statistically significant. Toward the end of the series, when a substantial proportion of states had adopted popular controls, we see that turnover and loss rates in states with and without popular controls track each other fairly closely. With this more fine-grained analysis, we do not see patterns that would lead us to conclude that direct election reforms contributed much to the instability of this period. In sum, the high turnover that we observed in the early-20th century does not appear to have been rooted in direct election of senators.

8.3.2 Direct Election and Senators' Voting Behavior

One possible reason that senators did not suffer harsher fates at the polls or more disruption in their careers is that they may have adapted their behavior in the Senate to fit new electoral demands. To date, there has been no published work that has focused directly and systematically on the impact of the change to popular elections on the behavior of senators.[21] Consequently, the existing literature has very little to tell us about the way indirect elections mediated voter preferences, particularly with respect to floor voting behavior. Poole and Rosenthal's (1997, 73–74) general analysis of the stability in voting behavior for senators and House members over the entire history of the Congress suggests the impact may be minimal, but a more focused analysis would substantially contribute to our knowledge about the effects of electoral institutions on legislative behavior.

---

[21] Several works in progress have found effects, however. Bernhard and Sala (2004) have found that direct election led to moderation in senators' voting behavior as an election nears. Lapinski (2000a) has found that senators tended to stay on committees rather than transfer after the 17th Amendment. Schiller (2003) has found that patterns in bill sponsorship behavior changed in response to direct election.

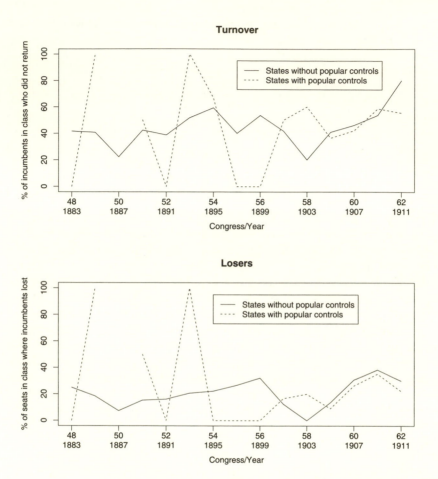

Figure 8.8 Turnover in States with and without Popular Controls, 48th–62nd Congress

Although direct election has been seen as a watershed change in the representative institutions of the United States, its significance would be challenged if we do not find changes in voting behavior in its wake. Changes that other studies have found with respect to the demographic characteristics of the institution's membership would be for the most part cosmetic, especially in terms of substantive representation. One claim that has emerged from the few existing studies of direct election is that it led to the Senate becoming more like the House, which might have led the Senate to shift more toward the House direction on the rules-based/relation-based continuum. A hypothesis that immediately follows from this claim is that senators' voting behavior became more similar to that of their House counterparts when the electoral institutions used to select them converged. With the 17th Amendment, senators would be selected by ordinary voters, just like House members. We might then predict a greater correlation between the voting behavior of representatives and senators from a given state if the reforms established a tighter electoral link between senators and their constituents. An alternative hypothesis, however, is that there would not be a greater correlation between senators and House members after direct election because senators had already established connections with ordinary voters, presumably to win support from state legislators. Riker (1955) contends that the rise of the public canvass in the 1830s meant that Senate candidates had to establish popular bases among voters in order to win office. The canvass involved candidates for the Senate campaigning with state legislators "who were more or less formally pledged to vote for them" (Riker 1955, 463). The support that Senate candidates received from state legislators was a result of the connections that these candidates had established directly with voters through popular campaigning. Thus, Senate candidates might have established direct electoral connections with ordinary voters well before institutional changes formally gave those voters a direct voice in selecting senators.

To adjudicate among these competing hypotheses, we compare roll call voting scores of senators and the relevant House state delegations. Note that this approach is superior to simply examining changes in voting scores of senators in isolation. Underlying changes in the electorate might have led senators to alter their behavior even in the absence of direct election reform. The Progressive Era was a period of rapid, extensive economic and societal change, so it would not be surprising if preferences in the polity shifted more quickly than usual. If changes in preferences in the electorate did occur, then this should be reflected in the behavior of members of both the House and the Senate. Members of the House, who have always been directly elected, provide a benchmark for determining if direct election changed the relationship between senators and their constituents with respect to roll call voting behavior.

To conduct this analysis we use common space NOMINATE scores computed by Keith Poole. These scores are similar to the more widely used NOMINATE scores, but members of the House and Senate share a common metric, enabling cross-chamber comparisons.[22] For a general analysis, we regress the score of a given senator on the average score for the House members of his state's delegation.[23] To compute these averages, we weight each House member's score by the percentage of the total votes in the state he received. This weighting captures the electoral clout of a given representative and is necessary due to variation in the way House members were

---

[22]These data cover the 46th through the 74th Congress (1879–1936). Common space scores are available for subsequent congresses, but the series breaks after the 74th.

[23]Levitt (1996) adopts a similar approach to predicting senators' voting behavior, but his purposes lead him to adopt a somewhat different specification. His model includes both the mean ideological scores for the entire House state delegation and the mean of the same party House delegation. He also includes variables to measure party leadership preferences, which we cannot include in our model since formal leadership positions did not exist for many of the congresses in the period we cover.

elected during the period covered by our analysis. Some states had at-large districts in addition to districts that covered smaller portions of the state.[24] Similarly, in some states representatives ran on a "general ticket," which meant that there were no congressional districts and each representative competed in a statewide election.[25] House members from at-large or general ticket states faced exactly the same geographic constituencies—to use Fenno's (1978) terminology—as senators and thus should be weighed more heavily in terms of the electoral connection.[26]

One potential problem with using common-space NOMINATE scores is that they are constant across a legislator's career. If a senator altered his voting behavior to adjust to changes in electoral institutions during his career, those changes would be muted since we have only a single score for his entire career. Any effects for direct election for a senator who served both before and after the 17th Amendment would be attenuated. One way to address this problem is to restrict our investigation to those senators whose terms of service ended before or started after the 17th Amendment took effect. This might introduce selection bias if the reasons senators are present in the institution is related to being out of step with their constituents in the way they vote. To address this potential problem, we use a selection framework where we include in a our model an equation that predicts whether or not a senator in a given congress continued to serve after 1912. The variables in this model include age, seniority, a dummy indicating a southern senator, and the percentage of the vote that the presidential candidate of the senator's party received in the state in the previous election. These variables capture the likelihood that the senator would retire or lose a reelection bid.[27]

If direct election tied senators more closely to ordinary voters, and if we assume that House members' behavior was a more direct reflection of their

---

[24]These kind of at-large districts were often temporary, existing as stopgap measures until new districts could be drawn after increases in the size of a state's delegation (Martis 1982). It is possible that representatives from these districts would not be worried about seeking reelection in them.

[25]In some cases, these were also stopgap measures taken when redistricting efforts were not completed or failed, although several states used general tickets in multiple electoral cycles. States in our sample that selected representatives in this way for at least one election include Arizona, Idaho, Kentucky, Maine, Minnesota, Missouri, Montana, New Mexico, North Dakota, South Dakota, Utah, Virginia, and Washington.

[26]An alternative to using votes for the weights would be to use district population. Precise district population figures are not available from the census for the elections we cover. County-level data on population can be aggregated to correspond to district population, but this requires dealing with many confounding issues (e.g., cities that have many districts but one county). In any case, we view votes as superior to population figures because of variations in political participation across regions. Although a particular district may have a large population, senators may discount the preferences of individuals living there if they tend not to turn out to vote.

[27]We do not display the results of the congress-by-congress selection analysis, since doing so would require numerous tables. Seniority was the most consistent predictor, having statistically significant and negative effects in each congress. The other variables also did fairly well as predictors, although they did not always have statistically significant effects.

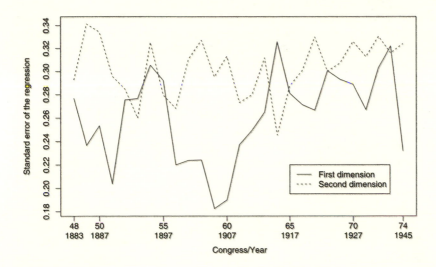

Figure 8.9 Predictive Power of House Delegation Voting Scores for Senate Voting Scores

constituents' preferences, then we should find that the voting behavior of a state's House delegation should have more predictive power for the voting behavior of the state's senators after the reform was adopted. If it does not, then this casts doubts on arguments about the impact of direct election on senators' voting behavior. Figure 8.9 reports the standard error of the regression from the model estimated congress by congress.[28] The predictive power of the voting behavior of House state delegations on the first and second dimensions does not appear to have increased in response to the implementation of the 17th Amendment. The first dimension values for the standard error of the regression during the congresses when senators were directly elected are at about the same levels as in prior congresses. The fit for the second dimension appears to have decreased somewhat after 1912.[29]

Interestingly, the model fit for the scores on the first dimension improves starting in the late 1890s, but this trend reverses in the congresses immedi-

---

[28] We report the standard error of the regression instead of R-squared because the latter is inappropriate for comparing model fit across different samples (see Achen 1982, 58–63).

[29] We also tried using the average scores for the House members of the senator's party and the opposite party in the state's delegation as explanatory variables. One problem with this approach is that many states in the sample—particularly in the South and in states with at-large districts—have no House members who do not share the senator's party affiliation. These states essentially have to be dropped from the sample, which, given the specific nature of the missing data problem, raises serious concerns about selection bias. Nevertheless, the results obtained from this analysis were similar to what we report here. We also tried accounting for whether or not a given senator was up for reelection. The results were generally the same, although the decline in predictive power was not as pronounced for the second dimension.

ately prior to the adoption of the 17th Amendment. The improved model fit from 1897 to 1910 corresponds to a period in which numerous states adopted some form of popular control, suggesting that the reforms at the state level may have boosted Senate responsiveness, at least temporarily.[30] The adoption of these reforms or the anticipation of their adoption may have tied senators more closely to ordinary voters, much in the way that House members were tied to them.

To investigate the impact of state level reforms, we could not rely upon common space scores because we lack variation when we separate out senators in office before and after adoption of said reforms. Instead, we examine the relationship between House state delegation votes and senators' votes on final passage for significant legislation. This does not require us to employ sample selection methods since, unlike common space scores, individual votes do not have the problem of a lack of within-senator variation. We compute a variable that is the proportion of yea votes cast by the relevant delegation (weighted in the same fashion as discussed above) and interact this variable with a dummy indicating whether a state adopted some form of popular control (we also include the main effect for the dummy). We then check to see if the model fit is significantly improved by adding the interaction term. We estimate separate probit models for the 48th through the 62nd Congress. The p values for the likelihood ratio test that the interaction between the direct election dummy and the House voting delegation variable significantly improves the fit of the model are reported in Figure 8.10. The likelihood ratio tests indicate that the addition of variables measuring state-level reforms significantly improves the fit of the model at the .1 level or better in only ten out of thirty-one votes in our sample. Of particular note is the weak explanatory power of state-level reforms after the mid-1890s, which is the period when most states adopted such reforms. Thus, it does not seem that state-level reforms are driving the increase in correlation between House and Senate voting behavior that we see during these congresses. We do not find strong, sustained effects for direct election reforms across the congresses where they should matter. Although the Senate may have become more like the House descriptively as a result of direct election reforms, our empirical analysis leads us to conclude that the Senate did not do so with respect to voting behavior.

8.3.3 Direct Election and Support for Reforms Regarding Rules of Debate

On the whole, direct election of senators does not seem to be a significant predictor of variation in senators' voting behavior. It could still be the case, however, that senators may have become more sensitive to popular pressure on the issue of obstruction. While votes on rules changes are usually not the most salient to the public, Dion's (1997) argument about the adoption

---

[30] According to Lapinski (2000b), twenty-one states adopted some form of popular control—mostly direct primaries—between 1905 and 1910.

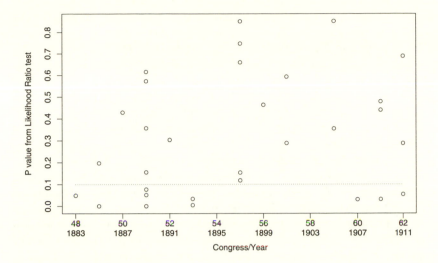

Figure 8.10 Impact of State-Level Direct Election Reforms on Final Passage Votes, 48th–62nd Congress

of cloture in 1917 raises the question of whether or not senators worried about constituents' responses to their votes on rules concerning obstruction. While no vote on the rules had as high a profile as the vote to adopt cloture in 1917, an earlier vote gives us the opportunity to determine if state level reforms provided an incentive for senators to vote in favor of restrictions on debate.

As discussed in Chapter 3, a particularly noteworthy precedent limiting obstruction occurred during Robert La Follette's high-profile filibuster of the Aldrich-Vreeland Currency Bill of 1908. The Senate voted 35-13 to endorse Nelson Aldrich's point of order against La Follette's use of successive quorum calls to stall action and then voted by the same margin to table the ensuing appeal by La Follette.[31] These votes not only paved the way for passage of the highly salient currency bill, they also were viewed as an important constraint on future filibusters. It is difficult to argue that senators at the time were not aware of both the practical and the symbolic importance of the establishment of this precedent. Combined with precedents allowing the counting of quorums, this change would seriously hamper future filibusterers. The *New York Times* noted that, "[t]o those who gave close attention to the filibuster the change in the interpretation of the Senate rules was considered of far greater importance than the fate of the Currency bill" ("No Campaign Issue in Currency Bill," *New York Times*, June 1, 1908, p. 2; see also "Filibuster Is Doomed," *Washington Post*, June 1, 1908, p. 4).

---

[31] Recall that Senate rules and precedents required that "business" take place between successive quorum calls. Aldrich's point of order held that debate does not constitute "business."

How much did the introduction of popular electoral controls have to do with this landmark change in the Senate rules regarding debate? An examination of the votes on the establishment of the precedent indicates that the answer is "not much." These were party-line votes, with all Republicans save La Follette and Norris Brown (R–NE) in favor of the limitation of the use of quorum calls. Including party as an explanatory variable in a standard binary regression model of the vote prevents assessment of the effects of popular electoral controls because the party variable produces perfect separation in the data. Substituting first- and second-dimension DW-NOMINATE scores for party also leads to sample separation, with the first-dimension score driving the results.

To circumvent this problem, we estimated a penalized-likelihood logistic regression, which enables estimation of the model including variables that preclude inference with a standard logit model (see Firth 1993; Heinze and Schemper 2003; Zorn 2005). We estimated two equations, including either party (=1 for Democrats; =0 for Republicans) or first- and second-dimension DW-NOMINATE scores and a dummy variable indicating the presence of popular control mechanisms in a senator's state. The results, reported in Table 8.5, indicate that either party or ideology is the key predictor of support for the restriction on debate, while popular electoral controls did not have an effect that is statistically distinguishable from zero (see columns 1 and 2). However, the presence of direct election reforms is highly correlated with partisan affiliation. All Democrats save one were elected from states with some form of popular control, while half of the Republicans were elected from such states. Yet party/ideology clearly trump popular control, as Republicans who were elected from states with such controls were not more likely to vote for the limitation than were those who were not subject to such controls.

One striking feature of the vote is how many senators abstained—81% of Democrats and 40% of Republicans. While it was not uncommon to have a high abstention rate during filibusters, particularly during attempts to deny a quorum, it may be that Democrats believed that they could not vote against the attempt to limit debate because of future retribution at the polls. However, the data indicate that this is not likely. Columns 3 and 4 of Table 8.5 report logit regressions where the dependent variable is whether the senator abstained or participated in the vote. Again we see that behavior is better predicted by either ideology or party than by popular electoral controls.[32] Party is clearly more important to the model than popular control, especially when one considers that the latter had little effect on Republicans from states that had such controls in place.

The reason the Democrats were not more vocal in their opposition to the bill and the attempt to limit obstructionist tactics appears to be a combination of fear that the Republicans would push even more extreme

---

[32]The popular control variable is not statistically significant even when it is the only variable included in the specification.

Table 8.5 Analysis of Vote Establishing Precedent against Repeated Quorum Calls

	Yea/Nay		Abstain	
	1	2	3	4
Constant	3.555	0.991	−0.178	0.883
	(1.476)		(0.358)	(0.525)
Party	−4.566	—	2.124	—
	(1.729)		(0.591)	
1st Dim. DW-NOMINATE score	—	8.088	—	−2.691
		(3.791)		(0.710)
2nd Dim. DW-NOMINATE score	—	−0.895	—	−0.082
		(−7.626)		(0.424)
Popular control	−1.554	−1.516	−0.534	−0.649
	(1.629)	(−6.910)	(0.522)	(0.578)
Log-likelihood	−7.91 ($p < .001$)	−4.18 ($p < .001$)	−55.59 ($p < .001$)	−49.79 ($p < .001$)

Notes: N = 43. Table entries are logit maximum likelihood coefficients with standard errors in parentheses. The estimates reported in columns 1 and 2 were obtained using a penalized log likelihood correction.

rules changes if the obstruction persisted and concern about GOP retaliation through other legislation. After the filibuster had failed,

> [Democratic] leaders hastened to explain that the willingness of the Republican machine to ride roughshod over the minority cut some figure in their complaisance. They were, or affect to have been, mightily afraid that the adoption of a cloture rule would have resulted if they had joined the filibuster. They also profess to have been greatly afraid that Republicans would pass the bill reducing southern representation in Congress ("Pass Currency Bill by Aldrich Strategy." *New York Times*, May 31, 1908, p. 1)

The Republicans had gone to great lengths to prevent the success of the filibuster, including disregarding or very narrowly interpreting existing rules. The size and intensity of the majority party made the threat of further rules changes credible. The Democrats, who held only one-third of the seats in the chamber, decided it was better to vote against the Republican bill but allow it to pass than to attempt obstruction to maintain the status quo. Their decision not to support the filibuster by Progressive Republicans or to vigorously oppose the clampdown on obstruction appears to have been due more to their concerns about meeting public demands for policy and their fears of a more severe rules change, and less about the negative views of the public with regard to obstruction ("No Campaign Issue in Currency Bill," *New York Times*, June 1, 1908, p. 2). This appears to be a classic instance in which bill supporters signaled their commitment to passage through the pursuit of new precedents restricting obstruction, while potential supporters of the filibuster—Democrats ambivalent about the bill—surrendered rather than risk more extreme rules changes.

8.4 CONCLUSION

In this chapter, we have attempted to determine why the Senate chose to adopt a formal rule for ending debate in 1917. While the Senate still relied on relation-based legislating to a significant degree and still allowed individual senators extensive individual prerogatives in debate, the acceptance of the formal limits imposed by the cloture rule marked an important break with Senate tradition. Informal conventions and the threat to resort to stricter, formal rules, which had been reasonably effective at keeping obstruction in check, no longer seemed to be working well at the turn of the century. While several factors contributed to the breakdown of norms, we have argued that the size of the Senate was the key culprit. A dramatic increase in the membership of the Senate due to the addition of new states undercut the conditions necessary for relation-based legislating to work effectively. The increase in size was exacerbated by other changes in the institutional, political, and economic context, which hindered interpersonal relations and communication among senators. The Senate's rising workload also appears to have contributed to increased demands for formal rules limiting debate.

Although direct election has been offered as a main suspect among the causes of institutional change within the Senate, we have presented systematic evidence that leads to the conclusion that the impact of direct election was limited in this regard. This reform did not increase instability in Congress nor did it alter senators' behavior in ways that would lead one to conclude that it instilled senators with a greater desire for rules-based legislating. Direct election may have caused the Senate to become more like the House descriptively, but on the behavioral dimensions that are relevant for obstruction, there was a great deal of continuity as the buffer of state legislatures was gradually stripped away during the late-19th and early-20th centuries.

It is important to point out that the cloture rule that was adopted in 1917 preserved many aspects of the system that made obstruction-as-wars-of-attrition generally beneficial. By still permitting extended but costly debate, the cloture rule allowed filibusters to continue to be fought as wars of attrition. This stood in stark contrast to a proposal that was presented by Senator Robert Owen (D–OK), who was chair of a special committee on the modification of the Senate's debate rules, to the Democratic caucus at the beginning of the 64th Congress. Owen's proposal would have enabled any senator to move at any time that a vote on a measure in question and its amendments take place in two days. In other words, if the motion was approved, it would be in order to move the previous question after two days of debate. There was not much support for Owen's proposal, in part because some senators thought "that many weeks should elapse after the new rule was invoked before the final vote came on any measure." Such an interval would have allowed for ample debate time while still requiring senators who supported or opposed the measure to incur the costs of engaging in extended debate ("Owen Outlines Fight for Cloture," *New York Times*, December 1, 1915).

The 1917 cloture rule gave bill supporters a new outside option, where if they could demonstrate supermajority support, a filibuster could be halted after allowing some time for deliberation. It was still costly to resort to cloture, since the procedure required building broad coalitions, guaranteed delay by requiring time for the cloture petition to ripen, and allotted floor time to be consumed by post-cloture debate. But the rule helped to reduce uncertainty, especially that presented by late-session obstructive efforts that took advantage of the adjournment deadline. The cloture rule did so by creating a sufficient but not a necessary condition for ending debate.

This helps us to understand why the Senate did not go further in limiting obstruction. Subsequent attempts to restrict debate were considered in the congresses following the 65th, but did not pass. There simply did not appear to be majority support for a stricter cloture rule (Koger 2002, Ch. 7). In the next chapter, we begin to consider the cloture rule's impact on lawmaking, which helps to explain why there was not more support in the Senate in the 1920s to 1940s for proposals to tighten Rule XXII.

Chapter Nine

Cloture Reform Reconsidered

9.1 INTRODUCTION

In this chapter, we investigate the impact of cloture reform, assessing the degree to which the rule affected lawmaking in the Senate. A central component of our theory is that legislators will move to a more rules-based system when relational legislating falters. This need not mean a complete shift from informal constraints to formal rules; instead, explicit rules can be adopted that limit the most troublesome shortcomings of relation-based governance, without completely displacing reliance upon norms and informal understandings. A thorough test of our theoretical arguments requires us to demonstrate that legislators do indeed benefit from this kind of formalization. We also need to explain why senators did not move farther along the rules/relation-based continuum in the first half of the 20th century by adopting either a stricter cloture rule or more severe limits on debate.

As with many filibuster-related issues, there are widely divergent opinions about the actual impact of the cloture rule. On the one hand, some—mainly at the time of its enactment—supported it as a meaningful reform that addressed the serious problems created by the lack of rules limiting debate in the Senate. On the other hand, some—mostly after its enactment—claimed that it was ineffective, amounting to little more than a perfunctory response to the intense public pressure that senators experienced as a result of the successful obstruction of a popular bill. In this chapter, we adjudicate among these different perspectives on cloture reform.

Even though the 1917 cloture rule was far from the previous question rules that existed in the House of Representatives and many other legislatures (Luce 1922), some observers at the time thought the rule would be an effective solution to the problems presented by unlimited debate. *The Washington Post* claimed that as a result of the amendment to the rules, "[t]he organized filibuster of a few men as recognized in the Senate is dead" ("Senate Votes Rule to End Filibusters," March 9, 1917, p. 1). While acknowledging that the rule "probably cannot be successfully used to prevent the spectacular one-man filibusters by which senators have talked bills pending in the closing hours of a session to a legislative grave" unless they are foreseen, the *Post* contended that "an organized affair which must be planned two days or more ahead of a session's end can be disposed of easily." *The New York Times* argued: "It is difficult to overestimate the importance of the new rule, both on measures of immediate interest and on the general course of legislation," adding that "the real importance of the rule lies in its almost unlimited potential effect on future legislation" ("Alters Rule of 100 Years," March 9, 1917, p. 1). In the floor debate on the amendment to Rule XXII, a few senators even argued that the new rule would be too effective, limiting debate to such a degree that it would diminish the Senate's role in the separation of powers system (p. 1).

Woodrow Wilson, who helped mobilize mass opinion in support of cloture, is reported to have "expressed warm support for the proposal" ("Change Is Opposed by Few," *New York Times*, March 8, 1917, p. 2). Wilson's reaction is significant. He had gone to unprecedented lengths for a president to vilify filibustering senators, launching an all-out public relations campaign against those who defeated the Armed Ship Bill and the rules of the Senate that allowed them to do so. For example, at a luncheon for the Democratic National Committee at the White House, Wilson "threw aside all reserve in expressing his opinion of those Senators who blocked passage of the Armed Neutrality bill." *The New York Times* characterized Wilson's remarks as an "outburst" that "both surprised and pleased" the attendees, as the president "castigated those Democrats who joined with Republicans in the Senate to embarrass the Administration at a time when the highest order of patriotism was necessary to enable the Government to cope with a delicate situation" ("President Repeats He Is Angry over Defeat of Armed Ship Bill," March 7, 1917, p. 1).[1] His support of the proposal suggests he thought it would be effective against the behavior he so vociferously attacked.[2]

In the aftermath of the cloture reform of 1917, the rule has been almost universally denigrated by close observers of the Senate. Byrd (1988, 124) claims that as early as November 1918, "it was becoming clear that the cloture rule was not going to be effective." Baker (1995, 46) contends that "the adoption of Senate Rule XXII did provide an easier mechanism to terminate excessive debate with a vote of cloture, but it proved so difficult to muster the required two-thirds majority needed to terminate debate that filibustering was not seriously hindered." White (1968, 60–61) argues that "the rule bore within itself the seeds of its own nullification" because it applied only to halting debate on a "measure," and President Pro Tem Arthur Vandenberg (R–MI) ruled in 1948 that this meant that cloture could not be applied to a motion to proceed to consider a bill.[3] Although the

---

[1] Albert Cummins (R–IA), who supported cloture reform, also characterized Wilson's behavior as "an unparalleled and unprecedented outburst" (*Congressional Record*, March 8, 1917, p. 34).

[2] Or at least his expected utility for this proposal appears to have been greater than what he would have obtained from pushing for a majority cloture proposal, since the chances of such a proposal passing were much less. It is also worth noting that with the war emergency heightening dramatically in March 1917, Wilson may have chosen not to devote more resources to the Senate rules fight beyond his initial public campaign.

[3] The problem was that bill opponents could obstruct the motion to proceed to consideration of a bill, and the cloture rule did not apply to such motions. Vandenberg declared at the time that ". . . in the final analysis, the Senate has no effective cloture rule at all. . . . [A] small but determined majority can always prevent cloture, under the existing rules" (U.S. Congress. Senate. Committee on Rules and Administration 1985, 20).

Senate reformed its rules in 1949 to apply the cloture rule to motions as well as measures, this change was part of a compromise that raised the threshold to alter the rules to two-thirds of the entire Senate, and therefore it meant that "cloture was in practical fact at least as far off as ever, and the Senate in plain fact retained what amounts to unlimited debate" (White 1968, 64). Rogers (1926, 177) argued that the cloture procedure was "so cumbersome as to be possible only in emergencies." Luce (1922, 295) also expressed doubts about the rule's effectiveness, since "very rarely does either party control two thirds of the votes of the Senate." Haynes's (1938, v. 1, 420) views on the impact of cloture in the decade after it was adopted are mixed, but he nevertheless claims that the rules still lent themselves to "practices which have been injurious to legislation and have greatly discredited the Senate in the opinion of the public." In an interesting point that he does not develop but we view as crucial to this debate, Haynes (1938, v. 1, 405) argues that "the efficacy of this rule for the most part inheres in the consciousness that it is available rather than in its actual use." Overall, the gist of these views is that legislation that could have been killed with a filibuster before the reform stood the same risk after the reform.[4]

Other critics of the cloture rule note the infrequency with which it was applied at all, let alone applied successfully. From the 66th to the 86th Congresses (1919–1960), only twenty-three cloture votes took place, and of those, only four were successful (Oppenheimer 1985, 398; Baker 1995, 46). Between 1927 and 1962, the Senate had an unbroken string of unsuccessful cloture votes—fourteen in all. By these measures, the 1917 rule did not appear to arm senators with a practicable weapon against obstruction.

If these views are correct, why did senators even bother to amend Rule XXII? To be sure, the reform apparently served to placate a fearful public incensed about the successful end-of-session filibuster of the widely popular Armed-Ship Bill. It was also viewed at the time as a first step toward majority cloture. *The New York Times* reported, "But everyone believes, and many Senators said on the floor of the Senate today, that before long the rule inevitably will be amended so as to give to a bare majority the power now given to two-thirds. Then a direct vote in the Senate can be obtained almost as easily and quickly as in the House" ("Alters Rule of 100 Years," March 9, 1917, p. 1).

The symbolic importance of the 1917 reform is unassailable, yet the prevailing conventional wisdom that its substantive impact was nil is questionable. If that view is correct, why did Wilson, who clearly had public opinion on his side in the reform effort, settle for the two-thirds rule rather than support the majority cloture provision that was considered in the Democratic caucus?[5] Although Wilson the political scientist had lauded the Senate's rules protecting unlimited debate in *Congressional Government* ([1885]

---

[4]See also Dion (1997) and Koger (2002).

[5]For details on the proposals considered in the Democratic caucus, see "President Considers Convoying Instead of Arming Merchantmen; Caucuses Approve Closure Rule," *New York Times*, March 8, 1917, p. 2.

1956), Wilson the president vigorously opposed them, and would be plagued by the obstruction they allowed throughout his presidency.[6] Perhaps he was simply being a practical politician and knew that there was not support for a more severe cloture rule. But this begs the question why enough support to amend the cloture rule did not develop in the Senate in the next couple of decades.

In the years following the reform, the Senate did not reduce the threshold further as many had thought it would. This was not for lack of trying. Shortly after the new rule was adopted, the Senate in 1918 considered a resolution by Oscar Underwood (D–AL) to re-introduce the previous question and limit debate during the conduct of World War I. Although the resolution was reported out favorably by the Rules Committee and a unanimous consent agreement was adopted to bring it to a vote, it was rejected by the Senate on a vote of 41 nays to 34 yeas. In the 67th Congress (1921–1923), five resolutions for limiting debate were introduced, yet none made any headway beyond the committee stage (U.S. Congress. Senate. Committee on Rules and Administration 1985, 17).

9.2 A SIMPLE MODEL OF CLOTURE

Our reconsideration of the cloture rule is motivated by the puzzle of why members would have created and maintained a procedure that critics have charged offered no real benefits to them. We develop a simple model that shows how senators might have benefited from a cloture rule even though they rarely resorted to invoking the procedure. The model contemplates how senators can trade off a decrease in the uncertainty of passage for an increase in the size of coalitions necessary to pass legislation. In this sense, cloture may have constituted a kind of insurance policy for risk averse legislators, which protected them from the risk they faced when considering legislation late in the session, when obstructionists had a particular advantage.

This trade-off can be modeled by considering a legislative entrepreneur's expected utility from passing legislation with and without cloture. The legislative entrepreneur (LE) can add individuals to the coalition, which increases the probability that her proposal will pass, but this comes at the cost of receiving fewer benefits from the legislation if enacted. The decrease in benefits can be viewed in terms of having to share with each additional legislator some piece of a fixed pie. The LE may have to provide a project to a senator's state, which means fewer funds for projects in the LE's own state. Or the decrease in benefits may be thought of as an adjustment of the proposal spatially in a way that moves the policy outcome in a direction closer to the ideal point of a senator who is hesitant to join the coalition,

---

[6]Although Woodrow Wilson ([1885] 1956, 220) had a change of heart once he found himself on the business end of the filibuster, his view from the ivory tower on the absence of the previous question from the Senate was positive: "that imperative form of cutting off all further discussion has fortunately never found a place there."

but away from the LE's ideal point. The question then is to what extent is the LE willing to compromise on the substance of the proposal in order to enhance its prospects for passage.

Let η denote coalition size (as a proportion), such that $\eta \in [.5, 1]$. We restrict η to this range because values of η below .5 are not relevant for our purposes, since we are interested only in coalitions that meet the necessary, but possibly not sufficient, threshold of a majority for passage.[7] Define π as the probability of passage of a piece of legislation, and B as the benefit obtained from passing legislation.[8] Both π and B are functions of η. Specifically, let

$$\pi(\alpha) = \left(\frac{\eta - .5}{.5} \right)^{\alpha}.$$

This gives non-linearly increasing π, with the α parameter indicating how much an additional coalition member beyond 51% of the chamber contributes to the probability of passage. We assume $\alpha \in (0, 1]$, such that as α approaches 1, the marginal increase in probability from adding a legislator to the coalition increases. This form for π has properties that are intuitively appealing for representing the functional relationship between coalition sizes and probabilities of passage. When $\eta = .50, \pi = 0$ (i.e., you need at least a minimum majority to have any chance of passing legislation) and when $\eta = 1, \pi = 1$ (i.e., you are assured of passing legislation when all members of the chamber are part of the supporting coalition). Having a minimum majority does not guarantee passage because various (unmodeled) factors may affect a bill's chances for passage, such as obstruction by opponents or being crowded out by other items on the agenda.

We let

$$B = \frac{1 - \eta}{.5},$$

which gives linearly decreasing B, such that B is maximized at a coalition of .51 and $B = 0$ when the coalition is unanimous.[9] We also assume $B = 0$ if the legislation fails to pass.

The expected utility for the LE can then be written as

$$EU = \pi B + (1 - \pi)0 = \pi B. \tag{9.1}$$

Plots of the LE's expected utility make clear the trade-off between coalition size and benefits. Figure 9.1 plots expected utility for $\alpha = 0.1$. With this value of α, the baseline probability for a coalition size of .51 is fairly high, and the marginal increase in probability from adding new coalition members

---

[7]We also put to the side cases where ties occur. In these situations, the ties would be broken by the vice president, but this has little relevance for our main concerns.

[8]In order to keep the model as simple as possible, we are "black boxing" the various decisions and actions of senators that would determine the values of η and π.

[9]Technically, B is maximized when the coalition size is $.5 + \varepsilon$, where ε is some small number. But given the small size of the Senate, the .51 threshold is accurate enough for our purposes.

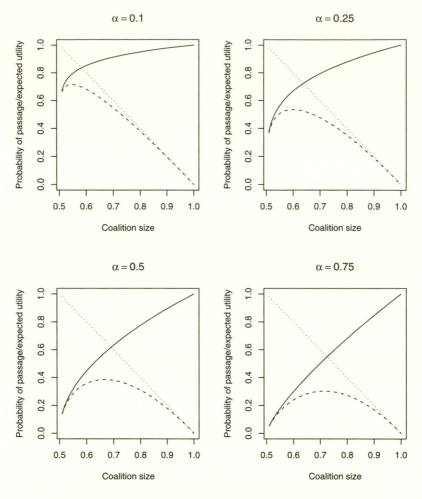

Figure 9.1 Expected Utility of Passage (— π; · · · B; - - - πB)

is fairly small after .6. *EU* is maximized at .55, which should lead the LE to put together close to minimum majority coalitions. As α increases, it is more beneficial to build bigger coalitions. For $\alpha = 0.5$, a coalition of .67 maximizes the expected utility of the LE, and thus we should expect to see supermajority coalitions. For higher α, coalitions are predicted to be oversized—*EU* is maximized at .71 for an α of 0.75. Note that the loss in benefits from adding another member to the coalition is the same across these different scenarios; all that changes is the contribution of each coalition partner to the probability of passage.

Our interpretation of the 1917 cloture rule is that it makes the probability function π jump upward at $\eta = .67$. That is, building a coalition that exceeds the supermajority threshold specified by the rule makes it sharply more probable (although not certain) that the legislation will pass. By building a supermajority coalition, LEs insure themselves against some of the vicissitudes of the legislative process. Should a filibuster develop against the legislation, the LE has the votes to invoke cloture. However, being able to invoke cloture does not guarantee that the legislation will pass, since obstructionists may be able to run out the clock depending on how much time is left in the legislative session and how many other, more salient pieces of legislation remain to be addressed.

In the presence of the cloture rule, the expected utility would be

$$EU_C = \pi(\alpha)B \cdot 1[\eta < .67] + \pi(\alpha^*)B \cdot (1 - 1[\eta < .67]) \qquad (9.2)$$

where $1[\cdot]$ is the indicator function and $\alpha^* < \alpha$, which serves to scale up the probability, making it more likely for the bill to pass if the coalition supporting it exceeds the two-thirds threshold. Plots are again useful to illustrate the logic. Figure 9.2 shows the effects of cloture for different values for α and α^*. When $\alpha = .1$, there is very little gain from having a two-thirds cloture rule. The jump that occurs in π does not produce a big enough increase in πB to exceed the maximum that existed without cloture.

However, for the other values of α^*, the maximum of πB is greater than the maximum without cloture. When $\alpha = .25$ and $\alpha^* = .1$, an LE realizes a gain in expected utility when she increases the size of her coalition to two-thirds. The prediction for this situation then is a larger coalition than what the LE would have put together without a cloture rule. When $\alpha = .5$ and $\alpha^* = .25$, we do not expect to see any difference in the LE's behavior. Her utility is maximized with a two-thirds coalition now as it was before. The model predicts a *decrease* in coalition sizes when $\alpha = .75$ and $\alpha^* = .5$, since the maximum of the expected utility function drops to .67 with cloture, down from .71.[10]

While it is difficult to tell which situations best characterize lawmaking in the late-19th and early-20th centuries, our analyses of significant legislation and tariff bills indicate that the one represented by α in the vicinity of .25 may have been fairly common. There are numerous cases where legislation passed with coalitions below the threshold established by the 1917 cloture rule. The increase that we observed in the average coalition size after the adoption of cloture is consistent with this view. While we acknowledge that other factors may have contributed to this increase, no one has yet offered a theoretical framework that explicitly demonstrates how these factors operate. We address alternative explanations for the increase in coalition sizes later in this chapter.[11]

---

[10]We explored other kinds of functional forms, including introducing nonlinearity into the benefit function, but the general predictions produced by the model were essentially the same as the ones discussed here.

[11]We expect there to be some variation in α values depending on whether the legislation is considered early or late in a congress. Legislation considered earlier should have lower αs because time constraints had less bite then, and so smaller coalitions could generally

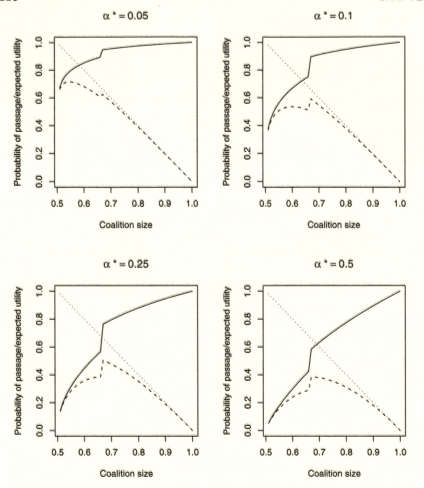

Figure 9.2 Expected Utility of Passage with a Two-thirds Cloture Rule (— π;
···B; - - - πB)

Another important point that emerges from the model is that the number of times cloture was sought and invoked successfully are not necessarily
good indicators of the impact of cloture reform (cf. Beth 1995). Once the
cloture rule establishes a threshold for passage, expected-utility-maximizing
LEs have a clearer target to aim for and should adjust their coalition-building
behavior accordingly. In many cases, this would mean building bigger coalitions in an attempt to preempt obstructive efforts. Would-be obstructionists
have less incentive to filibuster if they know that cloture can be invoked on
them. While there are various benefits to filibustering, the price that legis-

expect a high probability of passage. This is consistent with the empirical finding that
lopsided coalitions were less common early in pre-cloture congresses than in the final thirty
days (see Table 4.3).

lators have to pay to engage in this activity in terms of effort, opportunity costs, and the loss of goodwill may be too dear if there is a considerable chance the filibuster will be defeated without it affecting policy substantively. Thus, the cloture rule alters the strategic calculations of legislators so that LEs should build bigger coalitions in order to head off potential filibusters, and those who might have engaged in obstruction before might instead channel their resources into other activities that have more promise of a substantive return. Intense minorities may still filibuster, and such activity can still reveal beneficial information, since filibusters after the 1917 rule continued to be costly for several decades and the cloture rule itself allowed considerable latitude for debate. Our model then lays out the theoretical logic behind Haynes's assertion that the cloture rule was efficacious because legislators knew they could credibly resort to it if they built large enough coalitions, not because they actually had to apply it with great frequency.

An additional prediction that emerges from the model is that the variance of coalition sizes should decrease after the adoption of cloture. This would hold if values of α equal to or greater than .25 generally represent the lawmaking situations that LEs face, and if members in a specific situation know the distribution—but not actual value—of α. We believe that such uncertainty is particularly likely near the end of a congress. The time constraints imposed by the March 4 deadline and the rush to address pending items during lame duck sessions should have made it more difficult for LEs to ascertain how much support was necessary to gain passage. The availability of the cloture procedure reduced this uncertainty.[12]

Coalition sizes on significant legislation offer a way to test this prediction. While the change in the first moment in the distribution of coalition sizes noted above supports our theoretical conjectures, we should also see a change in the second moment if our argument about uncertainty is correct. That is, the variance of coalition sizes on significant legislation should be smaller after 1917 than it was prior to enactment of the cloture rule. We expect this to hold only for lame duck sessions, given the heightened threat that obstruction presented at that stage.

The data do support this prediction, although we need to be careful about our inferences due to small sample sizes. As reported in Table 9.1, the variance of coalition sizes in lame duck sessions prior to cloture reform was 0.017 (for six bills), but then decreased to 0.013 (for four bills) after cloture reform. Although this difference appears small, a nonparametric test of equal variances based on squared ranks, which is particularly well suited for samples of this size (Conover 1999, 300–3), indicates the difference in variances is significant at the .1 level.[13] If we include voice votes taken at the

---

[12] Of course, the cloture rule would not have reduced uncertainty in the very last days of a congress, since the procedure required three days for the cloture petition to "ripen" and allowed for some post-cloture debate.

[13] The nonparametric test is more appropriate for this sample than is the standard F test, which relies on asymptotic properties. Small sample sizes raise concerns about the power of statistical tests used with them, where power refers to the probability of rejecting

end of a congress and treat them as unanimous, this increases the sample size to twenty-one in the pre-cloture period (with coalition size variance equal to .025) and eight in the post-cloture period (with coalition size variance equal to .01). The nonparametric test with the larger sample size also leads us to reject the null of equal variances (at the .01 level).[14] These results are consistent with the argument that one goal of cloture reform was to reduce the uncertainty created by obstruction toward the end of a congress, particularly as norms of restraint started to break down.

Since coalition sizes are bounded above by 1, one might worry that an increase in the average coalition size would necessarily lead to a reduction in the variance. But our argument implies that cloture reform would have a significant impact on the variance only at the end of a congress. We should not see a significant difference between the variance of coalition sizes for legislation passed *earlier* in pre-cloture congresses and the variance in post-cloture congresses.[15] Consistent with our hypothesis, the pre-cloture and post-cloture variances differ only to the fourth decimal place, with the former equaling .0174 and the latter equaling .0171. Conover's (1999, 301) T_1 statistic is only -0.04, which has a p value of 0.484. We clearly cannot reject the null of equal variances across the two periods (even though coalitions on average became larger for legislation considered prior to the end of the congress).[16]

This analysis supports our arguments about the impact of cloture reform. While our model is relatively sparse, we believe that it illuminates one of the central strategic features of the cloture rule. By providing a sufficient—

---

the null when it is false. A small sample means low power (i.e., we would be unlikely to reject the null when it is false). Since we reject the null here, this should not be too great of a concern. While appropriate caution is necessary in drawing conclusions based on the sample we have, we wish to emphasize that the nonparametric approach is superior in this case to the parametric approaches that political scientists are more accustomed to.

[14] If we treat voice votes as being near unanimous (i.e., as if the size of the supporting coalition was 90%), the same results obtain.

[15] Even though we see an increase in average coalition size after 1917 both early and late in a congress, this does not mean we will also see changes in the variance for legislation passed early. The cloture rule created a sufficient but not necessary threshold for passing legislation. Earlier in a congress, LEs can choose to resort to the cloture process, but it becomes more of a necessity late in a congress. We might see LEs building bigger coalitions earlier on in order to avoid some potential problems, but they could still generally expect to get away with smaller coalitions because of costs and other constraints on obstruction. As a result, we might see an increase in the average coalition size earlier in a congress, but we would not necessarily see a reduction in their variance.

[16] Even though the sample sizes for legislation not passed at the end of a congress are large enough to use standard statistical methods, we report the Conover test for consistency and comparability. A similar pattern occurs with votes on appropriations bills. The variance of coalition sizes on appropriations bills considered in lame duck sessions was 0.023 (for six bills) in the pre-cloture era and 0.020 (for four bills) in the post-cloture period. The Conover test indicates that we can reject the null of equal variances at the .1 level. We consider the analysis of appropriations bills to be confirmatory, but we note that the small number of bills on which roll call votes occurred raises concerns about the selection process by which recorded votes instead of voice votes were held. We undertake a much more detailed analysis of the effects of cloture on the appropriations process in Chapter 10.

Table 9.1 Test of Equal Variances for Coalition Sizes on Major Legislation Considered Near the End of a Congress, 1881–1946

	Roll call votes only		Roll call and voice votes	
	Pre-cloture	Post-cloture	Pre-cloture	Post-cloture
N	6	4	21	8
Variance	0.017	0.013	0.025	0.01
Test Statistic*	138		−2.26	
Significance Level	.1		.01	

Notes: *The test statistic for roll call votes only is T defined by Conover (1999) on p. 301. The statistic for roll call and voice votes is T_1 (defined on the same page), which is used because of ties in the rankings of coalitions sizes.

but not a strictly necessary—condition for passing legislation, it allowed legislative entrepreneurs to reduce the uncertainty posed particularly by late-congress filibusters by building a larger supportive coalition. The result was an increase in the average and a reduction in the variance of coalition sizes when bills came up for consideration near final adjournment.

It is important to emphasize that we are not arguing that uncertainty reduction was the sole motivation for adoption of cloture reform. Senators were clearly also responding, in part, to intense public pressure and criticism of the institution. The gradual development of support for debate limitations over several decades suggest that the public outrage at the demise of the Armed-Ship Bill in 1917 was not solely responsible for the change; instead, efforts to change the rules became more common as the Senate grew in size and relation-based legislating gradually frayed. A series of high-profile, end-of-congress filibusters over several years had demonstrated that the Senate's traditional reliance on norms of restraint had lost its effectiveness, creating an environment of heightened uncertainty that also undermined the Senate's prestige and brought down waves of public wrath on senators.[17]

The extremely short floor debate in 1917 provides little in the way of direct evidence concerning senators' intentions. The debate lasted only six hours and took place at a time when the nation was consumed by national security concerns. The near unanimous vote for the rule change suggested senators saw little need to explain or justify the innovation during the floor debate. Comments during the debate hint that at least some senators understood that uncertainty reduction was an important feature of the reform. During an exchange between William Stone (D–MO) and Hoke Smith (D–

---

[17]See Schickler (2001) for a discussion of the role of the intersection of multiple member interests in shaping institutional innovations in Congress.

GA), Stone, asked Smith whether under the new rule he could get a vote on bills that President Wilson identified as being blocked by obstruction. Smith replied, "I think we can on any one of them" (*Congressional Record*, March 8, 1917, p. 31). Smith then asked a question of Stone—which was more of an assertion—whether the Senate could have passed a water power bill, which was blocked by less than one third of the Senate at the end of the previous congress, if they had a rule like the one under consideration. This exchange implies that Smith believed there would be less uncertainty about the passage of legislation as long as coalitions were big enough to invoke cloture. In commenting on the two-thirds threshold set by the rule, Lawrence Sherman (R–IL) attributed senators' support for this threshold to the belief that it is "entirely safe when two-thirds desire a roll call that it should be had" (*Congressional Record*, March 8, 1917, p. 21). Sherman's statement indicates that he believed the rule would decrease uncertainty about getting to a vote on final passage by providing a clear threshold for coalitions to exceed.[18] Sherman lambasted the president for misrepresenting the power of the filibuster, claiming that no meritorious bills had been killed by filibuster, except for some that had been considered during the final weeks of a congress. A similar sentiment was expressed by Reed Smoot (R–UT), who claimed filibusters that were not supported by at least one third of the chamber were unsuccessful "unless [they] were conducted during the last few days of the short session of Congress" (*Congressional Record*, March 8, 1917, p. 38). These comments suggest that senators viewed the two-thirds cloture rule as a way to limit the damage wrought by end-of-congress filibusters by relatively small minorities.[19] Such statements suggest that at least some senators thought that the absence of debate rules had left them vulnerable to a handful of members wreaking havoc by taking advantage of the intense time pressures late in a congress. Haynes's assertion that the true value of the rule rested in its deterrent value also suggests that others understood what we claim to be the logic behind the 1917 rule. We acknowledge that the paucity of statements regarding senators' intentions in 1917 makes our explanation of the goals of cloture reform tentative. However, the evidence presented here (and in Chapter 4) strongly suggests that the logic we outline illuminates the actual impact of the reform and the reasons that senators did not opt to tighten the rule substantially in the decades following 1917.[20]

---

[18]Sherman supported the cloture rule but feared it would set a precedent for majority cloture.

[19]The historical record provides surprisingly little direct evidence concerning the motivations for cloture reform. For example, the committee report issued for the cloture proposal in 1916, which was essentially the rule adopted in 1917, is simply the text of the proposal and includes no explanation for the logic behind it. The contemporary view of the reform given by the *Washington Post* (cited above) is consistent with our argument, since it basically states that the cloture rule removes the uncertainty of ending obstruction by a small group of senators.

[20]Our model of cloture reform might strike some as functionalist. The statements that we cite from contemporaries about how they thought the cloture rule would work undercuts this criticism, since they essentially say informally what we have spelled out formally in our model. In addition, we are not arguing that uncertainty reduction was

9.3 ALTERNATIVE EXPLANATIONS FOR INCREASES IN COALITION SIZES

Our theory is not the only potential explanation for why legislators would work to build supermajority coalitions. A set of alternative theories focus on how governing by supermajorities, while undoubtedly more burdensome, has potential advantages. Groseclose and Snyder (1996) demonstrate formally that a vote-buying strategy that involves putting together supermajorities can be less costly than a strategy of building minimal winning coalitions. Caplin and Nalebuff (1988) show that majorities of 64% (or greater) can solve problems of cycling and the unraveling of legislative bargains. Yet these theories do not offer explanations as to why we would observe the variation in coalition sizes that exists historically. In the remaining sections of this chapter, we discuss other theories of legislative institutions and behavior that may offer alternative explanations for the patterns that we have attributed to concerns about obstruction and attempts to address it through rules changes. While other factors undoubtedly come into play, we argue that these alternative explanations do not undercut our claims about the importance of obstruction and cloture reform.

9.3.1 Partisan Arguments for Changes in Coalition Sizes

Some might argue that increases in coalition sizes have little to do with concerns about obstruction and the advent of cloture, and instead are due to some larger factors in the political environment. The first half of the 20th century was a period of declining party unity and declining party polarization, suggesting that there might be a partisan explanation for the increase in coalition sizes. Figure 9.3 shows that party unity—measured with Rice cohesion scores—was generally lower for both the Republican and Democratic parties during the first few decades of the 20th century, regardless of whether they were in the majority or the minority. However, it is not clear that there is a sound theoretical basis for expecting declining partisanship to yield larger coalition sizes. Instead, if party unity is declining, then it might suggest that coalitions should decrease in size if they are primarily party based, since more members of the majority party are not voting with the party.[21] The extant formal literature on party government, such as Cox and McCubbins's (2005) cartel agenda model, are not designed to yield predictions concerning coalition sizes.[22]

---

the sole motivation for cloture reform; rather, this goal illuminates an important aspect of cloture's adoption and subsequent impact.

[21] If minority party cohesion were falling more rapidly than majority party cohesion, one might expect bigger coalitions. However, Figure 9.3 suggests that majority cohesion fell slightly more than minority cohesion in the 1920s–30s.

[22] The cartel agenda model makes predictions about how often each party will be rolled on a final passage vote. A "roll" occurs when a majority of the party's members vote against a bill that passes. The majority party should never be rolled in their complete information model. The minority party will be rolled often, with the roll rate an increasing

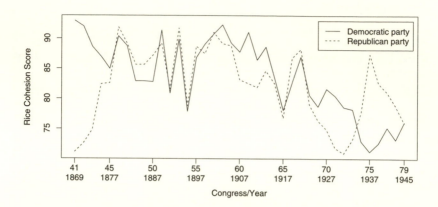

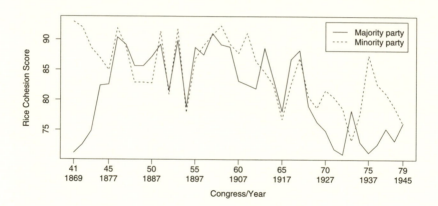

Figure 9.3 Party Unity Scores

Empirically, it does not appear to be the case that the increase in coalition sizes after 1917 is attributable to the decline in party voting. The correlation between coalition size on final passage votes and standard measures of party voting are relatively weak: −.23 for majority party cohesion and −.26 for the average percentage of the majority party who voted with their party on the set of party votes.[23] Perhaps more importantly, when either the Rice cohesion score or party voting measure are entered into the regression models

_____

function of the distance of the minority party median from the floor median. But depending on the precise distribution of status quo points, as well as the exact distributions of member ideal points, the cartel agenda model could yield predictions of either increasing or decreasing coalition sizes given a fall in party polarization.

[23] If one instead uses a NOMINATE-based measure of polarization, such as the distance between the party medians on the first dimension divided by the standard deviation of all senators' NOMINATE scores, the correlation with coalition size is just −.22.

predicting coalition size (see Table 4.2), each is statistically insignificant and the results for the other variables in the equation are qualitatively the same as in the original analysis. Thus, the finding that coalition sizes increased after the 1917 cloture rule is not attributable to changing patterns of party polarization or party voting.

It is also hard to see how a conditional party government (CPG) argument would explain the increase in coalition sizes. The CPG perspective claims that when parties are unified and homogeneous, majority party leaders are endowed with powers to further the party's interests. Parties became less unified and less homogeneous during the first few decades of the 20th century, which implies it would have been more difficult for party leaders to build party-based coalitions. But again the empirical observation that party unity and strength declined does not explain the pattern of coalition sizes we observe. Moreover, while there certainly is the perception that leadership influence varied significantly during this period, Gamm and Smith (2001a) demonstrate that these fluctuations are not consistent with the CPG perspective.

9.3.2 Unanimous Consent Agreements

A key feature of modern Senate procedure is the use of unanimous consent agreements (UCAs) to limit debate. UCAs are worked out by the majority leader in order to facilitate the legislative process, typically prior to the consideration of legislation on the floor. Yet prior to 1914, these agreements had little if any formal force as a constraining device, since they were not recognized as orders of the Senate and therefore could be violated with impunity (Gamm and Smith 2000; Roberts and Smith 2004). The 1914 rules change that obligated presiding officers to enforce the provisions of UCAs occurred within close proximity of the cloture rule change, and might have affected coalition sizes in ways that could easily be wrongly attributed to the cloture rule. The greater reliability of UCAs post-1914 might have led legislative entrepreneurs to craft compromises to legislation in such a way that it made senators more amenable to giving up some of their prerogatives in order to get to a final passage vote on legislation. Such compromises might have involved making legislation palatable enough that senators would be indifferent between spending resources to filibuster it and voting against it on the floor. Similar to the logic we spelled out for the impact of cloture reform, compromise would also serve to increase coalition sizes.

To examine the relationship between UCAs and coalition sizes, we added an indicator for the presence of a UCA to our regression for coalition sizes on significant legislation reported in Chapter 4 (see Table 4.2). The UCA indicator equals 1 if an agreement to limit debate in some fashion was entered into on a given piece of legislation, and equals 0 otherwise.[24] The results are reported in Table 9.2. First of all, the inferences on the variables from the

---

[24]The data were collected from the *Congressional Record* and *Senate Journal*. Post-1914, the *Journal* clearly indicates whether or not a UCA was in effect.

Table 9.2 Pre- and Post-1917 Cloture Reform Effects of New Presidential
Regime and UCAs on Sizes of Winning Coalitions on Major
Legislation, 1881–1946

	1	2
Constant	0.844	0.847
	(0.017)	(0.017)
Pre-1917 Senate	−0.097	−0.097
	(0.027)	(0.028)
New Regime × Pre-1917 Senate	−0.063	−0.064
	(0.033)	(0.034)
New Regime × Post-1917 Senate	−0.062	−0.062
	(0.031)	(0.031)
UCA	−0.076	−0.085
	(0.024)	(0.025)
Pre-1914 Senate	—	−0.013
		(0.036)
UCA × Pre-1914 Senate	—	0.100
		(0.084)
Adjusted R^2	.186	.182
F value	10.13 ($p < .001$)	6.97 ($p < .001$)

Notes: $N = 161$. OLS coefficients with standard errors in parentheses.

previous regression essentially remain unchanged. While the t statistic on
the pre-1917 regime switch interaction decreases somewhat, the coefficient
is still significant at conventionally accepted levels. The coefficient on the
UCA indicator is bounded away from 0, although it has the sign opposite of
what we would expect. Coalition sizes were *smaller* on legislation where a
UCA was in effect. This suggests that securing UCAs did not involve forging
compromises in ways that would increase coalition sizes. In order to account
for the fact that UCAs were essentially non-binding before 1914, we added a
pre-1914 dummy and interacted it with our UCA dummy. These regression
results are reported in column 2 of Table 9.2. The pre-1914 indicator is not
statistically different from 0 nor is its interaction with the UCA dummy,
suggesting that the advent of the era of binding UCAs has little to do with
the patterns in coalition sizes that we have observed. The inferences on the
other variables in the model are essentially unchanged.

Looking at post-1914 bills, we see that coalition sizes for significant bills that did not have UCAs were larger than those that did. The former had a mean of approximately .80, the latter a mean of .73, which is a statistically significant difference according to a Wilcoxon test. It does not appear that UCAs drove the increase in coalition sizes. If anything, it appears that UCAs were not necessary for bills where there was likely widespread agreement in the first place. It also appears that UCAs were used differently during this period than they are today. Rather than structure floor debate before a bill was brought to the floor, UCAs between 1914 and 1946 were generally entered into after a piece of legislation had been brought to the floor and been under debate for a period of time. If we delete two outlier UCAs that postponed consideration of legislation until a later session, 46% of the UCAs in our sample imposed debate constraints on either the same day they were entered into or on the following day. The mean number of days between the establishment of UCAs and the date when the constraints took effect was four (the median value was three days). These measures indicate that UCAs were not used for the purposes of forging compromises, but as a coordination device for disposing of business after floor time had already been devoted to legislation.

9.3.3 Agenda Change

Another alternative explanation that we consider for why coalition sizes became larger after cloture is that the congressional agenda changed. Congress may simply have dealt with issues that enabled legislative solutions that attracted larger majorities. Thus, the quantitative change in coalition sizes is due to a qualitative change in what those coalitions passed, or so the argument would go. To assess the validity of this argument, we perform the following counterfactual analysis: based on available data, what would we expect coalition sizes to look like after 1917 if the agenda during that period was the same as the pre-cloture agenda?

One way to assess changes in the nature of the agenda is to look at issue codes that indicate the subjects that the significant legislation in our sample addresses. We rely on two well-known sets of issue codes—developed by Clausen (1973) and Peltzman (1984)—for classifying roll call votes.[25] Figure 9.4 reports the proportion of significant bills passed in each congress between the 47th and the 79th that fell into Clausen's different categories.[26] We conducted tests of equal proportions to see if there were any differences in the proportion of significant bills enacted before and after cloture and found differences for only two out of the five categories. Social welfare legislation

---

[25] The roll call votes on final passage of significant legislation thus provide the issue codes. We employ Poole and Rosenthal's (2000) roll call data to match votes and their codes with significant legislation. We do not use Poole and Rosenthal's own issue codes because the large number of categories they specify (ninety-nine) does not permit parsimonious analysis of changes in the kinds of issues considered.

[26] Clausen's codes included a miscellaneous category that we do not report because none of the significant bills in our data set fell into this category.

appears to have been considered more frequently as part of the "significant" agenda ($\chi_1^2 = 3.27; p = 0.07$), while civil liberties legislation was considered less frequently ($\chi_1^2 = 3.49; p = 0.06$) after 1917. The increase in the proportion of significant social welfare legislation is clearly due to the New Deal, but as we stated in Chapter 4, we get the same result of an increase in coalition sizes even accounting for differences due to the sea change in American politics that was the New Deal. In fact, the average coalition size on these kinds of bills (.79) was somewhat smaller compared with bills in the other categories (.81) in the post-cloture period (although this difference is not statistically significant). Furthermore, civil liberties legislation had a mean coalition size of .81 in the pre-cloture era, which is greater than the mean coalition size of all legislation in the pre-cloture period. This suggests that if civil liberties legislation had been as uncommon in the pre-cloture period as it was in the post-cloture period, average coalition sizes would have been even smaller in the earlier period.

Figure 9.5 reports the proportions for the codes created by Peltzman. Again, there do not generally appear to be substantial differences before and after cloture in the share of the significant legislative agenda across most of the categories. According to tests of equal proportions, the exceptions are "Budget, General Interest" ($\chi_1^2 = 8.75; p = 0.003$) and "Defense Policy, Budget" ($\chi_1^2 = 2.56; p = 0.1$) legislation, which became more prevalent on the significant agenda. "Budget, Special Interest" legislation became less prevalent after 1917 ($\chi_1^2 = 2.70; p = 0.1$). Yet the average coalition size for the legislation that became more prevalent (.81) is virtually identical to the average coalition size for all other significant bills (.80) passed after the adoption of cloture. There is not a significant difference between average coalitions for "Budget, Special Interest" legislation and the other categories either before or after cloture, indicating that the declining prevalence of this type of legislation was not responsible for the observed increase in average coalition sizes after 1917.

As additional evidence that the increase in coalition sizes is not due to changes in the agenda, we refer to the analysis in Chapter 4 that showed coalitions on appropriations bills also increased during this period. The set of appropriations bills under consideration stayed fairly constant between the two eras. While the infrequency of roll call votes on spending bills requires us to be very cautious about making inferences based on them, the next chapter explores other ways in which an analysis of appropriations reveals the impact of cloture reform.

9.3.4 Changes in the Distribution of Preferences in the House and Senate

One interesting feature of the data we have examined on significant legislation is that coalition sizes on this kind of legislation in the House increased as well over the time period under investigation. As Table 9.3 reports, average coalition sizes in the House were very close to those in the Senate in the pre-

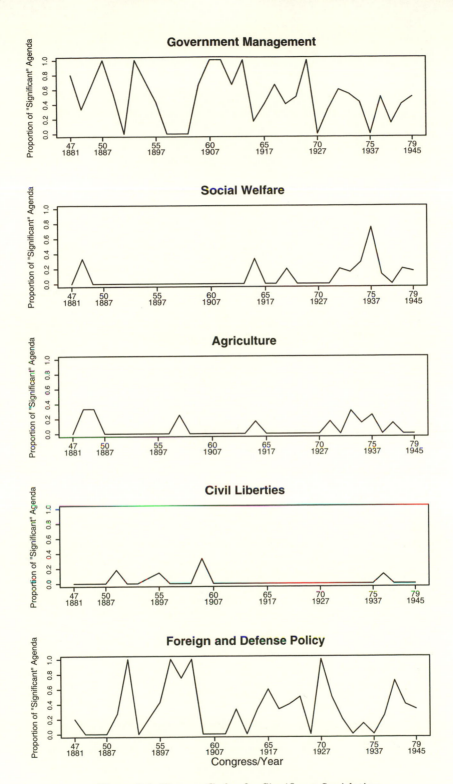

Figure 9.4 Clausen Codes for Significant Legislation

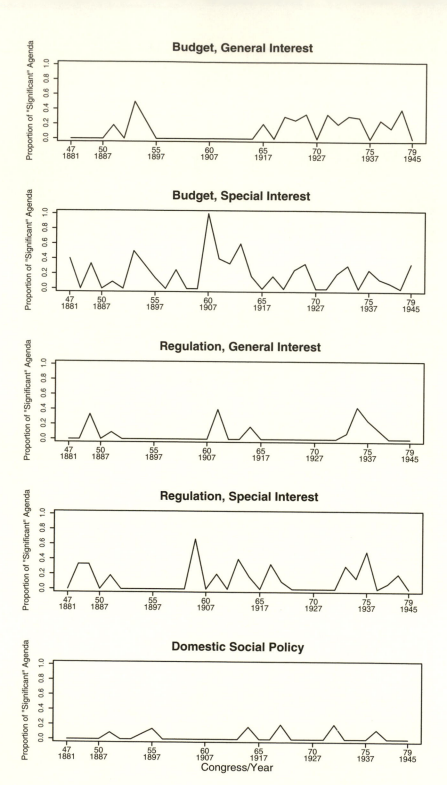

Figure 9.5 Peltzman Codes for Significant Legislation

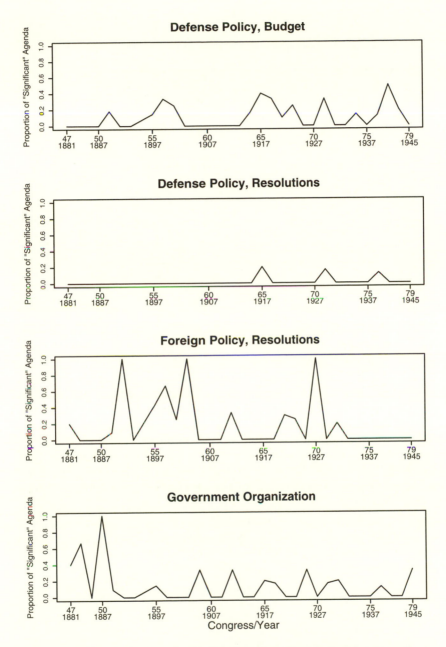

Figure 9.5 Peltzman Codes for Significant Legislation (continued)

Table 9.3 House Coalition Sizes on Major Legislation, 1881–1946

	Average percentage voting in favor	Percentage enacted with fewer than 2/3 voting in favor	Percentage enacted with fewer than 2/3 voting in favor
47th–64th Congress (1881–1917)	74	37	23
65th–79th Congress (1917–1946)	83	11	1

Notes: The number of laws is fifty-two for 47th–64th Congresses and eighty-six for 65th–79th Congresses.

and post-cloture periods. In fact, average coalition sizes in the House were slightly larger overall, and that chamber was more likely to pass significant legislation with supermajorities than was the Senate either before or after 1917. This result is surprising given that the institutional structure of the House, particularly after the adoption of the Reed rules in 1890, gave so much more leverage to the majority party to work its will. Coalition sizes were fairly broad prior to the Reed rules—74% on average compared with 80% afterward (although we have data on only fifteen pieces of pre-Reed legislation). Yet 27% of the significant legislation passed before the adoption of the Reed rules in the 51st Congress had fewer than 60% voting in favor, while only 7% of legislation enacted after this point had coalitions of this size. This is striking considering that the Reed rules were supposed have eliminated the effectiveness of obstructive tactics, yet coalitions appeared to be generally broader in that chamber. Given the virtual elimination of minority dilatory tactics in the 1890s, we would expect that coalitions in the House would be getting smaller, other things equal.[27]

The bicameral organization of Congress ensures that behavior of the two chambers will be correlated to a certain degree. More specifically, the size of coalitions that are formed in the two chambers to pass legislation in identical form should depend on the preference distributions of House and Senate members. If members of one chamber start to build larger coalitions to pass bills—and the preference distribution in the other chamber is nearly identical

---

[27]Ancillary regressions revealed that the pre-cloture variable had smaller effects relative to the Senate, and that partisan factors appeared to have played a larger role in determining coalition sizes in the House.

to that in the first chamber—then coalition sizes will tend to increase in both the House and Senate.

At a minimum then, for House coalition sizes to increase with Senate coalition sizes in line with our explanation, we should see convergence in the preference distributions of the two chambers. A formal test is available to assess whether or not the preference distributions in the two chambers did in fact became more similar. We conducted this test—known as the Mann-Whitney or Wilcoxon test of equal distributions—using the first dimension common space NOMINATE scores in each congress from the 46th through the 74th. The null hypothesis in this nonparametric test is that the two distributions are equivalent.[28] The p values across the congresses in our sample are displayed in Figure 9.6. The null is rejected (at the .1 level or better) far more frequently in the pre-cloture period than in the post-cloture period.[29] Nine out of nineteen pre-cloture congresses (47%) did not have statistically equivalent distributions, as opposed to only one—the 73rd (1933–1934)—out of ten post-cloture congresses.[30] Thus, a minimal condition for coalition sizes in the House to track coalition sizes in the Senate is met, although admittedly this does not tell us definitively whether the House responded to increases in Senate coalition sizes. The increase in House coalition sizes raises questions about the degree to which the cloture rule was causally responsible for the patterns we see in the data during this period. However, the potential alternative explanations we have considered have each been found empirically lacking. While the House comparison suggests agenda change might be responsible, the analysis in Section 9.3.3 refutes that explanation.

9.4 CONCLUSION

The prevailing conventional wisdom in the congressional literature is that the cloture reform of 1917 was merely symbolic and had little substantive import for the way the Senate did business in the few decades that followed

---

[28]The ideological distributions within the House and the Senate look like bimodal normal mixtures, with the two modes representing the modes for each party. Since it is nonparametric, the Mann-Whitney test is appropriate for these kinds of distributions (see Conover 1999, 272).

[29]These congresses are the 46th, 47th, 49th, 50th, 51st, 53rd, 54th, 55th, and 59th. We do not have a prediction about whether the distributions need to be similar in the pre-cloture period. We report the test results for both the pre- and post-cloture periods in order to demonstrate that there has been variation across the House and Senate in terms of the overlap of ideological distributions and that the pattern we see in the post-cloture period is not a foregone conclusion.

[30]This result does not seem to be due to divided versus unified control of Congress. In the pre-cloture period covered by the data, there were five congresses with divided control, but in only one of those do we reject the null of equal distributions. In the fourteen congresses with unified control, we reject the null for six of them. The differences in these proportions are not statistically significant, indicating no association between divided control and chamber preference distributions. In the post-cloture period covered by our analysis, only two congresses experienced divided control, but in neither of them is the null of equal distributions rejected.

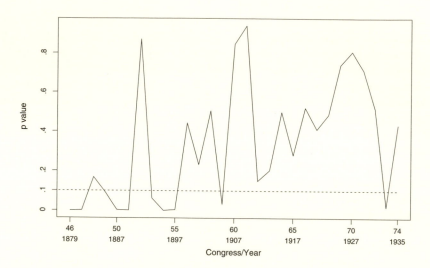

Figure 9.6 Test of Equal Distributions of Preferences in the Senate and House

the reform. However, we have shown theoretically how cloture reform's impact might have rested in its reduction of the uncertainty that legislative entrepreneurs faced when trying to push legislation near final adjournment. The rule had the potential to increase the Senate's efficiency in passing legislation by providing a clear threshold for cutting off debate and bringing legislation to a final vote. We have reported empirical evidence that is consistent with these theoretical conjectures. The reduction in variance of coalition sizes on significant legislation indicates that the adoption of the cloture rule had a substantive impact on the operation of the Senate, contrary to what the conventional wisdom would have us believe. By adopting the cloture rule senators meaningfully addressed the crisis they confronted at the turn of the century while preserving the essential nature of the Senate as a relation-based institution. Furthermore, we have shown that more general patterns in lawmaking are consistent with our arguments about the impact of cloture and are not explained by alternative theoretical perspectives.

This chapter and the previous chapter represent a movement in our analysis toward a *theory of institutions*. Diermeier and Krehbiel (2003) define an institutional theory as one in which "institutional features are taken as exogenous and behavioral postulates are fixed," whereas in a theory of institutions, institutional features become objects of collective choice. In previous chapters, we have considered how senators behaved under different institutional settings and what the consequences were for policy making at a macrolevel. In the last two chapters, we have considered why senators chose to change one of the most important features of their institution—the rules regarding debate—and adopt supermajority procedures for forcing a vote on legislation. Our primary concern is to understand Senate history, but our model of cloture reform can easily be applied to other legislatures. Although we have placed an emphasis on the uniqueness of Senate rules and procedures, it is obviously not the only legislature that relies on supermajority thresholds to get its work done. Indeed, one needs only to walk to the other end of the Capitol Building to find a legislative body that has adopted supermajority procedures as part of its rules. Even the strictly majoritarian House often conducts business under suspension of the rules, which requires two-thirds support. The House resorts to this procedure, which bars amendments not included in the motion and limits debate to forty minutes, in order to expedite the passage of legislation (Smith 1989, 37–40). In adopting this procedure, members of the House seemed to be making exactly the same trade-off that we argued senators made when they adopted the 1917 cloture rule. There are still some ways for procedurally savvy individuals to inhibit progress on legislation in the tightly structured House. One interpretation for why House members adopted this procedure is that it gives them protection from some of the uncertainty of the floor stage in exchange for compromising on the substance of legislation. Such compromise would be necessary to attract broader coalitions that can invoke the procedure, which in turn makes legislation less susceptible to parliamentary mischief. The analysis in this chapter can be extended to investigate whether similar motivations have led other legislative bodies in the United States and abroad to adopt supermajority procedures.[31]

Indeed, our theoretical conjectures throughout this book can be applied in comparative analysis to test their broader validity. In an innovative comparative investigation of legislative organization by Taylor (Forthcoming), chamber size is shown to be a robust predictor of centralized agenda control: small chambers are more likely to allow considerable individual latitude to shape the agenda, while large chambers tend to adopt rules that provide for tight control. This is consistent with the Senate's historical experience, in which the increase in size undermined the chamber's ability to operate under an informal, relation-based system that provided little formal infrastructure for limiting senators' behavior.[32]

The implications that our study has for comparative analysis is made all the more relevant by two recent cross-national trends: the widespread adoption of democratic forms of governments in former autocracies and a revivification of upper chambers in new and established democracies.[33] Of

---

[31] One preliminary investigation at the state level suggests our argument and results are indeed generalizable in this regard. Cody (2004) examines the impact of the adoption of a cloture rule by the Nebraska legislature in 1992. Similar to our analysis, he finds that coalition sizes after the adoption of the cloture rule were larger than before its adoption.

[32] Carruba and Volden's (2000) formal model also reveals that bodies with larger memberships require restrictive procedures as cooperation becomes costly.

[33] Massicotte (2001, 154) points out that in the period of 1950–1979, nineteen countries abolished second chambers, seventeen created or restored them, while nine countries created and then abolished the second chamber within this period. However, in the period from 1980 to 1999, only six second chambers were abolished, while eleven were restored and fourteen were created anew.

the one-hundred democracies in existence in 2003, almost half (forty-four) made their transitions to this form of government in the previous twenty years. When such transitions are made, nations must decide what form their legislatures will take, not only in terms of bicameralism versus unicameralism, but also in terms of internal organization of the legislature. Rules regarding debate are a key part of internal organization and present an interesting challenge to states that do not have particularly strong traditions of vigorous and open political deliberation. A lack of restrictions on debate might be particularly attractive for these countries philosophically, if not practically. Our analysis indicates the conditions under which sparse debate rules can be supplemented by informal constraints, enabling a legislature to accomplish its policymaking duties while allowing individual legislators considerable latitude for potentially informative discussion. Indeed, nascent legislatures might be well served by institutional designs that consist of a few basic rules around which they can develop and adapt, perhaps formalizing what works informally when strains begin to appear. Simply grafting complex designs that have developed in long-standing democracies onto legislatures in emerging democracies could be far less desirable than letting these institutions evolve from a limited, informal procedural infrastructure. While economically developing countries in particular may feel the need for fast-acting legislatures, our study cautions them about the potential value of parliamentary delay. The fact that upper chambers—which have traditionally played the role of retarding the activities of lower chambers with more direct ties to the mass public—have been resurgent recently in established democracies suggests that countries with lengthy experiences with republican governments are rediscovering the potential benefits of delay in decision making.

Legislatures must be relatively small and must not be subject to extreme time pressures in order for this kind of experimentation to be viable. The Senate's experience suggests that resorting to more formal rules—including limitations on debate—will be increasingly attractive for larger chambers confronting a higher workload. Thus, our study points the way for more general, comparative investigation of the relationship between debate rules and lawmaking.

Chapter Ten

The Impact of Cloture on the Appropriations Process

10.1 INTRODUCTION

In this chapter, we pursue the issue of the impact of cloture further by examining the appropriations process in the Senate. The failure to pass appropriations bills, especially due to obstruction, was a major concern of senators in the period under examination. They perennially confronted the problem of passing appropriations before the fiscal year expired, which was necessary to keep the federal government operating. We argue that the cloture rule was a key component of a set of institutional reforms that addressed the ability of the Senate to fulfill its charge in fiscal policymaking despite its sparse procedural infrastructure.

In debates about obstruction, concerns about appropriations were constantly expressed. In his campaign in 1925 against the rules that allowed filibusters, Vice President Charles Dawes asked whether "the power to kill legislation providing the revenues to pay the expenses of government should, during the last few days of a session, ever be in the hands of a minority, or perhaps one senator? Why should they ever compel the President of the United States to call an extra session of Congress to keep in functioning activity the machinery of the Government itself" (*Congressional Record*, 69th Cong., special session, pp. 3–4). According to Haynes (1938, v. 1, 395), "appropriations bills engrossed so much of the Senate's time that the necessity of some limitations on debate first became convincing in regard to them." The death of appropriations bills at the hands of obstructionists often prompted calls for cloture reform. For example, a cloture proposal introduced by Senator Orville Platt in 1901 was reported to be in response to the successful filibuster of a Rivers and Harbors appropriations bill in the previous congress ("To Limit Debate in the United States Senate," *New York Times*, March 6, 1901, p. 5). Rogers (1926, 183–84) argued that the power of the filibuster came through its effects on the appropriations process: "It is through their ability to hold up the appropriation bills that a filibustering minority can win a victory." It is important to note that these concerns were not just about filibusters of appropriations bills, but also about how filibusters of any legislation would affect the Senate's ability to pass spending measures.[1]

---

[1]Indeed, one of the reasons that the opposition to Jefferson Smith's filibuster in *Mr. Smith Goes to Washington* was so fierce was that his obstruction against the measure to expel him from the Senate for corruption was preventing the passage of an urgently needed appropriations bill.

The filibuster that defeated the Armed-Ship Bill in 1917 took with it several regular appropriations bills and a general deficiency bill, which amounted to about $511 million worth of stalled funds ("$511,000,000 in Bills Blocked by Senate," *New York Times*, March 5, 1917, p. 2).

In a series of articles on the failure to pass appropriations bills by the fiscal year deadline in 1912, the *New York Times* painted a dire picture of the resulting disruption. The *Times* contended that government departments would be in violation of the law if they continued to operate without the passage of appropriations bills that provided them with funds ("Convention Halts Department Funds," July 1, 1912, p. 4).[2] It was noted how the "most serious phase of the situation is the prospect that all the letter carriers and the rural free delivery carriers . . . may have to stop work until Congress acts . . . . [T]he 28,000 letter carriers in cities, 41,000 rural carriers, 33,000 clerks in post offices, 16,000 railway mail clerks, and upward of 8,000 other clerks in the service will be out of work and the public service will be prostrated" ("Dilatory Senate Halts Money Bills," June 27, 1912, p. 1). The *Washington Post* reported that 25,000 civilian employees in every navy yard in the country would be laid off without pay because of the failure to pass the Navy spending bill ("Ties Up U.S. Business," June 26, 1912, p. 11). The need to work through the summer on the appropriations bills was also problematic because it would keep members of Congress from the "pressing political business for most of them at home" ("The Delays in Congress," *New York Times*, July 9, 1912, p. 8).

The uncertainty that filibusters presented to the appropriations process was a primary concern in the efforts to reform Senate procedure. If our argument that the cloture rule served as an uncertainty-reducing mechanism is correct, then this should be reflected in the Senate's ability to process appropriations bills. We investigate whether the cloture rule led to increased efficiency in the appropriations process by more clearly prescribing a threshold for bringing debate to an end and legislation to a vote. We argue that cloture was part of a set of reforms enacted during this period that helped the Senate deal with problems that obstruction presented in the enactment of fiscal policy.

An examination of Senate action on appropriations is important beyond our interest in filibuster politics because, while several studies have undertaken historical analyses of the appropriations process in the House (e.g., Stewart 1989 and Kiewiet and McCubbins 1991), the process in the Senate has received scant scholarly attention. In part due to its traditional role of moving first in the process, the House has been seen as the dominant congressional partner in spending decisions. The Senate is depicted as reactive, serving as a "court of appeals," for claimants on the federal treasury who seek more funds than provided in the legislation initially passed by the House (Fenno 1966). Yet the role of the Senate in the appropriations process is far from trivial. This chapter helps to illuminate the part that the

---

[2]See also "Crisis in U.S. Cash," *Washington Post*, June 27, 1912, p. 5.

Senate's unique rules and procedures have played in spending decisions and the ability of the federal government to meet its fiscal obligations.

Studies of obstruction have not delved deeply into its effects on Congress's power over the purse strings of government. Yet one of the factors that is most important for understanding obstruction—time constraints—is particularly relevant for spending bills. Appropriations faced deadline problems that were more complex than those faced by other kinds of legislation. In order to meet the government's fiscal obligations and maintain operations, Congress had to pass appropriations by the beginning of the fiscal year, which occurred on July 1 during the period we examine. Congress would typically not be in session when the deadline passed for fiscal years that began in odd-numbered years. After adjourning on March 4, Congress would usually not meet again until December of that year. As a result, Congress had to pass appropriations bills by the March 4 adjournment date if it was to provide funds before the new fiscal year started.[3] Since Congress did not start considering appropriations bills for even-numbered fiscal years until the lame duck sessions, this made time constraints especially relevant.[4]

For fiscal years that began when Congress was conducting its regular session, the Senate nonetheless often struggled to complete work on spending bills. In fact, Congress was less likely to meet the fiscal year deadline for these years. Although members may have been less concerned about failing to meet the deadline when they knew they would still be in session to rectify the problem, it is worth noting that such failures were by no means unproblematic. The failure to meet the deadline would still mean that the relevant government entities would run out of money to fund their operations and Congress would have to go through the effort of passing continuing appropriations in addition to regular appropriations to keep these entities functioning.[5]

We posit that the cloture rule should have enhanced the Senate's ability to meet the relevant deadlines that it faced for passing spending bills. Although cloture was rarely invoked, we have presented evidence that senators built bigger coalitions after the rule was adopted, which is consistent with our argument that they were attempting to preempt filibusters. If such preemption was occurring, then it should have been easier for the Senate to pass appropriations in a timely manner. In this chapter, we investigate systematically whether or not this is the case.

---

[3]Special sessions could have been called to pass bills that failed of enactment before the deadline. While the Senate would often meet in special sessions shortly after the previous congress had adjourned in order to process presidential nominations, floor speeches and newspaper reports indicate that members of Congress were particularly averse to holding these kind of sessions to perform general legislative activities.

[4]Even-numbered fiscal years started on July 1 of odd-numbered calendar years.

[5]The standard practice was to pass a stopgap measure that would provide one-twelfth of the amount appropriated for the previous fiscal year. While this would enable the government to continue to write checks, it also fostered uncertainty regarding what obligations the government could incur, especially for commitments that extended beyond the one-month period allotted by the measures.

10.2 INSTITUTIONAL CHANGE RELEVANT TO THE APPRO-PRIATIONS PROCESS

Our analysis needs to be sensitive to other institutional changes during this period that are relevant to the appropriations process. These include some of the most important institutional changes involving the appropriations process in Congress's history. The two main changes are the passage of the Budget Act of 1921 and the decentralization and recentralization of committee jurisdictions over appropriations.[6]

While studies that focus on the impact of these institutional changes on the appropriations process in the House are plentiful, almost no systematic research has been conducted on the appropriations process in the Senate during this period—or for subsequent periods for that matter. Fenno's (1966) landmark book, *The Power of the Purse*, is essentially the only study that has examined the Senate process in any depth. Although Fenno's analysis is somewhat time-bound, covering the Senate only in the mid-20th century (1947–1965), a few major themes emerge from his research that have theoretical relevance for the study of obstruction in earlier periods and point to important factors that any empirical model of the appropriations process should account for. It is essential to assess whether the features that Fenno saw as central to the process in the Senate in the mid-20th century mattered in earlier periods.

One of Fenno's major conclusions was that the most important part of the appropriations process was the committee stage. The overall parameters of debate and deliberation were set in committee, and primarily in the House Appropriations Committee (HAC). The Senate Appropriations Committee (SAC) was also central to the process, but less so than HAC. A key difference between HAC and SAC, however, concerns the relationship between the committees and their parent chambers. The relationship between HAC and its parent chamber was characterized by tension, predominantly because of the committees' exclusivity, isolation, and tight-fisted control over the government's purse strings. Many House members complained about HAC's refusal to fund projects or programs that they believed were meritorious—or at the very least electorally beneficial.

The relationship between SAC and its parent chamber was much more cordial. Fenno hypothesized that this difference was rooted both in the greater openness of the committee in the Senate and the fact that a higher percentage of senators held seats on SAC, making it more representative. This made the committee much more accessible and rendered committee and chamber preferences over appropriations much more consonant than in the House. To paraphrase Fenno (1966, 614), "SAC is the Senate."

---

[6]It is unclear how the move to direct election during this period may have affected the appropriations process. Our analysis in Chapter 8 indicating that direct election had only limited effects on legislative behavior, however, suggests that it would not have had a substantial impact on the Senate's ability to meet appropriations deadlines.

This observation has theoretical relevance for our investigation of the Senate's ability to process appropriations. The greater representativeness of SAC should lead to less conflict on the Senate floor, since the bill that the committee reports is more likely to be in line with the preferences of non-committee members. Although the standard rules of floor debate grant substantial leeway to non-committee members to amend or obstruct SAC's proposals, it may be that senators see little need to do so because of their agreement with the committee. The greater representativeness of SAC should mean that it better anticipates what latent obstructors would object to once the bill reaches the floor and preempt them by making adjustments to the bill in committee.

This raises two important questions about SAC during the period we are interested in: First, how representative was SAC? Second, to what extent were the committee's proposals amended on the floor? Finding answers to these questions is complicated by the shifts in committee jurisdictions over spending bills that occurred in 1899 and 1922. In 1899, the Senate carved up most of SAC's jurisdiction and redistributed it to other committees. A similar devolution had taken place in the House in 1885 (Brady and Morgan 1987; Stewart 1989). This decentralization of appropriations stood in contrast to the centralizing efforts of party leaders that took place about the same time (Rothman 1966). The institutional change was largely driven by junior senators who sought more power over the Senate's proceedings (Schickler 2001; Schickler and Sides 2000). The effects of the decentralization in terms of which committees were given the authority to report appropriations bills are displayed in Table 10.1.

In early March 1922, the Senate reversed course and reinstated SAC's jurisdiction over all spending bills. However, committees that had appropriations jurisdiction after the 1899 divestiture were allowed to have three members serve ex officio on SAC when bills that had been a part of their turf were under consideration at SAC. They also could send one conferee to take part in conference committee deliberations.[7] The ex officio provision contributed considerably to the representativeness of SAC that Fenno reported. An important question for our analysis then is to what degree were the committees that received parts of SAC's jurisdiction representative of the larger chamber? The issue of the representativeness of committees, especially those that craft spending bills, has garnered considerable attention in the congressional literature. Proponents of the distributive perspective of legislative organization contend that committees are generally unrepresentative of their parent chambers. According to this work, committees consist of homogeneous preference outliers produced through a system of self-selection to committees that enables those with the greatest electoral stake in the committees' jurisdictions to obtain their preferred assignments (Shepsle 1978, 1979; Shepsle and Weingast 1987; Weingast and Marshall 1988). This view

---

[7]The District of Columbia committee was also granted this right. The ex officio provision was in effect until 1974, when Congress again transformed the appropriations process with the passage of the Budget and Impoundment Control Act.

Table 10.1 Senate Appropriations Decentralization of 1899

Appropriation bill title	Committee of jurisdiction
Agriculture	Agriculture and Forestry
Army	Military Affairs
Diplomatic and consular	Appropriations
District of Columbia	Appropriations
Fortification	Appropriations
Indian	Indian Affairs
Legislative, etc.	Appropriations
Military Academy	Military Affairs
Navy	Naval Affairs
Pension	Committee on Pensions
Post office	Post Offices and Post Roads
River and harbor	Commerce
Sundry civil	Appropriations

Source: *Congressional Record*, January 29, 1899, p. 1212

has been challenged by both the informational and partisan perspectives on legislative organization. The former argues that committees should be microcosms of the parent chamber in order to facilitate the communication of policy-relevant information (Krehbiel 1991), while the latter argues that committees should be representative of the (majority) party caucus, so that committees will be more effective and loyal agents of the party (Cox and McCubbins 1993; Kiewiet and McCubbins 1991). This dispute launched numerous empirical efforts using different measurement approaches to try to determine just how representative committees are in practice (Krehbiel 1990; Groseclose 1994; Hall and Grofman 1990; Maltzman 1997).

Studies of committee representativeness have focused mainly on the post–World War II period. Unfortunately, available data limit the extent to which we can address the issue of SAC's representativeness in earlier periods. Most importantly, existing data on committee rosters for the period under investigation does not include the names of the ex officio members of SAC. This makes it difficult to determine without possible error the ideological makeup of the panels that make spending decisions.[8] However, since we know the number of ex officio members from each of the legislative committees, we

---

[8] Fenno (1966, 508) claims ex officio members were the two senior majority members and the ranking minority members of the substantive committee, but it is not clear that this was the universal practice, given each committee could select its ex officio representatives under the rules.

can compute the percentage of the chamber that is eligible to participate in SAC deliberations.[9] While this measure is undoubtedly a crude one, it seems to fit well with the notion of representativeness that Fenno discussed, long before more sophisticated measures of committee ideology were developed. The key idea of inter-locking committee memberships is still tapped by this measure, and addresses our concern about committee-floor conflict on appropriations bills.

Figure 10.1 displays time series for the percentage of the Senate's membership that was involved in spending decisions for devolved and non-devolved appropriations bills. While there was a general upward trend in the representativeness of the funding committees by this measure, the trend appears to have accelerated somewhat with the recentralization of appropriations. Thus, the inter-locking memberships that Fenno discussed extend back at least to the recentralization, and given the close proximity of this institutional change to the the enactment of cloture, it is imperative to account for these changes to the committee system in our analysis.[10]

By comparison, the percentage of House members involved in appropriations decisions at the committee stage was much smaller both before and after the recentralization in that chamber. The legislative committees that lost jurisdiction to HAC when appropriations were recentralized in 1920 were not compensated as in the Senate, resulting in much grumbling and resentment of the committee (Stewart 1989, 205). As a consequence, the relationship between HAC and its parent chamber remained turbulent after the committee regained its lost authority.

The degree of harmony between the appropriating committees and the Senate should be reflected in the degree to which committee proposals were amended on the floor; in turn, the degree to which conflict spills out onto the floor should affect the Senate's ability to process legislation. Much has been made of the extent to which HAC recommendations have remained intact once the committee reports out bills. Fenno (1966) examined appropriations for thirty-six bureaus from 1947 to 1962, finding that HAC's recommendations were accepted without modification in the overwhelming majority of cases. The same seemed to be true of SAC. Kiewiet and McCubbins (1991, 149–52) extended Fenno's analysis to cover fiscal years 1947 to 1985, and found that the appropriations committees "appear to get most of what they want on the floor," since "amendments tend to be small in percentage terms" or "lacking in substance." A key difference between the appropriations process during the post-war period and the period we cover is that unanimous consent agreements had become a much more common way of doing business in the Senate and may have limited the range of amendments that could have

---

[9]This, of course, does not mean that all SAC members participate in committee deliberations to the same degree (cf. Hall 1996).

[10]Committee overlap existed to a more limited extent before the creation of ex officio seats on SAC. In the five congresses preceding the decentralization, the relevant legislative committees averaged between 0 and 1.8 members who also sat on SAC.

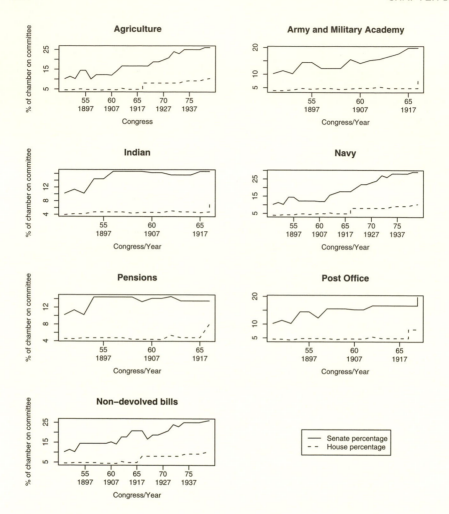

Figure 10.1 Percentage of Senate and House Involved in Appropriations Decisions

been offered on the floor (see Fenno 1966, 591). As a result, it is plausible that more amendments occurred in the earlier period.

But throughout the 20th century, one major issue was that the Senate almost invariably raised the dollar amount included in House bills. Anecdotal evidence indicates this tradition extended far back into congressional history. MacNeil (1963, 394) notes that House members complained of the Senate's additions to appropriations bills as early as the 1860s, and that by the end of the 19th century, this tradition appears to have been well established (see also Reinsch 1907, 112 and Rogers 1926, 111).

For our analysis, it is important to know whether this was the case systematically, and if so, whether the increases occurred during committee deliberations or during the amendment process on the floor. If they occurred during the latter stage, then this may have made it difficult for the Senate to process bills by the relevant deadlines. The wide open floor procedure in the Senate would have provided ample opportunity for senators to try to insert pork barrel projects into a bill through floor amendments. Indeed, the threat of obstruction may be one of the causal factors behind the more generous bills that came out of the Senate. The first reported case where a senator explicitly threatened to filibuster an appropriations bill in order to increase spending was when "Pitchfork" Ben Tillman (D–SC) claimed he would talk a 1903 deficiency bill to death unless funds to reimburse his state for expenses incurred during the War of 1812 were reinserted into the bill. His successful threat prompted Joseph Cannon—then House Appropriations chair—to deliver a rousing speech on the floor, charging that the rules of the Senate subjected the House to "legislative blackmail" ("Mr. Cannon Stirs the House," *New York Times*, March 5, 1903, p. 2; Burdette 1940, 72). Rogers (1926, 170–71) discusses this and one other incident where senators successfully had items inserted into appropriations bills in response to their threats of obstruction, and cites a statement made in 1913 by Senator Charles Thomas (D–CO) in which he claimed there were "scores of others which have disfigured our consideration of appropriations bills" during his service in the chamber (see also Matthews 1960, 259).

The degree to which the Senate modifies House bills might have been particularly problematic after the passage of the Budget Act. Kiewiet and McCubbins (1991, 172–73) argue that the Budget Act was largely prompted by a new interest in economy that stemmed from a dramatic increase in the federal debt due to World War I and changes in the source of revenues for the federal government—namely, the decline in tariffs and the rise in corporate and personal income taxation. This interest in economy had great potential to conflict with the long-standing Senate tradition of upping amounts in the bills that were referred to it. MacNeil (1963, 394–95) argues that the creation of the Budget Bureau and the restoration of all appropriations bills to HAC were an attempt by the House to reassert itself against the Senate, which had dominated the appropriations process since the decentralization of 1885. These steps were viewed as a way for the traditionally more frugal chamber to cut back on profligate spending, consistent with the mood of economy that prevailed at the time. The desire to impose spending discipline in the 1920s might have led to floor conflict if SAC had increased appropriations in the allegedly fiscally conservative House bill. If the increases in appropriations happened at the SAC stage, then economy-minded non-SAC senators might have tried to alter bills when they had a crack at them at the floor stage.

While anecdotally the Senate appears to have long been the more generous chamber when it came to spending decisions, we do not know the extent to which this was the case systematically. The existing literature is also silent on whether the deference to SAC extends either back in time or to the committees that obtained part of SAC's jurisdiction from 1899 to 1922. Figure 10.2 sheds light on the dynamics of both intra- and inter-chamber conflict over alterations to regular appropriations bills. It shows

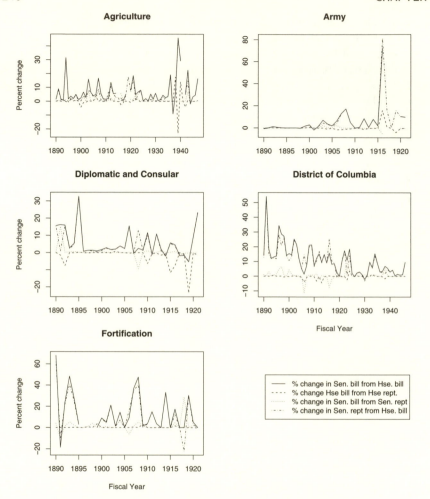

Figure 10.2 Changes to Appropriations Bills

the percentage change in the bill reported by the relevant appropriations committee and the bill that passed on the floor in each chamber, as well as the difference between the initial bills passed by the House and the Senate (i.e., before their differences were worked out in conference).[11]

Although there is substantial variation across appropriations types, one pattern that is evident from the figures is that the bill that passes the Senate

---

[11]These plots represent the main categories of appropriations bills that existed for most of the period covered by our analysis. Some series end after the 66th Congress because these specific bill titles ceased to exist after the passage of the Budget Act. The data are from tables that appear in the Senate document *Appropriations, New Offices, Etc.* From 1890, this document regularly included tables compiled by the clerks of HAC and SAC, which contain information about the amounts in and the progress of appropriations bills. A few outlying years are deleted from the plots in order to make them more readable.

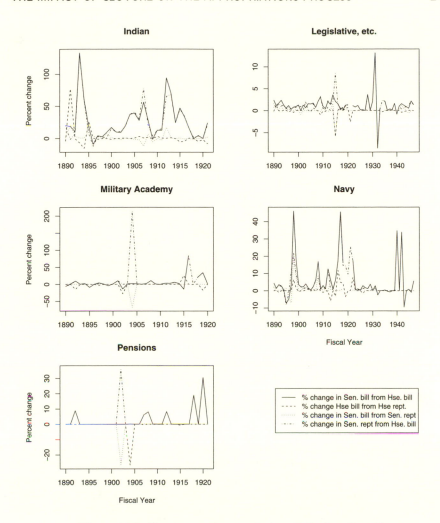

Figure 10.2 Changes to Appropriations Bills (continued)

typically has a larger amount than the House bill, but the Senate bill hews closely to that reported by the relevant Senate committee. Indeed, it is difficult to discern the dotted-dashed line representing the change between the House bill and the Senate committee bill, since it is mostly covered by the solid line representing the difference between the final Senate bill and House bill in Figure 10.2. Consistent with what Fenno found in the mid-20th century, appropriating was done almost entirely in committee and not on the floors of the chambers. The lines representing the difference between the bills passed by the chamber and the bills reported out of committee rarely depart from zero. The increases in House bills that occurred in the Senate appear to have largely been the result of committee deliberations.[12]

---

[12]The average percentage difference between bills that passed the House and bills that were reported from SAC is 7.2. By contrast, the difference between SAC bills and bills that passed the Senate is just 1.2.

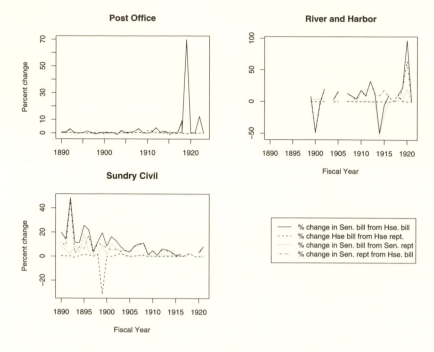

Figure 10.2 Changes to Appropriations Bills (continued)

At least in terms of dollar amounts, it was unusual for major changes to happen on the Senate floor, as the recommendations of the appropriating committees were for the most part accepted despite the lack of rules that would have restricted amendments. Nonetheless, this does not mean that the threat of obstruction on the floor by senators, who were either upset about being stiffed by the committee over funds they sought or disquieted by SAC larding up a bill, was not an issue. Fenno (1966, 520) quotes a SAC staffer who suggests that this was indeed a concern of appropriating committees:

> You can do a lot of things in the House that you can't do in the Senate. If you get up to speak on appropriations there, they can shout you down. But over here, you got to listen to what a senator has to say no matter who he is. If you don't, he'll filibuster you and hold up an appropriation bill for three days.

The openness of the Senate committee and the interlocking memberships that existed appeared to have enabled the committee to anticipate what trouble non-committee members could have caused on the floor and to modify bills in ways that preempted moves to change the bills through floor amendments.

10.3 CLOTURE AND APPROPRIATIONS DEADLINES

The discussion in the previous section sets the stage for a quantitative analysis of the impact of cloture on the ability of the Senate to process appropriations bills by deadlines established by the end of congresses and the beginning of the fiscal year. The analysis includes all regular appropriations bills that were considered from 1890 to 1946, which is essentially the same period covered by the data on significant legislation.[13] The dependent variable in our analysis takes on a value of 1 if the Senate *failed* to pass a bill for a given appropriations category by the relevant deadline, and is 0 otherwise. The key explanatory variable we are interested in is a dummy variable that equals 1 for bills considered prior to the adoption of cloture and equals 0 for post-cloture bills. If our hypothesis regarding the effectiveness of the cloture rule is correct, we should observe a positive coefficient on this variable. This is an admittedly crude measure and could account for numerous changes that occurred around the time that cloture was adopted. As discussed in the previous section, the most important changes that happened in close proximity to the cloture rule concerned the recentralization of the jurisdiction over appropriations in HAC and SAC and the Budget Act of 1921. While we could model the effects of these changes with their own dummy variables, such variables would obviously be highly correlated with each other and the dummy variable indicating the existence of a cloture rule. Including all of these dummies in our model would make it difficult to sort out the effects of the various changes in institutions that occurred. Fortunately, we can do better by including more precise measures that capture theoretically relevant features of these institutional changes.

A key change under the Budget Act was to centralize in the Bureau of the Budget the processing of agency requests for funds before they were submitted to Congress. This was intended to bring about efficiency in the process as well as to promote fiscal discipline by reining in agencies that submitted overly large spending requests. The centralization should have reduced the amount of time that it took to process the spending bills, which would have made it easier for the Senate to meet appropriations deadlines. Just as importantly, it also would have given senators more time to resort to the cloture procedure if they thought it necessary. Table 10.2 shows one measure that indicates increased efficiency that followed passage of the Budget Act in terms of the average number of days between important junctures in the process and the deadline. Post–Budget Act, there were on average more days between the deadline and the reporting of bills from HAC, their passage on the House floor, and the reporting of bills by SAC. The process prior to the point of reaching the Senate floor moved more quickly after 1921, which gave senators more time to consider bills on the floor.[14] Since we are mainly

---

[13]See footnote 11 for the source of the appropriations amounts and data on the progress of bills. We do not include deficiency appropriations bills in our analysis since these did not have the same kind of deadline constraints as regular appropriation bills.

[14]The increased efficiency is not due to the elimination of lame duck sessions in 1933

Table 10.2 Efficiency in the Appropriations Process, 1890–1946

	Pre-Budget Act ($N = 389$)	Post-Budget Act ($N = 242$)
Avg. number of days between report from HAC and deadline	83	100
Avg. number of days between House passage and deadline	69	94
Avg. number of days between report from SAC and deadline	48	71

Note: Data are based on all regular appropriations bills.

interested in the processing of bills on the Senate floor, we include in our specification the variable measuring the number of days between the reporting of the bill by SAC and the relevant deadline.[15] Including this variable allows us to account for one of the main ways in which the Budget Act induced efficiency. We expect this variable to have a negative coefficient, since the longer it takes to get through the committee stage in the Senate (i.e., the less time between the report of the committee and the deadline), the more difficult it should be to process the bill on the floor before either the congress or the fiscal year expires. Note that by including this variable we are also accounting for the amount of time it took the bill to make its way through the House, since the Senate did not begin to consider appropriations bills until the House had passed them.[16]

As Figure 10.2 shows, most modifications to House bills happened in SAC and not on the Senate floor. To the extent that these changes might have provoked discord on the floor, it should show up in the differences between the bill that passed the House and the bill reported by SAC. That is, economy-minded senators in the post–Budget Act world may have taken issue with increases in spending that occurred in committee, and might have tried to use their prerogatives on the floor to strip out spending that they viewed

---

nor is it due to longer sessions in the 1930s. If we exclude congresses after the 20th Amendment took effect, the average number of days between the important junctures and the deadline is greater across the board. Thus, it appears that the values for these measures increased after the Budget Act but then decreased after the 20th Amendment took effect.

[15] In a few cases, the bill was reported from SAC after the deadline. These bills are dropped from the sample so that the floor is not penalized for the late action of SAC.

[16] Including variables that measure the number of days between reporting or passage of the bill in the House produces essentially the same results as we report below.

as wasteful. The exercise of their prerogatives would have inhibited the progress of the bill toward final passage. To capture this possible effect, we include in our model a variable measuring the difference between the amount in the bill reported by SAC and the amount that passed the House. The greater this difference, the more potential conflict there might be on the floor as the competing interests of economy allegedly embodied in the House bill clashed with the increases that SAC had historically made to bills.[17] We expect a positive coefficient on this variable, which would indicate that greater differences led to more conflict and more difficulty in passing bills in the Senate.

The other major institutional changes that are crucial to account for concern the changing nature of committee jurisdictions over appropriations. The larger the percentage of the Senate that sat on the relevant appropriating committees, the smoother the floor stage of the process should have gone. In particular, the recentralization in 1922 and the concomitant increases in SAC's effective size should have made it more likely that the Senate would have met the deadlines as floor and committee agreement would have increased. The variable in our model that captures this effect is the percentage of members of the Senate who sat either on SAC or the relevant legislative committee between 1899 and 1922. This variable should have a negative effect—that is, increases in the percentage of the chamber serving on the committee should decrease the probability of a failure to meet the deadline.

Alternatively, one could argue that the recentralization might have had negative effects on the meeting of deadlines. Stewart (1989, 120) argues that one of the reasons for the devolution of appropriations bills from HAC was that members of Congress believed the committee was "severely overworked, as indicated by the tardiness with which appropriations bills were reported in the 48th Congress." Reconstituting SAC's jurisdiction might have led to similar difficulties after 1922. We doubt that this is the case because, first, the Budget Bureau should have made life much easier for both HAC and SAC, and, second, the enlargement of SAC meant that workload would have been distributed more widely for particular bills. Nevertheless, the sign of the coefficient on the committee-to-chamber ratio variable will settle this question.

The point about workload suggests another variable that should be included in our model. If the decentralization of appropriations was in part motivated by concerns about committee workload, then it may be the case that devolved bills were dealt with more expeditiously since this spread out the work at the committee stage. This, of course, assumes that the newly acquired jurisdiction could be handled along with the committees' other legislative duties. To account for possible effects of the decentralization (as opposed to recentralization), the model specification includes a variable that

---

[17]One could argue that it was the Budget Bureau more than HAC or the House that sought fiscal discipline. Data on appropriations estimates from the executive are harder to come by for the period we examine. If we use data on estimates instead of what HAC reported, we obtain similar results, but our sample size is reduced by about half.

indicates whether a bill was considered by a committee other than SAC in a given fiscal year. The inclusion of this variable helps to allay concerns that the change in appropriations jurisdiction in 1922 alone is responsible for the observed impact of cloture.

We include several other variables to account for additional factors that might have affected the Senate's ability to process appropriations in a timely fashion. The amount of general legislative demands that were placed on the Senate is one such factor, which we capture by employing Binder's (1997, 218–19) measure of workload, described in Chapter 7.[18] The partisan and ideological makeup of the Senate may also have effects on its efficiency. A partisan view of appropriations might hold that the more unified the majority party is, the better able it will be to enforce discipline and meet appropriations deadlines. Given the centrality of spending decisions to the construction of a favorable party label, unity should be promoted and exploited to keep the appropriations process functioning as smoothly as possible and to the benefit of the majority party (cf. Cox and McCubbins 1993; Kiewiet and McCubbins 1991). As discussed in Chapter 9, there was substantial variation in the unity of Senate parties during the period we cover. The conventional wisdom is that parties became uncharacteristically strong at the end of the 19th and beginning of the 20th centuries (Rothman 1966), but then unity declined substantially as we moved into the 1910s and 1920s. Considering the timing of this decline, it seems essential then to attempt to account for this variation to make sure it is not spuriously causing bias in the results for the other variables. Invoking the usual caveats about the difficulties of measuring party influence, we include in our model the standard measure of majority party unity, the Rice cohesion score.

Finally, we account for potential ideological conflict that would cause delays in processing appropriations bills. Binder (2003) argues that intrachamber dissension is an essential component to understanding whether or not Congress passes legislation on its agenda. The more ideologically polarized the chamber is, the harder it will be to forge agreements within the chamber, and by extension the harder it will be to pass legislation in a timely fashion. To account for these possible effects, the model includes Binder's measure of moderation/polarization. Using first-dimension DW-NOMINATE scores, this measure is a count of the number of senators who are closer to the chamber median than to the median in their party, weighted by the distance between the party medians. The more senators who are located in this interval, holding distance constant, the greater the number of "moderates" in the chamber, which should promote bipartisanship and less conflict on the floor.

Descriptive statistics for the variables in the model are reported in Table 10.3. Overall, about 3% of the bills in our sample failed to pass the Senate

---

[18]We also tried the number of requests for legislative action submitted to the Congress by the president (available in the *Database of Historical Congressional Statistics* compiled by Swift, Brookshire, Canon, Fink, Hibbing, Humes, Malbin, and Martis 2000). The general results reported below were unchanged when this variable was employed.

Table 10.3 Descriptive Statistics for Analysis of Passage of Appropriations Measures, 1890–1946

Variable	Mean	Median	Std. Dev.	Min.	Max.
Failure to meet deadline	0.033	0	0.180	0	1.000
Pre-cloture indicator	0.537	1.000	0.499	0	1.000
Days between committee report and deadline	56.884	45.000	44.664	1.000	169.000
% difference between House and Senate bill	0.072	0.014	0.183	−0.498	2.140
% of chamber on appropriating committee	27.224	16.667	16.228	10.000	47.917
Non-SAC bill	0.273	0	0.446	0	1.000
Senate Workload	0.576	0.526	0.480	−0.102	86.000
Majority Party Unity	61.491	62.802	10.160	42.936	77.553
Polarization/Moderation	30.278	23.134	16.039	10.893	76.100

Note: N = 631.

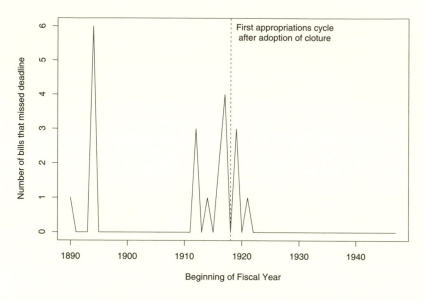

Figure 10.3 Missed Appropriations Deadlines

by the relevant deadline. By this measure, the Senate was fairly efficient at processing spending bills. If anything, though, this probably reflects the urgency that senators felt to meet fiscal deadlines. Seven percent of the bills in our sample were "near misses," beating the deadline by less than three days.[19]

A plot of the number of bills that missed their deadline appears in Figure 10.3. The plot shows that meeting the deadlines became more of an issue in the years around the adoption of cloture. It hints that the cloture rule had begun to address the problem of missed deadlines prior to the Budget Act, but that the rule was not a sufficient solution on its own.[20] While the Senate experienced multiple failures in the fiscal years leading up to the adoption of cloture, a decline in the number of bills that failed to meet deadlines appears to have begun with the adoption of cloture. But the number of failures did not go to zero until the Budget Act was implemented.

In order to account for potential correlation among appropriations, we estimated the model using generalized estimating equations (GEEs) (Liang

---

[19]About 15% of the bills in our sample failed to be enacted into law by the relevant deadline. More detailed data and a more complex model would be required to determine the effects of cloture on enactment of appropriations bills, since presidential vetoes and the conference procedure would need to be taken into account.

[20]This is consistent with Dixit's (2004, 40) argument that "new institutions of governance cannot be expected to leap frog to perfection," and that a transition period is likely to occur as individuals get used to new formal rules introduced to a relation-based system.

and Zeger 1986; Zorn 2001). GEEs relax assumptions about the independence of observations, which helps to account for possible unobserved correlation among particular bills.[21] The results of the GEE probit analysis are reported in Table 10.4.[22] The coefficient on the main variable of interest, the pre-cloture indicator, is statistically different from zero and has the expected sign. The marginal effect for this variable indicates that prior to the adoption of the cloture rule, a bill had a probability of failure of .03, with 95% confidence bounds [0.008, 0.094]. While this probability is small, it is important to keep in mind that it was fairly uncommon for spending bills to fail, but the potential for disruption was significant when they did.[23] After cloture the probability of failure is essentially zero.

The results on the other variables support the position that the cloture rule worked in tandem with other reforms to address one of the main problems that obstruction presented for the Senate—the ability to fulfill its constitutional duty in funding the operations of the federal government. The 1921 Budget Act and the recentralization of appropriations both appear to have had effects on efficiency. The earlier a bill makes it out of committee (and by extension the faster it moves through the earlier stages of the process), the more likely it is to meet the deadline. If the bill is reported from committee thirty more days before the deadline, its chances of failure drop by about 2 percentage points (with 95% confidence bounds of [.002, .072]). In addition, as the percentage of the chamber that sits on the relevant appropriating committee increases, the Senate fares better in meeting deadlines. If this variable increases by 5 percentage points from its median value, it gives a probability of failure of .01 [.001, .029]. Neither the percentage difference between the House and the Senate bill nor the consideration of a bill by a legislative committee appears to affect the likelihood of missing the deadline.

Of the ideological measures, party cohesion does not appear to affect whether or not a bill meets the deadline, and the moderation measure has effects that are in the opposite direction of what was expected.[24] The coef-

---

[21] Because of the dichotomous nature of the dependent variable, we are limited in our attempts to account for correlation among observations and observation-specific effects. Because of changes in bill titles we do not have the same number of observations per cross-sectional unit, which renders panel and time-series cross-section methods less useful. For the GEE analysis we cluster on bill title. We also tried clustering on fiscal year, but that washed out nearly all of the effects that we report below. This is not surprising since our main variables of interest mostly vary by fiscal year.

[22] Unfortunately, we cannot conduct a similar analysis using the House as a control series to further assess the impact of cloture because the House passed all of the bills in our sample by the relevant deadlines. However, this reinforces the point that apart from the House passing bills late in the game (but before the deadline), the problem with meeting the deadlines rested with the Senate.

[23] The severity of problems caused by missing deadlines most likely varied across bills, although it is not clear how to rank bills in this regard. While failure to pass an Army or Navy appropriations bill might endanger national security, the failure to pass a Post Office appropriations bill might provoke the most ire among constituents whose mail service would be disrupted. The GEE analysis should help to account for correlation induced by these kinds of unobserved factors.

[24] Binder (2003, 80), who examines lawmaking in the post–World War II era, suggests that her measure may have different effects for earlier time periods. Political parties

Table 10.4 GEE Probit Analysis of Passage of Appropriations Measures, 1890–1946

Variable	Coefficient	Std. Err.	p value
Constant	−4.744	2.207	0.032
Pre-cloture indicator	0.932	0.501	0.063
Days between committee report and deadline	−0.011	0.005	0.029
% difference between House and Senate bill	0.625	0.479	0.192
% of chamber on appropriating committee	−0.128	0.040	0.001
Non-SAC bill	0.070	0.264	0.792
Senate Workload	−1.029	0.633	0.104
Majority Party Unity	0.026	0.026	0.315
Polarization/Moderation	0.110	0.030	0.000
Wald χ^2_8	22.86	$(p = .003)$	
Expected percent correctly predicted	93		

Note: $N = 631$.

ficient on the workload variable also has a sign different from expectations, although it misses statistical significance at the .1 level. While we acknowledge the limitations of using the crude measure of a dummy variable for measuring the effects of cloture, the results on the other variables that we include in the model and the accounting for unobserved correlation among observations should allay concerns that the effects we find for cloture are spuriously generated by other institutional or contextual factors.

10.4 CONCLUSION

The first quarter of the 20th century was a period of remarkable institutional innovation. Fundamental changes occurred in how senators were elected and how they conducted business once they got to Capitol Hill. These changes were responses to conditions inside and outside the Congress that presented senators with new difficulties in achieving their various goals. Our general argument about the 1917 cloture reform was that it helped to reduce the uncertainty induced by the Senate's relative lack of limitations on debate. In analyzing the appropriations process, we have refined this argument by

in congresses of yesteryear may have had greater stakes in legislative accomplishments than do parties of today. Polarization might have led to (or been a symptom of) more disciplined parties that sought to establish substantive legislative records for an advantage in electoral competition.

claiming that cloture was part of a set of reforms that addressed problems related to obstruction and fiscal policy. The proximity of events and the coarseness of available data makes it difficult to separate out the unique and independent effects of these various changes. Nevertheless, we contend that cloture had important effects on the appropriations process in conjunction with other changes that occurred during this period and thus had more of an impact than is generally believed.

For the threat of cloture to be effective, bills had to be moved through the earlier stages of the appropriations process more quickly. Given the amount of time that it took for a cloture petition to ripen and the amount of post-cloture debate permitted under the rule, filibusters could still successfully obstruct bills considered in the final few days before the relevant fiscal year deadline. For cloture to have been a credible threat, it would have been necessary to bring legislation to the floor earlier in the annual appropriations cycle. The Budget Act appears to have promoted that kind of efficiency and thus worked in tandem with the cloture rule in helping to surmount the challenges presented to senators during this period. While the adoption of the cloture rule in 1917 did not solve by itself the problems presented by obstruction, its effects were not merely symbolic.

Chapter Eleven

Conclusion

One of the key questions we have tackled in this study is why a legislature would choose to allow a minority of its members to block the passage of legislation. A closely related question is under what conditions does it make sense to explicitly grant permission to a minority to obstruct through a supermajority cloture rule, as opposed to allowing individual members latitude to obstruct but not spelling out a specific threshold for forcing a final vote.

We have argued that the Senate relied upon an informal system of regulating filibuster battles prior to adoption of the cloture rule in 1917. Filibusters played out along the lines of game-theoretic models of wars of attrition, in which the relative resolve levels of the majority and minority were crucial. These filibusters had the advantage of eliciting credible information about how much each side cared about the policy issues at stake. Delay was costly, but the willingness to bear these costs indicated the depth of support for each side, and thus allowed the Senate to account for preference intensity. However, as the Senate grew in size and workload, this informally governed system became increasingly problematic. In particular, obstruction in the days before final adjournment became a serious danger to legislation as norms against small minorities capitalizing on the deadline decayed. The 1917 cloture rule established a formal threshold for ending filibusters, thus providing an additional option for bill supporters when confronted with obstruction. We have argued that the rule was particularly well suited to reducing the uncertainty posed by late-session filibusters by small minorities. Yet the post-1917 system retained elements of the old war-of-attrition filibuster politics. As long as time constraints were not too pressing—as at the end of a congress—bill supporters still had the recourse of attempting to sit out the filibuster rather than simply building a supermajority coalition. This meant that obstructionists were still forced to bear the costs of filibustering if they hoped to succeed. As a result, battles over obstruction continued to have the potential to reveal credible information about intensity.

Obstruction remains a central feature of today's Senate even though the conduct of filibusters has been transformed in recent decades so that they are no longer fought as wars of attrition. Instead, it is widely accepted that legislation of any importance requires at least sixty votes to pass, since sixty votes are necessary to invoke cloture.[1] If the supporting coalition

---

[1] As noted previously, budget legislation is an important exception due to statutory debate limitations that restrict obstruction. Congress has on occasion enacted similar statutory limitations for other types of legislation, such as trade bills (Binder and Smith

behind a piece of major legislation is not large enough to invoke cloture, the legislation is not likely even to make it to the floor. Sitting out filibusters is no longer a realistic option. While the *legislative* workload of the Senate is undoubtedly one reason why delay is not tolerable, an equally if not more important reason is that the demands that are placed on senators' time in addition to that devoted to legislating are so overwhelming (Oppenheimer 1985). Electoral demands are quite severe, both in terms of senators' need to spend time in their home states as well as the perpetual drive to raise campaign funds. The "Tuesday to Thursday Club"—members of Congress who are in Washington only Tuesday through Thursday—once derisively described a subset of easterners who could afford to travel back home for long weekends, often to look after their law practices or business interests.[2] This club is no longer exclusive, however, as most legislators have joined. As such, floor votes are rarely scheduled for Mondays and Fridays, and time for serious floor debate is limited.

Fund-raising demands are particularly acute. In order to retain a seat in today's Senate, an incumbent must raise millions of dollars, even in the smallest and least populous states with relatively inexpensive media markets. While incumbents have an easier time raising money than challengers, senators still have to allocate a significant amount of their time collecting contributions in the relatively small increments allowed under the law.[3] Even when senators are in Washington, a significant portion of their time is devoted to attending fund-raising events where they interact with lobbyists and others who have interests before the Congress (Jackie Koszczuk, "Nonstop Pursuit of Campaign Funds Increasingly Drives the System," *CQ Weekly*, April 5, 1997, pp. 770–74).[4] The amount of face time with constituents and contributors that senators believe is essential for reelection has dramatically increased the opportunity costs of waiting out filibusters, so much so that this option is no longer viable.

Hence, filibusters are no longer fought as wars of attrition. The contemporary context of lawmaking in the Senate has essentially eliminated the informational benefits that used to accrue from these kinds of battles. The essential component that is now missing is that filibustering is virtually costless for bill opponents. With costless filibustering, undertaking obstruction no longer signals that a proposed policy is particularly harmful to its foes.

1997, 185–95). Most of these involve situations where the Senate must approve or disapprove executive actions or proposals stemming from authority delegated to the executive.

[2]See Morris Udall, "Is Congress Sick?" *Congressman's Report*, February 21, 1964 (http://www.library.arizona.edu/branches/spc/udall/congrept/88th/640221.html, accessed July 25, 2004).

[3]Even if individual limits on donations were raised significantly, it is doubtful that this would make much difference since individuals and political actions committees rarely give the legal limit (Ansolabehere, de Figueiredo, and Snyder 2003).

[4]Henry Lee Myers's (D–MT) account of his daily routine as a senator serving in the early-20th century indicates that even back then a senator's schedule was packed (Myers 1939, Ch. 2). Yet of the many activities that Myers lists as part of his routine, one notable absence is fund-raising.

Returning to the calculus outlined in Chapter 2, if bill opponents know that the costs of fighting obstruction are prohibitive, then the resolve level of bill supporters becomes essentially irrelevant. No matter how high the resolve, the bill supporters will quickly move on to other matters unless they have the sixty votes required to invoke cloture. As a result, bill opponents with even modest resolve levels will threaten to filibuster, knowing that the majority will not devote extended floor time to the fight. Thus, filibustering has become costless for bill opponents for the simple reason that the opportunity costs of waiting out a filibuster have become overwhelming when senators are confronted with extraordinarily tight scheduling constraints (Oppenheimer 1985). As such, the available strategies for bill supporters are either to build a sixty-vote coalition or to withdraw the bill.

It is worth emphasizing that the much-discussed multi-tracking system devised by Mike Mansfield and Robert Byrd in the early 1970s is more a symptom of this transformation to costless filibustering than its cause.[5] Several scholars have argued that the tracking system makes filibusters costless because bill opponents are no longer forced to hold the floor for extended periods. Instead, the obstructed measure is simply moved onto a different track, which enables other legislation to be considered (Binder and Smith 1997; Ornstein 2003). This reduces the collateral damage of filibusters, and thereby lessens the negative externalities associated with obstruction. More importantly, it means that bill opponents need hold the floor only for the (extremely short) period when the obstructed bill is considered on the floor.

The key premise underlying this argument is that prior to tracking, filibustering essentially brought the floor of the Senate to a halt with respect to other legislative business. For example, Oppenheimer (1985, 406) states that "prior to implementation of the track system, the Senate was confined to considering a single piece of legislation on the floor. A filibuster delayed not only the bill being debated, but all other legislation awaiting floor consideration." Oleszek (2001, 202) similarly claims that "[b]efore the initiation of the track system, legislative business halted during filibusters." Journalistic accounts echo this view: "Before the introduction of tracking, a filibuster would stop the Senate from moving on to any other legislative activity" (Lawrence Hunter, "Bring in the Cots" *Washington Times*, final ed., June 22, 2003, p. B03). Senators have also promulgated this perception. For example, in an oft-cited floor statement about tracking, Alan Cranston (D–CA) argued that "[a]ll Senate business would grind to a complete halt against the barrier of a filibuster" during the "one-track system days" (*Congressional Record*, January 21, 1975, p. 928).

---

[5]There is a good deal of confusion over multi-tracking and what its impact has been on the Senate. For example, Ornstein (2003) claims that double tracking began in 1961, while Oppenheimer (1985, 406) claims the practice did not start until 1972 and Oleszek (2001, 202) dates the practice to the early 1970s. Binder, Lawrence, and Smith (2002, 419, n. 10) trace the start of this approach to 1970, a date that they confirmed with the assistant parliamentarian who served at that time.

Notwithstanding this common view, it is simply not the case that a filibuster necessarily stopped progress on all other legislation prior to the tracking system. It is true that the rules provide that the Senate stay on an item once it begins consideration, making that item the "pending business" or the "unfinished business" should the Senate adjourn during its consideration. But the Senate typically did not take up unfinished business until the afternoon, spending the earlier part of the day processing other matters. In practice, filibusters stopped all other business only when a majority wanted to keep the legislation on the floor and fully engage in a war of attrition. It was quite common for the Senate to temporarily put aside obstructed measures and dispense with less controversial items. For example, consider the obstruction of the Elections Bill in 1890–1891. During the height of the filibuster on that bill, the Senate still managed to take care of a substantial amount of business, passing numerous bills granting pensions and relief to private individuals and authorizing the construction of public buildings throughout the Union, as well as more significant bills like the one authorizing the construction of the Baltimore and Potomac Railroad. Senators could simply vote to postpone consideration of an obstructed bill until a later date or displace it with another measure, and the approval of such motions required only a majority.[6] Thus, prior to multi-tracking, obstructed measures did not necessarily bring the Senate to a halt unless a majority wanted to keep the item continually on the floor. Multi-tracking undoubtedly has its advantages in terms of accommodating senators' packed schedules and making the transition between major items more seamless.[7] But the unwillingness of majorities of fewer than sixty senators to engage in wars of attrition and incur the attendant costs is essentially what has made filibustering costless for minorities. As such, the tracking system can be viewed as routinizing and systematizing this new mode of operations, rather than as its source.

Therefore, it is the choice of a majority not to engage obstructing senators in a war of attrition. The system of filibusters as wars of attrition involved trade-offs: delay in the passage of legislation in exchange for policy and electorally relevant information. In an age of frequent and widespread public opinion polling, extensive staff resources, and what are essentially permanent electoral campaign enterprises, the potential value of filibusters

---

[6] Unanimous consent might have been necessary in some cases, but unanimous consent is also necessary to put a bill onto a separate track. The minority could have obstructed the vote on the motion to postpone (since it is debatable) to make life more troublesome for the majority, but minorities generally seemed pleased to have the item in question removed from the floor.

[7] One problem with pulling items from the floor temporarily is that it may require a motion to proceed to go back to those items, and such a motion is subject to a filibuster and would possibly require an extra cloture vote. Our view of multi-tracking is supported by former parliamentarian Robert Dove. He claims that multi-tracking is nothing but "window-dressing" that does little to address the problem of minority obstruction and simply permits senators to claim credit for working on a bill even if it is clear that little progress will be made due to obstructive opposition (Robert Dove, telephone interview, October 24, 2005).

as information revelation devices appears to be minimal even if it were still costly to engage in this activity. Nevertheless, the great irony appears to be that filibusters have become costless for the minority because the costs to the majority of engaging in wars of attrition have become prohibitively high.[8]

If lawmaking through filibuster politics no longer offers politically valuable information to senators, why does supermajority rule persist in the Senate? One plausible answer is the stickiness of inherited institutions. As Binder and Smith (1997) argue, it would require a two-thirds majority to defeat a filibuster of a rules change providing for majority cloture, essentially dooming reform absent an overwhelming majority. As long as at least one-third of senators perceive that eliminating obstruction will lead to policies that they oppose being enacted, supermajority rule will persist.

Inherited institutions are undoubtedly important, but their stickiness itself is not a complete explanation for the refusal of the Senate to move toward majority rule. As we have emphasized throughout this book, a committed majority could use new precedents to eliminate the tactics available to obstructionists. As we discuss below, such a strategy would entail substantial risks and costs—and the 1917 cloture rule, by codifying a procedure for overcoming filibusters, likely increased those costs. Nonetheless, a simple majority of the Senate with the cooperation of a sympathetic presiding officer could curb obstruction. Thus, the striking feature of Senate history is that such a committed majority has *never* been manifested.[9] Since there have repeatedly been floor majorities that have seen their short-term policy preferences stymied by obstruction, this lack of support for majority cloture cannot be attributed simply to members' immediate policy goals. Instead, bids to eliminate the filibuster in the contemporary Senate run up against individual senators' personal power goals. The right of unlimited debate makes each senator a more prominent player on the national political stage.

---

[8]The intense time pressures confronting senators has greater impact for a majority fighting obstruction than it does for senators undertaking a filibuster. The reason is that obstructionists need only be certain to have a handful of senators on or near the floor in order to block progress. By contrast, the majority must have fifty-one senators available at all times to maintain a quorum. This asymmetry underscores why filibustering has, in practice, become essentially costless to the minority (cf. Binder and Smith 1997, 216).

[9]As discussed below, a majority took this position in 1975, but this action was quickly rescinded by a subsequent majority vote. One might ask why pro–civil rights senators did not use precedents to stop filibusters of their proposals by southerners if this was a feasible approach. The reason is simply that committed majorities did not exist who favored such a change. Consider post-1917 civil rights proposals. It is reasonable to assume that if a majority (let alone a supermajority) did not favor invoking cloture on a specific legislative proposal, then a majority would not be in favor of establishing an anti-obstruction precedent that would affect not only the proposal in question, but all legislation brought before the Senate. Of the eight cloture votes pertaining to civil rights measures that were held between 1917 and 1964, not one attracted even a majority of the chamber. It is inconceivable then that a majority could have been found to support a change by precedent. When this approach was attempted during the debate over the 1957 Civil Rights Act, a majority simply opposed it, voting to table a motion to adopt rules for the session, which if considered could have led to majority cloture.

As Sinclair (1989) documents, senators use filibusters to make a name for themselves with donors, interest groups, and constituents. They threaten obstruction to extract concessions of all sorts from the White House and bill proponents. Even as costless filibustering eviscerates the potential informational value of obstruction, it makes the filibuster an even more valuable tool for individualistic senators in an era of candidate-centered elections.

At the same time, the contemporary context of sharp party polarization and narrow majorities in the Senate heightens the potential damage wrought by the filibuster to the majority party's legislative agenda. The prospects of moving toward majority rule will depend ultimately on whether the frustration of the majority party's agenda will become so troublesome that a floor majority will be motivated to bear the risks, uncertainty, and personal power costs of undertaking what has come to be known as the "nuclear option"—that is, eliminating minority rights through that venerable stratagem of rulings from the chair. Recent battles concerning judicial nominations lead us to expect that demands for majority cloture will only increase as partisan polarization persists. Thus far, enough minority senators have shown the willingness to compromise when confronted with the "nuclear" threat. But it is plausible that the space for compromise will vanish when confronted with a series of high-profile Supreme Court appointments in a political environment of intense interest group mobilization.

11.1 THE BATTLE FOR MAJORITY CLOTURE IN TODAY'S SENATE

The curious case of the 108th Congress's all-night session concerning judicial nominees—discussed in Chapter 1—by no means suggests that filibusters as wars of attrition are making a comeback. Instead, the use of a single all-night session to garner headlines points to how much things have changed with respect to obstruction. The strategy of waiting out filibustering senators is now futile, and as a result, the information-revelation component of filibusters has disappeared. It was highly unlikely that new information about senators' preferences or resolve was going to be revealed from the highly staged event.[10]

Nevertheless, the obstruction of the judges does share an important feature with filibusters of old in that senators have contemplated changing the rules to overcome successful obstruction. As noted in Chapter 1, Republicans have considered either passing an amendment to the standing rules or establishing new precedents—that is, the "nuclear option." Majority Leader Bill Frist

---

[10]Instead, this case indicates that the blame-game component of obstruction that we discussed in our analysis of tariff politics in Chapter 6 remains important. One of the most significant motivations for holding the event was that "the debate allowed both parties to begin honing their election-year pitches to swing voters about which side is to blame if the Senate's work is left undone" (Gebe Martinez and Keith Perine, "Talkathon a Practice for 2004," *CQ Weekly*, November 15, 2003, p. 2817).

initially pushed a rules change that would gradually reduce the number of votes required to end debate on presidential nominees from sixty to fifty-one over successive cloture votes.[11] Similar proposals have been introduced in the past, but have never attracted much support.[12] Frist's proposal did not have the two-thirds support required to invoke cloture against an assured minority filibuster had the proposal come to the floor, with even members of the majority party concerned about the new limitations the rule change would impose (John Cochran, "Senators Uneasy with Proposal to Alter Filibuster Rule on Judicial Nominations," *CQ Weekly*, June 28, 2003, p. 1605). The threat of this rule change was simply not credible, and thus did little to curtail the obstruction of the nominees.

11.1.1 Going Nuclear

The apparent futility of changing the rules by passing a resolution led Republican leaders to threaten to use rulings by the presiding officer to eliminate supermajority requirements for nominations. Again, the "nuclear" approach is not new and, as we noted in previous chapters, was contemplated in the pre-atomic age, serving as a significant deterrent to obstruction. While such a rules "revolution" would require less support than a formal rules change, the threat posed to obstructionists lacked credibility in the 108th Congress because it did not appear that a simple majority supported the establishment of the precedent (Keith Perine, "Partisan Rancor Continues to Jam Judicial Nominees," *CQ Weekly*, May 15, 2004, p. 1121). The increase in the Republican's majority to fifty-five seats in the 109th Congress made the threat much more real, especially considering the sympathies of the newly elected senators who came out firmly in favor of the change (Nick Anderson, "New GOP Senators May Back Filibuster Limits," *Los Angeles Times*, December 27, 2004. p. A23). Senator Arlen Specter (R–PA), who became the chair of the Judiciary Committee in the 109th, issued a press release stating that he would use his "best efforts to stop any future filibusters" and noting that "if a rule change is necessary to avoid filibusters, there are relevant recent precedents to secure rule changes with 51 votes" (Helen Dewar, "GOP Senators Elicit Pledge Not to Block Antiabortion Judges," *Washington Post*, Friday, November 19, 2004, p. A06). Specter's statement was issued as his ascension to the chairmanship was challenged by conservatives who were concerned he would not be an ardent supporter of President George W. Bush's nominees.[13]

---

[11] See S. Res. 138, *Congressional Record*, May 9, 2003, p. S6002.

[12] The first time such a proposal was introduced appears to have been in October of 1951 (U.S. Congress. Senate. Committee on Rules and Administration 1985). Binder and Smith (1997) advocate this reform as a solution to the problems of the contemporary Senate. Our arguments about the benefits of information revelation through filibusters do not lend support to this reform, simply because the rule would not require a bill to be kept on the floor between cloture votes and thus there is no real cost to the majority of invoking this procedure.

[13] The previous chair, Orrin Hatch (R–UT), had also come out in favor of pursuing this parliamentary tactic for judicial nominations, although he opposed it for general

The failure to attract even a majority has prevented proponents of the nuclear strategy from succeeding previously. From the 1950s through the 1970s, senators challenged the supermajority provisions of the Senate repeatedly when a new congress convened. The attempts sought to take advantage of the unique context that exists at the opening of a new congress by asserting that simple majorities should be allowed to make decisions about new rules. At the beginning of the 83rd Congress (1953–1954), Senator Clinton Anderson (D–NM), who led the charge for this approach during the 1950s and 1960s, moved to consider the adoption of new rules, with the intention of maintaining the status quo for all rules save Rule XXII. He proposed to change that rule to allow for cloture by a majority of senators. After several days of debate, the Anderson motion was tabled on a vote of 70-21. Anderson made a similar motion at the beginning of the 85th Congress. The proposal had more support this time and won a sympathetic advisory opinion from Vice President Richard Nixon regarding the constitutionality of Rule XXII, but it still lost on a vote to table by 55-38.

Similar attempts in the 1960s were based on the assertion that it was unconstitutional to require two-thirds to invoke cloture on proposals to change the rules. A key decision was made at the start of the 91st Congress (1969–1971), when Vice President Hubert Humphrey ruled that if only a majority—not two-thirds—of those present and voting agreed to limit debate on a proposal to change the rules at the beginning of a congress, then the chair would rule that cloture had been invoked (*Congressional Record*, January 15, 1969, p. 920). In doing so, Humphrey violated precedent by issuing a ruling on a constitutional question.[14] The Senate then voted 51-47 to invoke cloture, and Humphrey followed through with his ruling. However, upon appeal of this decision, the Senate voted 53-45 to reverse it, maintaining the status quo that two-thirds was necessary to end debate on a proposed rule change. An effort in the 92nd Congress by Jacob Javits (R–NY) to question the ruling of the chair on the two-thirds requirement to invoke cloture on a rules change was also defeated 55-37 by a tabling motion (U.S. Congress. Senate. Committee on Rules and Administration 1985, 22–30). While the Senate did not change precedents regarding the continuing nature of the body or the constitutionality of Rule XXII, the key constraint was the absence of a floor majority willing to embrace such an approach.

The closest the contemporary Senate came to a rules revolution happened in 1975 during the effort to pass Senate Resolution 4, which proposed to lower the cloture threshold in Rule XXII from two-thirds to three-fifths. In the face of a filibuster of the resolution, James Pearson (R–KS), a co-

---

legislation (see "Hatch Addresses Christian Coalition Road to Victory 2004 Conference," September 24, 2004, available from http://hatch.senate.gov).

   [14]This suggests again the space for maneuver within the body of senate rules and precedents for those seeking to use rulings from the chair. According to former parliamentarian Dove, Humphrey's disregard for precedent in this case was unusual for the 20th century Senate, though he noted it was much more common in the 19th century (Robert Dove, telephone interview, October 24, 2005).

sponsor of the measure, made a motion stating that the rules change was a constitutional issue arising under Article I, Section 5 and "superseded the rules specifying that the Senate is a continuing body" as well as the existing cloture rule. Thus, he moved that if a majority voted in favor of his motion to end debate on the motion to proceed to the consideration of S. Res. 4, the chair would immediately move that question (i.e., the question on the motion to consider, not on the actual adoption of the resolution) (*Congressional Record*, February 20, 1975, p. 3835). Majority Leader Mike Mansfield announced his intention to move that Pearson's motion was out of order, but held in abeyance because his point of order was subject to a tabling motion that would have precluded debate (and if approved would have established a precedent for majority cloture). Vice President Nelson Rockefeller submitted Pearson's motion to the Senate for decision, which had the effect of empowering the Senate to invoke cloture on S. Res. 4 by a majority vote. After some debate, the Senate voted to table Mansfield's point of order against Pearson's motion, 51-42. This was the first instance in which a majority of the Senate voted to establish a precedent that would enable cloture by majority vote, although at the time there was disagreement about the impact of the vote on the Senate's rules. Whatever the case, the vote did not translate immediately into a victory for the reformers. Senator James B. Allen (D-AL), one of the most influential figures in the politics of filibusters in the 1970s, used a parliamentary tactic that enabled him to continue the filibuster on the resolution.[15]

A few days later, a compromise was reached that would require three-fifths of the chamber to invoke cloture, rather than three-fifths of those present and voting as was originally proposed. An essential part of the solution to the impasse, however, involved a reversal of the vote to table Mansfield's point of order, thereby eliminating the precedent that had presumably been established for majority cloture. The Senate voted to reconsider the tabling motion on February 26 by a vote of 53-38, and then rejected the motion itself 40-51 ("Senate Close to Accord on Filibuster Change," *Congressional Quarterly Weekly Report*, March 8, 1975, p. 502). The compromise reform eventually passed, although the opponents of the original proposal forced its supporters to follow the existing procedures under Rule XXII and invoke cloture by a two-thirds vote. The opponents of cloture reform clearly thought it important to prevent a precedent for majority cloture from remaining on the books, while reform supporters—who were divided on the question of majority cloture itself (as opposed to three-fifths cloture)—thought it better to accept this compromise than to attempt to quash Allen's continued obstruction by pushing for ever-more restrictive precedents. This case again makes clear that a committed majority, though, can change the rules in this

---

[15] Allen raised a point of order that Pearson's motion was complex and therefore, under Senate rules, should be divided into parts for debate and voting. The vice president ruled that the motion was divisible, and then Allen proceeded to filibuster the separate parts ("Reformers Lose Chance to Modify Filibuster," *CQWR*, February 22, 1975, p. 412). No appeal or vote took place on this ruling.

fashion, while underscoring the necessity of the majority being unified on the ultimate goal of majority rule.[16]

It is worth emphasizing that the contemporary Senate has not been completely averse to the establishment of precedents to limit the use of obstruction short of reducing the cloture threshold. The last significant change brought about through new precedents occurred in the 95th Congress (1977–1978) during a successful attempt to crack down on post-cloture filibusters. Senator Allen had perfected this technique and other senators had followed his lead in employing it ("Gas Filibuster Recalls Past Obstructions," *Congressional Quarterly Weekly Report*, October 8, 1977, 2137). Rule XXII at that time limited debate after cloture had been invoked to one hundred hours by allotting each senator one hour. But this limit did not apply to quorum calls and to consideration of amendments submitted prior to the cloture vote, leaving a large loophole in the rule. This resulted in long delays even after successful cloture votes.

Majority Leader Byrd initially sought to use an ordinary rules change to close the loopholes that permitted post-cloture filibusters. He was the lead sponsor of S. Res. 5, which proposed to reduce the time for post-cloture debate to fifty hours and limit dilatory quorum calls. Although Byrd worked with Minority Leader Howard Baker, Jr. (R–TN) on a compromise after the resolution met with a preliminary Republican filibuster, the proposal subsequently stalled (Thomas P. Southwick, "Senate Filibusters Cloture Rule Change; Nears Compromise," *Congressional Quarterly Weekly Report*, May 14, 1977, p. 893).[17]

Nonetheless, Byrd seized upon a post-cloture filibuster later in that congress as an opportunity to accomplish some of the same goals through establishing new precedents. During consideration of a bill that would deregulate natural gas, Senators Howard Metzenbaum (D–OH) and James Abourezk (D–SD) forced consideration of numerous amendments submitted before cloture was invoked in order to drag out the debate. After an exhausting two weeks of debate which included a thirty-six hour session, three precedents

---

[16] Allen's obstruction could have been quashed through rulings from the chair along the lines of the original ruling on Pearson's motion, but this would have required a coalition of fifty-one senators to stick together over a series of votes. While a floor majority agreed on the need to reduce the cloture threshold to three-fifths, there was less widespread support for going further in eliminating minority rights. Rockefeller created a controversy on February 26 by refusing to recognize Allen, who sought to ask a parliamentary question. Both Democratic and Republican senators criticized Rockefeller's apparent violation of precedents regarding the paramount right of recognition ("Reformers Consider Filibuster Compromise," *Congressional Quarterly Weekly Report*, March 1, 1975, p. 448).)

[17] In response to a post-cloture filibuster led by Allen in the 94th Congress, then-Majority Leader Mike Mansfield warned that "the actions of the minority on this bill will inevitably lead next year to a major attempt in the Senate to alter Rule XXII to provide for majority cloture" (quoted in "Senate Passes Compromise Anti-trust Bill," *Congressional Quarterly Weekly Report*, June 19, 1976, p. 1591; see Binder and Smith 1997, 142). While Mansfield's prediction was not borne out, a change in the rules was clearly on the mind of his Majority Whip, Robert Byrd, who joined Mansfield during that congress in criticizing the post-cloture filibusters.

were established that limited post-cloture filibusters. The first and arguably most important ruling required the presiding officer to take the initiative to rule dilatory amendments out of order, rather than waiting for a senator to make a point of order. The ruling had broad support and was upheld on a vote of 79-14. The second ruling allowed senators to rescind amendments offered prior to cloture and prevented other senators from calling up amendments that had been rescinded. This ruling was slightly less popular, with 59 senators voting in favor and 34 senators voting against. The last ruling extended a long tradition of cracking down on dilatory motions and quorum calls, holding that a dilatory motion or a request for the yeas and nays did not constitute business, which would help to prevent repeated quorum calls. The vote to uphold this decision was 74-21.

Although these rulings had broad support, the manner in which the first was implemented was highly controversial. Byrd called up thirty-three of Abourezk and Metzenbaum's amendments in rapid succession, and Vice President Walter Mondale ruled each out of order. In doing so, Mondale ignored other senators seeking recognition to appeal the decisions of the chair, recognizing only Byrd until the amendments were dispensed with. This move angered senators because it threatened the right of recognition—one of the fundamental sources of senators' power. Tempers flared and harsh words were exchanged, hearkening back to some of the most heated filibusters of the 19th and early-20th centuries. Eventually, Byrd calmed the furor by assuring his colleagues that a precedent regarding recognition rights had not been established. The filibuster was broken, the gas bill was passed, and perhaps most importantly, the rules of the game had been changed in three important ways to make it more difficult to obstruct, all without the adoption of a resolution (Alan Berlow, "Filibuster Fallout: Byrd's Role and Precedents," *Congressional Quarterly Weekly Report*, October 8, 1977, pp. 2127–28; Bob Rankin, "Senate Continues Dismantling of Energy Plan," *Congressional Quarterly Weekly Report*, October 8, 1977, pp. 2119–38).[18]

11.2 CONFRONTATION, COMPROMISE, AND THE GANG OF FOURTEEN

In the 109th Congress, the debate over judicial nominees and the Senate's rules consumed Washington to a degree that matches some of the fiercest and most dramatic filibuster fights. Although the Republicans' initial attempt to publicize the obstruction of the judicial nominees through the 108th Congress's all-night session fell more or less flat, the issue took on much greater

---

[18]The rules were changed by resolution in 1979 to limit post-cloture filibustering further by allowing only 100 hours for all actions (speeches, motions, reading of amendments, etc.) after cloture was invoked. This allotment was reduced to 30 hours in 1985 (Bach 2001, 12). Gold and Gupta (2004, 265–69) cite two other instances during Byrd's tenure as majority leader where dilatory tactics were limited by establishing new precedents. These concerned consideration of nominations and the reading of the *Journal*.

salience in the following congress. Bush renominated seven of the filibustered nominees, setting the stage for a showdown. The debate eventually shifted from one about whether the Republicans could invoke the nuclear option to whether they would. Procedurally, there were several different scenarios under which the Republicans could impose majority cloture on judicial nominees. All of these involved violation of past precedents to a degree, but Republicans seemed to be more than willing to undertake them.[19] The real question was whether or not the Republicans had the necessary majority to win key votes on rulings from the chair.

Senate leaders elevated the issue to the top of the agenda, and the mass media devoted significant column space and air time to the filibuster and the nuclear option. Liberal and conservative groups became involved to a much greater degree, helping to escalate the rhetoric and intensify the controversy.[20] Leaders of conservative groups sent a clear signal that their support of Frist's presidential ambitions (and those of other Republican hopefuls) were tied to the confirmation of the judges.[21] Interestingly, the conflict took on an aspect of Fearon's (1994) model that was largely absent from earlier filibusters: audience costs for backing down seemed to be central to the dynamics of the conflict (see Chapter 2). Democratic and Republican leaders preferred confrontation to compromise because they would be penalized by their allied interest groups should they be seen as caving in.

Although none of the nominations in question were brought to the floor until May 2005, the conflict over them took on a war-of-attrition-like quality. Each side expended resources to convince the other and the public that their position was the right one, hoping that the other side would relent. As the conflict came to a boil, it remained unclear whether Frist had the votes to succeed in his efforts to end the filibuster. He did not appear to have the support of moderates Susan Collins (R–ME), Olympia Snowe (R–ME), Lincoln Chafee (R–RI), and maverick John McCain (R–AZ). A few other Republicans, such as Chuck Hagel (R–NE) and John Warner (R–VA), were non-committal, expressing concern about the long-term impact on the functioning of the Senate. Vice President Dick Cheney stated that he would support Frist's efforts, meaning that Frist needed only 50 votes (if everyone voted) to invoke the nuclear option since Cheney would break the tie in addition to issuing the necessary rulings (David D. Kirkpatrick, "Cheney

---

[19] For a comprehensive discussion of these scenarios, see Beth (2005).

[20] One conservative group, Progress for America, intended to raise $5 million for an anti-filibuster ad campaign, which was comparable to the amount that it raised for a campaign promoting President Bush's social security reform efforts (Charlie Savage, "Ad Wars Mount as Republicans Ready Ban on Senate Filibusters," *Boston Globe*, April 21, 2005, 3rd ed., p. A6).

[21] For example, Richard Lessner, executive director of the American Conservative Union, stated: "If Senate Majority Leader Bill Frist hopes to capture the Republican nomination for president in 2008, then he has to see to it that the Bush judicial nominees are confirmed. . . . If he fails, then he is dead as a presidential wannabe" (quoted in Charles Babington, "Frist Likely to Push for Ban on Filibusters; Failure Risks Conservatives' Ire; Success May Prompt Legislative Stalemate," *Washington Post*, April 15, 2005, p A04).

Backs End of Filibustering," *New York Times*, April 23, 2005, p. A1).[22] Both sides claimed the other lacked the necessary votes, but it was clear that a vote on the nuclear option would have been extremely close. Much of the posturing seemed to be aimed at convincing wavering Republicans that the votes were there and that it would look bad for them to have broken with their party only to end up on the losing side.

As the Senate prepared for another all-night session on May 23—complete with cots set up in the Capitol—the conflict was defused, at least temporarily, by an eleventh-hour compromise agreement entered into by a group of fourteen senators.[23] The "Memorandum of Understanding on Judicial Nominations" explicitly stated that the Democratic signatories would vote to invoke cloture on three nominees—Priscilla Owen, Janice Rogers Brown, and William Pryor. It made no promises about two other contested nominees, William G. Myers III, and Henry Saad, presumably dooming their chances of reaching the bench. In exchange, the Republican signatories would oppose "any amendments to or interpretation of the Rules of the Senate that would force a vote on a judicial nomination by means other than unanimous consent or Rule XXII" in the 109th Congress. The agreement stated that "nominees should only be filibustered under extraordinary circumstances, and each signatory must use his or her own discretion and judgment in determining whether such circumstances exist." The agreement also sent a clear signal to President Bush about the privileged role of senators in the nomination process, encouraging him to consult with senators from both parties prior to submitting nominees to the Senate.

The nuclear threat had succeeded in gaining important concessions from the Democrats. Owen, Brown, and Pryor were regarded by the Democrats—and their interest group allies—as extremists who would provide conservatives with enhanced control of several appeals courts. Yet the deal had prevented the imposition of majority rule. Thus, as it has in every previous instance when the prospect of imposing de jure majority rule through precedents was on the table, the Senate balked. A key question is why a clear majority did not emerge in support of Frist's maneuver. An important strategic consideration for senators concerned the Democrats' response to the execution of the nuclear option and what the impact of such a move would have on individual senators' personal power goals. Democrats threatened to respond with full parliamentary force to an attempt to use rulings from the chair to curtail filibusters of judicial nominations, using every weapon

---

[22]It is not clear that Cheney would have had to cast the decisive vote in the case of a tie. The volume of Senate precedents published in 1909 states: "It has universally been held that upon the question of an appeal from the decision of the chair a tie vote sustains the decision" (U.S. Congress. Senate 1909, 449).

[23]Only twelve appear to have been necessary to prevent the success of the nuclear option. The group included moderates as well as more extreme senators. The Republicans included Mike DeWine of Ohio, Susan Collins, Lindsey Graham of South Carolina, Lincoln Chafee, John McCain, John Warner, and Olympia Snowe; the Democrats included Ben Nelson of Nebraska, Mark Pryor of Arkansas, Robert Byrd, Joe Lieberman of Connecticut, Mary Landrieu of Louisiana, Ken Salazar of Colorado, and Daniel Inouye of Hawaii.

in their arsenal to bring all non-essential work in the chamber to a halt (John Cochran, "Senators Uneasy With Proposal to Alter Filibuster Rule on Judicial Nominations," *CQ Weekly*, June 28, 2003, p. 1605). Indeed, the widespread legislative destruction Frist's maneuver would unleash is in part why the approach is referred to as the nuclear option. At a time when the parties are highly polarized and seats in the Senate are almost evenly split between parties, the supermajority requirements in the Senate are the most potent resource the Democrats possess to stop the Republicans from rolling them on key agenda items. The threatened Democratic response meant that Republicans risked sacrificing their substantive legislative agenda if they pursued the nuclear option with respect to judicial nominations. The widespread prerogatives that senators possess, which leads to the chamber's heavy reliance on unanimous consent to get things done, would in theory enable the minority to tie the institution in knots and prevent progress on legislative priorities.

If the Democrats went to this extreme, Republicans would then have had two choices: either accept the resulting legislative paralysis and hope to win the ensuing public relations war by blaming the Democrats for the lack of accomplishments or push the fight further by using the same revolutionary tactics to curtail or remove the remaining obstructive tools used by the Democrats. There was a great amount of uncertainty regarding how the public would respond if the Democrats slowed the institution to a crawl. The conventional wisdom is that Republicans' charges of obstruction worked in the battle over the passage of the Homeland Security Act, hurting Democrats at the polls in 2002 and helping the Republicans regain majority control of the Senate. Two years later, newly elected Senator John Thune (R–SD), whose successful campaign against then–Minority Leader Tom Daschle involved labeling him as the "chief obstructionist" on the Democratic side, believed his victory would convince enough Democrats to relent on the obstruction of judicial nominees (Charles Babington, "109th Congress Convenes with Larger GOP Majorities," *Washington Post*, January 5, 2005, p. A3). Senator Specter, in his effort to secure the Judiciary chairmanship, claimed that he expected the Senate to avoid "judicial gridlock" given the "election results demonstrating voter dissatisfaction with Democratic filibusters" ("GOP Senators Elicit Pledge Not to Block Antiabortion Judges," Helen Dewar, *Washington Post*, Friday, November 19, 2004, p. A06). Comparisons have been made to the shutdown of the federal government in 1995–1996, which proved to be a public relations disaster for the Republicans. Democrats might have experienced a similar backlash if their obstruction was perceived to cause hardship for voters. Thus, Republican claims concerning public impatience with obstruction had merit. Indeed, Democrats themselves showed signs of reluctance to fulfill their threats of retaliation. As the events progressed through the spring, Democrats leaked to the press that they would allow various specific types of bills to pass (Michael Crowley, "The Day After, " *The New Republic*, April 18, 2005, p. 10). Eventually, party leaders signaled that their main retaliation would be to attempt to add popular Democratic programs as non-germane amendments to GOP bills, rather than using their prerogatives to stop all Senate action.

Yet, public opinion polling gave indications that the Republicans faced a potential backlash for going nuclear. A report by the Gallup Organization indicated that a majority of Americans opposed attempts to eliminate the filibuster. While the complexities of the issue and the obscurity of the Senate's internal workings require caution in interpreting responses to queries about support for the filibuster, the report indicated that the results were consistent across a broad range of question formats and wordings (Newport 2005). The poll also indicated that the issue was not one that the public was devoting much attention to. Of the 148 news stories in the past fifteen years that Gallup had asked respondents whether or not they were following closely, the filibuster controversy ranked near the bottom. Nevertheless, there were some indications that Republican senators were concerned that the issue would increase in salience and work against them. Republican Conference Chairman Rick Santorum (R–PA) was reported to have advocated delay in pursuing the nuclear option after internal party polls indicated a lack of support among the public (Alexander Bolton, "Santorum Reads Nuke Polls, Applies the Brakes," *The Hill*, April 21, 2005, p. 1). Yet, in the end this was seen as a reason to redouble public relations efforts in support of the nuclear option rather than a signal to abandon it.[24]

One sense in which existing rules weakened the GOP hand is that the cloture rule, by specifying a process through which the rules can be changed (that is, with a two-thirds vote), afforded plausibility to Democratic claims that the GOP was "breaking the rules" in enforcing the nuclear option. Prior to 1917, advocates of new precedents curbing obstruction could argue that in the absence of any rule providing a mechanism to end debate, the Senate could not reasonably allow minorities to prevent the creation of rules governing debate. In other words, in the absence of rules specifying a threshold for ending debate, would-be reformers could (and did) argue that majority rule is the appropriate default option and should be assumed to hold. By contrast, the 1917 cloture rule, by specifying the supermajority required to change the rules, undermined this argument. In today's Senate, implementing the nuclear option appears to run afoul of the explicit rules of the Senate in a manner that did not hold prior to 1917. It is critical to emphasize that a floor majority can still choose to go nuclear, but doing so poses heightened political risks since it can effectively be portrayed as violating a long-standing explicit rule of the Senate.

With the public response unclear and possibly muted, a more serious concern to senators appeared to be the diminution of their personal power if

---

[24]Santorum claimed that the reason the public opposed the nuclear option was that they perceived (incorrectly in his view) the filibuster as part of the system of checks and balances. Research that argues that the electorate deliberately attempts to balance out polarized parties by choosing divided government (Fiorina 1996; Alesina and Rosenthal 1995) provides support for the argument that the public might reject the concentration of power that eliminating long-standing features of the Senate would entail.

filibustering of judicial nominees was eliminated. Attempts to crack down on senators' prerogatives with respect to judicial nominees in particular collide with a formidable institutional tradition where extreme deference has been given to the smallest of minorities. The tradition of "senatorial courtesy," where presidents consult with senators from relevant states before making judicial appointments, extends back to the presidency of George Washington. Since the early-20th century, this tradition of deference to individual senators has been institutionalized to a degree through the "blue slip" process in the Judiciary Committee, which can lead to a nomination being killed in committee.[25] Democrats defended their obstruction of an up-or-down vote on judicial nominees in part by claiming that Republicans pursued essentially the same strategy on a much larger scale for President Bill Clinton's nominees by killing them in committee.

If Republicans had pursued and won the vote to impose majority rule on nominees and Democrats created a parliamentary quagmire without relenting, the imposition of additional precedents severely limiting individual prerogatives might have been necessary if key elements of the majority party's agenda were to be passed. A full crackdown would have required the majority to place limits on the right of recognition and impose new germaneness requirements. But taking such extreme steps would conflict with individual senators' reluctance to reduce rights that they themselves might need to draw upon in the future.

The elimination of filibusters for judicial nominees thus raises the specter that senators as individuals will lose powerful resources with respect to other Senate decisions. Whatever approach is used to impose majority rule would establish a precedent that a majority could draw on in the future to curtail filibusters of substantive legislation. Just as nuclear weapons cannot be uninvented, precedents established under the nuclear option become available for subsequent legislative battles. Precedents can be reversed, but this simply reinforces the point that supermajority requirements ultimately depend on remote majoritarian decisions. Given how the conflict over the filibuster

---

[25]When a nomination is under consideration by the committee, blue slips are given to the senators from the relevant state. In the case of circuit courts that cover more than one state, seats are informally parceled out to the states covered so that senatorial courtesy can operate. Generally, however, blue slips are seen as less relevant for nominees to this level of the federal judiciary (Goldman 1997; Giles, Hettinger, and Peppers 2001). If the blue slips are returned with the word "disapprove" circled or not returned at all, the nomination is in danger. The blue slip procedure is not laid out in formal rules and it is largely up to the discretion of the committee's chair to determine the extent to which disapproval, either explicitly or implicitly conveyed via a blue slip, affects a nomination's fate. Some chairs have halted a nomination in response to only one negative blue slip, others have required both senators to disapprove, while in other cases nominations have moved forward despite disapproval by the relevant senators (Jennifer A. Dlouhy, "Blue Slips Seen in New Light," *CQ Weekly*, July 12, 2003, p. 1736). Binder and Maltzman (2004) conduct a systematic investigation of the blue slip procedure and find that the threat of a blue slip delays the making of nominations in the first place, subject to certain qualifications. Nevertheless, although blue slips have not granted senators absolute vetoes over nominees, individual senators expect to hold significant sway in this area of Senate decision making.

of a handful of judicial nominees escalated despite a low level of salience with the general public, one can only imagine the pressure that senators would face to go nuclear on something that the public cared about and followed intensely. The continuing trend of sharp party polarization indicates that the controversy over judges is likely to spill over into other areas, with threats of eliminating supermajority requirements to follow.

With control of the Senate shifting back and forth between the parties in the past decade, senators are highly uncertain about whether they will be in the partisan majority or minority during their careers. In any case, even majority party members have regularly used their extensive prerogatives to affect policy and increase their individual importance in the political system. This suggests a significant role for inherited institutions, but one that is more complex than the suggestion that preexisting rules block the majority from ending obstruction. Instead, a floor majority has the capacity to curtail minority rights, but doing so will involve substantial costs and uncertainties that the floor majority must be willing to bear. The heaviest is the concern that senators will be eliminating a weapon they would want to employ in future legislative or nomination battles. For example, John McCain expressed his concerns by stating, "If we don't protect the rights of the minority . . . if you had a liberal president and a Democrat-controlled Senate, I think that it could do great damage" (Ronald Brownstein, "McCain Sees 'Slippery Slope' in Filibuster Ban," *Los Angeles Times*, April 11, 2005, p. A9). Fighting back against a minority's efforts to paralyze the institution would most likely require a more extensive clamping down on individual prerogatives, which exacerbates concerns about the long-term effects of the crackdown once today's majority finds itself in the minority.

What implications do these conclusions have for the theory of pivotal politics and our extensions of it? Krehbiel's pivotal politics model takes the rules of the Senate as fixed and exogenous. It makes sense to assume that most of the time participants do take the rules of the game as a given. Institutions structure expectations about how the underlying interactions will typically be configured. However, these elemental institutions are still subject to a form of remote majoritarianism. If existing institutions are producing outcomes on highly salient issues that are unsatisfactory to a majority of the Senate, the rules themselves are subject to change. The cases that we reviewed in this chapter reemphasize the malleability of Senate procedures when confronted by a committed majority. While the sixty-vote threshold specified in Rule XXII does appear to generate true filibuster pivots, it is important to remember that supermajority requirements are a remote majoritarian choice. A committed majority can change the rules if it wants to, but it has to be willing to bear the costs—both short term and long term—of doing so. A majority currently seems committed to having a pivot be the 60th percentile senator—as well as maintaining extensive individual prerogatives—but these can be changed and the threat of change may temper the extreme use of individual prerogatives. To fully understand the role that the filibuster pivot plays in lawmaking today, future theory building efforts in the pivotal politics mode need to consider the endogeneity of rules in more depth and how the median as a meta-pivot in legislatures with supermajority rules affects behavior under those rules.[26]

11.3 DESIRABILITY OF REFORM

Is this imposition of majority rule, whether for judicial nominees or other legislative matters, desirable normatively speaking? In answering this question, it is worth putting into context the claims that the filibuster regularly induces the sort of legislative paralysis that makes reform imperative for the Senate to function at all. Debates about the use of obstruction in the Senate are often marked by dramatic assertions about how dysfunctional the institution has become. Journalistic accounts of today's Senate make the situation out to be appallingly bad. Even in the early-20th century, when obstruction was minimal compared with today's standard, there were calls for the abolition of the Senate because of its perceived inability to act. The hyperbole from a century ago should serve as a reality check on similar claims made today.

Those who claim the Senate is dysfunctional might point to such recent innovations as "holds" as evidence that the institution is broken, arguing that they are tantamount to a *liberum veto*. Holds are not part of the standing rules of the Senate; they are informal requests made to the majority leader to delay or prevent consideration of an item, typically in the form of a request to be informed before the item is brought up. The evidence that holds are equivalent to an individual veto is mostly anecdotal (e.g., see Sinclair 1989, 130). More systematic investigation has, at least preliminarily, indicated that holds are bargaining tools rather than a veto prerogative. Evans, Lipinski, and Larson (2003) analyzed holds from two congresses using records kept by former Senate Majority Leader Howard Baker and found that generally measures with holds on them tended to pass. Tiefer (1989, 563–66) also argues that a hold is not an "absolute veto," although it can serve as a powerful bargaining chip. Instead, holds are akin to a threat to filibuster, and therefore will be effective only if the majority leader believes that the sixty votes necessary for cloture cannot be assembled or if the item is of such low salience to most senators that it would not be worth the floor time required to go through the cloture process.[27]

---

[26]It is, in principle, possible for supermajority rules to be invulnerable to change by a floor majority. For example, if the Constitution mandated supermajority decision making (as it does for treaty ratification and convictions in impeachment trials), remote majoritarianism within the Senate would not hold.

[27]It also may be the case that senators have an incentive to exercise some measure of restraint in their use of holds, due to the threat of tit-for-tat holds and the fear of removal of this informal prerogative if it is pushed too far. Although workload and demands on senators' time have made it easier to obstruct, they may also make it easier to punish individuals who push their individual prerogatives too far. To extend the atomic metaphor, senators of today have been likened to nuclear-armed states, given their potential for

On the question of judicial nominees, it would be difficult to say that fil-ibusters have severely damaged the system of advice and consent in terms of approval rates. Of the nominations made during the 108th Congress, the Senate confirmed 81% by the end of the congress. The remaining va-cancies on the circuit and district courts constituted only 4% of the total seats.[28] Compare this statistic with the vacancy rate at the end of the 103rd Congress—the last time there was unified control of the federal government. The vacancy rate then was 7.4%, which the Clinton administration claimed constituted "full employment" in the federal judiciary.[29] By this measure, the number of vacancies on the bench does not appear to be severe, espe-cially when only a few of these vacancies are due to obstruction. The Senate processed numerous nominees during the time that a handful were blocked. This hardly seems like the kind of crisis that would justify the potential havoc wreaked should the majority go nuclear. According to the Senate Judiciary Committee, as of March 28, 2005, all but one of the nominees to the District Court that had been reported to the floor had been confirmed. Sixty-seven percent of circuit court nominees who made it out of committee were confirmed. Vacancies on the circuit court appear to be due more to the failure of the president to nominate individuals than to the failure of the Senate to hold up-or-down votes on the nominees.[30]

While many perceived the battle over appeals court nominees as a dress rehearsal for future Supreme Court nominations, there is more to the con-flict than concerns about who will fill the next few vacancies on the high court, although those concerns are certainly important. Overall, the judi-cial nomination process has undoubtedly become more contentious in the past two decades. Goldman (2005, 895–98) has developed an index of ob-struction of nominees, which "is determined by the number of nominees who remained unconfirmed at the end of the congress, added to the num-ber for whom the confirmation process took more than 180 days, which is then divided by the total number of nominees for that congress." Starting around the 100th Congress, obstruction of nominees has increased progres-sively. Prior to the 107th Congress, obstruction mostly took the form of stalling during the committee stage. Presidents of one party saw several of their nominees blocked by a Judiciary Committee controlled by the opposite party. Democrats obstructed some of President George H. W. Bush's nomi-

wreaking havoc on one another by exploiting their individual prerogatives (cf. Sinclair 2001, 15). But contrary to the conventional wisdom about the dysfunctional Senate, this could in principle deter the abuse of these prerogatives and promote cooperation to a significant extent.

[28]These data are from http://www.usdoj.gov/olp/judicialnominations.htm (accessed January 26, 2005).

[29]See "Judicial Nominations," Statement of Senator Orrin G. Hatch before the Exec-utive Business Meeting of the Senate Committee on the Judiciary, September 28, 2000 (http://judiciary.senate.gov/oldsite/9282000_ogh.htm, accessed July 25, 2004).

[30]Of course, one could argue that the administration had not nominated individuals out of fear that they would be filibustered. This seems unlikely given the willingness of the administration to engage in confrontation over appointments to the bench.

nees when they controlled the Senate, but then Republicans set records for obstruction of President Clinton's nominees after they took over the upper chamber. When the Democrats regained a narrow majority in the 107th, the index peaked for the period with respect to appeals court nominees but dropped for district court nominees as Democrats focused their efforts on obstructing the former. After Republicans were returned to majority status for the 108th Congress, the index has remained high, largely due to the Democrats' filibustering appeals court nominees. Obstruction was further exacerbated by presidential election politics, with upticks in the index for even-numbered congresses (i.e., those preceding a presidential election year).

Judging from floor voting patterns from the 101st through 107th Congress (see Table 11.1), nominees who made it to the floor during this period were generally not controversial enough to produce opposing coalitions of the size that would have been necessary to block them permanently by a filibuster. In the 101st to the 105th Congress, nearly all nominees for both the district and circuit courts were confirmed on voice votes. Except for three nominees, all of those who received recorded votes had the support of greater than three-fifths of the chamber.[31] Another way to interpret these numbers is that Republicans and Democrats were able to work out compromises across nominees to avoid the kind of showdown the Senate recently experienced.

Such compromises, however, proved more difficult to come by since the return to unified party government in 2003. One reason that the traditional, informal consultations behind the advise and consent process no longer defuse conflict over nominees—and that conflict has boiled over into the public arena—is that the judiciary has become a much more important arena for policymaking (Farhang 2005). In addition to ruling on highly controversial regulatory and federalism issues, the courts have played a central role in adjudicating hot-button social issues that sharply divide the parties, such as abortion and gay rights. This helps to explain why the fight escalated to the point that it had in spring 2005 even though ordinary voters seemed to be paying little attention to it. The polarization that exists in the Senate has combined with increased stakes over appointments to the judiciary to bring the Senate to the brink of a historical confrontation with the potential to change the institution and the American polity in a profound and irreversible way.

---

[31] Ronnie L. White, an African American nominated to the District Court by Clinton, was rejected on the floor on a party-line vote in the 106th. He was the first judicial nominee to be defeated on the floor since Robert Bork in 1987 (Karen Foerstel, "Uproar Over Rejected Jurist May Doom Other Nominations," *CQ Weekly*, October 9, 1999, p. 2367). Dennis Shedd, a top aide of Senator Strom Thurmond (R–SC), was approved for a seat on the U.S. Court of Appeals for the 4th Circuit by a vote of 55-44 in the 107th. An attempt to invoke cloture on the nomination of Ted Stewart to the District Court failed on a party-line, 55-44 vote. Stewart, who was a close friend of then-Judiciary Chair Orrin Hatch, was blocked from a vote by Democrats in retaliation for the blocking of two nominees for the 9th Circuit, Richard Paez and Marsha Perzon. Stewart was later confirmed on a vote of 93-5 after a deal was struck to allow other Clinton nominees to come to the floor. Paez was confirmed, 59-39.

Table 11.1 Floor Voting Patterns on Judicial Nominations, 101st–
107th Congress

Congress	Proportion Voice Votes	Avg. Coalition Size	Min. Coalition Size	Number of Cloture Votes
101	0.99	0.91	0.91	0
102	0.98	0.82	0.63	1
103	0.98	0.72	0.62	1
104	1.00	N/A	N/A	0
105	0.81	0.94	0.62	0
106	0.76	0.84	0.46	3
107	0.94	0.93	0.56	2

Note: Data are from roll call records and Rutkus and Sollenberger (2004).

The bottom line is that the fight over filibusters of judicial nominees is
merely symptomatic of a long-simmering conflict in the war over control
of the courts. Eliminating the filibuster would not address the underlying
problem, which involves a lack of willingness to compromise between two increasingly polarized parties over an increasingly politicized judiciary. While
the recent fight was over a small handful of nominees, the conflict is likely to
spread to a larger proportion of nominees in the future. Invoking the nuclear
option would further deteriorate relations between senators and open up the
possibility of majority rule for a broader range of legislative matters in the
Senate.

The primary legislative impact of obstruction today is to expand the "gridlock interval" to include an additional ten senators (up to the 60th percentile
senator) on the opposite side of the status quo from the president.[32] This
expansion of the gridlock interval often has a major impact on policy—
including the defeat of bills that otherwise would have had sufficient support
to be enacted on an up-or-down vote. But it is by no means clear that this
additional hurdle for passage has rendered the Senate unable to govern, just
as there is little evidence that obstruction rendered the pre-cloture Senate
ineffective.[33] The Senate has responded when supermajority requirements
have become overly burdensome by relaxing them for certain policy areas.
Provisions of the Budget Act of 1974 allowing a majority to pass major

[32] As noted in Chapter 2, since veto threats mean that a two-thirds majority is necessary to move policies away from the president's ideal point, the filibuster pivot on the
president's side of the status quo is not relevant.

[33] There may be principled reasons rooted in democratic theory to enact majority cloture. Our claim is simply that the legislative impact of the sixty-vote cloture requirement,
though significant, is bounded and can be analyzed usefully through the gridlock interval
lens (Krehbiel 1998).

budgetary changes have provided a safety valve that has allowed narrow majorities to legislate on the particularly salient issue of taxes.[34]

The increased polarization of the Senate has cast the impact of the filibuster in sharper relief. Polarization and narrow majorities require that more substantial concessions (often painful to core constituencies) need to be made on policy in order to bridge the ideological divide between senators in the two parties. This need to compromise may, in practice, enhance the extent to which Senate outcomes reflect the public's views. Opinion polls show that senators are more polarized than the general public. If the Senate median is more extreme than the median voter in the polity, supermajority requirements can prevent the movement of policies away from the more moderate preferences of ordinary citizens.[35]

Even if one concedes that the filibuster has not paralyzed the Senate and rendered it unable to govern, one must still consider whether supermajority procedures are consistent with the Constitution, especially in light of their exploitation to block judicial nominees. Some have argued that the Constitution implies that only a majority is necessary for those items where a supermajority was not specified as necessary. Therefore, they conclude that the obstruction of judicial nominees, which has translated into a supermajority requirement for confirmation, is unconstitutional.[36] Yet the Constitution also allows the Senate to decide its own rules and does not restrict the Senate from adopting supermajority requirements for any decisions not explicitly specified in the founding document. We have argued that a majority of senators could eliminate supermajority requirements through rulings of the chair, but the bottom line is that a majority of the Senate has never fully committed to going to this extreme.[37] The binding constraint precluding a revolution to date in the 109th Congress is that Republicans have not been able to garner a floor majority for this approach, suggesting that remote majoritarianism still exists concerning Senate rules. True, a majority may not have formed because it would be afraid of what a minority would do in response, but that is a question of preferences regarding policy and

---

[34]Senators have used this reform to get other priority bills enacted with less than supermajority support by attaching these items to budget measures (e.g., see Daniel J. Parks, "Byrd Seeks a Way to Stop Tax Bill from Passing by Simple Majority Vote," *CQ Weekly*, March 10, 2001, p. 533). These tactics can also make for some ugly behind-the-scenes institutional politics. Decisions about what can and cannot be including in reconciliation packages are made by the Senate's parliamentarian under the so-called Byrd Rule adopted in 1985. As a result, parliamentarians have recently found themselves at the forefront of epochal legislative battles and in the middle of some of the most acrimonious controversies (Andrew Taylor, "Senate's Agenda to Rest on Rulings of Referee Schooled by Democrats," *CQ Weekly*, May 12, 2001, p. 1063).

[35]This is assuming that the status quo is at or near the ideal point of the median voter in the electorate.

[36]For example, see William Kristol, "Break the Filibuster," *Weekly Standard* 10, no. 32, May 9, 2005.

[37]The violation of precedents that would be required to do this in the contemporary Senate does raise additional concerns about the status of precedents and their relationship to the rule of law.

not constitutional principles. The majority could fully clamp down on the minority as was done in the House over a century ago, but to do so would likely require a majority of senators to agree to give up the wellspring of their power by curtailing the right of recognition and other prerogatives. At this moment, an insufficient number of senators seem willing to start down the path that would lead to quotidian majority rule. As a result, much like the Senate of the 19th century, today's Senate continues to accord the minority the opportunity to stand in the way of the majority.

Beyond constitutional concerns, one might also question whether super-majority rule is consistent with basic norms of democratic governance. When one considers the severe malapportionment of the Senate with respect to pop-ulation, however, it is problematic to assume that a move toward majority rule within the institution would help the representation of majority views within the electorate. The diverse, heterogeneous nature of the American electorate adds to the justification for incorporating hurdles that encourage today's majority to consider the views of minority interests. Finally, from a separation of powers standpoint, supermajority rule in the Senate is one of the few remaining barriers to presidential dominance in a context of highly polarized parties and unified control of Congress and the presidency.

11.4 PROSPECTS FOR CHANGE

In conclusion, we offer speculation about what it would take for senators to impose de jure majority rule on the judicial confirmation process and other legislative matters. The compromise over judicial nominees reached in May 2005 was a temporary one, and the conflict promises to flare up again in the future. Several conditions would need to be met before a floor majority would commit to the nuclear option with respect to judicial nominees. First, there would need to be a cohesive majority of fifty or more senators who share a strong commitment to enacting a specific set of highly salient policies but that lack the sixty votes necessary for cloture. Pro–nuclear option Republi-cans know that they cannot count on the support of the moderates (namely, Chafee, Collins, and Snowe) and mavericks like McCain in their party. It is also questionable whether a handful of senators concerned about the main-tenance of institutional traditions—whether for the institution's sake or for more narrowly self-interested motivations—will go along.[38] If these senators maintain their positions against the nuclear option, the Republicans would have to enlarge their majority with senators who would be willing to vote for it. But a larger majority for Republicans could produce enough votes to invoke cloture on controversial nominees, since the defectors on the nuclear option have voted with their party on cloture votes. This would render the question moot.

---

[38] Even staunch conservative Trent Lott (R–MS), who came out strongly against the judicial filibusters, was reportedly working behind the scenes to facilitate the compromise so that the nuclear option could be avoided ("Work on Nominees Puts Lott Back In Spotlight," *Chattanooga Times Free Press*, May 29, 2005, p. A5).

But even if a cohesive majority confronted obstruction on a highly salient set of issues, it may not be sufficient for the nuclear option to be invoked. It would also be necessary for the minority to persist in obstruction, even as threats of a crackdown are raised. Given incomplete information about the majority's resolve and given the imperative to position-take for attentive interest groups and constituents, this condition may not be too difficult to overcome in the contemporary context.[39] Beyond such short-term policy calculations, however, it would be necessary to overcome individual members' personal power interest in preserving their prerogatives, and the prominence and status such prerogatives accord them in the political system. Furthermore, members of the current majority would need to value their present policy gains more than the potential policy losses should they find themselves members of a much less powerful minority in the future. Given that party control of the Senate has changed hands several times in the past two decades, such concerns are rather palpable.

Finally, the majority would need to believe that it would hold its own in the public relations battle that would ensue should it attempt the nuclear option. Contrary to the way contemporary filibusters are conducted, using the nuclear option to crack down on obstruction *would* involve a war of attrition, with the parties blaming each other for the impasse in the hope of winning over the public. Republicans would accuse Democrats of causing gridlock, rendering the government incapable of meeting policy demands. Democrats would accuse Republicans of a power grab, steamrolling and trampling on the rights of the minority. The minority might well be advantaged in this public relations battle by the shift toward more formal rules since 1917. Today's Senate rules explicitly require a two-thirds vote to invoke cloture on a rules change. By contrast, the pre-1917 rules included no such requirement. As a result, a revolution in the pre-cloture era would have meant claiming that the ambiguous rules needed to be reinterpreted. Doing so today would require circumventing a clearly written rule. To the extent that the public might object to an explicit, unilateral reversal of existing rules, the revolution strategy is likely a more risky one to implement today.

The continuing trends of increasing polarization, declining comity, and erosion of norms in the Senate do not bode well for future compromises over the chamber's rules. One of the scenarios most likely to take the Senate to

---

[39] For example, Democratic interest groups would likely be up in arms if the party surrendered on a high-profile filibuster—say, of a Supreme Court nominee—and attributed this surrender to fear of Republicans' use of the nuclear option. Still, the compromise reached in May 2005 suggests that at least some Democrats were willing to risk such charges, though they were able to claim that they had gained some concessions in the deal. Indeed, the same moderate Democrats from Republican-leaning states who would be the swing voters in any GOP effort to gain sixty votes for cloture on a judicial nominee are also the Democrats least likely to worry about alienating liberal interest groups and most concerned with appearing reasonable to their constituents. Five of the seven Democratic signatories represented states that went for Bush in 2004, suggesting that they were concerned about possible electoral repercussions for continuing to support the judicial filibusters.

the brink again involves Supreme Court nominations. The stakes will be a great deal higher for a Supreme Court nominee, leading senators to feel more intensely than they did about the appeals court nominees. Democrats will likely assert that it is justifiable to filibuster a Supreme Court nominee who would threaten the Court's current delicate balance in favor of abortion rights (Carl Hulse, "Amid Vows of Opposition, Senate Braces for Disarray," *New York Times*, July 2, 2005, p. A12). The replacement of the late Chief Justice Rehnquist with John Roberts did not threaten this balance, since it was not likely to change the extant ideological equilibrium on the Court. As a result, Democratic opposition to Roberts was tepid. But Samuel Alito's nomination to replace the moderate, pro-choice Sandra Day O'Connor holds the potential to move the Court significantly to the right on abortion restrictions, among other issues. While there likely would still be a one vote margin opposing outright reversal of *Roe v. Wade*—even if Alito and Roberts were both to vote to overturn—the new justices could well tip the balance in favor of new restrictions on access to abortion.[40] Therefore, the possibility of a Democratic filibuster loomed in early January 2006, as confirmation hearings for Alito were set to begin. For Democrats, a key question will likely be whether the seven moderate party members who agreed to filibuster judicial nominees only in "extraordinary circumstances" will conclude that the Alito case meets this test. If just five Democrats refuse to back a filibuster, the GOP can impose cloture to defeat a filibuster if the majority party remains unified. Even if 41 Democrats can hold together to defeat cloture, however, the threat of Republicans' exploiting the "nuclear option" may serve as a deterrent to obstruction. For the Republicans, the pressure from religious conservatives and the White House to use whatever means necessary to confirm Alito will prove staggering. If religious conservatives feel betrayed by Republican senators who do not go all out in support of an anti-*Roe* nominee, they may withdraw support from these senators and possibly even actively support primary challengers. Fear of alienating the religious conservative base may well result in the kind of intensely committed majority that would be necessary to execute the nuclear option and impose de jure majority rule on judicial nominees. Two of the seven Republican members of the "Gang of Fourteen"—Lindsey Graham and Mike DeWine— have already indicated that they do not believe Alito's nomination qualifies as an "extraordinary circumstance," hinting that they would support the nuclear option in response to a filibuster. It is impossible to predict at this time whether a sufficient number of Democrats would relent when faced with such a threat, or whether enough moderate and maverick Republicans would buck their leadership once again. Whatever the case, obstruction and conflict over rules of procedure in the Senate promise to remain at the center of the politics of the nation for the foreseeable future.

---

[40]More generally, it is highly plausible that replacing O'Connor with Alito would shift the Court to the right on numerous other issues, including affirmative action and gay rights.

Bibliography

Achen, Christopher H. 1982. *Interpreting and Using Regression*. Number 29 in Quantitative Applications in the Social Sciences. Newbury Park, CA: Sage.

Aldrich, John. 1995. *Why Parties? The Origins and Transformation of Party Politics in America*. Chicago: University of Chicago Press.

Alesina, Alberto and Howard Rosenthal. 1995. *Partisan Politics, Divided Government, and the Economy*. New York: Cambridge University Press.

Alexander, De Alva. 1916. *History and Procedure of the House of Representatives*. Boston and New York: Houghton Mifflin.

Alter, Alison B. and Leslie Moscow McGranahan. 2000. "Reexamining the Filibuster and Proposal Powers in the Senate." *Legislative Studies Quarterly* 25 (2): 259–84.

Ansolabehere, Stephen, John M. de Figueiredo, and James M. Snyder. 2003. "Why Is There So Little Money in U.S. Politics." *Journal of Economic Perspectives* 17 (1): 105–30.

Atkinson, Charles R. 1911. *The Committee on Rules and the Overthrow of Speaker Cannon*. New York: Columbia University Press.

Axelrod, Robert. 1986. "An Evolutionary Approach to Norms." *American Political Science Review* 80 (December): 1095–1111.

Bach, Stanley. 2001. "Filibusters and Cloture in the Senate." Congressional Research Service Report.

Baker, George, Robert Gibbons, and Kevin J. Murphy. 2002. "Relational Contracts and the Theory of the Firm." *Quarterly Journal of Economics* 117 (February): 39–84.

Baker, Ross K. 1995. *House and Senate*. New York: W. W. Norton. 2nd edition.

Baron, David P. 1991. "Majoritarian Incentives, Pork Barrel Programs, and Procedural Control." *American Journal of Political Science* 35 (1): 57–90.

Bawn, Kathleen and Gregory Koger. 2003. "Intensity, Effort, Endogenous Rules and Obstruction in the U.S. Senate." Paper presented at the Annual Meeting of the Midwest Political Science Association.

Beeman, Richard R. 1968. "Unlimited Debate in the Senate: The First Phase." *Political Science Quarterly* 83: 419–434.

Bensel, Richard F. 1984. *Sectionalism and American Political Development, 1880–1980*. Madison: University of Wisconsin Press.

Bensel, Richard F. 1990. *Yankee Leviathan: The Origins of Central State Authority in America, 1859–1877*. New York: Cambridge University Press.

Bensel, Richard F. 2000. *The Political Economy of American Industrialization, 1877–1900*. New York: Cambridge University Press.

Bernhard, William and Brian R. Sala. 2004. "The Remaking of an American Senate: The 17th Amendment and Ideological Responsiveness." Paper presented at the annual meetings of the Southern Political Science Association, New Orleans, Jan. 8–10.

Beth, Richard S. 1994. "Filibusters in the Senate, 1789–1993." Congressional Research Service Memorandum.

Beth, Richard S. 1995. "What We Don't Know about Filibusters." Paper presented at the Annual Meeting of the Western Political Science Association.

Beth, Richard S. 2005. "'Entrenchment' of Senate Procedure and the 'Nuclear Option' for Change: Possible Proceedings and Their Implications." Congressional Research Service Report.

Binder, Sarah A. 1997. *Minority Rights, Majority Rule*. New York: Cambridge University Press.

Binder, Sarah A. 2003. *Stalemate: Causes and Consequences of Legislative Gridlock*. Washington, DC: Brookings Institution.

Binder, Sarah A., Eric D. Lawrence, and Steven S. Smith. 2002. "Tracking the Filibuster, 1917 to 1996." *American Politics Research* 30 (4): 406–22.

Binder, Sarah A. and Forrest Maltzman. 2004. "The Limits of Senatorial Courtesy." *Legislative Studies Quarterly* 24 (February): 5–22.

Binder, Sarah A. and Steven S. Smith. 1997. *Politics or Principle? Filibustering in the United States Senate*. Washington, DC: Brookings Institution.

Bliss, C. and Barry Nalebuff. 1984. "Dragon Slaying and Ballroom Dancing: The Private Supply of a Public Good." *Journal of Public Economics* 27: 772–87.

Brady, David, Richard Brody, and David Epstein. 1989. "Heterogeneous Parties and Political Organization: The United States Senate, 1880–1920." *Legislative Studies Quarterly* 2 (14): 205–23.

Brady, David and David Epstein. 1997. "Intraparty Preferences, Heterogeneity, and the Origins of the Modern Congress: Progressive Reformers in the House and Senate, 1890–1920." *Journal of Law, Economics, & Organization* 13 (1): 26–49.

Brady, David, Judith Goldstein, and Daniel Kessler. 2002. "Does Party Matter? An Historical Test Using Senate Tariff Votes in Three Institutional Settings." *Journal of Law, Economics, and Organization* 18 (1): 140–54.

Brady, David W. and Mark Morgan. 1987. "Reforming the Structure of the House Appropriations Process: The Effects of the 1885 and 1919–1920 Reforms on Money Decisions." In Mathew McCubbins and Terry Sullivan, editors, *Congress: Structure and Policy*, New York: Cambridge University Press. Pages 207–34.

Brady, David W. and Craig Volden. 1998. *Revolving Gridlock*. Boulder, CO: Westview Press.

Buchanan, James M. and Gordon Tullock. 1962. *The Calculus of Consent: Logical Foundations of Constitutional Democracy*. Ann Arbor: University of Michigan Press.

Burdette, Franklin L. 1940. *Filibustering in the Senate*. Princeton: Princeton University Press.

Byrd, Robert C. 1988. *The Senate, 1789–1989: Addresses on the History of the United States Senate*. Washington, DC: U.S. G.P.O.

Cameron, Charles M. 2000. *Veto Bargaining: Presidents and the Politics of Negative Power*. Cambridge: Cambridge University Press.

Campbell, Andrea C., Gary Cox, and Mathew D. McCubbins. 2002. "Agenda Power in the U.S. Senate, 1877–1986." In David W. Brady and Mathew D. McCubbins, editors, *Party, Process, and Political Change in Congress*, Stanford: Stanford University Press. Pages 146–65.

Canon, David T. and Charles Stewart. 2002. "Parties and Hierarchies in Senate Committees." In Bruce I. Oppenheimer, editor, *U.S. Senate Exceptionalism*, Columbus: Ohio State University Press. Pages 157–81.

Caplin, Andrew and Barry Nalebuff. 1988. "On 64%-Majority Rule." *Econometrica* 56: 787–814.

Caro, Robert A. 2002. *Master of the Senate: The Years of Lyndon Johnson*. New York: Knopf.

Carpenter, Jesse T. 1990. *The South as a Conscious Minority, 1789–1861.* Columbia: University of South Carolina Press.

Carrubba, Clifford J. and Craig Volden. 2000. "Coalitional Politics and Logrolling in Legislative Institutions." *American Journal of Political Science* 44 (2): 261–277.

Chamberlain, Lawrence H. 1946. *The President, Congress and Legislation.* New York: Columbia University Press.

Clausen, Aage. 1973. *How Congressmen Decide: A Policy Focus.* New York: St. Martin's Press.

Cody, Scott. 2004. "Shifting Pivots: Cloture Rules and Legislative Outcomes in the Nebraska Legislature." Paper presented at the Midwest Political Science Association Annual Meeting, April 15–18, 2004, Chicago, Illinois.

Collie, Melissa P. 1988. "Universalism and the Parties in the U.S. House of Representatives, 1921–1980." *American Journal of Political Science* 32 (4): 865–83.

Conover, W. J. 1999. *Practical Nonparametric Statistics.* New York: John Wiley & Sons. 3rd edition.

Cooper, Joseph. 1962. *The Previous Question: Its Standing as a Precedent for Cloture in the United States Senate.* Senate Document 87–104. Washington, DC: G.P.O.

Cooper, Joseph and Elizabeth Rybicki. 2002. "Analyzing Institutional Change: Bill Introduction in the Nineteenth-Century Senate." In Bruce I. Oppenheimer, editor, *U.S. Senate Exceptionalism,* Columbus: Ohio State University Press. Pages 182–211.

Cox, Gary and Mathew D. McCubbins. 1993. *Legislative Leviathan.* Berkeley: University of California Press.

Cox, Gary W. and Mathew D. McCubbins. 2005. *Setting The Agenda: Responsible Party Government in the U.S. House of Representatives.* Cambridge: Cambridge University Press.

Crofts, Daniel W. 1968. *The Blair Bill and the Elections Bill: The Congressional Aftermath to Reconstruction.* Ph.D. thesis. Yale University.

Crook, Sara Brandes and John R. Hibbing. 1997. "A Not-So-Distant Mirror: The 17th Amendment and Congressional Change." *American Political Science Review* 91: 845–853.

Cushing, Luther Stearns. 1866. *Elements of the Law and Practice of Legislative Assemblies in the United States of America.* Boston: Little, Brown and Company.

Dell, Christopher and Stephen W. Stathis. 1982. "Major Acts of Congress and Treaties Approved by the Senate, 1789–1980." Congressional Research Service Report No. 82–156 GOV.

Diermeier, Daniel and Keith Krehbiel. 2003. "Institutionalism as a Methodology." *Journal of Theoretical Politics* 15 (2): 123–44.

Dion, Douglas. 1997. *Turning the Legislative Thumbscrew*. Ann Arbor: University of Michigan Press.

Dixit, Avinash K. 2004. *Lawlessness and Economics: Alternative Modes of Governance*. Princeton: Princeton University Press.

Donald, David Herbert. 1996. *Charles Sumner*. New York: Da Capo Press.

Ellickson, Robert C. 1991. *Order Without Law*. Cambridge: Harvard University Press.

Elster, Jon. 2000. "Rational Choice History: A Case of Excessive Ambition." *American Political Science Review* 94: 685–95.

Engstrom, Erik J. and Samuel Kernell. 2003. "The Effects of Presidential Elections on Party Control of the Senate under Indirect and Direct Elections." Presented at the History of Congress Conference, University of California at San Diego, December 5–6.

Epstein, David and Sharyn O'Halloran. 1996. "The Partisan Paradox and the U.S. Tariff, 1877–1934." *International Organization* 50 (2): 301–24.

Evans, C. Lawrence, Daniel Lipinski, and Keith J. Larson. 2003. "The Senate Hold: Preliminary Evidence from the Baker Years." Paper presented at the Annual Meeting of the Midwest Political Science Association, April, Chicago, Illinois.

Farhang, Sean. 2005. *The Litigation State: Public Regulation and Private Lawsuits in the American Separation of Powers System*. Ph.D. thesis. Columbia University.

Faulkner, Harold U. 1929. "The Development of the American System." *Annals of the American Academy of Political and Social Science* 141: 11–17.

Faulkner, William. 1950. *Requiem For A Nun*. New York: Random House.

Fearon, James. 1994. "Domestic Political Audiences and the Escalation of International Disputes." *American Political Science Review* 88 (September): 577–92.

Fenno, Richard F. 1966. *The Power of the Purse: Appropriations Politics in Congress*. Boston: Little, Brown.

Fenno, Richard F. 1978. *Home Style: House Members in Their Districts*. Boston: Little, Brown.

Fiorina, Morris P. 1996. *Divided Government*. Boston: Allyn and Bacon. 2nd edition.

Firth, David. 1993. "Bias Reduction of Maximum Likelihood Estimates." *Biometrika* 80 (1): 27–38.

Fudenberg, Drew and Jean Tirole. 1991. *Game Theory*. Cambridge: MIT Press.

Gamm, Gerald and Steven S. Smith. 2000. "Last Among Equals: The Senate's Presiding Officer." In Burdett A. Loomis, editor, *Esteemed Colleagues*, Washington, DC: Brookings Institution Press. Pages 105–37.

Gamm, Gerald and Steven S. Smith. 2001a. "The Dynamics of Party Government in Congress." In Lawrence Dodd and Bruce Oppenheimer, editors, *Congress Reconsidered*, Washington, DC: CQ Press. 7th edition. Pages 245–68.

Gamm, Gerald and Steven S. Smith. 2001b. "The Senate Without Leaders: Senate Parties in the Mid-19th Century." Paper presented at the Annual Meeting of the American Political Science Association.

Gamm, Gerald and Steven S. Smith. 2002a. "Emergence of Senate Party Leadership." In Bruce I. Oppenheimer, editor, *U.S. Senate Exceptionalism*, Columbus: Ohio State University Press. Pages 212–240.

Gamm, Gerald and Steven S. Smith. 2002b. "Policy Leadership and the Development of the Modern Senate." In David W. Brady and Mathew D. McCubbins, editors, *Party, Process, and Political Change in Congress*, Stanford, CA: Stanford University Press. Pages 287–314.

Gamm, Gerald and Steven S. Smith. 2003. "Steering the Senate: The Consolidation of Senate Party Leadership, 1879–1913." Paper presented at the Congress and History Conference, Massachusetts Institute of Technology, May 30–31.

Gibbons, Robert. 1992. *Game Theory for Applied Economists*. Princeton University Press.

Giles, Michael W., Virginia A. Hettinger, and Todd Peppers. 2001. "Picking Federal Judges: A Note on Policy and Partisan Selection Agendas." *Political Research Quarterly* 54 (3): 623–42.

Gilligan, Thomas W. and Keith Krehbiel. 1987. "Collective Decisionmaking and Standing Committees: An Informational Rationale for Restrictive Amendment Procedures." *Journal of Law, Economics, and Organization* 3: 287–335.

Gold, Martin B. and Dimple Gupta. 2004. "The Constitutional Option to Change Senate Rules and Procedures: A Majoritarian Means to Overcome the Filibuster." *Harvard Journal of Law and Public Policy* 28 (1): 206–72.

Goldman, Sheldon. 1997. *Picking Federal Judges: Lower Court Selection from Roosevelt through Reagan*. New Haven, CT: Yale University Press.

Goldman, Sheldon. 2005. "Judicial Confirmation Wars: Ideology and the Battle for the Federal Courts." *University of Richmond Law Review* 39: 871–908.

Greif, Avner. 2000. "The Fundamental Problem of Exchange: A Research Agenda in Historical Institutional Analysis." *European Review of Economic History* 4: 251–84.

Groseclose, Timothy. 1994. "Testing Committee Composition Hypotheses for the U.S. Congress." *Journal of Politics* 56: 440–58.

Groseclose, Timothy and Nolan McCarty. 2001. "The Politics of Blame: Bargaining before an Audience." *American Journal of Political Science* 45 (1): 100–119.

Groseclose, Timothy and James Snyder. 1996. "Buying Supermajorities." *American Political Science Review* 90 (2): 303–15.

Hall, Richard L. 1996. *Participation in Congress*. New Haven, CT: Yale University Press.

Hall, Richard L. and Bernard Grofman. 1990. "The Committee Assignment Process and the Conditional Nature of Committee Bias." *American Political Science Review* 84: 1149–66.

Hansen, Mark. 1990. "Taxation and the Political Economy of the Tariff." *International Organization* 44: 527–51.

Haynes, George H. 1906. *The Election of Senators*. New York: Henry Holt and Co.

Haynes, George H. 1938. *The Senate of the United States: Its History and Practice*. Boston: Houghton Mifflin Company.

Heinze, Georg and Michael Schemper. 2003. "A Solution to the Problem of Separation in Logistic Regression." *Statistics in Medicine* 21 (21): 2409–19.

Heitshusen, Valerie and Garry Young. 2001. "Critical Elections, Divided Government, and Gridlock: Assessing Major Policy Change, 1874–1946." Paper presented at the Macro-Politics of Congress Conference, June 1–3.

Herron, Michael. 2000. "Post-estimation Uncertainty in Limited Dependent Variable Models." *Political Analysis* 8 (1): 83–98.

Hirshson, Stanley P. 1962. *Farewell to the Bloody Shirt*. Bloomington: Indiana University Press.

Hiscox, Michael J. 2002. *International Trade and Political Conflict*. Princeton: Princeton University Press.

Hoar, George F. 1903. *Autobiography of Seventy Years*. New York: C. Scribner's Sons.

Huitt, Ralph K. 1961. "Outsider in the Senate: An Alternative Role." *American Political Science Review* 55 (3): 566–75.

Huitt, Ralph K. 1962. "On Norms, Roles, and Folkways." *American Political Science Review* 56 (1): 142.

Inter-university Consortium for Political and Social Research and Carroll McKibbin. 1997. "Roster of United States Congressional Officeholders and Biographical Characteristics of Members of the United States Congress, 1789-1996: Merged Data [Computer file].". 10th ICPSR ed. Ann Arbor, MI: Inter-university Consortium for Political and Social Research [producer and distributor].

James, Scott C. and David A. Lake. 1989. "The Second Face of Hegemony: Britain's Repeal of the Corn Laws and the American Walker Tariff of 1846." *International Organization* 43: 1–29.

Kehl, James A. 1981. *Boss Rule in the Gilded Age: Matt Quay of Pennsylvania*. Pittsburgh: University of Pittsburgh Press.

Keller, Morton. 1977. *Affairs of State: Public Life in Late Nineteenth Century America*. Cambridge: Belknap Press of Harvard University Press.

Key, V. O. 1949. *Southern Politics in State and Nation*. New York: A. A. Knopf.

Kiewiet, D. Roderick and Mathew D. McCubbins. 1991. *The Logic of Delegation: Congressional Parties and the Appropriations Process*. Chicago: University of Chicago Press.

King, Gary. 1998. *Unifying Political Methodology*. Ann Arbor: University of Michigan Press.

King, Gary, Michael Tomz, and Jason Wittenberg. 2000. "Making the Most of Statistical Analyses: Improving Interpretation and Presentation." *American Journal of Political Science* 44 (2): 347–61.

Koger, Gregory. 2002. *Obstruction in the House and Senate*. Ph.D. thesis. UCLA.

Kohlmeier, A. L. 1938. *The Old Northwest as the Keystone of the Arch of American Federal Union*. Bloomington, IN: Principia Press.

Krehbiel, Keith. 1986. "Unanimous Consent Agreements: Going Along in the Senate." *Journal of Politics* 48 (3): 541–64.

Krehbiel, Keith. 1990. "Are Congressional Committees Composed of Preference Outliers?" *American Political Science Review* 84: 149–63.

Krehbiel, Keith. 1991. *Information and Legislative Organization*. Ann Arbor: University of Michigan Press.

Krehbiel, Keith. 1996. "Institutional and Partisan Sources of Gridlock: A Theory of Divided and Unified Government." *Journal of Theoretical Politics* 8: 7–40.

Krehbiel, Keith. 1998. *Pivotal Politics*. Chicago: University of Chicago Press.

Kreps, David and Robert Wilson. 1982. "Reputation and Imperfect Information." *Journal of Economic Theory* 27 (2): 253–79.

Lambert, John R. 1953. *Arthur Pue Gorman*. Baton Rouge: Louisiana State University Press.

Lapinski, John S. 2000a. "Congress, Legislative Performance, and American Political Development." Paper presented at the Annual Meeting of the American Political Science Association, Washington, DC.

Lapinski, John S. 2000b. *Representation and Reform: A Congress Centered Approach to American Political Development*. Ph.D. thesis. Columbia University.

Lawrence, Eric D. 2005. "The Publication of Precedents and Its Effect on Legislative Behavior." Unpublished manuscript.

Lee, Frances E. and Bruce I. Oppenheimer. 1999. *Sizing Up the Senate: The Unequal Consequences of Equal State Representation*. Chicago: University of Chicago Press.

Levitt, Steven D. 1996. "How Do Senators Vote? Disentangling the Role of Voter Preferences, Party Affiliation, and Senator Ideology." *American Economic Review* 86 (3): 425–41.

Liang, Kung-Yee and Scott L. Zeger. 1986. "Longitudinal Data Analysis Using Generalized Linear Models." *Biometrika* 73: 13–22.

Lodge, Henry Cabot. 1893. "Obstruction in the Senate." *North American Review* 157 (444): 523–29.

Long, J. Scott. 1997. *Regression Models for Categorical and Limited Dependent Variables*. Thousand Oaks, CA: Sage Publications.

Lowi, Theodore J. 1964. "American Business, Public Policy, Case Studies, and Political Theory." *World Politics* 16 (4): 677–715.

Lowi, Theodore J., Benjamin Ginsberg, and Kenneth A. Shepsle. 2002. *American Government: Power and Purpose.* New York: Norton. 7th edition.

Luce, Robert. 1922. *Legislative Procedure.* Boston: Houghton Mifflin Company.

Lyman, Horace S. 1903. *History of Oregon,* volume 4. New York: North Pacific Publishing Society.

MacMahon, Arthur W. 1930. "Second Session of the Seventy–First Congress." *American Political Science Review* 24 (4): 913–46.

MacNeil, Neil. 1963. *Forge of Democracy: The House of Representatives.* New York: David McKay.

Maltzman, Forrest. 1997. *Competing Principles: Committees, Parties, and the Organization of Congress.* Ann Arbor: University of Michigan Press.

Martis, Kenneth C. 1982. *The Historical Atlas of United States Congressional Districts, 1789–1983.* New York: Free Press.

Martis, Kenneth C. 1989. *The Historical Atlas of Political Parties in the United States Congress, 1789–1989.* New York: Macmillan.

Massicotte, Louis. 2001. "Legislative Unicameralism: A Global Survey and a Few Case Studies." *Journal of Legislative Studies* 7 (1).

Matthews, Donald R. 1960. *U.S. Senators and Their World.* Chapel Hill: University of North Carolina Press.

Matthews, Donald R. 1961. "Can the 'Outsider's' Role Be Legitimate?" *American Political Science Review* 55 (4): 882–83.

Mayhew, David R. 1991. *Divided We Govern: Party Control, Lawmaking, and Investigations, 1946–1990.* New Haven: Yale University Press.

Mayhew, David R. 2003. "Supermajority Rule in the U.S. Senate." *PS: Political Science and Politics* 36 (1): 31–36.

McCall, Samuel W. 1911. *The Business of Congress.* New York: Columbia University Press.

McCarty, Nolan, Keith Poole, and Howard Rosenthal. 2002. "Congress and the Territorial Expansion of the United States." In David W. Brady and Mathew D. McCubbins, editors, *Party, Process, and Political Change in Congress,* Stanford, CA: Stanford University Press. Pages 392–451.

McElroy, Robert McNutt. 1930. *Levi Parsons Morton*. New York: G. P. Putnam's Sons.

Meinig, D. W. 1993. *The Shaping of America: Continental America, 1800–1867*, volume 2. New Haven, CT: Yale University Press.

Merriam, Charles E. and Louise Overacker. 1928. *Primary Elections*. Chicago: University of Chicago Press.

Miller, William Lee. 1996. *Arguing About Slavery: The Great Battle in the United States Congress*. New York: Knopf.

Myers, Henry Lee. 1939. *The United States Senate: What Kind of Body?*. Philadelphia: Dorrance and Company.

Nevins, Allan. 1947. *Ordeal of the Union*, volume 2. New York: Charles Scribner's Sons.

Newport, Frank. 2005. "Public Favors Keeping Filibuster Rule in U.S. Senate." Gallup News Service, http://www.gallup.com/ (accessed May 9, 2005).

Nichols, Roy F. 1948. *The Disruption of American Democracy*. New York: MacMillan Company.

Nichols, Roy F. 1963. *Blueprints for Leviathan: American Style*. New York: Atheneum.

North, Douglass C. 1990. *Institutions, Institutional Change, and Economic Performance*. New York: Cambridge University Press.

North, Douglass C. and Andrew R. Rutten. 1987. "The Northwest Ordinance in Historical Perspective." In David C. Klingaman and Richard K. Vedder, editors, *Essays on the Economy of the Old Northwest*, Athens: Ohio University Press.

O'Halloran, Sharyn. 1994. *Politics, Process, and American Trade Policy*. Ann Arbor: University of Michigan Press.

Oleszek, Walter J. 2001. *Congressional Procedure and the Policy Process*. Washington, DC: CQ Press. 5th edition.

Oppenheimer, Bruce I. 1985. "Changing Time Constraints on Congress: Historical Perspectives on the Use of Cloture." In Lawrence C. Dodd and Bruce I. Oppenheimer, editors, *Congress Reconsidered*, Washington, DC: Congressional Quarterly. 3rd edition. Pages 393–413.

Ornstein, Norman J. 2003. "Reform Is Needed, but Tread Carefully." *Roll Call* (May 21).

Ostrom, Elinor. 1998. "A Behavioral Approach to the Rational Choice Theory of Collective Action." *American Political Science Review* 92 (1): 1–22.

Ostrom, Elinor and James Walker. 1991. "Communications in a Commons: Cooperation without External Enforcement." In Thomas R. Palfrey, editor, *Laboratory Research in Political Economy*, University of Michigan Press. Pages 287–322.

Ostrom, Elinor, James Walker, and Roy Gardner. 1992. "Covenants with and without a Sword: Self Governance is Possible." *American Political Science Review* 86 (2): 404–16.

Palfrey, Thomas R. and Howard Rosenthal. 1988. "Private Incentives in Social Dilemmas." *Journal of Public Economics* 35 (April): 309–32.

Palmquist, Bradley. 1999. "Analysis of Proportions Data." Paper prepared for the Annual Meeting of the Political Methodology Society, Texas A & M University.

Peltzman, Sam. 1984. "Constituent Interest and Congressional Voting." *Journal of Law and Economics* 27 (April): 181–210.

Petersen, R. Eric. 2001. "Is It Science Yet? Replicating and Validating the *Divided We Govern* List of Important Statutes." Paper presented at the Annual Meeting of the Midwest Political Science Association, Chicago, IL.

Pierce, Edward L. 1969. *Memoir and Letters of Charles Sumner*, volume 4. New York: Arno Press and New York Times.

Pierson, Paul. 2000. "Path Dependence, Increasing Returns, and the Study of Politics." *American Political Science Review* 94 (2): 251–67.

Poage, George R. 1936. *Henry Clay and the Whig Party*. Chapel Hill: University of North Carolina Press.

Polsby, Nelson W. 1968. "The Institutionalization of the U.S. House of Representatives." *American Political Science Review* 62 (1): 144–68.

Polsby, Nelson W. 1986. *Congress and The Presidency*. Englewood Cliffs, NJ: Prentice Hall. 4th edition.

Poole, Keith T. and Howard L. Rosenthal. 1997. *Congress: A Political-Economic History of Roll Call Voting*. New York: Oxford University Press.

Potter, David M. 1976. *The Impending Crisis, 1848–1861*. New York: Harper and Row.

Ragsdale, Lyn. 1996. *Vital Statistics on the Presidency: Washington to Clinton*. Washington, DC: Congressional Quarterly.

Ransom, Roger L. 1989. *Conflict and Compromise: The Political Economy of Slavery, Emancipation, and the American Civil War*. New York: Cambridge University Press.

Reinsch, Paul S. 1907. *American Legislatures and Legislative Methods*. New York: Century Co.

Richards, Leonard L. 2000. *The Slave Power: The Free North and Southern Domination, 1780–1860*. Baton Rouge: Louisiana State University Press.

Riker, William H. 1955. "The Senate and American Federalism." *American Political Science Review* 49 (2): 452–69.

Riker, William H. 1964. *Federalism: Origin, Operation, Significance*. Boston: Little, Brown.

Riker, William H. 1982. *Liberalism Against Populism*. Prospect Heights, IL: Waveland Press.

Roberts, Jason M. and Steven S. Smith. 2004. "The Evolution of Agenda-Setting Institutions in Congress: Path Dependency in House and Senate Institutional Development." Paper presented at the History of Congress Conference, Stanford University, April 9-10.

Rogers, Lindsay. 1926. *The American Senate*. New York: Alfred A. Knopf.

Rohde, David W. 1988. "Studying Congressional Norms: Concepts and Evidence." *Congress and the Presidency* 15 (Autumn): 139–45.

Rohde, David W. 1991. *Parties and Leaders in the Postreform House*. Chicago: University of Chicago Press.

Rosenthal, Howard L. and Keith T. Poole. 2000. "United States Congressional Roll Call Voting Records, 1789–1990: Reformatted Data." [Computer file]. 2nd version. Pittsburgh, PA: Keith T. Poole, Carnegie Mellon University, Graduate School of Industrial Administration [producer]. Ann Arbor, MI: Inter-university Consortium for Political and Social Research [distributor].

Rothman, David J. 1966. *Politics and Power: The United States Senate, 1869–1901*. Cambridge: Harvard University Press.

Rutkus, Denis Steven and Mitchel A. Sollenberger. 2004. "Judicial Nomination Statistics: U.S. District and Circuit Courts, 1977–2003." Congressional Research Service Report.

Sala, Brian R. 2002. "Time for a Change: Pivotal Politics and the 1935 Wagner Act." Paper presented at the Annual Meeting of the Midwest Political Science Association.

Schattschneider, E. E. 1935. *Politics, Pressures and the Tariff: A Study of Free Private Enterprise in Pressure Politics, as Shown in the 1929–1930 Revision of the Tariff*. New York: Prentice Hall.

Schickler, Eric. 2001. *Disjointed Pluralism: Institutional Innovation and the Development of the U.S. Congress*. Princeton: Princeton University Press.

Schickler, Eric and John Sides. 2000. "Intergenerational Warfare: The Senate Decentralizes Appropriations." *Legislative Studies Quarterly* 25: 551–75.

Schiller, Wendy J. 2003. "The Electoral Connection: Career Building and Constituency Representation in the U.S. Senate in the Age of Indirect Elections." Paper presented at the History of Congress conference held at the University of California at San Diego.

Schiller, Wendy J. and Charles Stewart. 2004. "U.S. Senate Elections before 1914." Presented at the Congress and History Conference, Stanford University.

Seager, Robert and Melba Porter Hay, editors. 1888. *The Papers of Henry Clay*. Lexington: University Press of Kentucky.

Sell, Jane and Rick Wilson. 1991. "Levels of Information and Contributions to Public Goods." *Social Forces* 70 (Sept.): 107–27.

Shepsle, Kenneth A. 1978. *The Giant Jigsaw Puzzle*. Chicago: University of Chicago Press.

Shepsle, Kenneth A. 1979. "Institutional Arrangements and Equilibrium in Multidimensional Voting Models." *American Journal of Political Science* 23: 27–59.

Shepsle, Kenneth A., Eric S. Dickson, and Robert P. Van Houweling. 2003. "Bargaining in Legislatures with Overlapping Generations of Politicians." Harvard University, Typescript.

Shepsle, Kenneth A. and Barry R. Weingast. 1981. "Political Preferences for the Pork Barrel: A Generalization." *American Journal of Political Science* 25 (1): 96–111.

Shepsle, Kenneth A. and Barry R. Weingast. 1987. "The Institutional Foundations of Committee Power." *American Political Science Review* 81: 85–104.

Shepsle, Kenneth A. and Barry R. Weingast. 1994. "Positive Theories of Congressional Institutions." *Legislative Studies Quarterly* 19: 149–79.

Silbey, Joel H. 1967. *The Shrine of Party: Congressional Voting Behavior, 1841–1852*. Pittsburgh, PA: University of Pittsburgh Press.

Sinclair, Barbara. 1989. *The Transformation of the U.S. Senate*. Baltimore, MD: Johns Hopkins University Press.

Sinclair, Barbara. 2001. "The New World of U.S. Senators." In Lawrence Dodd and Bruce Oppenheimer, editors, *Congress Reconsidered*, Washington, DC: CQ Press. 7th edition. Pages 1–18.

Sinclair, Barbara. 2002. "The '60-Vote Senate'." In Bruce I. Oppenheimer, editor, *U.S. Senate Exceptionalism*, Columbus: Ohio State University Press. Pages 241–61.

Smith, Steven S. 1989. *Call to Order: Floor Politics in the House and Senate*. Washington, DC: Brookings Institution.

Smith, Steven S. 1995. *The American Congress*. Boston: Houghton Mifflin.

Stanwood, Edward. 1903. *American Tariff Controversies in the Nineteenth Century*. Boston: Houghton Mifflin.

Stephenson, Nathaniel W. 1930. *Nelson W. Aldrich, A Leader in American Politics*. New York: C. Scribner's Sons.

Stewart, Charles III. 1989. *Budget Reform Politics: The Design of the Appropriations Process in the House of Representatives, 1865–1921*. Cambridge: Cambridge University Press.

Stewart, Charles III. 1992. "Responsiveness in the Upper Chamber: The Constitution and the Institutional Development of the Senate." In Peter F. Nardulli, editor, *The Constitution and American Political Development: An Institutional Perspective*, Urbana: University of Illinois Press. Pages 63–96.

Swift, Elaine K. 1996. *The Making of an American Senate, 1787–1841*. Ann Arbor: University of Michigan Press.

Swift, Elaine K., Robert G. Brookshire, David T. Canon, Evelyn C. Fink, John R. Hibbing, Brian D. Humes, Michael J. Malbin, and Kenneth C. Martis. 2000. "Database of Congressional Historical Statistics [Computer file]." Ann Arbor, MI: Inter-university Consortium for Political and Social Research [producer and distributor].

Tarbell, Ida M. 1911. *The Tariff in Our Times*. New York: MacMillan.

Taussig, F. W. 1931. *The Tariff History of the United States*. New York and London: G. P. Putnam's Sons.

Taylor, Andrew J. Forthcoming. "Size, Power, and Electoral Systems: Exogenous Determinants of Legislative Procedural Choice." *Legislative Studies Quarterly*.

Taylor, George Rogers. 1951. *The Transportation Revolution, 1815–1860,* Volume 4 of *The Economic History of the United States.* New York: Rinehart and Company.

Tiefer, Charles. 1989. *Congressional Practice and Procedure: A Reference, Research, and Legislative Guide.* New York: Greenwood Press.

Tirole, Jean. 1988. *The Theory of Industrial Organization.* Cambridge: MIT Press.

Unger, Nancy C. 2000. *Fighting Bob La Follette: The Righteous Reformer.* Chapel Hill: University of North Carolina Press.

Upchurch, Thomas Adams. 2004. *Legislating Racism: The Billion Dollar Congress and the Birth of Jim Crow.* Lexington: University Press of Kentucky.

U.S. Congress. Senate. 1909. *Precedents: Decisions on Points of Order with Phraseology in the United States Senate, from the First Congress to the Sixtieth Congress, 1789–1909.* Washington, DC: U.S. G.P.O. 61st Cong., 1st sess.

U.S. Congress. Senate. 1913. *Precedents: Decisions on Points of Order with Phraseology in the United States Senate, from the First to Sixty-Second Congress Inclusive, 1789–1913.* Washington, DC: U.S. G.P.O. 62nd Cong., 3rd sess.

U.S. Congress. Senate. 1992. *Riddick's Senate Procedure: Precedents and Practices.* Washington, DC: U.S. G.P.O. 94th Cong., 1st sess.

U.S. Congress. Senate. Committee on Rules. 1883. *Report of the Committee on Rules Relating to the Rules of the Senate and the Joint Rules of the Senate and House of Representatives and the Senate Manual.* Washington, DC: U.S. G.P.O. Committee Report, no. 2. 48th Cong., 1st sess.

U.S. Congress. Senate. Committee on Rules and Administration. 1985. *Senate Cloture Rule.* Committee Print, no. 99–95. 99th Cong., 1st sess.

Valelly, Richard M. 2004a. "Counterfactualizing American Political Development: What We Can Learn from the Federal Elections Bill of 1890." Prepared for presentation at the Miller Center, University of Virginia, December 3.

Valelly, Richard M. 2004b. *The Two Reconstructions: The Struggle for Black Enfranchisement.* Chicago: University of Chicago Press.

Van Deusen, Glyndon G. 1937. *The Life of Henry Clay.* Boston: Little, Brown and Company.

Von Holst, Herman. 1893. "Shall the Senate Rule the Republic?" *Forum* 16: 263–71.

Weingast, Barry R. 1979. "A Rational Choice Perspective on Congressional Norms." *American Journal of Political Science* 23 (2): 245–62.

Weingast, Barry R. 1998. "Political Stability and Civil War: Institutions, Commitment, and American Democracy." In *Analytic Narratives*, Princeton: Princeton University Press. Pages 148–93.

Weingast, Barry R. N.d. "Institutions and Political Commitment: A New Political Economy of the American Civil War Era." Unpublished manuscript.

Weingast, Barry R. and William Marshall. 1988. "The Industrial Organization of Congress." *Journal of Political Economy* 96: 132–63.

White, William S. 1968. *Citadel: The Story of the U.S. Senate*. Boston: Houghton Mifflin.

Willis, H. Parker. 1910. "The Tariff of 1909, II: The Legislative History of the Act." *Journal of Political Economy* 18 (January): 1–33.

Wilson, Woodrow. [1885] 1956. *Congressional Government: A Study in American Politics*. New York: Meridian Books.

Wirls, Daniel. 2005. "Tocqueville's Shadow: Exploring Myth and Reality about Deliberation in the Antebellum Congress." Paper prepared for presentation at the Congress and History Workshop, Washington University in St. Louis, May 13–14.

Wolfinger, Raymond E. 1971. "Filibusters: Majority Rule, Presidential Leadership, and Senate Norms." In Raymond E. Wolfinger, editor, *Readings on Congress*, Englewood Cliffs, NJ: Prentice Hall.

Zelizer, Julian E. 2004. *On Capitol Hill: The Struggle to Reform Congress and its Consequences, 1948–2000*. New York: Cambridge University Press.

Zorn, Christopher J. W. 2001. "Generalized Estimating Equation Models for Correlated Data: A Review with Applications." *American Journal of Political Science* 45: 470–90.

Zorn, Christopher J. W. 2005. "A Solution to Separation in Binary Response Models." *Political Analysis* 13 (2): 157–70.

Index

PRINCETON STUDIES IN AMERICAN POLITICS: HISTORICAL, INTERNATIONAL, AND COMPARATIVE PERSPECTIVES

Filibuster: Obstruction and Lawmaking in the U.S. Senate by Gregory J. Wawro and Eric Schickler

Disarmed: The Missing Movement for Gun Control in America by Kristin Goss

When Movements Matter: The Townsend Plan and the Rise of Social Security by Edwin Amenta

Shaping Race Policy: The United States in Comparative Perspective by Robert C. Lieberman

How Policies Make Citizens: Senior Political Activism and the American Welfare State by Andrea Louise Campbell

Managing the President's Program: Presidential Leadership and Legislative Policy Formulation by Andrew Rudalevige

Shaped by War and Trade: International Influences on American Political Development edited by Ira Katznelson and Martin Shefter

Dry Bones Rattling: Community Building to Revitalize American Democracy by Mark R. Warren

The Forging of Bureaucratic Autonomy: Reputations, Networks, and Policy Innovations in Executive Agencies, 1862-1928 by Daniel P. Carpenter

Disjointed Pluralism: Institutional Innovation and the Development of the U.S. Congress by Eric Schickler

The Rise of the Agricultural Welfare State: Institutions and Interest Group Power in the United States, France, and Japan by Adam D. Sheingate

In the Shadow of the Garrison State: America's Anti-Statism and Its Cold War Grand Strategy by Aaron L. Friedberg

Stuck in Neutral: Business and the Politics of Human Capital Investment Policy by Cathie Jo Martin

Uneasy Alliances: Race and Party Competition in America by Paul Frymer

Faithful and Fearless: Moving Feminist Protest inside the Church and Military by Mary Fainsod Katzenstein

Experts and Politicians: Reform Challenges to Machine Politics in New York, Cleveland, and Chicago by Kenneth Finegold

Bound by Our Constitution: Women, Workers, and the Minimum Wage by Vivien Hart

Prisoners of Myth: The Leadership of the Tennessee Valley Authority, 1933-1990 by Erwin C. Hargrove

Political Parties and the State: The American Historical Experience by Martin Shefter

Politics and Industrialization: Early Railroads in the United States and Prussia by Colleen A. Dunlavy

The Lincoln Persuasion: Remaking American Liberalism by J. David Greenstone

Labor Visions and State Power: The Origins of Business Unionism in the United States by Victoria C. Hattam